T0350307

Strategic Use of Information Technology for Global Organizations

M. Gordon Hunter
University of Lethbridge, Canada

Felix B. Tan
Auckland University of Technology, New Zealand

IGI PUBLISHING

Hershey • New York

Acquisition Editor:	Kristin Klinger
Senior Managing Editor:	Jennifer Neidig
Managing Editor:	Sara Reed
Assistant Managing Editor:	Sharon Berger
Development Editor:	Kristin Roth
Copy Editor:	Angela Thor
Typesetter:	Jennifer Neidig
Cover Design:	Lisa Tosheff
Printed at:	Yurchak Printing Inc.

Published in the United States of America by
IGI Publishing (an imprint of IGI Global)
701 E. Chocolate Avenue
Hershey PA 17033
Tel: 717-533-8845
Fax: 717-533-8661
E-mail: cust@igi-pub.com
Web site: http://www.igi-pub.com

and in the United Kingdom by
IGI Publishing (an imprint of IGI Global)
3 Henrietta Street
Covent Garden
London WC2E 8LU
Tel: 44 20 7240 0856
Fax: 44 20 7379 0609
Web site: http://www.eurospanonline.com

Library of Congress Cataloging-in-Publication Data

Strategic use of information technology for global organizations / M. Gordon Hunter and Felix Tan, editors.
   p. cm.
   Summary: "This book provides valuable insights into the role of the CIO, his interaction within the organization and external relationships with vendors and suppliers. It emphasizes the need for balance between management and technology in the role of CIO, and focuses on this role as an expert on information technology, and a leader in the appropriate application of IT"--Provided by publisher.
   Includes bibliographical references and index.
   ISBN 978-1-59904-292-3 (hardcover) -- ISBN 978-1-59904-294-7 (ebook)
   1. Information technology--Management. 2. Strategic planning. I. Hunter, M. Gordon. II. Tan, Felix B., 1959-
   HD30.2.S794 2007
   658.4'038--dc22
                          2007007261

British Cataloguing in Publication Data
A Cataloguing in Publication record for this book is available from the British Library.

The views expressed in this book are those of the authors, but not necessarily of the publisher.

Strategic Use of Information Technology for Global Organizations

Table of Contents

Preface vi

Section I:
Global Themes

Chapter I
Creating and Developing a Program of Global Research 1
Detmar W. Straub, Georgia State University, USA
Karen D. Loch, Georgia State University, USA

Chapter II
Global Programs of Research: Maintenance and Extensibility 33
Detmar W. Straub, Georgia State University, USA
Karen D. Loch, Georgia State University, USA

Chapter III
IT Software Development Offshoring: A Multi-Level Theoretical
Framework and Research Agenda 59
Fred Niederman, Saint Louis University, USA
Sumit Kundu, Florida International University, USA
Silvia Salas, Florida International University, USA

Chapter IV
Experiences Conducting Cross-Cultural Research 85
    M. Gordon Hunter, University of Lethbridge, Canada

Chapter V
The Challenge of Web Site Design for Global Organizations 103
    Dianne Cyr, Simon Fraser University, Canada
    Carole Bonanni, University College of the Fraser Valley, Canada
    John Bowes, School of Interactive Arts and Technology, Canada
    Joe Ilsever, Douglas College, Canada

Chapter VI
Understanding E-Government Development: A Global Perspective 137
    Keng Siau, University of Nebraska – Lincoln, USA
    Yuan Long, Colorado State University – Pueblo, USA

Section II:
Regional Themes

Chapter VII
Strategic Alliances and E-Commerce Adoption in Regional SMEs:
A Comparative Study of Swedish and Australian Regional SMEs 156
    R. C. MacGregor, University of Wollongong, Australia
    L. Vrazalic, University of Wollongong, Australia

Chapter VIII
E-Business Integration by SMEs in the Manufacturing Sector:
A Data Envelopment Analysis Approach 201
    Roman Beck, Johann Wolfgang Goethe University, Germany
    Rolf T. Wigand, University of Arkansas at Little Rock, USA
    Wolfgang Koenig, Johann Wolfgang Goethe University, Germany

Chapter IX
Small Firms and Offshore Software Outsourcing: High Transaction
Costs and Their Mitigation 218
    Erran Carmel, American University, USA
    Brian Nicholson, Manchester Business School, UK

Chapter X
Information Systems Effectiveness in Small Businesses: Extending a
Singaporean Model in Canada 245
    Ana Ortiz de Guinea, Queen's University, Canada
    Helen Kelley, University of Lethbridge, Canada
    M. Gordon Hunter, University of Lethbridge, Canada

Chapter XI
E-Government Implementation Framework and Strategies in
Developed and Developing Countries 275
    Y. N. Chen, Western Kentucky University, USA
    H. M. Chen, Shanghai Jiaotong University, China
    W. Huang, Ohio University, USA
    R. K. H. Ching, California State University, USA

Chapter XII
Organizational Learning Process: Its Antecedents and Consequences
in Enterprise System Implementation 300
    Weiling Ke, Clarkson University, USA
    Kwok Kee Wei, City University of Hong Kong, Hong Kong

Chapter XIII
Knowledge Management and Electronic Commerce Supporting
Strategic Decisions: The Case of Taiwan 325
    Wen-Jang Kenny Jih, Middle Tennessee State University, USA
    Marilyn M. Helms, Dalton State College, USA
    Donna T. Mayo, Dalton State College, USA

Chapter XIV
An Evaluation System for IT Outsourcing Customer Satisfaction
Using the Analytic Hierarchy Process: The Case Study in Korea 354
    YongKi Yoon, Yonsei University, Korea
    Kun Shin Im, Yonsei University, Korea

About the Authors 383

Index 392

Preface

The introduction and use of information systems impacts the organization. Information technology is leading to a freer exchange of information within and between organizations. Further, the process of globalization, facilitated by information technology, is also precipitating organizational change. These major factors affecting organizations may be viewed from two perspectives. Internally, organization staff, structures, and processes will, of necessity, change. Externally, changes will result relating to suppliers and customers.

Internally, staff must know the capabilities of information technology and how it may be applied to more effectively perform their role within the organization. While various structures are being adopted, one common aspect relates to establishing a learning environment to facilitate the acquisition and application of intellectual knowledge. Finally, information technology must be employed in a flexible manner in order to respond to inevitable change.

Externally, organizations are establishing strategic partnerships with suppliers. Information technology is being employed to ensure an efficient relationship between each entity's business processes. Further, organizations must now do more than provide customer satisfaction. It is now incumbent upon organizations to delight their customers to such an extent that customers will remain loyal for quite some time. Also, as customers realize the possibilities of products and services, they become more sophisticated and demand improved quality, service, and reliability. Information technology enables organizations to respond by learning about customers' wants and anticipating or rapidly responding to those needs.

Many of these issues are addressed by the chapters included in this volume. The chapters presented here are organized into themes relating to manuscripts that take a global or regional perspective.

Global Themes

The two chapters at the beginning of this section report on an international program of research based upon Arab culture and information technology policy. Chapter I, by Straub and Loch, describes the process of developing the program. Chapter II, also by Straub and Loch, discusses the extension of the program and a retrospective analysis of the overall process outlining a global perspective to the research. Chapter III, by Niederman, Kundu, and Salas, presents off shore software development as a global economic phenomenon. Then, Hunter, in Chapter IV presents suggestions for researchers to consider when conducting cross-cultural investigations. In Chapter V, Cyr, Bonanni, Bowes, and Ilsever discuss the aspects of trust, satisfaction, and loyalty in Web site design when different cultures are considered. This section concludes with Chapter VI where Siau and Long analyze factors affecting e-government using social development theories.

Regional Themes

The chapters in this section focus on one or a few specific locations within one region. The four chapters at the beginning of this section report on investigations of information technology use by small businesses. In Chapter VII MacGregor and Vrazalic compare the advantages for strategic alliances between small businesses in Sweden and Australia. Beck, Wigand, and Koenig, in Chapter VIII investigate e-commerce develops by small businesses in the manufacturing industry. In Chapter IX, Carmel and Nicholson investigate offshore outsourcing by small businesses. Another discussion of small businesses is included in Chapter X, by Ortiz de Guinea, Kelley, and Hunter, which extends a Singapore-developed information system's effectiveness model to Canada. In Chapter XI, Chen, Chen, Huang, and Ching compare e-government strategies in China and the United States of America. Ke and Wei, in Chapter XII, investigate the organizational learning process of two companies in

China. In Chapter XIII, Jih, Helms, and Mayo rely on various companies in Taiwan to study how e-commerce is impacted by knowledge management processes. Finally, in Chapter XIV, Yoon and Im base their investigations of customer satisfaction of information technology outsourcing on companies in Korea.

Acknowledgment

This book is made possible through the efforts of many people. We especially want to thank the authors of each chapter for contributing the results of their work and expanding our understanding of aspects related to global information management. Also, the people at IGI Global have been instrumental in providing assistance in the development of the book. We specifically appreciate the assistance of Dr. Mehdi Khosrow-Pour, Ms. Jan Travers, and Ms. Kristin Roth.

We dedicate this book to the hard working and loyal staff at IGI Global.

M. Gordon Hunter
Felix B. Tan
January 2007

Section I

Global Themes

Chapter I

Creating and Developing a Program of Global Research[*]

Detmar W. Straub, Georgia State University, USA

Karen D. Loch, Georgia State University, USA

Abstract

This is the first part of a two-part chapter that describes and analyzes a program of research (PR) in international IT studies begun in the fall of 1992 and continuing through 2004. The chapter presents the first two stages which span the years of 1992 through 2000, focusing on the creation and development process for a PR, examining the concept of a PR, the inception of our PR and its maturation both in terms of theory and methodology, research team dynamics, and program implementation. We offer guidelines for initiating and maintaining programs of research, highlighting the inevitable trade-offs that occur when high administrative work loads and intensive data gathering in the global setting, often involving long periods of time abroad, have to be balanced against the ability to carry out the research at all and the rarity of the data.

Introduction

This is the first part of a two-part presentation that traces the evolution of a program of research (PR) on Arab culture and national IT policy and how these variables affect various ICT (information and communications technologies) outcomes. This paper focuses on the creation and development of the PR. The second part is presented in Straub and Loch (2006). The program began in 1992 with a team of four faculty members at Georgia State University, three of whom were IS faculty and one of whom was a cultural anthropologist. Since the research domain set in the Arab world was familiar to only one of the faculty members, sharing of knowledge between the team members was critical, even as the team grew somewhat larger over data-gathering exercises in Jordan, Lebanon, Saudi Arabia, the Sudan, and Egypt. By the late 1990s, the research had reached a point where major U.S.-government National Science Foundation (NSF) funding was sought and acquired. Team membership had changed, as well, and the program shifted to an examination of other variables and explored new ways of measuring the established constructs. Over time, we adopted the acronym ACIT-APIT (Arab Culture and IT Transfer; Arab Policy and IT Transfer) as representative of the work; the URL for detailed information about the program is www.acit-apit.com.

As the team wrapped up its grant activity in 2004, our thinking was moving to new applications of models and methods. We are considering comparative studies in developing and lesser-developed countries across continents and will seek funding to support these endeavors. For example, IT policy and culture in other developing countries like South Africa and Brazil could offer fascinating contrasts to each other and to the experiences of lesser-developed countries such as Tanzania and Bolivia, where national IT policy is in its infancy and IT infrastructure is nascent.

The evolution of this program of research is idiosyncratic in that the program has changed considerably over the years due to personal and individual factors as much as by environmental factors. Nevertheless, there are some causal agents that seem to be generalizable, and the telling of the story could be of use to researchers pursuing global studies in determining how and if a program of research will allow them to reach their goals more efficaciously.

The PR story is divided into four stages. The first two stages are told in Part I. The second two are told in Part II. Guidelines and lessons learned are offered in each case as the nature of the research, including evolution of the model, methodology, and team composition developed during the 10-plus-year horizon.

Typical Characteristics of Programs of Research

Programs of research are systematic pursuits of knowledge. The problem to be solved is divided into interrelated elements, and research is organized along the critical paths of dependencies. Each phase of the program is intended to build on the discoveries of the prior stages (Schultz & Slevin, 1975; Williamson & Ouchi, 1981). In a hauntingly prescient analysis of what eventually happened 35 years later in the Human Genome Project, Platt (1964) discussed how a planned approach to biological research can accelerate our scientific knowledge base by finding true associations and by ruling out infeasible ones. Thus, one of the advantages of programs of research is that they presumably allow scientists to make faster progress toward understanding complex phenomena than would occur piecemeal, either by the same researchers or by a set of disparate researchers. In contradistinction to one-shot projects or even a thematically unified series of studies, PRs are expected to create a substantial stream of work, one that manifests itself in a series of working papers, conference proceedings, journal publications, book chapters, books, and presentations. Typical characteristics of programs of research are shown in Table 1 and discussed next.

1. **High-impact research questions:** Programs of research most often seek out big hits—areas where the social, economic, or disciplinary impacts are the greatest. This is why the research most readily funded by the NSF and other major scientific organizations tends to be programs of research. These organizations want to support work that will lead to the largest improvements in broad social and economic settings.

2. **Team-based/cross-disciplinary:** Assuming that programs of research are inclined to be ambitious in addressing high-profile research questions, it is clear that individuals or smaller groups of researchers may not possess the necessary expertise or skills to carry out the research. Programs of research, therefore, tend to be cross-disciplinary and composed of a relatively larger group of researchers. It is not uncommon to find that these teams are also cross-institutional, given that the right person to fill in the expertise needed for the project may not be found at one's own institution.

3. **Theory-based:** There are clear benefits to creating models and frameworks that are theory-based. They introduce ideas that have longevity, because they tap into the basic way social systems and computers work and interact. Programs of research are aligned well with this, since one of their prime objectives can be to uncover law-like relationships between concepts in the real world. There can be a downside to using theory when researchers have to develop constructs, linkages, and instrumentation from scratch. This occurs when prior approaches were not based on theory, and the only way to investigate the phenomenon

Table 1. Typical features of generic programs of research

Features	Commentary: Programs of research ...
1. High impact research questions	... can address high-impact issues, since they are ambitious and broadly conceived.
2. Team-based/cross-disciplinary	... almost always need to have disparate expertise, rare in single individuals, to carry out the goals of the program.
3. Theory-based	... can make intellectual contributions that go beyond empiricism to impacts that are long-lasting and core to the field.
4. Incremental accumulation of knowledge	... can plan to build on one's own work and related work that are inspired by the program or at least consonant with it.
5. Longevity	... can explore thoroughly a phenomenon over a relatively long period of time, using a variety of approaches and refining the explanatory models as time goes on.
6. Organic	... adapt to changes over time. Over time, most things change; programs of research are no exception.
7. Knowledge transfer	... can leverage learning of all team members with their complementary skill sets, but if key individuals leave the program, this can pose problems.
8. Continuity	... can roll over expertise from one project to the next, and repurpose intellectual capital to new needs.
9. Funding	..., given their typically ambitious objectives, may require funding, since their resource needs are high.

is to set the scientific validation process in motion from the very beginning (Straub, 1989).

4. **Incremental accumulation of knowledge:** Purposeful science builds on the work of others. While there is value in pure replication (Kuhn, 1970), most research is directed toward adding value to the knowledge base, even if it is incremental. Programs of research are excellent ways to make substantive enhancements in what we know about a phenomenon; they also are dedicated to building on their own work and on that of others that may have been inspired by the program, creating a sort of multiplier effect. Researchers also work in parallel, with little to no knowledge of the work of others, of course. But programs of research that have a reasonable dispersion of knowledge about their findings are more likely to lead to synergies and dovetailing of work.

5. **Longevity:** With the advent of a program of research, it becomes immediately obvious that this is a long-term effort. The research questions are ambitious and require multiple studies and varying approaches to address them. They require a team with depth in diverse content and methods. Single, one-shot studies cannot possibly carry out the goals of such a program. Even thematic streams of work are not as long-lived, in general. PRs present opportunities

to gather data at subsequent points in time, and offer one of the few options for this in academe.

6. **Organic:** In any human endeavor, it would be unreasonable to expect high consistency with complex projects and large groups of people working over long periods of time, which proves to be exactly the case in most PRs. Some avenues of work prove to be dry; others are fruitful. Some team members carry on year after year, while others drop in and out or graduate and move on. Nothing is so predictable about a program of research as the fact that it will change. When the team members understand this in advance, they are better prepared to deal with it when it inevitably occurs.

7. **Knowledge transfer:** Related to the inclination of programs of research to be team-based is the advantage that team members are continually educating each other from their diverse knowledge bases. Whereas this is crucial in any PR, it is particularly important in global studies, since knowledge of the cultural and national setting is so key.

8. **Continuity:** PRs are composed of teams of faculty members, doctoral students, and graduate assistants, as well as sometimes practitioners and staff members, all of whom develop a sense for the goals of the group and how to realize these goals. When the team moves on to another aspect of the overall program, it understands the problems and issues and can apply them to the new setting. This efficiency leads to effective additional problem solving, since the team can spend more time thinking through the challenges and not dwelling on logistics.

    There is a significant downside to continuity, in that this considerable resource base needs to be nurtured and supported. When the funding from one grant ends, the people are still there, and the team leaders need to find ways to fund the team.

9. **Funding:** Large-scale, long-term PRs require major funding by their very nature. Researchers can temporize for a period and fund programs with smaller, more numerous sources of funding, but the truly ambitious projects require large infusions of money.

Our PR, Lakatos, and Scientific Progress

Before launching into a fuller discussion of the experiences of our PR, it is important that we distinguish between what we are calling a program of research and PRs, as defined by some philosophers of science. For Lakatos (1970a, 1970b), for example, a program of research is a hard core of propositions and a set of ancillary hypotheses that can be falsified without threatening the PR. Lakatos' (1970a, 1970b) definitions and elaborations of PRs are part of a macro-level intellectual inquiry into the nature of science. In this inquiry, he questions the positions of Kuhn (1970) and Popper (1980, 1989) and affirms a latitude with predictions of ancillary hypotheses that prove to be false. In this regard, he is taking a stance similar to that of Cook and Campbell (1979) in their advocacy of a critical realist acceptance of falsification.

Our definition of a PR in this chapter goes well beyond issues concerning the intellectual core. We see it as a social experience and a set of methodologies. It also involves practices and interrelationships with other groups, such as funding agencies and research outsourcers. If there is a core in a PR, we assume that it would be associated with the identity of the researchers involved rather than the ideas per se. The discussion of PRs in this chapter should be evaluated in this context.

Key Dimensions for Global IT Programs of Research

PRs that are being carried out in the domain of global IT studies have another orthogonal set of distinctive characteristics that affects how and where research is conducted. Table 2 shows two dimensions—culture and model elements—that can affect choices in thoroughly exploring and gaining insight into the phenomenon of interest.[1] First, one can explore a single culture using a constrained model (Cell 1,1). In order to study a single culture, there are basic assumptions that are being made about culture and its influence on IT. In the context of ACIT-APIT work, we call this culture influence modeling, first introduced in Hill et al. (1994). The notion behind this form of modeling is that individual cultures have a range of

Table 2. Dimensions of global IT programs of research

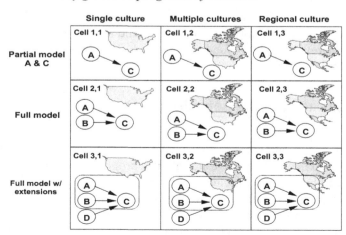

commitment to particular cultural values, and those persons that are most strongly committed to those values will have a predictable response to certain features of IT (sometimes it is also true that those least committed will have the opposite response, but we attempt to capture this in a construct that we term technological culturation in ACIT-APIT).

As the team broadens its scope and studies several cultures or subcultures (Cell 1,2) up to entire regions (Cell 1,3), the result is greater generalizability. The change in scope on the model dimension ranges from a severely restricted, parsimonious model to an expanded, less parsimonious model. This latter objective is worthwhile, since it allows the scientist to explain more. The risk is always that the model is poorly specified.

One might be tempted to think that the natural scientific progression through the matrix is to move methodically one level at a time across and downward through the culture and the model axes. This would enable a team to build effectively on knowledge gained from simpler models and fewer cultures. Theoretically and meth-odologically, this may be a reasonable plan. The ACIT-APIT program found that it was necessary to capitalize on research opportunities and to leap levels in the matrix. Table 3 depicts these changes to date. We began simply enough with qualitative studies in Jordan (Cell 1,1), but were soon thereafter presented with an opportunity

Table 3. Actual approaches taken in ACIT-APIT

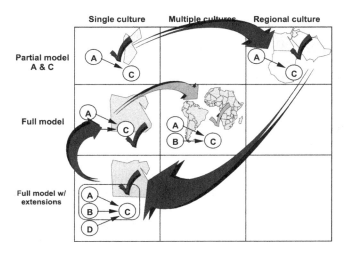

Note: N.B. Projects undertaken are shown in black checks and arrows; those for future research in grey.

to gather data from five Arab countries (Cell 1,3), and we felt that this would give us unprecedented access to valuable data. Subsequent to this work, we again were given access to superb data in a single country: Egypt (Cell 2,1). The model was expanded, and new data were collected for theory confirmation or disconfirmation (Cell 3,1). In working with our sources in Egypt, we found ever-increasing chances to gather more data, data that had never been accessed before. So we seized on this opportunity and garnered major funding to stay in Egypt for a longer period of time (Cell 2,1). Our future plans, as alluded to earlier, are to compare the full model performance across multiple cultures and two continents (Cell 2,2).

Table 3 also depicts a late movement of the team from the single culture, extended-model perspective (Cell 3,1) to a perspective involving multiple countries and the main model (yellow arrow to Cell 2,2). This is future work that we now are contemplating in two socioeconomically divergent African and South American cultures. This would provide a robust test of our theories.

Carpe Diem Principle

It might occur to the reader that opportunism was a strong factor in making decisions for the ACIT-APIT program of research. We would not deny this. In fact, we would argue that IS researchers, especially in global IT studies, need to be open to such possibilities. The fact of the matter is that there are huge barriers to conducting global IT work, and this problem is compounded if one decides to attempt a program of research. Change is inevitable and does not always evolve according to plan. Therefore, the team needs to be open to change and needs to welcome it when it comes. It also comes in the form of unexpected modifications in the human resources that are the basis of the program, as discussed next.

Changes in ACIT-APIT Team Over Time

In order to properly document the evolution of the program that is highlighted in this chapter, it is important to understand that the players in the project changed rather dramatically over time. The two authors of this chapter have been on board for the duration, but many others have made critical contributions at various points in the program life. Table 4 indicates team members, roles and expertise, and the period during which they were actively involved. The team was Georgia State University (GSU) faculty members and doctoral students, with the primary exceptions of Dr. Sherif Kamel (American University in Cairo), Dr. Khaled Wahba (Cairo University), and those who assisted in data collection in other Arab countries. Other team members not shown were those hired to gather data or those who cooperated with the various projects for a short time.

Table 4. Changes in team membership over duration of research program

Phase	Team Member	Role and Expertise	Period of Involvement
Stage 1: Inception (1992-1996)	William Cotterman	Background in IS; consulting, and study of Arab world for more than 20 years	1992-1996
	Detmar Straub	Background in IS; experience with Asian cultures and IT, particularly Japan	1992-1997
	Karen Loch	Background in IS; long-standing interest in international IT studies; fluent in French	1992-1997
	Carole Hill	Background in cultural anthropology; work in Costa Rica and health systems	1992-1997
	Kamal El Sheshai	Background in Decision Sciences and statistics; native Egyptian	1995-1997
Stage 2: Focusing (1997-1999)	Detmar Straub; Karen Loch; Carole Hill	See above	1997-1999
	William Cotterman	Retired from GSU in 1997	
	Kamal El Sheshai	Retired fr om GSU in 1997	
	Sherif Kamel	Background in IS; director of a quasi-government agency; on faculty at American University in Cairo; active in researching implementation of systems in Egypt; native Egyptian	1997-1999
	Greg Rose	Background in IS; experience with cultural aspects of time in Arab and other cultures; GSU doctoral student	1998-2000
Stage 3: InDepth (2000-2003)	Detmar Straub; Karen Loch Sherif Kamel	See above	2000-2004
	Carole Hill	Retired from GSU in 2001	2001
	Galen Sevcik	Background in accounting; active in researching financial systems; taught numerous times in Egypt	2002-2004
	Khaled Wahba	Background in systems engineering; colleague of Sherif Kamel; on faculty at Cairo University; native Egyptian	2002-2004
	Ricardo Checchi	Background in IT and engineering; GSU doctoral student	2002-2004
	Peter Meso	Background in IT in developing countries	2003-2004
Stage 4: Redirection (2004-???)	Detmar Straub; Karen Loch Galen Sevcik Peter Meso	See above	

Table 5. Dissemination of results during Stage 1

Results Dissemination	Team Involved	Themes/Comments	Years of Coverage
1. "The Impact of Arab Culture on the Diffusion of Information Technology: A Culture-Centered Model," *Proceedings of the the Impact of Informatics on Society: Key Issues for Developing Countries, IFIP 9.4,* Havana, Cuba, 1994.	Hill, Straub, Loch, Cotterman, and El-Sheshai	First exposition of the basic, underlying theoretical model. Initial specification of construct linkages.	1992-1994
2. "A Qualitative Assessment of Arab Culture and Information Technology Transfer," *Journal of Global Information Management*, 6(3), (1998), 29-38.	Hill, Loch, Straub, and El-Sheshai	Attempt to understand cultural barriers to IT adoption through an interpretation of numerous interviews that used "rapid assessment" qualitative techniques.	1992-1996
3. "Transfer of Information Technology to the Arab World: A Test of Cultural Influence Modeling," *Journal of Global Information Management*, 9(4), 6-28.	Straub, Loch, and Hill	The first quantitative examination of the evolving research model.	1992-1996

Stage 1: Inception (1992-1996)

As shown in Table 1, we believe that research programs may exhibit distinctive features at different points in time and that this can be a helpful framing of what often occurs as a program evolves. In fact, in the early periods of the program project, the scientists involved may not have even realized that, indeed, they were engaged in a systematic program of research. This may not even have been their original intention. It could have started from the simple desire to study an interesting phenomenon, and the modus vivendi was really coincidence.

This was certainly the case for the research program that serves as an illustration of a long-standing program, our ACIT-APIT PR. How such programs begin and then how they take on their initial form may be of interest to other researchers, so we describe this in the following. The output from Stage 1 is shown in Table 5.

Typical Activities in this Stage

The following activities characterized this stage. Each will be discussed next in greater detail.

1.   Formation of team

2.   Scoping of initial project, including consideration of research methodologies to be employed

3.   Literature review

4.   Creation of research model

5.   Development of instrumentation

6.   First data-gathering trips abroad

Formation of Team

Programs of research are, by definition, on a larger scale than ordinary one-shot projects and, therefore, almost always involve collaboration. Since research is a social construction, we would argue that nearly all research projects of this magnitude begin with collegial connections. Seldom do researchers seek out others for collaboration solely on the basis of their prior work; the personal connection is an all-important ingredient in the inauguration.

Late in the fall of 1992, Bill Cotterman and Detmar Straub, both of the CIS Department at Georgia State University (GSU), met to discuss a new stream of research in an international setting. Straub had spent six months the previous year living in Japan and was interested in how culture affected the use and diffusion of IT. Cotterman had consulted in the Arab world for over 20 years, spoke Arabic, and was equally convinced that IT methods and adoption in Arabic countries were affected profoundly by culture. It became immediately clear that a larger team to extend the breadth of expertise would be desirable in order to appreciate more fully the nuances of this phenomenon. Karen Loch was the first person invited to join the team because of her extensive international experience, contacts, and strong background in information systems. Subsequently, we invited Carole Hill to join the project. Both Bill and Karen had worked with Carole on international efforts for the University and were familiar with her work. Carole was in the Cultural Anthropology Department and had studied the impact of culture in the health care setting, both in the U.S. and in Costa Rico. Carole brought a fresh, non-business-school perspective to the project and expertise in qualitative research methodologies that extended the team's portfolio of expertise.

One of the first insights that Dr. Hill brought to the project, in fact, was the need to vary from the typical approach being taken in IS-cultural studies, particularly cross-cultural studies. These studies tended to base their hypotheses on universal cultural characteristics such as those advocated by Hofstede (1980). In fact, Straub and colleagues, using comparative data from Japan, Switzerland, Finland, Peru, Egypt, and the U.S., eventually would publish several chapters in this traditional vein (Straub, 1994; Straub, Keil, & Brenner, 1997). In contradistinction to this stance, Hill pointed out that anthropologists tended to explore cultural features distinctive to each culture. Thus, the philosophical and methodological approach that the team decided to pursue was termed culture-specific modeling. This direction was articulated in the first article emerging from the research stream (Hill et al., 1994) (Table 5, Article #1).

One additional team member joined in 1995. Kamal El-Sheshai was invited to join because of his strong statistical background and his linguistic ability as a native Egyptian. (We have found that it is always helpful, even crucial, to have native speakers on the team.)

Scoping of Initial Project, Including Consideration of Research Methodologies Employed

Initially, our objective simply was to study how culture impacted the diffusion of systems and IS methodologies in the Arab world. As the literature review progressed, this phenomenon became better specified, and the project became better scoped. Because the phenomenon appeared to involve a heavy component of sociopsychological processes, we used anthropological techniques to formulate our initial impressions. Hill was an invaluable team member in training us in what she referred to as rapid assessment techniques, which are intensive methods that allow the collection of anthropologically relevant data in a relatively short time period. They involve assessments from interviewing that go beyond the straightforward responses of the participants themselves. Probing, unstructured inquiries during the interviews became critical in this process. Systematic observation, such as layouts of the office spaces, were drawn up, usually after the meeting and before leaving the premises. These allowed us to assess the central or subsidiary position of the computer in people's work lives. We also learned to create real-time field notes that documented impressions of the setting, social interactions, and other factors that might impact computer use or systems development. These can be especially useful in cultures that are suspicious of tape recording their opinions and fact sharing. In fact, without such extensive field notes, much research within internationally based PRs could not be carried out.

Literature Review

We quickly discovered that there is an immense amount of literature that illuminates the culture of the Islamic world, and even more specifically, the Arab world. We focused on works, particularly books such as Bharat's The Arab Mind that spoke to these cultural dimensions. We were most interested in how Arabs think and respond unconsciously to their environment, and such works provided key insights. On the cultural anthropology side, a number of works by Hakken (1990, 1991, 1993a,

1993b) gave insight into how cultures could resist strongly the change that was encapsulated in assumptions in computer systems. Other works such as Antonelli (1986), Atiyyah (1989), and Goodman and Green (1992) covered specific problems that arose in diffusing IT in the Arab world. This period of rumination and sharing of concepts was lengthy. An immensely interesting part of this process was trying to determine a priori which cultural features under which conditions would prove to be inhibitors or, conversely, facilitators.

Creation of Research Model

Also in this stage, we developed a theoretical model that drove subsequent work and, in a variant form, does so to this day. The literature bespoke the conceptual basis for the study, but we advanced from this basic knowledge to identify key constructs that included constructs for culture, technological culturation, IT national policy and infrastructure, and systems outcomes.

Many of these theoretical elements were specified ab ovo, which framed the project from 1992 to the present time (see definitions of these constructs and their linkages in the Appendix). As this model evolved, linkages were specified and respecified, and the final research model included parsimonious links between three independent variables and one dependent variable, termed ICT outcomes or IT transfer. We hypothesized as well a downstream secondary effect of ICT transfer that is intuitive but not well studied; that is, socioeconomic effects.

In the first part of our study, we drew a linkage between technological culturation (originally termed acculturation) and culture and IT infrastructure/policy. This is shown as the working model in Figure 1. Later, a more elaborate model evolved, depicted in Figure 2. Implementation factors were considered besides cultural is-

Figure 1. Initial working research model (Source: Hill et al., 1994)

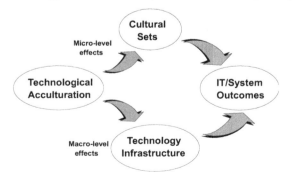

Figure 2. Overall emergent research model (Source: NSF model; www.acit-apit. com)

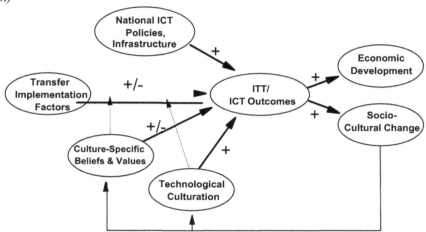

sues and basic infrastructure. As the program evolved and the knowledge about the phenomenon of cultural impacts on IT transfer increased, we altered our research model in order to expand the number of variables and posit feedback loops and moderating effects. While the overall model became less parsimonious over time (see Figure 3), we were able to plan for and to carry out feasible projects within the overall program by selecting domains of interest for particular studies and, in this fashion, engage in parsimonious testing. For the quantitative testing of relationships between culture, technological culturation, and ITT/ICT outcomes (a renaming of IT/System Outcomes in the working model), we employed the parsimonious model shown in Figure 3.

While this research model was intended to describe progression toward computing in any society, our research program focused on the Arab world, with special attention to studies in Egypt in the latter 1997-2003 period. Arab culture has some idiosyncratic features (often, but not always, orthogonal to Hofstede's [1980] cultural dimensions) that became the dominant theme of the research program, particularly in the early stages.

Figure 3. Parsimonious model for testing links in Stage 1 (Source: Straub, Loch, & Hill, 2001)

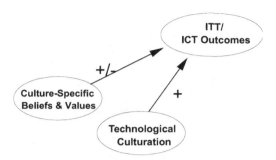

Development of Instrumentation

The project used several techniques in the early period. At the outset of the research, we convened three focus groups of Arab students who had lived less than six months in the United States or another developed country. An evolving set of open-ended questions was posed to each group, and the ensuing conversations were recorded and transcribed. Our goal was to ascertain beliefs, values, and attitudes about ITT. Because these individuals had lived in the U.S. for less than six months, they served as surrogates for the views and values of young Arab adults living in their home countries. Transcripts of focus groups were content analyzed for themes, constructs, and relationships and also used as the basis for development of a questionnaire instrument and interview questions.

The structured portion of the evolving research instrument consisted of a series of open-ended and closed-ended questions. Additionally, scenarios were to be incorporated for participant response. Each scenario, which described the development and implementation of different information systems in varying organizational settings, had embedded within it cultural beliefs and values that were drawn from the literature review and focus group results. Questions about the scenario tried to determine which of these beliefs were considered to be salient by the participants. In a pilot study of several dozen Arab-American business persons, participants were asked to read scenarios and to respond to a series of questions regarding their cultural beliefs and norms and their assessment of the likely success or failure of the information system described in the scenarios. Much thought was given to this, especially in the areas of language and instrument administration. English, for instance, was the language of choice for the early studies in Atlanta. Since the respondents in this stage were all native Arabic speakers with a high level of competency in the English language, this choice seemed to be reasonable. Language fluency questions verified our suppositions in this regard. But it also became clear

Figure 4. Amman, Jordan: Site of first major data gathering

that two versions of the instrument—one in Arabic and one in English—would be required for administration of the instrument in Arab countries.

This pretesting was followed by a two-month field study in Jordan (Figure 4). There, interviews were conducted with a variety of organizations, including government agencies, NGOs, MNC, and leading Jordanian private-sector firms. The interviewers administered the structured questionnaire instrument in person with influential players as well as gathered ethnographic and other qualitative data. The analysis of this qualitative data led to a published study (Hill, Loch, Straub, & El-Sheshai, 1998).

In studying culture and its impacts, anthropologists historically have preferred ethnographic techniques, and, for this reason, much of the foundation work in Jordan was qualitative. To empirically test the cultural influence model, however, we felt the need for a sample size of several hundred individuals. This is most efficiently achieved through a questionnaire. Additionally, we felt that the use of multiple methods and samples allowed us to better triangulate on the phenomenon of culture and IT.

Therefore, in the latter part of this stage, we also used a mailed questionnaire approach to gathering data. A mailed survey methodology has the advantage of gathering a relatively large sample, but it is important that the survey be pretested. Validation of the instrument with the Arab-American focus groups allowed us to prepare an English and Arabic form of the questionnaire. The Arabic version incorporated dialectical differences for each country in which the data were to be collected and then back-translated for accuracy. Four additional Arab countries—Egypt, Saudi Arabia, Lebanon, and the Sudan—were selected for data gathering. In Egypt, Saudi Arabia, Lebanon, and the Sudan, survey administration was handled by colleagues. This process resulted in a paper published in the *Journal of Global Information Management* (Straub et al., 2002).

Initial Data-Gathering Trips Abroad

To support the intensive data gathering in the early stage, we applied for numerous internal university grants (described later). Most of these grants were competitive, but they were not for large sums, and so our budgets were constrained. To deal with the financial restrictions, we tried to combine teaching, conference trips, and so forth in order to cover expenses. Trips that serve more than one purpose are highly desirable, since they amortize the expenses over multiple purposes. Straub and Sevcik taught in the Joint MBA program with Cairo University, which the team was able to leverage.

Trips to the Middle East were spotty in these early years, as Table 6 shows.

Team Processes

Global IT researchers may find it useful to hear more about operational and heuristic processes that our team adopted for its work. We began meeting for two hours on a weekly basis with task agendas that ranged from literature review to theory adaptation. The reading and discussion of the literature was handled much as in a book club. Everyone read the assigned articles, and then we debated the key points together while making notes for future use. This approach enabled us to develop the working model and then later to refine it.

In addition to discussion of the literature, the team found that planning tasks and preparing publicity documents were good uses of meeting time. Writing letters or e-mails to contacts or cover letters for conferences or journals were a joint effort, and the attention of several minds improved their quality greatly, we surmise.

We found that some tasks were best not performed as a team. Writing the first draft of papers and even subsequent rewritings were done best as an individual project by the lead author and then later emended by the other authors. Although the team

Table 6. Trips abroad for the ACIT-APIT program of research

Year	Dates	Venue; Purpose	Team Members
1994	November - December	Amman; research	Cotterman; Loch; Hill; Straub
1995			
1996			
1997	June 3-5	Cairo; research and conference	Loch; Straub; Hill
1998	May 18-31	Cairo; research	Straub;
	June 6-8	Cairo; research and conference	Straub; Loch
1999	March 4-15	Cairo; research	Straub; Loch
	April 11-May 23	Cairo; research and teaching	Straub
	October 7-13	Cairo; research	Straub
2000	April 12-June 5	Cairo; research and teaching	Straub
2001	February 2-March 14	Cairo; research and teaching	Straub; Loch
	June 1-7	Cairo; research and conference	Straub; Loch
2002	May 21-28	Cairo; research	Straub
2003	January 23-March 4	Cairo; research and teaching	Straub; Loch
	May 9-21	Alexandria; research and teaching	Straub
	August 12-19	Cairo; research	Straub; Loch; Sevcik; Checchi
2004	September 30 - October 7	Cairo; research	Straub; Loch; Sevcik; Checchi

often looked at data together in order to determine how to code transcripts or how to apply statistical tools, the work of coding and running statistical tests was always performed off-line.

Stage 2: Focusing and Theory Confirmation (1997-1999)

PRs may move from a first learning stage to a more confirmatory stage, once there is evidence that the basic interpretation of the phenomenon has merit. Our project took this turn. New antecedent variables and other contingencies were considered, as were variations of measurement. Our attention shifted to working regionally to working in one country, Egypt, because of the contacts that had been nurtured there and the welcoming environment for research. Sources of external funding also were sought out during this stage.

In the case of ACIT-APIT, we felt we had made some progress in qualitatively capturing key constructs through rapid assessment techniques. Culture notoriously is difficult to assess, but we believed that we had teased out some of the cultural

Table 7. Dissemination of results during Stage 2

Results Dissemination	Team Involved	Themes-Comments	Years of Coverage
1. "Predicting General IT Use: Applying TAM to the Arabic World," *Journal of Global Information Management, 6,* (1998), 39-46.	Rose and Straub	Work in the traditional exploration of culture and IT diffusion; predictions were borne out.	1997-1998
2. "Diffusing the Internet in the Arab World: The Role of Social Norms and Technological Culturation," *IEEE Transactions on Engineering Management, 50*(1), (2003), 45-63.	Loch, Straub, and Kamel	Addition of social norms to the ACIT-APIT model; exploration of organizational level of analysis.	1999
3. "The Role of Culture and IT Policy in the Developing World: The Case of Egypt and the Arab Culture," Iowa State University, 2001.	Straub	Annual Miller Lecture Invited Speaker. Basic description of ACIT-APIT program of research.	1992-2000
4. "E-Competitive Transformations," Presentation at the Information & Decision Support Center (Cabinet-level Agency) Conference, 2001.	Straub	Attended by more than 1,500 Egyptian business and government professionals, this conference was held February 12–15, 2001. Straub discussed the already apparent impacts of Egyptian government policy on privatizing the telecomm industry.	1995-2000
5. "Competing with e-Commerce (in Egypt)," Principal speech in one-day seminar sponsored by Magdy Hamish and the Arab Academy of Science and Technology, 2001.	Straub	There were approximately 150 business and government executives and managers in attendance, including the chairman of the IDSC, the CEO of the Central Bank of Egypt, the CEO of the Arab Contractors, and so forth. Straub stressed circumstances in Egypt, particularly policy initiatives, which could impact the development of e-commerce in Egypt.	1995-2000
6. Workshops/education/seminars for working adults in Egyptian academic institutions, 2001.	Straub	Lectures on the potential for Egypt to transfer critical IT capabilities from industrialized countries. Joint MBA program between Cairo University and Georgia State University.	1995-2000
7. Workshops/education/seminars for working adults in Egyptian academic institutions, 2001.	Straub	Lectures on e-business potential of Egypt for the Arab Academy for Science, Technology & Maritime Transport, Alexandria.	1995-2000

continued on following page

Table 7. continued

Results Dissemination	Team Involved	Themes-Comments	Years of Coverage
8. "Qualitative Research in IS: Innovative Methods for Research in the Middle East," *BITWORLD Conference 2001*, June 4-6, Cairo.	Loch	Explanation of the difficulties of carrying out qualitative and quantitative research in developing countries like Egypt.	1992-2000
9. "Challenges of Cross-Cultural Research in IS: Some Experiences," *BITWORLD Conference 2001*, June 4-6, Cairo.	Loch E	xplanation of the difficulties of carrying out qualitative and quantitative research in developing countries like Egypt.	1992-2000
10. "Qualitative Research in IS: Innovative Methods for Research in the Middle East," *BITWORLD Conference 2001*, June 4-6, Cairo.	Kamel	Explanation of the difficulties of carrying out qualitative and quantitative research in developing countries like Egypt.	1990-2000
11. "Studying Bits throughout the World: New Theoretical Approaches to Researching Culture in Developing Countries," Keynote Address. *BITWORLD Conference 2001*, June 4-6, Cairo.	Straub	Argument for a new theoretical approach to defining "culture" based on social identity theory	1992-2000
12. "Hurdles to Conducting Cross-Cultural Research," *BITWORLD Conference 2001*, June 4-6, Cairo.	Straub	Views on the difficulties of carrying out qualitative and quantitative research in developing countries like Egypt.	1992-2000
13. "International Information Technology Transfer: An Extended Study," Virginia Polytechnic Institute, Blacksburg, VA, September 27, 2002	Loch	Presentation of ACIT-APIT research to faculty and doctoral students	1995-2001
14. "Use of the Internet: A Study of Individuals & Organizations in the Arab World," *Global Information Technology Management Conference*, Memphis, TN, 2000	Loch, Straub, and Kamel	Reporting of results from preliminary interviews.	1995-1999

conflicts that were in play in Arab culture. So, we changed the project in order to assess culture through different means. We also tried to reconceptualize culture in order to find more acceptable instrumentation.

The output from this stage is shown in Table 7.

Typical Activities in This Stage

The following activities characterized this stage. Each will be discussed next in greater detail.

1.   Acquisition of internal grants

2.   Changes in team membership

3.   Reframing of project, including consideration of new research methodologies to be employed

4.   Continuing literature review

5.   Development of new instrumentation and retesting of research model

6.   Additional data-gathering trips abroad

Acquisition of Internal Grants

We began applying for grants to support the program within a year or two of inception. In Stage 1, these were proposals to Georgia State University. The history of these is shown in Table 8. Please note that the rejection rate was not insignificant, and that it took perseverance to lock down grants, both from the standpoint of internal and external applications.

Table 8. Funded grants history for supporting the ACIT-APIT PR

Grant Proposal Title	Years	Funding Agency	Amount
"Workshop on IT Policy in Egypt and Developing Countries" (NSF # INT-0322501)	2004	National Science Foundation (NSF)	$30,000
"GSU in the Middle East — Extending Our Reach in Egypt"	2002-2003	International Strategic Initiatives, GSU	$6,000
"IT Transfer to Egypt: A Process Model for Developing Countries" (NSF # DST-0082473)	2000-2003	National Science Foundation (NSF)	$390,000
"People & Information Technology Policy: The Human Link"	1998-1999	Research Initiation Grant, GSU	$5,000
"The Egyptian Initiative: Cross-Institutional Linkages: Georgia State University and the Mubarak Informatics Institute"	1997	International Strategic Initiatives, GSU	$4,000
"Transfer of Information Technology to Developing Countries"	1997	GSU Research Team Grant	$10,200
"Transfer of Information Technology to Developing Countries"	1997	Dean of Arts and Science; Dean of Business Administration	$7,000
"Impact of Arab Culture on the Diffusion of Information Technology: A Culture-Centered Pilot Study"	1994-1995	Research Initiation Grant, GSU	$5,000

Changes in Team Membership

The original team changed in Stage 2 for a variety of reasons. Drs. Cotterman and El-Sheshai both retired and served thereafter only in occasional consulting roles. Although we lost the Arabic language facility with these two departures, we gained it through the addition of Dr. Sherif Kamel, who headed up a quasi-governmental organization promoting IT and IT education in Egypt. To examine the use of systems in the Arab world through a traditional lens, doctoral student Greg Rose engaged in a pinpointed research project with Straub. This project complemented the work of the main project team but can be considered to be part of the overall program of research.

This stage demonstrates an organic movement of people in and out of the team that is common in many long-term programs. Professional lives undergo a large number of changes over multiple years, and constituency of the team is one of these inevitable processes.

Reframing of Project, Including Consideration of New Research Methodologies to be Employed

This stage called for alteration in how we were gathering data, since we became increasingly interested in triangulation and wanted to strengthen our methods as we ramped up for a proposal for the NSF to be submitted in February 1999. Data gathering techniques in the first stage were both quantitative and qualitative in nature, as indicated by the two major articles that described results in this stage (Article #2 and Article #3 in Table 4). We determined that the rapid assessment techniques used in Stage 1 could be used in a positivist analysis, as well, if the sample sizes were higher.

Thinking ahead toward an NSF proposal, which has the advantage of sponsoring multi-year work, we also created a phased research approach calling for varying qualitative and quantitative methods in different phases.

Continuing Literature Review

In this stage, we broadened our literature base in order to learn more about the role of national IT policy in developing countries. We knew the general outlines of our planned NSF proposal and policy issues were going to be a critical part of that inquiry.

The seminal work by King and colleagues (1994) is a good example of this. These IS scholars posit the effect of institutional commitment at the highest levels; that is,

Figure 5. Cairo, Egypt: Site of major data-gathering efforts in Stages 2 and 3

at the nation-state level, on the effective national deployment of IT. This fit in well with our notions that the IT infrastructure of a country, including its national policies dealing with computing and networks, would directly impact diffusion. One of the important papers that helped us to choose stakeholders with which to work was Gurbuxani et al. (1990). They argue that there are six stakeholder groups of importance in executing a national IT policy. These are multinational corporations (MNCs), trend-setting local firms, governmental agencies, non-governmental organizations (NGOs), professional and trade organizations, and educational institutions.

Unfortunately, the literature on IT national policy is relatively diminutive and not well accepted in the mainstream of IS research, and there was not an extensive literature to work with in this domain. The paucity of this literature is evidenced in Checchi et al. (2003), and, for obvious reasons, we tried to view this paradoxically as both a deficiency and as a fertile field for future work.

Since we also knew that ongoing work in the program involved data gathering in Egypt and that the NSF grant was to be focused on Egypt with its seat of government in Cairo (Figure 5), we found works like Nidumolu et al. (1996) to be highly useful. This chapter presents three different theoretical perspectives on the success of decision support systems disseminated throughout the Egyptian governorates.

Development of New Instrumentation and Retesting of Extended Research Model

We used Stage 1 instrumentation in the extended model tested in this stage. The measurement of outcomes was based on previous measures, and we repeated the scales for the technological culturation construct, even though this variable was not proving to be entirely dependable. To tap into the essence of the TC construct, we decided to add a direct assessment to the previous surrogate characterization. Thus, these new questions asked respondents explicitly about their exposure to hardware, software, the Internet, and IT training that had been imported from other non-Arab countries. This seemed to represent an improvement in measurement properties (Loch, Straub, & Kamel, 2003).

In addition to exploring a parsimonious model that used only the variables posited in the emergent model in Stage 1 (Figure 2) (Straub et al., 2001), we experimented in Stage 2 with subsets of measures for ITT/ICT outcomes; namely, system usage. This work (Loch et al., 2003) drew from one link in the emergent model—TC to ITT/ICT Outcomes—and hypothesized a new linkage from social norms to outcomes. This extended model, with its sundry measures, is shown in Figure 6. The extension of the model to include social norms (SN) substantiated strong connections between social influences like TC and SN and acceptance of systems. Measures were similar to those used in previous research. Specific cultural obstacles also were identified in this study through the qualitative analysis.

The decision to test the theory in at least one new context proved to be extremely helpful. First, it confirmed the causal linkages. Second, it reinforced the qualitative results that came out of Stage 1.

Additional Data-Gathering Trips Abroad

The project team visited the Middle East many times during the course of the project, and we were able to dovetail various interests in carrying this out, starting in Stage 2. First, we sought local university funding, which was instrumental in advancing the work. In order to secure funding beyond the official university sources, we gave presentations to the deans of the School of Arts and Sciences, where Professor Hill had her appointment, and the College of Business, where Loch and Straub had their appointments. The deans were favorably impressed with the work to date and with the prospects for future external funding and were willing to support the project, as well. It was helpful that the Dean of Arts and Sciences was Egyptian, and his initial offer of funding was generous. The Dean of Business soon thereafter established parity in supporting the project. This funding enabled us to make several trips to the Middle East to gather data.

Team Processes

In Stage 2, we continued to meet on a weekly basis but added an hour to the meeting time. There have been many times since making this change that the best work

Figure 6. Model for testing additional link to Stage 1 model (Source: Loch et al., 2003)

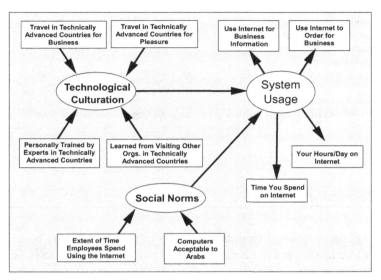

of the day occurred during the last hour. Sometimes, it is necessary to have a long warm-up period before generating the most productive ideas.

During this stage, we began to use more formalized project planning tools and techniques, such as prioritizing tasks and assignment of off-line work. This became especially critical for the planning of the NSF proposal. These proposals are relatively complex, and submission of materials has to be orchestrated carefully in order to meet the deadlines. Proposals that are one day late are not considered, so it is an important item of business. In order to garner as many perspectives as possible on costs, we worked on proposal budgets as a team.

In addition, we had to reorganize to try for the NSF grant for the subsequent year. We were pleased to be ranked in the highly competitive top category for our first submission in February 1999, but the program director was not able to stretch funds for all proposals in the category, and so we were not funded. To try to make sure that the proposal would be even stronger when we resubmitted in February 2000, we visited relevant program directors in Washington, DC, and changed the proposal in accordance with their suggestions. Some of these suggestions included strengthening the ties to Egyptian organizations. This grantsmanship is described in greater detail in Part II of this chapter.

Table 9.

#	Lessons Learned: DOs
1.	Be creative regarding funding.
2.	Leverage funds—internal and external.
3.	Commitment to team members.
4.	Build relationships.
5.	Process is slow, organic.
#	**Lessons Learned: DON'Ts**
1.	Ill-advised for junior faculty to play a lead role due to the length of time to publication.

Lessons Learned: Part I

Table 9 lists lessons learned from this program of research. It may be noted that several of these lessons are not limited to Part I but are applicable to international programs of research.

All research is dependent on available resources. This is true particularly for international research. Be creative about the sourcing of funding to keep the project alive. We utilized every internal option available to us. Internal grants are a good source for preliminary funds. These smaller dollars allowed us to establish a foundation on which we were able to successfully secure more significant funding from third parties over a multi-year period. We also found internal funds as an effective vehicle to bridge between funds obtained by third-party funds.

Team members must be committed; a core group is essential to the longevity of the project. Loch and Straub have been core members since the inception of this inquiry. A churn of team members creates gaps in project experience and slows down the whole research process. Team members that work well together are also part of the success process.

Related to the importance of working together as teams is the focus on building relationships. The import of strong relationships between and among members of the research team is captured by an adaptation of the adage for successful real estate development to "relationships, relationships, relationships." An international PR is fully dependent on relationships of team members and personal networks that each one might represent that is key for access to the target sample.

Global IT programs of research are inherently difficult. The distance, time difference, and time delays, not to mention the funding challenges to keep the PR alive, are challenging. We found, as well, that there was a lack of body of work on which to draw. Nevertheless, it has been phenomenally rewarding. In Part II, the story continues, reviewing the PR's development and delineating steps leading to third-party funding.

References

Antonelli, C. (1986). The international diffusion of new information technologies. *Research Policy, 15*(3), 139-147.

Atiyyah, H. S. (1989). Determinants of computer system effectiveness in Saudi Arabian public organizations. *International Studies of Management & Organization, 19*(2), 85-103.

Baba, M. (1995). The cultural dimensions of technology-enabled corporate transformation. In M. J. Santos, & R. D. Crus (Eds.), *Technological innovation and cultural processes: New theoretical perspectives.* Mexico, D.F.: National University of Mexico.

Bertolotti, D. S. (1984). *Culture and technology.* Bowling Green, OH: Bowling Green State University Popular Press.

Brooks, F. P. (1995). *The mythical man-month: Essays on software engineering, anniversary edition* (2nd ed.). Boston: Addison-Wesley.

Checchi, R. M., Hsieh, J. J. P-A., & Straub, D. W. (2003). Public IT policies in less developed countries: A critical assessment of the literature and a reference framework for future work. *Journal of Global Information Technology Management, 6*(4), 45-64.

Cook, T. D., & Campbell, D. T. (1979). *Quasi-experimentation: Design and analysis issues for field settings.* Boston: Houghton Mifflin.

Culnan, M. J. (1986). The Intellectual development of management information systems 1972-1982: A co-citation analysis. *Management Science, 32*(2), 156-172.

Cunningham, R. B., & Srayrah, Y. K. (1994). The human factor in technology transfer. *International Journal of Public Administration, 17*(1), 101-118.

Escobar, A. (1994). Welcome to Cyberia: Notes on the anthropology of cyberculture. *Current Anthropology, 35*(3), 211-231.

Gallupe, R. B., & Tan, F. B. (1999). A research manifesto for global information management. *Journal of Global Information Management, 7*(3), 5-18.

Goodman, S. E., & Green, J. D. (1992). Computing in the Middle East. *Communications of the ACM, 35*(8), 21-25.

Gurbaxani, V., King, J. L., Kraemer, K. L., McFarlan, F. W., Raman, K. S., & Yap, C. S. (1990, December 16-19). *Institutions and the international diffusion of information technology.* Paper presented at the 11th Annual International Conference on Information Systems, Copenhagen, Denmark.

Hakken, D. (1990). Has there been a computer revolution? An anthropological view. *The Journal of Computing and Society, 1*, 11-28.

Hakken, D. (1991). Culture-centered computing: Social policy and development of new information technology in England and in the United States. *Human Organization, 50*(4), 406-423.

Hakken, D. (1993a). *Computing myths, class realities: An ethnography of technology and working people in Sheffield, England.* Boulder, CO: Westview Press.

Hakken, D. (1993b). Computing and social change: New technology and workplace transformation, 1980-1990. *Annual Reviews of Anthropology, 22*, 107-132.

Hassan, S. Z. (1994). Environmental constraints in utilizing information technologies in Pakistan. *Journal of Global Information Management, 2*(4), 30-39.

Hill, C. E., Loch, K., Straub, D. W., & El-Sheshai, K. (1998). A qualitative assessment of Arab culture and information technology transfer. *Journal of Global Information Management, 6*(3), 29-38.

Hill, C. E., Straub, D. W., Loch, K. D., Cotterman, W., & El-Sheshai, K. (1994, February 21-23). *The impact of Arab culture on the diffusion of information technology: A culture-centered model.* Paper presented at the Impact of Informatics on Society: Key Issues for Developing Countries, IFIP 9.4, Havana, Cuba.

Hofstede, G. (1980). *Culture's consequences: International differences in work-related values.* Beverly Hills, CA: Sage.

Kamel, S. (1995). IT diffusion and socio-economic change in Egypt. *Journal of Global Information Management, 3*(2), 4-16.

Kedia, B. L., & Bhagat, R. S. (1988). Cultural constraints on transfer of technology across nations: Implications for research in international and comparative management. *Academy of Management Review, 13*(4), 559-571.

King, J. L., Gurbaxani, V., Kraemer, K. L., McFarlan, W. F., Raman, K. S., & Yap, C. S. (1994). Institutional factors in information technology innovation. *Information Systems Research, 5*(2), 139-169.

King, J. L., & Kraemer, K. L. (1995, March). Information infrastructure, national policy, and global competitiveness. *Information Infrastructure and Policy, 4*, 5-28.

Kraemer, K. L., Gurbaxani, V., & King, J. L. (1992). Economic development, government policy, and the diffusion of computing in Pacific area countries. *Public Administration Review, 52*(2), 146-156.

Kransberg, M., & Davenport, W. (1972). *Technology and culture: An anthology.* New York: Schocken Books.

Kuhn, T. S. (1970). *The structure of scientific revolutions* (2nd ed.). Chicago: University of Chicago Press.

Lakatos, I. (1970a). Criticism and the growth of knowledge. In J. T. Schick (Ed.), *Readings in the philosophy of science* (pp. 91-195). New York: Cambridge University Press.

Lakatos, I. (1970b). Falsification and the methodology of scientific research programs. In I. Lakatos & A. Musgrave (Eds.), *Criticism and the growth of knowledge* (pp. 91-196). Cambridge: Cambridge University Press.

Loch, K., Straub, D., & Kamel, S. (2003). Diffusing the Internet in the Arab world: The role of social norms and technological culturation. *IEEE Transactions on Engineering Management, 50*(1), 45-63.

Lucas, H. C. (1978). Empirical evidence for a descriptive model of implementation. *MIS Quarterly, 2*(2), 27-41.

Mendoza, R. H., & Martinez, J. L., Jr. (1981). The measurement of acculturation. In J. A. Baron (Ed.), *Explorations in Chicano psychology* (pp. 1-83). New York: Praeger.

Nidumolu, S. R., Goodman, S. E., Vogel, D. R., & Danowitz, A. K. (1996). Information technology for local administration support: The governorates project in Egypt. *MIS Quarterly, 20*(2), 197-224.

Platt, J. R. (1964, October 16). Strong inference. *Science, 146*, 347-353.

Popper, K. R. (1980). *The logic of scientific discovery.* London: Hutchinson.

Popper, K. R. (1989). *Conjectures and refutations: The growth of scientific knowledge* (5th ed.). London: Routledge.

Robey, D., & Zeller, R. L. (1978). Factors affecting the success and failure of an information system for product quality. *Interfaces, 8*(2), 70-75.

Schultz, R. L., & Slevin, D. P. (Eds.). (1975). *A program of research on implementation.* American Elsevier.

Straub, D. W. (1989). Validating instruments in MIS Research. *MIS Quarterly, 13*(2), 147-169.

Straub, D. W., & Loch, K. D. (2006). Global programs of research: Maintenance and extensibility. *Journal of Global Information Management, 14*(2), 29-51.

Straub, D. W., Loch, K. D., Evaristo, R., Karahanna, E., & Srite, M. (2002). Toward a theory-based measurement of culture. *Journal of Global Information Management, 10*(1), 13-23.

Straub, D. W., Loch, K., & Hill, C. (2001). Transfer of information technology to the Arab world: A test of cultural influence modeling. *Journal of Global Information Management, 9*(4), 6-28.

Williamson, O. E., & Ouchi, W. G. (1981). The markets and hierarchies program of research: Origins, implications, prospects. In A. H. Van de Ven, & W. F. Joyce (Eds.), *Perspectives on organizational design and behavior* (pp. 347-406). New York: John Wiley.

Endnotes

*   This material is based upon work supported by the National Science Foundation under Grant #DST-0082473. Any opinions, findings, and conclusions or recommendations expressed in this material are those of the author(s) and do not necessarily reflect the views of the National Science Foundation.

[1]   This depiction is purely for the sake of illustration. It is not clear that there is such a regional culture of the Americas north of Guatemala. This viewpoint is not unrelated to the Global Information Management framework proposed by Gallupe and Tan (1999). The concept of single and multiple cultures is explored in their framework, and they also talk about single variable studies and compare these with more complex models.

Appendix

Definition of Constructs and Linkages in Funded NSF Grant #DST-0082473

National IT Policies (POL). Refers to specific technology policies that guide the development of information systems in a specific country. The overall construct reflects the level of support for technological development within a given nation. For this reason and due to the fact that there is a lively exposition centered around the link of government policy with ITT (Gurbaxani et al., 1990; Kamel, 1995; King et al., 1994; King & Kraemer, 1995; Kraemer, Gurbaxani, & King, 1992), POL is modeled as predicting ITT/system outcomes in a specific Arab developing country; namely, Egypt. The model is intended to be robust so that it can be adapted easily in later studies to consider the multi-country case.

Transfer Implementation Factors (IMPLEMENT). Refers to the set of antecedents generally studied in the literature, such as user training, top management support, and championing of systems projects. For this research project, key elements of IMPLE-MENT are derived from the literature for further study in the developing world (Culnan, 1986; Lucas, 1978; Robey & Zeller, 1978).

Culture-Specific Beliefs and Values (CULTURE). Defined as specific patterns of thinking that are reflected in the meanings people attach to their behavior (Baba, 1995; Hofstede, 1980). Hofstede (1980) refers to culture as a learned phenomenon that results in the "collective programming of the mind" (p. 25). In our model, it refers to those specific beliefs, values, and meanings that are thought to have a downstream effect on the use of information systems. CULTURE is demonstrated through social actions and becomes crystallized in social institutions. Bertolotti (1984) pointed out over a decade ago that the culture of a country or region greatly affects the acceptance of technology through its beliefs and values regarding modernization and technological development. Over two decades ago, Kransberg and Davenport (1972) stated that "an advance in technology not only must be congruent with the surrounding technology but must also be compatible with the existing economic and other cultural and social institutions of society." Ignoring the cultural context can result in delays or, at worst, failures in the ITT process (Baba, 1995). Fundamentally, the study of the relationship between technology and culture is "particularly concerned with the cultural constructions and reconstructions on which the new technologies are based and which they in turn help to shape" (Escobar, 1994).

The study, therefore, intends to discover how Egyptians practice technology in their everyday lives.

continued on following page

Technological Culturation (TC). Refers to exposure and experiences that individuals have with technology developed in other countries. In anthropological studies, acculturation typically refers to the assimilation by members of one society of the values and beliefs of a pre-existing culture or by the adoption of some of their cultural characteristics (Mendoza & Martinez, 1981). These earlier studies assumed that the more developed countries unilaterally gave new technology to lesser-developed countries. The beliefs that help people make sense out of the world and that guide their social world are always changing. They change and learn in response to internal and external events. TC refers to those changes that occur as a result of external stimuli, specifically technology stimuli. Traditional theoretical bases of this concept assume that the transfer of information and technology flows from a dominant culture to a subordinate one. It is this assumption that prompted some anthropologists to abandon the concept as one born out of colonialism.

In the present research, which studies CULTURE and TC in the context of the Arab world, TC designates beliefs and behaviors that originate outside traditional Arab culture and society and are incorporated into the belief sets of Arabs. The assumption is that the cultural-social lives of our respondents influence their attitudes toward and use of technology. The theoretical framework assumes that Arabs continually negotiate their technological world within the context of their culture and that the contact between these worlds is transforming in nature.

In the IT arena, TC occurs when people become informed or educated about computer systems and application software that are not presently diffused within their own culture. These experiences range from formal experiences such as long-term studying in a technically advanced culture to informal experiences such as travel abroad.

ITT/System Outcomes (ITT). Refers to the actual use or intention to use new technology within specific institutions/organizations of a country as well as to the success or failure of the diffusion of new technologies (Cunningham & Srayrah, 1994; Hassan, 1994; Kedia & Bhagat, 1988). It also can refer to the outcomes of a system development methodology or process during which systems are specified, designed, and implemented. As shown in Figure 2, the model formulates relationships between CB, TC, POL, IMPLEMENT, and ITT. It further proposes that technological culturation and cultural beliefs have a moderating influence on the relationship between IMPLEMENT and ITT.

This work was previously published in the Journal of Global Information Management, 14(2), 1-28, April-June 2006.

Chapter II

Global Programs
of Research:
Maintenance and Extensibility[*]

Detmar W. Straub, Georgia State University, USA

Karen D. Loch, Georgia State University, USA

Abstract

This is the second part of a two-part chapter that describes and analyzes a program of research (PR) in international IT studies that began in the fall of 1992. The first part spans the years 1992 through 2000 and discusses the concept of a PR, the inception of our PR, and its maturation in terms of theory and methodology, research team dynamics, and program implementation. Part II focuses on the time frame of 2000 to 2004. The work undertaken during this second period is distinctive in two areas: the examination in detail of the full range of all constructs in the final research model; and grantsmanship, which was essential to the life of the PR. Specifically, a multi-year NSF grant funded the core of in-depth work undertaken between 2000 and 2003. A second NSF grant permitted us to work with domain experts from around the world to push the stream of research forward. In Part II, we also offer a retrospective analysis, based on our experience, on the PR effort. Pros and cons are articulated and then extrapolated into practical lessons learned that will be useful to others in similar undertakings. We offer guidelines for initiating and maintaining programs of research, highlighting the inevitable trade-offs that occur when high administrative work loads and intensive data gathering in the global setting, often involving long periods of time abroad, have to be balanced with the ability to carry out the research at all and the rarity of the data. Finally, we look forward to what we term Stage 4—the period of redirection—which is the bridge to the next program of research.

Introduction

This is the second part of a two-part presentation that traces the evolution of a program of research (PR) on Arab culture and national IT policy and how these variables affect various ICT (information and communications technologies) outcomes. In Part I, Creating and Developing a Program of Global Research (Straub & Loch, 2006), we described the background leading up to this period. Each team member brings different and complementary assets to the project. Loch had long-term established relationships with a key individual in Egypt, Sherif Kamel, without whom we would not have been able to do this work. Kamel was instrumental in opening the doors for interviews at all levels. Straub and Sevcik both taught in the Robinson Joint MBA program with Cairo University, which permitted the team to leverage its funds and gave it considerable on-the-ground experience and contact with its partners. Kamel had been involved in the development of the ICT sector in Egypt. He was exceptionally knowledgeable of the players and had access to them. It was 1999. At this point, we knew two things. First, we were committed to continuing the line of inquiry. Second, we knew we must seek major third-party funding to sustain the work.

Stage 3: In-Depth (2000-2003)

We published a series of articles reporting our initial findings in the first two stages, inception and theory confirmation. We felt that the next natural step in the development of what we now knew to be a program of research was a large-scale grant, especially from a prestigious source like the National Science Foundation (NSF) in the U.S. Competitive grants, such as NSF grants, convey many benefits to awardees.

The competitive nature of the grant means that awards presumably go to ideas that are acceptable science and will lead to high impacts, both in scholarly and social terms. In addition to the funding, which is necessary to carry out the research, the winning of an NSF grant can lead to participation in NSF panels and reviewing, which extends the knowledge base and social network of team members. The impact on the research is indirect but decidedly valuable.

While not the place for a detailed discussion on grant programs and their respective funding agencies, it merits mentioning that many developed countries have governmental funding and even private funding available. The Canadian government, for example, provides reasonably good levels of funding for researchers at Canadian institutions. This is equally true of Asian schools, such as those in Singapore and Hong Kong, as well as for countries belonging to the European Union.

Table 1. Dissemination of results during stage 3

Results Dissemination	Team Involved	Themes-Comments	Years of Coverage
1. *An Instrumentation Process for Measuring ICT Policies and Culture*, Proceedings of the Information and Communications Technologies and Development Conference, Kathmandu, Nepal, 2002.	Checchi, Sevcik, Loch, and Straub	How the instruments and interview scripts were developed for the NSF grant	1999-2002
2. *Bounded Rationality and Sectoral Differences in Diffusion of National IT Policies*, Proceedings of the IFIP WG 9.4 - 2003 Conference, Athens, Greece 2003.	Meso, Checchi, Sevcik, Loch, and Straub	Analysis of Stage 1 data to validate a bounded rationality interpretation of policy awareness	1999-2002
3. "Public IT Policies in Less Developed Countries: A Critical Assessment of the Literature and a Reference Framework for Future Work," *Journal of Global Information Technology Management*, 6(4), (2003), 45-64.	Checchi, Hsieh, and Straub	Creation of meta-model for policy research in the future via a meta-analysis of the IT national policy literature in major journals	1994-2002
4. "Toward a Theory-Based Measurement of Culture," *Journal of Global Information Management*, 10(1), (2002), 13-23.	Straub, Loch, Evaristo, Karahanna, and Srite	Based on attempts to capture culture in scenarios in ACIT-APIT program of research, a musing on how culture can be measured	1942-2001
5. "Transferring Technology to the Developing World," In M. Khosrow-Pour (Ed.), *Encyclopedia of Information Science and Technology, Vol. 5* (pp. 2846-2850), Hershey, PA: Idea Group Reference, 2005.	Petter, Sevcik, and Straub	Review of ACIT-APIT work and that of other scholars working in this stream	1992-2002
6. *Measuring Success in e-Commerce*, ECIS 2002, Gdansk, Poland. Keynote Speaker.	Straub	Details on the Egyptian experience with the Internet from data in the program	
7. *Studies and Research in Egypt: 1992-2002*, Information and Decision Support Center, Cairo, Egypt. Speaker.	Straub	Details on the Egyptian experience with the Internet from data in the program	

The output from this stage is shown in Table 1.

Typical Activities in this Stage

The following activities characterized this stage. Each will be discussed next in greater detail.

1.   Acquisition of external grants
2.   Changes in team membership
3.   Continuing literature review
4.   New instrumentation and retesting of refined and expanded research model
5.   Numerous trips abroad
6.   Team processes

Acquisition of External Grants

The application for the main NSF grant in February 1999 was the largest funding we had attempted to date. The proposal, which can be viewed at http://ACIT-APIT.com, was ranked among the highly competitive proposals, but funding ran out before it could be financed. Therefore, we were in the position of reapplying with a different set of reviewers for the following year's competition.

The reviews of the proposal were extremely valuable, and we gained additional insights on how to strengthen the proposal by visiting with the NSF program directors in Washington, DC. One of the points the reviewers made was that commitments from high-profile Egyptian stakeholders would send a strong signal that the proposed work actually could be accomplished. When we resubmitted the proposal, these letters of commitment were in place. Had we not already worked closely with many of these stakeholders, the chances of obtaining the letters and, therefore, the chances for funding would have been greatly reduced.

In the summer of 2000, the team was notified that it had been awarded NSF Grant #DST-0082473. After a process of trimming back the budget, the final award was $390,000 for 30 months. Loch was the principal investigator (PI) on this grant.

Near the end of this stage, we applied for and were awarded a second NSF grant. This $30,000 grant, NSF #INT-0322501, funded a two-day forum on advancing theory on IT national policy in Cairo in October 2004. It permitted the team to cover the expenses of U.S.-based researchers in this general research area to gather in Cairo to assist in forging new directions in theory-making. The details of the forum may be found at: http://acit-apit.com. The first day of the forum was an informational session open to the public. All individuals with whom we had worked or who had participated in some fashion in the study were invited. Keynote speakers from the Ministry of Communications and Information Technology (MCIT) and the American University in Cairo were part of the forum program. The second day constituted a workshop of high-profile academics and well-positioned policymakers. Plans are to produce a report that may be able to lead research in IT national policy in the future.

Changes in Team Membership

Team membership changed radically in this stage with the loss of our cultural anthropologist, Dr. Carole Hill. Even though she retired during the first year of the funding of the main NSF grant, she stayed on with the project for another year.

The team was fortunate to obtain the involvement of Dr. Galen Sevcik, Associate Professor of Accounting at GSU, as the third PI on the project. Sevcik was versed in Egyptian culture as a result of several years of teaching in Cairo. He had been working with us voluntarily on the project before Hill's retirement and converted to a more active role when she ceased working on the grant. As a result of his interest, we modified our data collection in Stages 2, 3, and 4 to capture the organizational department of the respondents. When gathering policy reactions in Stage 2, we actively tried to match firm financial and IT officers so that we could exploit Sevick's expertise. He was highly involved in the development of the instrumentation and an active participant in the downstream analysis and writing tasks. He was also the PI for the second NSF grant for the forum.

Dr. Khaled Wahba formally joined the on-the-ground team at this time. He served as the coordinator of Stages 3 and 4 of the grant. With his background in systems engineering, Wahba was able to utilize his expertise and position in a semi-governmental agency to gain access to the Egyptian institutions that were required for a major interviewing schedule. Our long-time colleague, Dr. Sherif Kamel, continued to play a key role in this effort, with contacts to IT policymakers and critical C-level corporate officers that went back to the 1980s.

With the NSF support, we were able to involve a doctoral student in the program full time. Ricardo Checchi, an Argentine CIS doctoral student with an engineering background, grew into a role as a key participant in the instrument development process and developed an interest in the stream of research as a secondary thrust to his primary agenda of working on digital supply networks. Checchi has been an author on three important papers for the project (Checchi et al., 2003; Checchi, Sevcik, Loch, & Straub, 2002; Meso, Checchi, Sevcik, Loch, & Straub, 2003).

The last member to join the team post NSF in 2003 was Dr. Peter Meso, an assistant professor of CIS at GSU. Meso specializes in the developing country domain and authored an important paper for the project on sector effects in awareness of IT national policies. He joined the project to work on data analysis and writing results; he presented these results at an IFIP conference in Athens in 2003 (Meso et al., 2003).

Continuing Literature Review

Work in this stage delved more deeply into scholarly work in IT policy. This was the first time that we were analyzing the full model. A meta-analysis by Checchi et al. (2003) scanned the IT policy literature and summarized the findings up to 2002. They offered a framework (Figure 1) that shows the importance of institutional actors in the policy formation process.

The other major literature developments during this period were possible new theory bases that supported the basic linkage between policy and diffusion. Among the most promising theory bases are regime theory (Koenig-Archibugi, 2003), stakeholder theory (Freeman, 1984; Frooman, 1999), and what we will likely term governance theory (Finkelstein, 1995; Koenig-Archibugi, 2003).

Figure 1. Framework for IT national policies research (Source: Checchi et al., 2003)

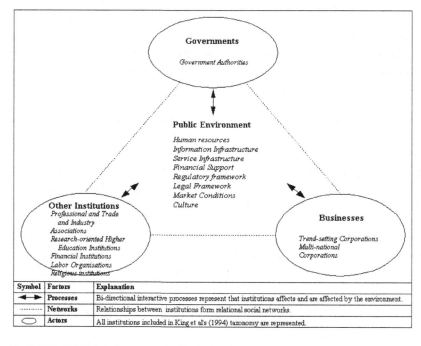

New Instrumentation and Retesting of Refined and Expanded Research Model

The process of developing instrumentation to measure the effects of culture and ICT government policy on the diffusion of computing (e.g., hardware, software, telecomm, applications) was a long and difficult challenge. The instrumentation was multi-method and included quantitative (structured, survey-like interview questions) and qualitative (open-ended interview questions) techniques. The proposal called for measures for four constructs: (1) national IT policies; (2) cultural-specific beliefs and values; (3) technological culturation; and (4) transfer implementation factors. Furthermore, the instrumentation needed to be different for each of the four stages of the project. Instrumentation was developed through multiple stages of the project, the first two stages focusing on policy creation and awareness of the policies by those individuals in a position to implement the policy.

Stage 1 identified ICT policies in place. The categorization of respondents was driven by Gubaxani et al.'s (1990) work first presented at ICIS in 1991. High-level Egyptian government officials, top-ranking business executives, and leaders of NGOs (non-profit, non-governmental organizations such as UN agencies) were sought for interviews about the range and importance of national policy initiatives relevant to IT. Stage 2 established the validity of the policy identification that surfaced in Stage 1 by assessing interviewees' awareness, perception of completeness, and merit of the policies. To gather information about perceptions of these governmental efforts, Stage 2 involved interviews with IT and financial managers.

Large-scale data collection was the goal of both Stages 3 and 4, the former using the technique of semi-structured interviews and the latter using a Web survey. In Stage 3 the final instrumentation was created and validated in four steps: (1) the hypotheses were stated, relevant policies were chosen, scenarios were drafted, and a preliminary version of the instrumentation was sketched out; (2) focus group interviews with Egyptians were conducted in which the policies and scenarios were presented and the participants' reactions were recorded; (3) the instrumentation was piloted both in Egypt and in the U.S. with Egyptians who had been in residence six months or less; and (4) the instrumentation was translated into Arabic. A qualitative assessment of content and construct validity was undertaken. The instrumentation proved to be acceptable and ready for use in the larger data collection stages.

As shown in Figure 2, the domain of the research model examined in the NSF grant included relationships that were tested previously in Stage 2 (see Figure 3). We used scenarios, as we had in Stage 2, to gather these data. The team also studied how the awareness of policy could affect the acceptance of that government effort. Since there was a large number of policies in place, the initial work in Stages 1 and 2 involved an identification of the most critical policies and those that were most heavily supported by the private sector and other Gurbuxani et al. (1990) stakeholders.

Figure 2. Overall emergent research model (Source: NSF model; www.acit-apit. com)

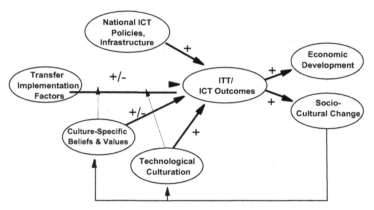

Figure 3. Parsimonious model for testing links in stage 1 (Source: Straub, Loch, & Hill, 2001)

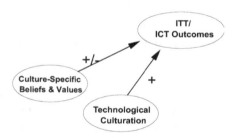

Numerous Trips Abroad

This stage involved the most intense period of travel in the history of the program of research. As can be seen from Table 2, there were six trips promised for data collection and administration of the NSF project in Cairo. Actually, we ended up making 10 trips during the full period of the grant (the grant was extended by six months, largely because of delays from the September 11, 2001, disaster) and the time immediately prior to the grant (this was used to lay the groundwork for the grant).

The early trips in the project were used for efficient gathering of policies from C-level officers in Egyptian firms or MNCs and from high-ranking officials in the Ministry

Table 2. Original work plan for NSF project

Research Task	2000			2001				2002			
	2nd	3rd	4th	1st	2nd	3rd	4th	1st	2nd	3rd	4th
Task #1: Refine qualitative instruments & interview scripts; Identify personnel; train research assistants	├	─┤									
Task #2: Qualitative data collection - research issue #1		├	─	─┤							
Task #3: Translation & data analysis & refinement of quantitative instrument				├	─┤						
Task #4: Qualitative & quantitative data collection - research issue #2						├	─┤				
Task #5: Translation & data analysis							├	─┤			
Task #6: Write-up & dissemination of results									├	─┤	
Annual Reports & Final Report					■				■		■
Meetings in Cairo	■	■		■	■			■			■
Meetings in Atlanta					■		■				

Year 1 | Year 2 | Year 3

of Communications and Information Technology and the cabinet-level Information and Decision Support Center. Later in the grant, the trips served three purposes. First, we engaged in primary data collection so that the team could get a feel for the data. Second, we coordinated activities with a research center at the American University in Cairo, the Social Science Research Center (SRC). This well-known institution among academic research groups in Egypt agreed to conduct the 200+ interviews mandated for the project and to collect the crucial data that we needed for both qualitative and quantitative analysis. Their participation in the project has proven to be absolutely essential, since the number of interviews was large, the interview script elaborate, and many of the interviews were conducted in Arabic. Training sessions for the interviewers were successful, and the SRC professionals did a superb job in collecting these data. It should be noted that there is an Egyptian law that mandated (1) that we have official governmental approval for the study and (2) that native Egyptians must conduct the interviews. Therefore, it was essential that we approach an organization such as SRC for this purpose. Once again, the role of relationships played an unanticipated role. Hill knew the second in command at SRC as a result of her work in cultural anthropology. We had established preliminary contact some years back; it now came to fruition.

Team Processes

The team continued meeting on a weekly basis and focused a lot of energy in creating instrumentation that would be effective in capturing the essence of the theoretical constructs being investigated in the NSF project. This process was described previously, but it is important for IS researchers to know that the means of gathering data are single points of success or failure for a project of this kind. Many methodological articles have pointed this out (Straub, 1989).

The other major task for the team was writing grants and handling the logistics for the forum in October 2004. It is hard to underestimate the amount of time and effort that can go into such endeavors. Grants typically have multiple sections, and whereas institutions can provide support by supplying the university boilerplates for describing the university environment, the presentation of scientific ideas is solely the domain of the researchers. Moreover, even something as simple as a two-page CV for each principal investigator and each senior consultant must be done by the individuals involved. The need to emphasize the most relevant characteristics of the individuals' backgrounds means that university support cannot be applied readily. Likewise, budgets are primarily the task of the researchers, although the university office of sponsored research is instrumental in explaining what is fundable and what is not.

In short, there is a huge amount of work associated with applying for a grant. If the grant is competitive, there is still the low probability of success. For this reason, the team must place the acquisition of grants high on its agenda and expect productivity on other parts of the program to fall off to virtually nil until the submission is complete. It also needs to be mentioned that the principal investigator in charge of the finances also has a gigantic task in tracking expenses once the grant is awarded. Most funding agencies have a monitoring mandate, and reports and adjustments in budgets are part of their oversight responsibility. This places major burdens on the team to respond to these requirements.

Stage 4: Redirection (2004-Present)

Given that we completed the formal data collection from the NSF research project as of the spring of 2004, we are currently analyzing data and preparing scientific papers. We subsequently completed a fourth data collection stage that was a Web-based survey. We anticipate that there are six to nine viable papers that can be written from the rich datasets in our possession. This process obviously will take several years to complete with analyzing data, writing papers, revising papers, and seeing them through to a publication venue.

The other major activity in this post-NSF research project period was the NSF-funded Forum on Advancing Theory in National IT Policy. The grant called for supporting the expenses of the ACIT-APIT team and a set of invited guests. The terms of the grant required that invited guests be associated with a U.S. university.

One of the goals of the forum was to bring together a group of IS scholars whose members have demonstrated interests in the role of IT national policy in socioeconomic and systems outcomes. The forum schedule, which can be viewed at http://acit-apit.com, included presentations as well as workshop sessions to accomplish these goals. The first day of the program was open to the public; the second day was intensive workshop sessions of invited participants dedicated to theory building.

Table 3. Pros and cons of programs of research

Themes	Pros of Global IT Research Programs	Cons of Global IT Research Programs
1. Creation of knowledge	Consistent publication stream / depth of knowledge base and insights	Major long-term commitment / risk of flagging interest (see HR)
2. Methods	Permits triangulation of methods and exploration with new methods	May require researchers to work with methods with which they are not necessarily intimately familiar (see HR)
3. Duration	Allows for a long-term perspective on the phenomenon	Can lead to myopia from ideological momentum about how to study and carry out the research
4. Funding	Benefits from major inflows of funding to support long stays abroad and data gathering in unfamiliar settings	Requires the continual acquisition of such significant funding
5. Complex task handling	Offers perhaps the only good way, from a financial standpoint, to study meso-level theories where work in foreign cultures is required	Must cope with complexity; grants, and high administrative workload due to this added complexity, resulting in delays
6. HR involvement	Allows long-term commitment, which makes it ideal for principal investigators who are secure in their positions and can afford years of research downtime before becoming productive again	Rules out the involvement of very junior faculty since the output from the program may not occur before tenure time
7. The international experience	Excitement of learning new cultures	Travel and time abroad costs

In this stage, we also were thinking ahead to expanding the scope of the research program for the future. As indicated previously in the discussion of funding initiatives, we anticipate that our next funding requests will move beyond the Arab world and examine continents and countries that are at very different points in development. In Africa, for example, South Africa and Botswana are moving forward rapidly in IT capability. Tanzania and other lesser-developed countries have an IT infrastructure that is at the lowest end of the scale. The contrast in national policy approaches could be fascinating, based on insights articulated in Chechhi et al. (2003). Generalizability of what we have learned about National IT Policy (its development and implementation) and insights on plausible explanations for policy success is what we can offer at this time.

Analysis of Pros and Cons

Table 3 highlights the pros and cons that have been hinted at or mentioned briefly throughout the chapter, and a brief analysis of these could be helpful as touchstones for researchers who are considering PRs. Irrespective of the lifecycle stage of the project, it is clear that programs of research can lead to a myriad of positive outcomes.

1. Creation of Knowledge

PRs typically create a unique research production flow, assuming, of course, that the team spends as much time on analyzing its rare data and communicating its findings as it does in pretesting and gathering the data. As the program changes in character and builds off prior discoveries, the insights likely become deeper and richer. The funding adds incentives to move forward consistently and to disseminate results of the project.

Conversely, programs require a long-term commitment in order to create knowledge. This can tax the participants, especially when there are problems that need to be resolved in the project. For some, it would be tempting to have only one-shot projects or thematic series of studies that readily could be abandoned, if they fell on hard times. Programs of research in global IT can be challenging, for example, because the mainstream journals generally are unreceptive to the work. Naturally, there are exceptions, but a simple glance at the last five years of MISQ, ISR, and JMIS indicate quite clearly that articles that truly are expanding our knowledge of global issues in IT are not forthcoming. It is, perhaps, anecdotal to speculate on why this might be the case, but there is little doubt that the theory bases in global IT are not as well developed as those in the mainstream. This very likely disadvantages this form of research.

2. Methods

The phenomenon of scientific interest remains basically the same for a PR, unlike one-shot projects that all have unique foci. This allows the team to try out different approaches to discovering new knowledge. The variation does not have to proceed between paradigms, as in quantitative and qualitative. It also can occur among techniques within the paradigm. In our case, for example, we coded responses to interview scripts for positivist analysis as well as survey data that tap into much larger samples.

The potential downside to this is that researchers need to work with techniques in which they are not schooled and that may be inimical to their personal dispositions. Learning curves are difficult, naturally. But there can be dead ends in methods that researchers were just simply not aware of a priori. A qualitative researcher, for example, may not feel comfortable with the need for larger samples in quantitative analysis. Hill, our cultural anthropologist, was not used to working with such large numbers. As she schooled us in anthropological approaches, we did the same for her with more quantitative approaches. Not all scholars can make this transition.

3. Duration

A PR typically extends over a period of time. This provides value in two ways: first, findings over time present a longitudinal perspective that can probe more deeply than is often the case with one-time, snapshot examinations of an issue; second, a consistent stream of publications, including both conference papers and journal articles, affords the researchers a strong profile and recognition of contribution over time. This is important in that tenure and promotion decisions typically pose the questions: Do the research streams in the portfolio demonstrate thematic unities, or are they all over the map?

The intellectual momentum that is created by doing things in certain ways and in thinking about the phenomena in certain ways also can lead to undesirable habits. Researchers can become myopic in ways that do not occur as readily in one-shot projects. One counterbalance to this tendency is the infusion of new team members with divergent perspectives. But the collective and conscious will of the ensconced team also sometimes can overcome this form of myopia.

4. Funding

In the case of the ACIT-APIT program of research and its international context, the funding challenges always remained a preeminent concern, since, if there were no funding, the ability to continue the work would be in jeopardy. Clearly, the need for funds comes from the research requirements, which include supporting long stays abroad and data gathering in unfamiliar settings. Being able to support a cadre of doctoral students is also a major benefit.

The primary challenge that we found in this area was the pressure to continually be seeking the next source of funding. Once one has acquired funding, the stakes rise, since you are finishing up the data analysis and publications for one project and, at the same time, allocating time and effort to the acquisition of funding for the next project.

5. Complex Task Handling

The complexity of ambitious projects may require PRs in order to come to any truly deep insights. Studying established relationships and simple linkages is relatively easy compared to complex models with constructs that resist ready measurement. Working in cultures foreign to your own is an added level of complexity that is made tractable with PRs but then requires the concomitant commitment for long periods of time.

The administrative workload from grants has been discussed previously. This notwithstanding, even PRs without major funding bring with them a greater burden of tracking the elements in several projects that are longitudinal in nature and carried out with different methods, in all likelihood.

6. HR Involvement

There is a time-in-rank consideration that the team needs to openly talk about and discuss. It is obvious that only under the most felicitous of circumstances will junior faculty benefit from the outputs of a program of research. It is more likely that there can be timely benefits from an ongoing program, but for those programs in the inception mode, it easily could be five years before the first scholarly production. For senior researchers, this is generally not as great of a problem, since these researchers are more likely to have other sources of productivity. The risk also is lower for senior faculty, if they are not counting on a stream of work from a program of research. When it comes, it is thus more in the vein of serendipity. The bottom line is that junior faculty members need to be very cautious about over-investing in a program of research, either their own or that of others. There are cases where it can work out, often in situations where major funding is not required to carry out the work, but it clearly involves a higher risk.

Team cohesiveness and evolution are also parameters that influence the success of the team. Team churn can contribute to delays and potential stoppage of the project. Team composition is also important, as each member has expertise in diverse areas, including methodologies, domain/discipline, culture, language, and key contacts that may be conducive to the ultimate success of the PR.

7. The International Experience

In conclusion, there can be no denying that global IT programs of research can be fascinating sources of knowledge and can deepen the emotional satisfaction of conducting research. Exposure to new cultures is a draw for many academics; it could be associated with the need of many IT scholars to learn, grow, and stay intellectually alive. The offset to exposure to new ways of thinking and doing is that it takes a toll on one's energies, time, and personal finances. This is especially acute for global IT studies. Time spent abroad is time spent away from families, in the majority of cases, and from other productive work. University budgets for travel do not necessarily cover all expenses, which is particularly true for enlightening but nonreimbursable trips to sites outside of the scope of research. In the ACIT-APIT program, for example, we have made many trips outside of the sites where we were collecting data. We have visited Luxor, Aswan, and Sharm el-Sheikl, for instance. Learning the culture of a people requires this kind of travel, but without the one-to-one mapping from research needs to locale, we took the conservative approach by funding these from personal finances.

Practical Lessons Learned

What are the practical lessons that we learned that can be communicated to scholars who are thinking of or are already engaged in a program of research? Many of those appearing in Table 4 have been discussed in this chapter. Others are stressed here for the first time. We have divided these lessons by stage, with a set of lessons applicable throughout the PR.

Table 4. Practical lessons learned

Stage	Item	To Be Sought Out	To Be Avoided
1. Inception	(a)	Familiarizing trip to locale of study	Book knowledge of the culture(s) alone
	(b)	Pretests and pilot tests of instrumentation	Insufficient time in face-to-face meetings to iron out measurement problems
2. Focusing	(c)	Commitment from as many stakeholders as possible	Poor team responsiveness
	(d)	Internal and external funding	Discouragement from rejection, especially for competitive grants
3. In-depth	(e)	Interim publications	Waiting for all the data
	(f)	Outsourcing critical elements and having backup strategies in case of default of partners	Easy ways out
4. Redirection	(g)	Other domains where confirmed theories and proven methods and instrumentation can be reapplied	Staying with the same domain because of momentum
	(h)	Stick-to-it-iveness	Relaxing
Throughout the program of research	(i)	At least one native speaker as team member, or someone fluent in the language of culture being studied; also those whose expertise complements the team, wherever possible	Too large a team
	(j)	An ambitious project that excites potential readers	Too large a project scope
	(k)	Theory-driven approach	Too much reliance on deduction and not open enough to inductive insights, as in a grounded theory approach

Stage 1. Inception

(a) The initial stage of a program of research requires the team to learn about the culture(s) under scrutiny and the possible theoretical approaches to the investigation. This book knowledge is indispensable from a scientific point of view. But it is also extremely helpful, if the team can make a probing trip to the locale concurrent with the at-home reading and thinking process. This kind of familiarizing trip yields deep insights into the nature and enactment of the culture that go far beyond book knowledge. It also invigorates the team by seeing the actual society to which the results of the work can be applied.

In the ACIT-APIT program, we were not able to travel to the Middle East before our first data gathering. We simply did not have the resources to carry this off. Had we known the value this would have imparted, though, we might have made greater efforts to win funding for this initial exposure.

(b) It took our team many years to recognize the benefits conferred by the pretests and pilot tests conducted in Atlanta before going to the Arab world. With instrumentation that had face validity before we ventured into real world settings, we undoubtedly saved effort in the long run. This was serendipity as much as anything, since we were not able to fund the familiarizing trip previously mentioned in (a). Had we been able to travel to the Middle East earlier, we might have been tempted to hazard our draft instrumentation in that setting, which could have been an impediment to the project rather than an enhancement.

There is a real temptation to skimp on instrumentation and to get on to data collection. We found that hard work on instrumentation was best handled in team meetings, and, if other researchers follow this approach, they may be inclined to allocate insufficient time in face-to-face meetings to iron out measurement problems. This process is a long and involved process, and it should not be short-shrifted.

Stage 2. Focusing

(c) We recommend that teams gain commitment from as many stakeholders as possible after the initial stage. In fact, some of the contacts that are made in the first stage can become part of a stakeholder community that is aware of your work and (hopefully) its value. Business contacts in the locale are obviously of tremendous importance, but governmental contacts can be critical, as well. In order for foreigners to conduct research in many countries outside the U.S., for example, it is helpful/necessary to have a government imprimatur. So, even if the domain of the work does not involve government, there are persuasive reasons for gaining its confidence and, indeed, for recognizing government policymakers and implementers as stakeholders.

Perhaps the most crucial stakeholders other than those mentioned are scholars and professors from the locale under scrutiny. Our experience was that there was a stakeholder base of interested academic parties and that some of these people make ideal teammates. Given the ambitious nature of programs of research, there is a lot of work that needs to be carried out in the locale itself. Making company contacts and setting up site visits are just the tip of that iceberg. Therefore, bringing local academics into the project is a mutually beneficial arrangement that should be viewed as highly desirable, perhaps even mandatory.

Once a community is nurtured, it is vital to maintain relations with stakeholders. We have made special trips to the Middle East at nontrivial expense to deliver talks or to present reports to such stakeholders. Here, again, the value of having local teammates becomes obvious. Without such support, it easily could occur that the stakeholder base loses track of (and perhaps interest in) the program of research.

(d) One non-insignificant reason for nurturing a stakeholder community is that letters of commitment often are decisive in acquiring funding, which is our second recommendation for this stage. Although especially true for international studies, there are many forms of research that cannot be conducted without resources. Gaining a sample base beyond your local, car-accessible region is only one of many arguments in favor of seeking sponsorship. Internal funding usually is easier to achieve than external funding, but the team needs to think about and plan for both. We used formal planning tools to help us through the application for the major external grant, but this is not as instrumental as simply making good, doable plans. Missing a deadline for many funding agencies means a year's delay.

Already discussed is the fact that there is high uncertainty in the funding route. It is easy to become discouraged by rejection, especially for competitive grants. Moreover, there is a sense that the team is not really being productive while preparing proposals, budgets, and so forth. There is some truth to this, but if the team is inventive, some work can be carried out with already acquired or limited funds while the grant decision is being made, so there can be output from the team to offset this sense of stalemate. Teams likely become more creative as time goes by in this regard.

Stage 3. In-Depth

(e) If the team wins a large, multi-year grant, we recommend that it plan immediately for interim publications. This, likewise, is useful for the annual reports to the funding agencies and for keeping up team morale. Items 1 through 7 in Table 1 were interim publications for the ACIT-APIT program while we were in the midst of the main NSF project. Our focus was on instrumentation, relatively straightforward analyses, and a meta-analysis of the policy literature. Web sites, of course, also are useful in disseminating information about the project, and they should be developed, but there is no real substitute for publications. Clearly, these can be conference papers, but opportunities for journal publications should not be eschewed.

The converse of this approach is to wait for all the data to come in. This really delays the publication stream by years. In our case, with an extension approved to a full three years, it would have been an unconscionable delay to publish information about the project. It also would have constituted a slighting of the stakeholders, in our opinion.

(f) It is difficult or, some might argue, impossible to carry out an ambitious PR abroad without outsourcing critical elements. Most academics do not have the ability to transfer their personal and professional life to another country for a long period of time (i.e., six months). Moreover, moving assumes that a social network is in place and that the researcher feels at home in that culture and, likely, even the native language. These are Herculean assumptions for most global IT researchers.

Our experience in this regard was the following. We were comfortable with outsourcing the major data collection in the NSF project to the SRC at the American University in Cairo. Not only did they possess an enviable reputation for carrying out excellent work in Egypt, but they also had an inherent interest in the project.

Nevertheless, it always should be in the back of scholars' minds that there may be hitches in the strategy, the data collection, or the personal interactions that doom an outsourcing arrangement. Being without backup plans is to be avoided at all costs. Hitches, in fact, can be the PR death knell, unless the team has explored options in advance. In our case, for instance, our Egyptian teammates were fully capable in a pinch of conducting the interviews rather than serving only as interview schedulers. This would have severely stressed our teammates' personal and professional resources but ultimately would have led to a successful conclusion. It is best not to have such a toll taken on one's partners, however, and so we were fortunate that backup strategies were not needed.

Stage 4. Redirection

(g) In the redirection stage, the team wants to seek out new areas for exploration. These new areas are other domains, where confirmed theories and proven methods and instrumentation can be reapplied. These can be far afield, as they were in our case, or they can be closer to what the program already has worked with. Our team is choosing to branch out into new cultures, but it is very possible that we could have delved even more deeply into the Arab world and used new methods to gain greater insights. As Table 5 shows, we also could have moved our approach to other Arab countries and back to the regional level.

In our opinion, a poor choice that a group can make at this point is to stay with what it has been doing simply out of momentum. There are challenges to learning new cultures that are not to be taken lightly, to be sure. But there can be an excitement in this, as well.

(h) There is a real and present risk that the team will begin to relax once the data has been collected in the major funding effort in this stage. Many people experience the same anti-climactic feeling with the completion of their dissertations. The sense

Table 5. Actual approaches taken in ACIT-APIT

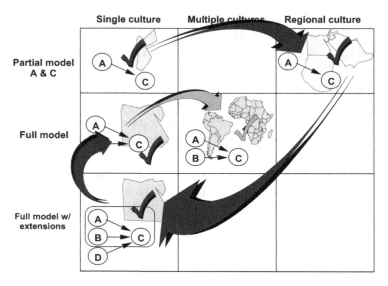

that the major work is done can lead to low levels of productivity and many years before the major dissemination of results takes place.

The team needs to dig deep and to get the resolution needed to pursue the daunting challenge of analyzing large amounts of data from the typically multiple stages of the project.

Throughout Program of Research

(i) We have found that, for global IT projects, you will need at least one native speaker as a team member. The requisite expertise is someone fluent in the language of the culture being studied and also, of course, astute enough to be conscious of the culture, to the extent that this is possible. We also actively sought out colleagues who had expertise that complemented that of the rest of the team, wherever possible. Hill, the ACIT-APIT cultural anthropologist, was an example of this in our situation.

There is a danger, of course, that the team grows too large because of the need to add specialties. When the team is too large, it likely will suffer from an intractable number of communication linkages (Brooks, 1995). Our team size has varied from three to seven (including the Egyptian partners), and we have felt comfortable at the high end of this range but probably would not want more teammates than this.

(j) PRs need to strike a delicate balance between having a large enough project scope to excite other scholars and not to exceed the capacity to deliver. This balance is not easy to achieve. We know that scope creep occurs in systems projects; it has been our experience that it also can occur in IT research projects. There is perhaps little more to be said on this except to note the obvious. The program will not be better in the long run, if it promises more than it can deliver. An unambitious project, on the other hand, will never get funded.

(k) Many IS scholars have a nearly fanatical belief in a theory-driven approach. We have become schooled in believing that deduction and prediction give our work enormous advantages, especially in publishing in the quantitative, positivist tradition. It is possible and even likely that this can lead to shortsightedness. Too much reliance on deduction, not being open enough to inductive insights, can stymie a program. The team needs to be open-minded about the conclusions it is drawing. Ideally, it might be desirable to step back intellectually at times and rediscover the roots of the phenomenon. This may strike many as a movement backward, but it could be as exciting as exploring new cultures. There is no denying that it brings with it its own set of risks, however.

Conclusion

This chapter has presented the experiences of a 10-plus-year program of research on Arab culture, national IT policy, and IT transfer. The difficulties and benefits of this program have highlighted issues that typify programs of work in the global arena.

We make no claims that our approach to the program has been either exemplary or one-of-a-kind. Others very likely could carry out their own programs and, perhaps, have done so already with greater aplomb and better results. We know that other universities consistently have pulled in large research grants for decades and that the research output from these projects has been considerable. Listing such programs is not really necessary, as most IS scholars are aware of them through community sources of information. Moreover, we would not want to emphasize these programs to the exclusion of other programs that are not as well known but are also highly successful.

But we do believe that what we have learned can be of value to anyone who is considering, initiating, or in the midst of a program. There is clear value to programs from a scientific point of view. In a sense, the work is inimitable, since it rapidly becomes specialized by virtue of the longevity, team, funding, and cumulative knowledge. The work can stimulate doctoral work and lead to high impact findings that make reputations. There is a joy in long-term collaboration that goes far beyond what is experienced in one-shot projects.

This notwithstanding, there are large costs to such a program. The benefits are often so long in coming that junior faculty cannot really count on value received before tenure time. Administrative overhead is killing. Time abroad stresses a person personally and professionally. The mainstream journal editors and reviewers are not as receptive, as one would hope, to topics in global IT research.

In the final analysis, global IT researchers will determine whether this makes sense for their own careers by evaluating their institutional environment and their personal disposition toward large-scale, long-term work in other cultures. For those who are entranced by such challenges, there is little that can rival the excitement and sense of satisfaction in programs of research in global IT studies.

References

Baba, M. (1995). The cultural dimensions of technology-enabled corporate transformation. In M. J. Santos & R. D. Crus (Eds.), *Technological innovation and cultural processes: New theoretical perspectives*. Mexico, D.F.: National University of Mexico.

Bertolotti, D. S. (1984). *Culture and technology.* Bowling Green, OH: Bowling Green State University Popular Press.

Brooks, F. P. (1995). *The mythical man-month: Essays on software engineering, anniversary edition* (2nd ed.). Boston: Addison-Wesley.

Checchi, R. M., Hsieh, J. J. P-A., & Straub, D. W. (2003). Public IT policies in less developed countries: A critical assessment of the literature and a reference framework for future work. *Journal of Global Information Technology Management, 6*(4), 45-64.

Checchi, R. M., Sevcik, G. R., Loch, K. D., & Straub, D. W. (2002, December). *An instrumentation process for measuring ICT policies and culture.* Paper presented at the Information and Communications Technologies and Development Conference, Kathmandu, Nepal.

Culnan, M. J. (1986). The Intellectual development of management information systems 1972-1982: A co-citation analysis. *Management Science, 32*(2), 156-172.

Cunningham, R. B., & Srayrah, Y. K. (1994). The human factor in technology transfer. *International Journal of Public Administration, 17*(1), 101-118.

Escobar, A. (1994). Welcome to Cyberia: Notes on the anthropology of cyberculture. *Current Anthropology, 35*(3), 211-231.

Finkelstein, L. S. (1995). What is global governance? *Global Governance, 1*(3), 367-372.

Freeman, R. E. (1984). *Strategic Management: A stakeholder approach.* Boston: Pitman Publishing.

Frooman, J. (1999). Stakeholder influence strategies. *Academy of Management Review, 24*(2), 191-205.

Gurbaxani, V., King, J. L., Kraemer, K. L., McFarlan, F. W., Raman, K. S., & Yap, C. S. (1990, December 16-19). *Institutions and the international diffusion of information technology.* Paper presented at the 11th Annual International Conference on Information Systems, Copenhagen, Denmark.

Hassan, S. Z. (1994). Environmental constraints in utilizing information technologies in Pakistan. *Journal of Global Information Management, 2*(4), 30-39.

Hofstede, G. (1980). *Culture's consequences: International differences in work-related values.* Beverly Hills, CA: Sage.

Kamel, S. (1995). IT diffusion and socio-economic change in Egypt. *Journal of Global Information Management, 3*(2), 4-16.

Kedia, B. L., & Bhagat, R. S. (1988). Cultural constraints on transfer of technology across nations: Implications for research in international and comparative management. *Academy of Management Review, 13*(4), 559-571.

King, J. L., Gurbaxani, V., Kraemer, K. L., McFarlan, W. F., Raman, K. S., & Yap, C. S. (1994). Institutional factors in information technology innovation. *Information Systems Research, 5*(2), 139-169.

King, J. L., & Kraemer, K. L. (1995, March). Information infrastructure, national policy, and global competitiveness. *Information Infrastructure and Policy, 4*, 5-28.

Koenig-Archibugi, M. (2003). Global Governance. In J. Michie (Ed.), *The handbook of globalisation* (pp. 318-330). Camberley, Surrey UK: Edward Elgar.

Kraemer, K. L., Gurbaxani, V., & King, J. L. (1992). Economic development, government policy, and the diffusion of computing in Pacific area countries. *Public Administration Review, 52*(2), 146-156.

Kransberg, M., & Davenport, W. (1972). *Technology and culture: An anthology.* New York: Schocken Books.

Lucas, H. C. (1978). Empirical evidence for a descriptive model of implementation. *MIS Quarterly, 2*(2), 27-41.

Mendoza, R. H., & Martinez, J. L., Jr. (1981). The measurement of acculturation. In J. A. Baron (Ed.), *Explorations in Chicano psychology* (pp. 1-83). New York: Praeger.

Meso, P., Checchi, R. M., Sevcik, G. R., Loch, K. D., & Straub, D. W. (2003, June). *Bounded rationality and sectoral differences in diffusion of national IT policies.* Paper presented at the IFIP WG 9.4 - 2003 Conference, Athens, Greece.

Petter, S., Sevcik, G., & Straub, D. (2005). Transferring technology to the developing world. In M. Khosrow-Pour (Ed.), *Encyclopedia of information science and technology* (Vol. V, pp. 2846-2850). Hershey, PA: Idea Group Reference.

Robey, D., & Zeller, R. L. (1978). Factors affecting the success and failure of an information system for product quality. *Interfaces, 8*(2), 70-75.

Straub, D. W. (1989). Validating instruments in MIS Research. *MIS Quarterly, 13*(2), 147-169.

Straub, D. W., & Loch, K. D. (2006). Creating and developing a program of global research. *Journal of Global Information Management, 14*(2), 1-28.

Straub, D. W., Loch, K. D., Evaristo, R., Karahanna, E., & Srite, M. (2002). Toward a theory-based measurement of culture. *Journal of Global Information Management, 10*(1), 13-23.

Straub, D. W., Loch, K., & Hill, C. (2001). Transfer of information technology to the Arab world: A test of cultural influence modeling. *Journal of Global Information Management, 9*(4), 6-28.

Endnote

*   This paper/material is based upon work supported by the National Science Foundation under Grant #DST-0082473. Any opinions, findings, and conclusions or recommendations expressed in this material are those of the author(s) and do not necessarily reflect the views of the National Science Foundation.

Appendix

Definition of Constructs and Linkages in funded
NSF Grant #DST-0082473

National IT Policies (POL). Refers to specific technology policies that guide the development of information systems in a specific country. The overall construct reflects the level of support for technological development within a given nation. For this reason, and due to the fact that there is a lively exposition centering around the link of government policy with ITT (Gurbaxani et al., 1990; Kamel, 1995; King et al., 1994; King & Kraemer, 1995; Kraemer, Gurbaxani, & King, 1992), POL is modeled as predicting ITT/system outcomes in a specific Arab developing country; namely, Egypt. The model is intended to be robust so that it can be adapted easily in later studies to consider the multi-country case.

Transfer Implementation Factors (IMPLEMENT). Refers to the set of antecedents generally studied in the literature, such as user training, top management support, and championing of systems projects. For this research project, key elements of IMPLE-MENT are derived from the literature for further study in the developing world (Culnan, 1986; Lucas, 1978; Robey & Zeller, 1978).

Culture-Specific Beliefs and Values (CULTURE). Specific patterns of thinking that are reflected in the meanings people attach to their behavior (Baba, 1995; Hofstede, 1980). Hofstede (1980) refers to culture as a learned phenomenon that results in the "collective programming of the mind" (p. 25). In our model, it refers to those specific beliefs, values, and meanings that are thought to have a downstream effect on the use of information systems. CULTURE is demonstrated through social actions and becomes crystallized in social institutions. Bertolotti (1984) pointed out over a decade ago that the culture of a country or region greatly affects the acceptance of technology through its beliefs and values regarding modernization and technological development. Over three decades ago, Kransberg and Davenport (1972) stated that "an advance in technology not only must be congruent with the surrounding technology but must also be compatible with the existing economic and other cultural and social institutions of society." Ignoring the cultural context can result in delays or, at worst, failures in the ITT process (Baba, 1995). Fundamentally, the study of the relationship between technology and culture is "particularly concerned with the cultural constructions and reconstructions on which the new technologies are based and which they, in turn, help to shape" (Escobar, 1994). The study, therefore, intends to discover how Egyptians practice technology in their everyday lives.

continued on following page

Technological Culturation (TC). Refers to exposure and experiences that individuals have with technology developed in other countries. In anthropological studies, acculturation typically refers to the assimilation by members of one society of the values and beliefs of a pre-existing culture or by the adoption of some of its cultural characteristics (Mendoza & Martinez, 1981). These earlier studies assumed that the more developed countries unilaterally gave new technology to lesser-developed countries. The beliefs that help people make sense out of the world and that guide their social world always are changing. They change and learn in response to internal and external events. TC refers to those changes that occur as a result of external stimuli, specifically technology stimuli. Traditional theoretical bases of this concept assume that the transfer of information and technology flows from a dominant culture to a subordinate one. It is this assumption that prompted some anthropologists to abandon the concept as one born out of colonialism.

In the present research, which studies CULTURE and TC in the context of the Arab world, TC designates beliefs and behaviors that originate outside traditional Arab culture and society and are incorporated into the belief sets of Arabs. The assumption is that the cultural-social lives of our respondents influence their attitudes toward and use of technology. The theoretical framework assumes that Arabs continually negotiate their technological world within the context of their culture and that the contact between these worlds is transforming in nature.

In the IT arena, TC occurs when people become informed or educated about computer systems and application software that presently are not diffused within their own culture. These experiences range from formal experiences, such as long-term studying in a technically advanced culture, to informal experiences such as travel abroad.

ITT/System Outcomes (ITT). Refers to the actual use or intention to use new technology within specific institutions/organizations of a country as well as to the success or failure of the diffusion of new technologies (Cunningham & Srayrah, 1994; Hassan, 1994; Kedia & Bhagat, 1988). It also can refer to the outcomes of a system development methodology or process during which systems are specified, designed, and implemented. As shown in Figure 2, the model formulates relationships between CB, TC, POL, IMPLEMENT, and ITT. It further proposes that technological culturation and cultural beliefs have a moderating influence on the relationship between IMPLEMENT and ITT.

This work was previously published in the Journal of Global Information Management, 14(2), 29-51, April-June 2006.

Chapter III

IT Software Development Offshoring:
A Multi-Level Theoretical Framework and Research Agenda

Fred Niederman, Saint Louis University, USA

Sumit Kundu, Florida International University, USA

Silvia Salas, Florida International University, USA

Abstract

The offshoring of IT development is a significant global economic phenomenon. It influences the lives and fortunes of individuals, organizations, and nations/regions. However, because offshoring so broadly affects different stakeholders, a multi-level theory is required so that influences that may positively affect one set of stakeholders while negatively affecting another are not misinterpreted by an overly narrow analysis. This chapter discusses how IT development is differentiated from other global labor sourcing and argues that it is worthy of investigation as an offshoring domain. The chapter proposes that the study of IT development offshoring needs to recognize precursors and results as they affect individuals, organizations, and nation/regions, and presents examples and discussion in each of these areas. The chapter further argues that the domain of IT development offshoring is incomplete without consideration of interactions between the individual and nation/region as well as between the organization and nation/region. The chapter concludes by considering the complexity of presenting a complete picture in this domain and suggesting some areas for future research.

Introduction

Offshore outsourcing (offshoring) is the practice of distributing work, particularly in the area of information technology (IT) services and development, to workers outside the national borders of the host country. It represents an extension to global proportion of outsourcing practices that have become widely practiced since the 1980s among organizations seeking to hire others to manage IT work or to develop new IT capabilities. Offshoring is not an issue limited to multinational corporations in the U.S., but a global issue that impacts organizations (Beylerian & Kleiner, 2003) and government agencies (Gruber, 2004; Harden, 2003) around the world.

This practice has received widespread attention, because it influences significantly economic activity for a diverse set of stakeholders. It shifts the equation of decision making for individual IT workers and those considering IT as a career, for organizations embarking on offshoring activities (or considering whether to do so), and for nations/regions competing to attract IT offshoring work or to retain that work domestically. This chapter argues that offshoring is a significant global, information-technology-related phenomenon of a magnitude that demands attention and understanding. It also argues that the range of stakeholders and the interaction among stakeholders suggest that comprehensive understanding of this phenomenon will require attention to each stakeholder group as well as the manner by which decisions and actions at each level have influence at different levels. Figure 1 presents a graphic representation of the relationships among stakeholder levels that will be discussed in this chapter.

Offshoring is of significant concern to IT workers, as it potentially affects both the number and kind of jobs available to them. In the U.S., total IT employment shrank significantly from its peak in 2000. Using the BLS, InformationWeek found that the number of Americans employed in technology has increase by 96,000 in the last year and a quarter (up to summer 2005). However, that is still 82,000 fewer jobs than at the end of June 2002 (Chabrow, 2005). For a period of time, unemployment among IT workers was higher than among U.S. workers overall for the first time since the invention of the computer (at least since statistics included IT workers) (Niederman, 2004). At approximately the same time, according to an Information Technology Association of America (ITAA) study in 2003, U.S. IT-producing companies have moved 12% of their IT work offshore, while non-IT-producing companies have moved approximately 3% of their IT work offshore. Matloff (2004, p. 28) references a study by Gartner Group projecting "that 25% of all U.S. IT jobs will move overseas by 2010, up from 5% today." As early as 2001, more than 40% of Fortune 500 companies reportedly were engaged in offshore outsourcing (Carmel & Agarwal, 2002).

The extent to which the decline in U.S. IT jobs is caused by offshoring is not clear. Other explanations of the dropoff include the completion of Y2K project staffing, the bursting of the dot-com investment bubble, and the general business downturn from the September 11, 2001, disaster. For individual IT workers, the globalization of the workforce presents a set of challenges and opportunities and a layer of uncertainty regarding the value of investment in particular skills and commitment to particular employers.

From the perspective of the individual organization, the offshoring of IT work represents a shift in utilization of capital-creating opportunities either to provide the same amount of IT services at lower cost or to increase the development and deployment of IT at the same cost. In turn, this can reduce costs for transaction overhead, for producing a given amount of goods or services, or for creating new or enhanced product offerings. These reduced costs allow for some combination of reinvestment in new research and development, lower prices or more options for customers, greater profits distributed to investors, or retention of capital for future investment. Of course the theoretical possibility of reducing costs and increasing benefits depends on organizations making a series of good choices, including

Figure 1. Levels of analysis and interactions

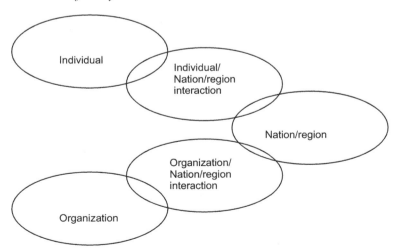

whether they are individually in a position to take advantage of offshoring, where to offshore, by what agency mechanism to offshore, and how to control and manage the process. Benefits are not automatic, and there is much concern about avoiding the risks and pitfalls that are inherent in the nature of offshoring.

From a national and regional perspective, offshoring implies a significant shift in the distribution of global resources. As jobs and wages move from one nation to another, there is a resulting shift in multiplier effects as those wages are spent in different localities. This may stimulate demand for other products among offshoring work recipient nations. This may, in turn, lead to a general rising wealth within the country receiving offshoring work. As a result, receiving offshoring work is of significant concern at the nation/region level. Individual countries have limited investment resources to encourage the development of new industries. Assessment of existing capabilities is a critical input into decisions regarding extension of these assets through new investment. A range of policies, including taxation and subsidies, protection of intellectual property, and investment in physical and human infrastructure, potentially can affect the ability to attract or retain IT development work and workers. This raises questions for nations/regions regarding the nature of existing assets; the investment and policy strategies most likely to yield benefits above costs; how to contain the risks to workers, private investors, and organizations; and projections for future needs of industry that might be addressed by their taxpayers.

At each of these three levels of analysis—the individual, the organizational, and the nation/regional—various constituents may be affected by decisions, actions, and results. Some individuals will position themselves for long and prosperous careers, while others will have jobs disappear and be forced to make career changes at potentially inopportune times. Some organizations will choose to participate in offshoring and gain significant cost, quality, or revenue advantages, while others may find projects bogging down or losing significant intellectual property. Some organizations will refrain from participating and will find themselves falling behind in their industry, while others will gain advantages or experience costly mistakes. Similarly, some nations will find their investment in infrastructure to support acquisition and retention of offshoring work, while others either will not profit from their investment or will find themselves falling behind.

In this chapter, we argue that there are significant research issues at each of these levels of analysis. Increased understanding regarding investments in skills, managing offshoring projects, and investing in infrastructure, for example, will be important in increasing benefits and limiting failures from offshoring activities. However, we further argue that a framework for offshoring research that only looks at these levels remains incomplete. A number of issues involve interplay of stakeholders among levels. For example, the outcomes of investment by nations in human and technical infrastructure will provide constraints as well as opportunities for individuals and organizations within those borders. The evaluation of decisions by nations regarding investment in offshoring infrastructure may be contingent in part on the nature of the existing workforce; the culture of the workers may determine the degree to which such investment is nurtured into successful enterprises. These relationships across levels may be non-linear or contingent. For example, an intermediate rate of taxation may allow nations to recoup costs of prior investment in human and physical infrastructure and to stimulate continuous improvement, but too high a level of taxation may render domestic offshoring work non-competitive and choke off expansion, while too low a rate may result in deteriorating infrastructure that eventually will not sustain growth.

In response to the complexity of the phenomenon of offshoring, developing an understanding of the precursors, mechanics, and results of offshoring in a comprehensive manner will require its examination from multiple perspectives. This topic requires the application of a multilevel theoretical lens to "bridge the micro-macro divide, integrating the micro domain's focus on individuals and groups with the macro domain's focus on organizations, environment, and strategy" (Klein, Tosi, & Cannella, 1999, p. 243).

The purpose of this chapter is to provide an initial step in assembling the relevant theoretical and empirical bases for developing a research agenda for offshoring. This study will take a broad perspective in considering what a comprehensive theory of offshoring would need to include. Theories from various streams of international business, strategy, and management, as well as empirical findings from MIS research, are presented in order to broaden our understanding of this wide-ranging topic and to provide a framework for future offshoring research. Discussion will begin with a consideration of why IT development is in itself worthy of special study and theorizing. What differentiates it from other offshoring services? The chapter then continues by examining issues within each of the three levels of analysis—individual, organizational, and nation/regional. It will continue with a discussion of some issues related to multiple levels. The chapter concludes with a brief synopsis and discussion of prioritization of future research work.

Why Focus on IT Development Offshoring?

IT development differs from other IT services, such as staffing of help desks or operations of data centers, in several ways. The process of developing new IT generally is complex and takes many steps, from initiation and planning to coding, testing, implementation, and maintenance. These elements are relatively constant, whether the new IT is specific to a given firm or a package to be sold across multiple customers, although the emphasis and complexity of each element may vary greatly between custom and package development. Typically, significant knowledge of an organization's other IT assets are required for custom development, because new applications generally are added to an overall portfolio of software that runs on specific hardware and telecommunications platforms. Similarly, high levels of expertise for testing systems across platforms, for balancing generic and innovative capabilities, for designing easy-to-learn and easy-to-use interfaces are crucial for package development. As a result, IT development represents a particularly complex and sophisticated work domain.

These characteristics suggest that IT development falls within what Erramilli and Rao (1993) called idiosyncratic services. Given their differences with less-specific IT activities, this particular domain provides an attractive subset of service activities for examination. Given the generally higher level of skills necessary for this sort of work, it represents an arena in which the economic impact of shifting geographic location of labor would have significant impact, not only on number of jobs but on the proportion of high-end work within a national portfolio. It is an area that pressures nations/regions to develop both technical and human resource infrastructures to be competitive in attracting and retaining highly skilled workers.

Because of the level of complexity and sophistication represented by IT development in contrast to other IT services, there is no reason to expect that decision making, actions, and outcomes that pertain to IT development also will apply to other IT services. From a research perspective, studies that mix offshoring of IT development and other IT services risk washing out genuine effects within each domain. We would argue that where studies span the different types of IT development and other services, separate analysis should be made within and across these domains to test whether, indeed, they behave differently.

This viewpoint is indirectly supported by the work of Murray and Kotabe (1999). One would expect, as they hypothesized, that such IT development activities, because they tend to be integrated with critical organizational processes, would be sourced internally by organizations. However, as results of their study did not support this hypothesis, it is likely that the core competency and expertise of the outsourcing company may lead to greater external sourcing of this sort of service. This suggests that organizations may perceive lower cost and lower or equivalent risk using the competencies of external firms, even for development of complex systems, than the costs and risks for providing these internally. Alternatively, they may perceive IT applications not as part of the core operations and procedures but rather as a technical supplement that supports their operations. This suggests an interesting, if not unique, service industry, where the nature of the service is clearly not a simple interchangeable commodity, and yet significant amounts of offshoring, in fact, do occur.

Examination of Issues within Levels

The Individual Level

Some IT professionals are affected by offshoring in terms of their immediate employment and long-term employment prospects. This shows up in layoffs but also in the creation of new job titles that have new skill demands. For example, a class of IT project managers is emerging for coordinating work between international sites. Individual effects also turn up in selection of careers among those entering the market, including students and those temporarily outside the job market (Niederman, 2004).

Human Capital Theory

Human capital theory largely is concerned with the mechanisms by which the application of human skills and abilities translate into individual and organizational profits. Some specific areas of interest include the investment in training made by individuals and organizations that result in higher levels of productivity for individuals and, as a result, increasing profits that can be divided between the individual and the organization. One particular concern of this line of research is the varied outcomes from training because, as an individual's skill and productivity increase, unless the payoff from that investment is recognized and rewarded by the organization, there is some chance of a different organization hiring that individual and profiting from the original company's training investment.

Taking current wage differentials between the U.S. and India for programmers, for example, that difference is explained logically by differences in overall economic standards between the two countries. Cost of living averages are so much lower in India that even receiving a fraction of the pay for Indian programmers in contrast to equivalent workers in the U.S. may result in little living standard difference. Another consideration is that, to the extent that the U.S. and India represent different labor markets, their supply and demand curves may differ significantly. In this explanation, there is a relatively small gap in supply and demand for programmers in the U.S. but a very high supply of programmers relative to demand in India, thus resulting in far lower pay in India for the equivalent work. Another explanation revolves around wage stickiness. In good times for employees (when demand is greater than supply), wages will rise, but in bad times, as supply exceeds demand, wages will freeze, and employers will be inclined to reduce the number of employees or to stop hiring, and to reduce total numbers through layoffs or attrition. New workers will be hired at lower wages, raises will be curtailed or diminished, and the average wage will stay the same. This analysis would lead to speculation that

India simply may have not gone through enough periods of upward wage pressure in order for labor costs to be equivalent to those in the U.S. It is also interesting to consider the effects of the overall economic strength of the U.S. and India and how those translate into currency exchange rates. In recent years, the U.S. dollar has weakened against key world currencies such as the Euro (although, at the time of this writing in July 2005, the dollar had made up some ground), which may tend to narrow the price differential between U.S. and Indian programmers, once currency differences are accounted for. It is also interesting to note that as offshoring gains momentum, more Indian programmers are hired, and their average wages can be expected to rise. Agrawal and Thite (2003) estimated that salaries have been rising at an annual 20% rate in recent years in India. Increasingly Indian firms are reported to be looking to China, Singapore, and Eastern European countries to offshore some of their workload.

In countries that predominantly are sending work overseas, the threat of offshoring can cause individuals to increase investment in their own knowledge base and skill levels through on-the-job means, such as volunteering for work with the latest technologies and off-the-job means such as courses, tutorials, volunteer work, and self-motivated projects. At the same time, the opportunity to expand work overseas may cause organizations to invest less money in training their own employees, who may become redundant in any case. This also may cause decision making among those entering the work force to emphasize jobs expected to be difficult to offshore. This, in turn, may create local labor shortages in both the near and long term with the unintended result of stimulating forecasts showing even more long-term benefit in moving jobs offshore. In another scenario, however, training dollars may not diminish overall but may shift from skills emphasizing the execution of development of new applications to planning and integrating new applications into the support of core competency areas within the firm.

Individual-Level Research Questions. Research questions pertaining to the individual level fall into three categories: (1) how does offshoring or, more generally, the integration of labor markets, affect IT workers' jobs in terms of human resource management variables, such as compensation, working conditions, and skill requirements? (2) Given that there is a significant effect of offshoring, how does it differentially affect IT workers in countries primarily offshoring work from those primarily receiving offshored work? and (3) For the individual IT worker, what strategies and approaches work best for maximizing opportunities created by offshoring and ameliorating associated risks? As a corollary to the third question, what skills and abilities provide the most likely return on investment for IT workers in both highly offshore sending and receiving countries?

The Organization Level

To Offshore or Not to Offshore. The decision of whether or not to offshore IT development is not monolithic. Organizations ultimately may offshore all of their IT development, or, to the extent that it can be deconstructed into modules, they may select particular pieces to outsource. If the organization is going to offshore some portion of its IT development, what should be retained in-house and what should be offshored? Knowledge creation and enhancement of human capital is thought largely to be the core driving force for success in today's global marketplace (Ambos & Schlegelmilch, 2005; Chaharbaghi & Nugent, 1996; Hatch & Dyer, 2004; Lev, 2004; Tirpak, 2005). Insights into the nature of knowledge and its use in organizations can affect our understanding of offshoring, particularly in opportunities for creating new intellectual property (or expanding the risk of losing it). Teece (2000), for example, addresses this issue in terms of the decision to outsource work for companies seeking innovation as a basis for competitiveness. This clearly would be the case in many instances for IT product companies, given that the work largely will be involved in the creation of their main products. Teece (2000) frames the offshoring question in global economics terms: under what conditions is it best to develop new products from internal development, joint venture, strategic alliance, long-term purchase agreement, or simply buying it on the market? The answer, he suggests, depends on the type of innovation—the degree to which it stands alone or is intertwined with other production, marketing, or scientific processes—and on its degree of newness. It depends on how difficult it is to replicate the knowledge or, conversely, to defend exclusive access to its use.

Offshoring Providers of Differing Structure. It is important to recognize that IT-producing firms may vary greatly. At the one end are firms like Microsoft and IBM that produce software products and services for arms-length customers in the open market. These products may be tailored for particular customers and implementations, but at their core are largely packages with standard content developed for application in many environments. At the other end are firms like Nestle or Proctor and Gamble that have evolved to consume predominantly software packages developed by companies like Microsoft and IBM but that also produce custom products to fill particular niches and to retain intellectual property regarding strategic business processes. The approach to offshoring can be expected to vary significantly for these firm types.

When offshoring is undertaken by a firm whose primary products are not IT (e.g., Boeing primarily makes airplanes and incidentally may spin off some software made for the purpose of supporting its primary product lines), the firm generally will outsource to development specialists. However, such specialists come in different flavors. Such outsourcing could be (1) to a domestic IT firm operating solely domestically, (2) to a domestic firm with multinational staffing, (3) to a foreign firm relative to the outsourcer (e.g., in the U.S., such firms would include Infosys or Tata Consulting) that may use labor in the same domestic market but is more likely to produce the work largely or exclusively in the outsourcing work receiver's primary country of activity (e.g., for Infosys or Tata Consulting, the work would be in India), or (4) to a foreign outsourcing firm that operates exclusively overseas relative to the outsourcing company. The selection of the type of offshoring provider will have managerial implications. These implications likely will include areas of cost and management requirements. It is likely that cost differentials would mirror different amounts of the outsourcing of the management of the offshoring process as well as the work. In interacting with a domestic offshoring firm, the preponderance or totality of cross-cultural relationship management would be handled by the offshoring work recipient. In interacting directly with a service provider in the offshore receiving country, much more of that level of management would need to be undertaken by the offshoring firm. As a result, one would expect that costs for this sort of management might be passed on by the domestic provider and, conversely, be absorbed as overhead or risk, if dealing directly with an overseas provider. The other arrangements should fall somewhere between the two extremes in both cost and management requirements.

How to Manage Offshoring Programs and Projects. When offshoring is undertaken by an IT development firm (e.g., Oracle, IBM, Microsoft), it typically would be a core service function and, therefore, should be expected to be sourced internally. However, this internal sourcing would involve staff across any of the geographic locations of the organization and, therefore, may be domestic or multinational in nature. The decision making for where to undertake work within the umbrella of a multinational development firm will be based on at least two factors: workload distribution at a current point in time (i.e., the availability of labor resources relative to the required work timeline) and the level of development for distributing projects globally or managing multinational projects. These approaches contrast sending an entire project overseas with the expectation of the return of completed project objectives vs. ongoing collaborative work among IT developers in multiple national locations. Each of these will have different managerial requirements, although both will necessitate the clear specification of expectations and requirements. The latter also will necessitate the technical and human communications skills, procedures, and execution for ongoing coordination of tasks.

The proliferation of offshoring and/or outsourcing has led to geographical, cultural, and institutional scattering of corporate activities globally, which, in turn, has led to increased transaction (Jones & Hill, 1988) and agency costs (Morck & Yeung, 1992). The issues of internal costs (opportunism, free rider, monitoring, bargaining, negotiation, bounded rationality) and external costs (political stability, financial- and market-related risks) has been of concern to organizations involved with international business activities. In short, the liability of foreignness (Coviello & McAuley, 1999; Zaheer & Mosakowski, 1997) has an important impact on the firm's offshoring activities as it seeks to minimize transaction costs.

If an organization decides to enter into offshoring operations, there are a number of managerial issues that logically affect the probability of successful completion. To the extent that offshoring remains a relatively new phenomenon, it is possible that best practices may become standardized and well-known. On the other hand, even individual organizational IT development and routine outsourcing have not developed a reputation for routine success. MIS projects, in general, are estimated to have as many as 80% unsuccessful outcomes in terms of delivery on time, at cost, and with expected features at a given level of quality. According to one Dutch study, in particular, "70-80 percent of the projects failed, either completely or partly" (Cozijnsen, Vrakking, & van IJzerloo, 2000). There is no guarantee that offshored projects will be more successful, particularly given the additional overlay of time, culture, financial, technical, and legal issues (Kobayashi-Hillary, 2005; Kliem, 2004). The stresses of offshored projects can have multiple effects: on the one hand, it is very easy for organizations to underestimate the difficulty of this sort of project, experience failure with an initial project, and terminate relationships and programs of offshoring; on the other hand, offshored projects, given the clearly additional complexities, might enforce a standardization, a use of methodology, and a formalization of communication that may eat away part of the gain from labor cost differential but represent a needed discipline for projects in general (and may return to the outsourcing company as new knowledge and best practice that lower lifetime costs of all project development).

A growing number of books presents the opinions and experiences of individuals, largely consultants, who have been involved in offshoring projects (although they do not necessarily focus specifically on IT development in contrast to other offshoring activities) and present useful lists of issues that managers need to address in preparing for commitment to offshoring activities. Kobayashi-Hillary (2004), for example, focuses specifically on offshoring to India and, in addition to a general introduction to Indian culture and business climate, describes several key concerns for offshoring managers. These concerns include outcome metrics and benchmarking service levels, the vendor selection process, developing legally binding contracts, securing intellectual property as well as transferring knowledge where appropriate, developing communication channels, and working with staffing for blending labor forces or integrating labor results. From a research perspective, each of these concerns represents a set of managerial decisions and implementations that can add to or detract from a successful offshoring program. The relationship among these may be complex in that excellent procedures for securing intellectual property may be rendered of little value without appropriate legal contracts and methods of enforcement, but excellent contracts and enforcement may have no value, if the original planning for securing intellectual property is flawed. In other words, an index of quality of these variables may be captive to some variables that doom a project to failure, regardless of the quality of all other factors, if they do not reach a sufficient quality threshold. Similarly, Robinson and Kalakota (2004) present a rich set of cases that illustrate their discussion of various issues and practices across a wide range of offshoring services, including IT development.

Another useful approach to studying the management of offshoring operations is to consider the extension of lessons learned from the more constrained cases of domestic outsourcing. Outsourcing, in general, is a well-researched area within the MIS scholarly community. The study of IT outsourcing, in general, has been researched widely. Lacity and Willcocks (1998, 2000) have addressed this sort of IT outsourcing in a series of detailed studies. A major finding of these studies suggests that selective outsourcing (e.g., outsourcing carefully selected subsets of the information technology function) generally produces better results in terms of cost savings than either completely outsourcing or not outsourcing at all.

Another source of guidance regarding the understanding of offshoring comes from consideration of the project and program level of IT management. The IT project control literature differentiates four modes of project control mechanisms: outcome-oriented, process-oriented, self-managed, and clan-managed (Kirsch, 1996). There is logic to these differentiations, and it might be possible to separate offshoring projects into these categories. Two issues, however, present themselves—are these mutually exclusive, and are these at the right level of analysis? Observed actual methods used for controlling projects may be categorized along these lines; these categories may generate specific behavioral actions that become available for managing these tasks. Do multicultural project teams require specific control techniques for successful outcomes?

If an organization decides to enter into offshoring, Carmel and Agarwal (2002) present a stage model of offshoring activity maturity. They suggest that firms move through the following stages: (1) no offshoring but internal advocates of the practice; (2) pilot projects for non-core IT processes; (3) leveraging of cost efficiencies through offshoring; and (4) offshoring as a strategic initiative. By implication, much of the risk of entering into offshoring arrangements come from jumping to sophisticated operational models without developing the requisite managerial skills and experience through smaller-scaled entry mechanisms. Kaiser and Hawk (2004) observe in practice the use of a similar stage model describing the sequence of changes for a particular relationship between a large U.S. multinational company and its Indian offshoring partner.

Organization-Level Research Questions. What types of IT development are most effectively offshored? Under what conditions is it best to use various types of partners for offshoring? How do organizations go about choosing the location for sending their offshoring work? What is the net effect of increasing transaction costs through adding cultural diversity relative to lower costs of labor to handle transactions? How can organizations project the transaction costs of starting offshoring relationships? How can organizations minimize transaction and other costs of offshoring through technical and human infrastructure and process management?

The Nation/Regional Level

The Location Decision—The Country Perspective. Davidson (1980) focuses directly on the role of country characteristics and experiences in determining foreign direct investment (FDI) location decisions. Important country variables include natural resources, transportation and infrastructure, tax and investment policies, market size and characteristics, labor costs, and government incentives. Each of these may influence the MNE's decisions of whether to make a foreign equity investment and where to locate such an investment (Porter, 1990). These factors also can be examined for clues to explain the relatively quick and extensive shift to offshoring of labor. As a service, rather than physical product, some elements, such as natural resources and transportation are likely to play a lesser role. However, labor costs, tax and investment policies, and government incentives are likely to be crucial. We would particularly suggest considering labor costs in the broadest sense of not only expenditures but also costs against benefits. Issues such as quality, turnaround speed, and maintainability of code will sustain or erode advantages simply from cost. We would argue that even straightforward programming from clear specifications has not yet reached the level of commodity.

Pries-Heje, Baskerville, and Hansen (2005) present a case highlighting barriers to development of offshoring capabilities in Russia. In conclusion, they identify four key barriers: (1) increased stress on foreign language training; (2) improved training for software development managers; (3) legislation to support more autonomous Russian software houses; and (4) enforcement of laws on intellectual property. Clearly, these recommendations span issues of human resource skills in language and management through governmental policies regarding property guarantees. These concerns are echoed in a similar work by Hawk and McHenry (2005), who differentiate between strengths and challenges for Russian firms going after high-end innovative projects and going after the lower-cost market.

Carmel (2003) presents what he calls the oval model of success factors for software-exporting countries. The model elaborates on an earlier model by Heeks and Nicholson (2002). The oval model consists of eight elements: (1) government vision and policies, including funding and tax benefits; (2) human capital, including traditions, quantity, composition, language, and managerial skills; (3) wages; (4) quality of life; (5) linkages that emerge among individuals, work groups, firms, and nations due to geographic, cultural, linguistic, or ethnic connections; (6) technological infrastructure; (7) capital from domestic or foreign sources; and (8) industry characteristics, such as number of firms, their size, associations, common vision and branding, and aspirational standards. As the author points out, the relationships among these variables are subtle. It is not clear that all are necessary for the creation of a successful national environment to support offshoring and that some may represent tradeoffs (e.g., lower wages may attract more business but a lower quality of life). Human capital also is not a simple variable, as it includes not only a threshold number of talented individuals but a concentration in particular skill and talent areas. Moreover, expenditures on training human capital may be lost, if the individuals choose to move to other nations/regions; on the other hand, attracting individuals following extensive training elsewhere may be an effective strategy (e.g., the H1B program bringing a large number of highly trained Indian IT professionals to the U.S.). Although Carmel's (2003) argument primarily is addressed to nation/regions and what they need to do to attract offshoring investment, from another perspective, it describes the factors that individual firms need to look for in countries where they are considering offshoring some of their work.

Much literature in the global information systems arena presents snapshots of particular countries or regions at a point in time in terms of their infrastructure or a particular element of their computing capabilities. Communications of the ACM published a series of articles on this topic (e.g., Burkhart et al., 1998; Tan et al., 1999; Goodman, 2003). Individually, these articles tend not to be highly theory-oriented; however, viewing them collectively tends to reveal patterns of development. One pattern pertains to the digital divide and the tendency for high per capita income countries to correlate closely with high information density. It is not clear the degree to which information density creates wealth vs. the degree to which wealthy people can afford to invest in information technology, or whether both attributes exist in a positive feedback cycle.

Carmel (2003) has produced a taxonomy of nations in terms of their software exporting sophistication. This model differentiates four levels of sophistication, which he calls tiers 1, 2, 3, and 4. These categories are differentiated by maturity in terms of how long they have been exporting software, the number of firms that suggests a critical mass; and cumulative export revenues. Tier 1, according to this schema, includes countries such as the U.S., Canada, UK, Germany, Japan, and Australia. It also includes India, Ireland, and Israel. Tier 2 includes only Russia and China. Tier 3 includes Brazil, Costa Rica, Mexico, the Philippines, Pakistan, the Czech Republic, and Hungary, for example. Tier 4 includes Cuba, Egypt, Vietnam, and Indonesia. Of course, this listing represents the placement of countries at a particular time period. A successful taxonomy provides the ability to compare current status and strategies for advancement within each category, excluding the substantial differences that such extreme contrasts in scale represent. Following the progress of countries within these various categories relative to the various key success factors, including human capital, governmental policies, and technology infrastructure, forms the basis for a natural experiment in order to consider and refine the relative value of different investments, given the various contingencies that differences among countries within each category represent.

Global Competition for Work. From the perspective of nations/regions, the offshoring issue is framed inversely to the issues facing individuals and organizations. The overriding questions are (1) whether to create an environment that supports offshoring (i.e., to invest in programs and policies with the intention of encouraging such transactions or creating the infrastructure to enable them) and (2) if creating such an environment, which investments will maximize probability of successfully attracting offshoring business while minimizing the risk of expenses that do not generate adequate return. There is an inherent risk that efforts to create such an environment will not yield all of the desired results. These come largely from the answers to several questions: (1) Will the business climate continue to stimulate offshoring in general? (2) Will investments be able to create a competitive environment when investments of competitors are only partially known? and (3) Even if strategies and intentions target the correct elements of the environment, will the implementation allow full realization of anticipated benefits?

On the other hand, the potential benefits of attracting offshoring business include the potential for generating foreign investment, highly paid jobs in relatively environmentally friendly industries, supplemental business activity supporting highly paid workers, additional educational and training opportunities, positive feedback between export and internal markets, and increased participation in world markets with resulting exposure to world-level standards and practices. A growing body of labor economics literature provides evidence from U.S. census data of a connection between investment in computer resources and higher wages and productivity in general (Dunne, Foster, Haltiwanger, & Troske, 2004). It shows an even stronger relationship between wage and skill increases in research and development relative to high-tech industries (Allen, 2001) but even here shows a significant role for computerization in changing the structure of skills and wages in the U.S. labor market.

Nations/regions already can be seen competing to serve as the target for offshoring ventures. Without necessarily intending to do so specifically for offshoring, India's investments in engineering and business education since its independence have created a human resources pool that has been competing successfully for IT development work on the world market. Other countries, such as Ireland, Singapore, Israel, New Zealand, and Finland, have been documented to support programs to stimulate IT development and related computer and telecommunications industries (Ein-dor, Myers & Raman, 1997; Watson & Myers, 2001). Arora and Gambardella (2004) contrast the approaches by India, Ireland, and Israel—developing software production capabilities largely through export—with strategies of Brazil and China that also have fueled significant growth but more largely through their domestic market. It is clear that simple replication of another country's successful strategy does not necessarily work. Nations do not start off on an even footing but vary with respect to natural resources, legacy infrastructure, and geographic positioning.

There are also natural advantages and risks of being a first mover to use any particular strategy to create business opportunity. For example, the first mover has the challenge of convincing potential clients of the viability of programs that have never existed; on the other hand, once those clients are convinced, there are no existing competitors, and the first mover may establish an unassailable body of knowledge and stable of clients. However, the first mover often has taken on significant investment in research and development, which the followers may be able to trim significantly while potentially finding relatively inexpensive but highly customer-satisfying improvements on the original idea. There may be room only for one or a few entities to succeed in a business environment such that many followers quickly may exhaust the original opportunity.

Nation/Region-Level Research Questions. How do nation/regions identify the key factors that will lead to success in competition for offshoring work (or for retaining work onshore)? How do nation/regions implement their investment strategies to maximize the return on their investment? How can nation/regions adapt strategies and learn from the successes and failures of others in improving their overall environment for support of offshoring?

Examination of Issues Between Levels

In this next section, we focus on issues that cross between organizations and national/regional entities and then on those between individuals and national/regional entities. Issues regarding offshoring between individuals and firms largely will involve the matching of new work opportunities with new skill configurations, and it is not clear that offshoring creates unique issues in this regard. As new factory equipment, for example, comes online, organizations have similar issues in identifying new skill needs and shuffling their workforce through a variety of mechanisms, including training, reassignment, hiring, and reduction in force, to make these adjustments. The specific offshoring issues of interest pertaining to these matters mostly will be at the individual level regarding the reaction of workers to a need for skills or at the organizational level of identifying and realigning job descriptions in response to new environmental demands.

Organization-Nation/Regional. Issues regarding the selection of a particular location for offshoring can be viewed as an interaction between organizations and nations/regions. Decision making with regard to selecting national sites for developing offshoring relations involves both the attributes of the firm and of the nation/region levels.

Cost and Other Factors. We see issues of cost and measuring costs as an interaction between organizations and locations. Dunning (1981) and Davidson (1980) suggest that labor is one of several key factors believed to influence where firms choose to locate business activity. However, we would argue that firms will vary on their ability to capitalize on labor cost differentials. Although offshore salaries can be substantially lower relative to some domestic economies, they do not represent the total cost comparison to domestic development. The full cost includes costs of vendor selection, transitioning the work, layoffs and retention, lost productivity, cultural issues, improving development processes, and managing the contract. One estimate puts these costs from 15% to 55% above the contract (Overby, 2003). Nations/regions with lower gross salary cost but less developed infrastructure, for example, may have equivalent total costs of production. Organizations with work that is more reliant on pure labor will observe a different cost structure than those more reliant on telecommunication or other infrastructure, as they evaluate different locations.

Organizations with many different kinds of projects also will have to decide whether there are more economic benefits optimizing the location of each project or reducing complexity and perhaps overall management costs by locating all offshoring in a single location, even if, project-by-project, some or all locations are non-optimal. Finally, there is the feedback loop, where an environment is so strong that many organizations select locating there, but the onslaught of organizations changes the profile of the environment, perhaps by pushing the environment's resources to or beyond capacity. We have noted earlier the estimates that India's salaries have increased an estimated 20% annually in recent years (Arora & Gambardella, 2004; Agrawal & Thite, 2003). This is a possible indicator that even with the excellent educational system and large population, the demand for IT workers may push the capacity of any given nation to deliver.

Organization-Nation/Region Relationship Research Questions. How do nations/regions anticipate the future competitive factors determining the location of offshoring work in order to invest effectively in these areas? How do organizations trade off the strengths and limits of nations/regions as they make their decisions regarding location of ongoing operations and for specific work allocation?

Individual-National Interaction. Unfortunately, even as offshoring brings prosperity to those receiving contracts, it provides upheaval for those left behind. It is argued that, in many cases, net employment of IT personnel in the organizations engaging in offshoring tends to remain constant with the bulk, if not the entirety, of staff moving into higher-end activities; for example, from programming to analysis and design. In this case, the individual employees, at a minimum, need to develop new skills and mindsets in order to adjust to the new opportunities. Some, of course, cannot make this adjustment. Of those, some find employment using their existing skills in other locations, not necessarily for the same level of compensation. In the end, although some IT personnel are ultimately without jobs, sometimes it is for significant periods of time and, at times, requires a change of career field for reentry into the labor market.

Recent compensation and job satisfaction surveys have found that although information technology (IT) employees' salaries have increased slightly in the last year, employee morale declined sharply and may be impacting the company's performance and productivity (Johnson, 2004). With the emerging trend of offshoring skilled jobs to cheaper labor markets on the rise, IT employee morale has declined dramatically in 75% of the organizations surveyed (out of 650) by the META Group in their 2004 IT Staffing and Compensation Guide (McGee, 2004). However, several organizations have learned by trial and error that there are hidden costs and repercussions associated with outsourcing that are not anticipated up front, including the impact to remaining employees or survivors (Brockner et al., 1986, 1993, 1995; Mishra, Spreitzer, & Mishra, 1998) and the long-distance relationship with the new foreign workers (Rao, 2004).

Although there is no leading theory on offshoring and the surviving employees, it is possible to integrate survivor's guilt/syndrome (downsizing) and the effect of cultural and geographic differences to encapsulate the impact of offshoring on the surviving employees. Survivors have feelings of fear, insecurity, frustration, anger, sadness, depression, and unfairness (Mishra & Spreitzer, 1998) as a result of an organizational layoff. These symptoms can cause employees to "become demotivated, cynical, insecure and demoralized" (Baruch & Hind, 2000, p. 29); they also can cause increased turnover and lower productivity (Brockner et al., 1995). In fact, numerous reports have been made in the U.S. of individuals whose jobs were outsourced, and, in some cases, the affected individuals were asked to train their lower-wage replacements (Worthen, 2003).

Furthermore, it was discovered in leading studies that specific physical and mental health risks for surviving employees are directly associated with downsizing, caused by "intensification of job strain, time pressure, reduction of social support, lack of control, role ambiguity and the uncertainty regarding job future" (Pepper et al., 2003). The study also found varying degrees of medical symptoms exhibited by employees, of which the variance was attributed to the employee's closeness to the layoff process. For example, if the employee was directly involved in the layoff process (i.e., notifying employees that they were being laid off, etc.), then they exhibited an increase in medical symptoms, as opposed to those employees who were separated from the process, which rarely exhibited medical symptoms at all.

Mechanisms found to link downsizing and health problems included changes in work situation, the impact of negative or lack of social support, and an increase in harmful habits (i.e., increased alcohol consumption) due to anxiety and stress (Kivimaki et al., 2000). A secondary effect of layoffs after the immediacy of mental and physical ailments is the decrease in productivity and increase in turnover. This negative impact on the organization stems from the reactions of surviving employees, which can be passive, such as worrying and anxiety (walking wounded) or as aggressive as outrage, anger, and cynicism (carping critics) (Mishra & Spreitzer, 1998). As a result, offshoring can create unanticipated costs for the organization with its remaining employees as well as affect the levels of productivity and innovation (Mishra & Spreitzer, 1998).

For those organizations that have decided to offshore, there are several steps that management can make to help reduce the employee' stress level and uncertainty and to bolster employee morale (Laribee & Michaels-Barr, 1994). First and foremost is honesty. Lack of real and meaningful communication is cited increasingly as the source of employee fear and insecurity (Gallagher, 2003). In addition, putting a transition plan in place and helping the laid-off employees find new work can mitigate the negativity inspired by outsourcing (Brockner, 1992). Other factors included how the announcement or communication surrounding the layoffs were framed (context) (Brockner et al., 1995), whether or not employees perceive that the decisions surrounding the layoffs were fair and procedural justice or "the fairness of the methods used to make or implement a resource allocation decision" (Brockner et al., 1995; Wiesenfeld et al., 2000).

There are also issues regarding the role of nations in mitigating the effects of IT worker layoffs that may result from offshoring or other causes. One approach suggested by Friedman (2005) would be the creation of an employment insurance that would supplement wages for individuals moving to new jobs. IT workers tend to be an independent bunch, noting the failure of periodic attempts to create unionization, at least in the U.S., and perhaps are more motivated by providing challenge and opportunity than safety nets. On the other hand, again in the U.S., surveys of job attributes sought by IT workers in recent years have moved significantly toward security and benefits relative to challenge (Sethi et al., 2004). Individual IT workers take significant risk in their choice of training and skill development; it could become a competitive advantage for nations seeking the middle level as well as highest quality IT workers to provide some kind of insurance to lessen the effects of periodic market adjustments.

Insourcing vs. Offshoring—Immigration Policies. From another perspective, organizations make the decision to offshore some IT work as a preference over insourcing IT workers from other countries. Although the number of IT workers coming to the U.S. through the H1-B visa program has diminished since peaking in the years 2000 and 2001, the program has had a significant impact on the American IT workforce. The H1-B visa is intended to supplement the U.S. workforce in critical areas, allows for a six-year stay in the U.S., and is based on sponsorship of a particular organization. It is estimated that as many as 80% of the Indian IT workers who come to the U.S. on this program end up becoming permanent residents or citizens (Agrawal & Thite, 2003). Assuming that skills and knowledge are embedded in this set of workers, on what basis do organizations decide whether to recruit workers rather than to relocate work to another country? Some likely factors include (1) evolving political risks involved in not using domestic workers to perform the task; (2) costs of labor and total cost of outsourcing IT work; (3) a threshold technical infrastructure, management, and labor force that allows a receiving country to be positioned to provide services; and (4) cultural similarities, particularly in terms of common language, that provide an advantage to countries like India and Singapore in receiving outsourcing assignments from English speaking countries in North America and Europe. However, formal analysis of the relative strength of these influences also should account for broader consideration of transaction costs as well as the legal and environmental factors noted by Dunning (1981) and Davidson (1980).

From the level of national policy, while there is risk of a brain-drain from talented individuals leaving their country of origin, some workers return home having received significant investment in their intellectual capital. Moreover, regardless of the costs and benefits to individual firms, there are many advantages for insourcing people relative to outsourcing jobs. These advantages include (1) the multiplier effect, as insourced people buy homes, cars, and food and otherwise stimulate the overall economy; (2) the potential for innovations by these folks to create new companies hiring U.S.-born as well as newcomers in additional jobs; and (3) a decreased risk of loss of intellectual capital to potentially competing organizations (Agrawal & Thite, 2003).

Individual-Nation/Region Research Questions. What responsibilities do nation/regions have for assisting those made redundant by jobs lost to offshoring and those survivors who might be affected by offshoring? What mechanisms are available to nation/regions for addressing individual worker issues, and how successful are they when applied? What are the trade-offs for countries between offshoring work and insourcing labor?

Conclusion

The offshoring of IT development is a significant global economic phenomenon. It represents an important component in worldwide global labor sourcing. Its importance derives from the high value-added products produced and the high skill and generally high compensation of its workers. It influences the lives and fortunes of individuals, organizations, and nations/regions. It is worthy of significant study both empirically to understand its dimensions and theoretically to understand key relationships, where practices, policies, and actions may influence outcomes. However, because offshoring so broadly affects different stakeholders, a multi-level theory is required so that influences that may positively affect one set of stakeholders while negatively affecting another are not misinterpreted by an overly narrow analysis. Such a multi-level theory is complex. It will need to incorporate or extract from theories that currently exist, illuminating issues at each stakeholder level. It also will need to build new conceptual, measurement, and theoretical viewpoints and tools in order to identify and quantify the interactions between various stakeholder levels, to consider non-linear relationships, and to identify feedback loops that may shift relationship strength and even direction across different time periods.

Although not discussed in this article, the authors observe at least two other possible levels of analysis that should be explored for a thorough examination of the offshoring phenomenon. Although not quite as clearly defined as the organization or nation/region, the industry level also offers opportunities for investigation into offshoring of IT development in contrast to offshoring of other tasks or domains. We have avoided this level of analysis in this article for the sake of parsimony and for limiting the scope of discussion specifically to a special type of labor sourcing. However, contrasting IT development with other industries would show what relationships prevail for all service sourcing and which ones are unique to particular industries. Also, there is a theoretical global perspective. In a simplistic two-nation situation, jobs leaving the U.S. and arriving in India, for example, would show up as a loss for the U.S. and a gain for India. However, as the situation includes more observable factors—Indians using profits to buy U.S. products and services—the sum total effects may create offsetting benefits and losses as well as present treacherous measurement issues, particularly if intangibles are considered; even at the same rate of compensation, some jobs are more hazardous or routine, for example, than others. Nevertheless, in principle, a kind of global scorecard, whether balanced or not, would address the net impacts of offshoring. Do all nations/regions benefit (to what extent are the benefits distributed within the nation/regions)? Do some benefit at the cost to others? Do the net benefits outweigh the net costs when all effects are calculated?

In this chapter, we have attempted to identify key issues and some directions for application of existing theory to the study of offshoring at three levels of analysis and have suggested relationships that cross the individual-nation/region and the organization-nation/region dimensions. For each of these, we have identified a set of critical research questions. These questions are formulated largely from the perspective of practice with the view that answers to these questions would have significant applicability. Much work remains to translate these over-arching questions into manageable examples, the measurement of which illuminates both cases and general principles pertaining to offshoring IT development labor. However, we believe that such work will have much value, as offshoring evolves from a special case of labor sourcing to a well-structured practice. We believe that this examination of this phenomenon can serve as a research agenda helping to define distinctions in types of offshoring, the presentation of high-level research questions, and the suggestion of the range of issues that comprise a full picture of the domain. Future research also should target the development of specific measures to replace the more general concept of outcomes related to each stakeholder level. For example, what are the appropriate measures for individual outcomes (e.g., income, mobility, job satisfaction, index of several variables)? What are the appropriate measures for the nation/region outcomes (e.g., GDP, percent of GDP derived from offshoring, performance relative to other countries? tax revenue generated from offshoring)? The definition of such variables will be needed to move to another level of testing the degree to which various policies have influenced particular outcomes.

References

Agrawal, N. M., & Thite, M. (2003). Human resource issues, challenges and strategies in the Indian software industry. *International Journal of Human Resources Development and Management, 3*(3), 249.

Allen, S. G. (2001). Technology and the wage structure. *Journal of Labor Economics, 19*(2), 440.

Ambos, B., & Schlegelmilch, B. (2005). In search of global advantage. *European Business Forum*, (21), 23.

Arora, A., & Gambardella, A. (2004). *The globalization of the software industry: Perspectives and opportunities for developed and developing countries* (Working Paper 10538). Cambridge, MA: National Bureau of Economic Research. Retrieved July 1, 2005, from http://www.nber.org/papers/w10538

Baruch, Y., & Hind, P. (2000). Survivor syndrome—A management myth? *Journal of Managerial Psychology, 15*(1), 29.

Beylerian, M., & Kleiner, B. H. (2003). The downsized workplace. *Management Research News, 26*(2-4), 97.

Brockner, J. (1992). Managing the effects of layoffs on survivors. *California Management Review, 34*(2), 9.

Brockner, J., Greenberg, J., Brockner, A., Bortz, J., Davy, J., & Carter, C. (1986). Layoffs, equity theory, and work performance: Further evidence of the impact of survivor guilt. *Academy of Management Journal, 29*(2), 373.

Brockner, J., Wisenfeld, B. M., & Martin, C. L. (1995). Decision frame, procedural justice, and survivors' reactions to job layoffs. *Organizational Behavior and Human Decision Processes, 63*(1), 59.

Brockner, J., Wiesenfeld, B. M., Reed, T., Grover, S., & Martin, C. (1993). Interactive effect of job content and context on the reactions of layoff survivors. *Journal of Personality and Social Psychology, 64*(2), 187.

Burkhart, G. E., Goodman, S. E., Mehta, A., & Press, L. (1998). The Internet in India: Better times ahead? *Communications of the ACM, 41*(11), 21.

Carmel, E. (2003). The new software exporting nations: Success factors. Electronic *Journal of Information Systems in Developing Countries, 13*(4), 1-12.

Carmel, E., & Agarwal, R. (2002). The maturation of offshore sourcing of information technology work. *MIS Quarterly Executive, 1*(2), 65-78.

Chabrow, E. (2005). *IT employment on upswing*. Retrieved July 5, 2005, from http://www.informationweek.com/showArticle.jhtml?articleID=160403526

Chaharbaghi, K., & Nugent, E. (1996). A new generation of competitors. *Management Decision, 34*(10), 5.

Coviello, N. E., & McAuley, A. (1999). Internationalisation and the smaller firm: A review of contemporary empirical research. *Management International Review, 39*(3), 223.

Cozijnsen, A. J., Vrakking, W. J., & van IJzerloo, M. (2000). Success and failure of 50 innovation projects in Dutch companies. *European Journal of Innovation Management, 3*(3), 150.

Davidson, W. H. (1980). The location of foreign direct investment activity: Country characteristics and experience effects. *Journal of International Business Studies, 11*(2), 9.

Dunne, T., Foster, L., Haltiwanger, J., & Troske, K. R. (2004). Wage and productivity dispersion in United States manufacturing: The role of computer investment. *Journal of Labor Economics, 22*(2), 397.

Dunning, J. H. (1981). *International production and the multinational enterprise.* London: Allen and Unwin.

Ein-Dor, P., Myers, M. D., & Raman, K. S. (1997). Information technology in three small developed countries. *Journal of Management Information Systems, 13*(4), 61.

Erramilli, M. K., & Rao, C. P. (1993). Service firms' international entry-mode choice: A modified transaction-cost analysis approach. *Journal of Marketing, 57*(3), 19.

Friedman, T. L. (2005). *The world is flat: A brief history of the twenty-first century.* New York: Farrar, Straus, and Giroux.

Gallagher, J. (2003). Full disclosure: Telling it like it is. *Insurance & Technology, 28*(8), 28.

Goodman, S. (2003). The origins of digital computing in Europe. *Communications of the ACM, 46*(9), 21.

Gruber, A. (2004). Fear of outsourcing. *Government Executive, 36*(1), 14.

Harden, B. (2003, June 10). Cuts sap morale of parks employees; Many fear losing jobs to outsourcing. *The Washington Post,* p. A.19.

Hatch, N. W., & Dyer, J. H. (2004). Human capital and learning as a source of sustainable competitive advantage. *Strategic Management Journal, 25*(12), 1155.

Hawk, S., & McHenry, W. (2005). The maturation of the Russian offshore software industry. *Information Technology for Development, 11*(1), 31-57.

Heeks, R., & Nicholson, B. (2002, May 29-31). Software export success factors and strategies in developing and transitional economies. In *Proceedings of the IFIP Working Group 9.4 Conference* (pp. 311-331). IIMB Bangalore, India.

Johnson, M. (2004). Bracing for backlash. *Computerworld, 38*(28), 18.

Jones, G. R., & Hill, C. W. L. (1988). Transaction cost analysis of strategy structure choice. *Strategic Management Journal, 9*(2), 159.

Kaiser, K. M., & Hawk, S. (2004). Evolution of offshore software development: From outsourcing to cosourcing. *MIS Quarterly Executive, 3*(2), 69-81.

Kirsch, L. J. (1996). The management of complex tasks in organizations: Controlling the systems development process. *Organization Science, 7*(1), 1.

Kivimaki, M., Vahtera, J., Ferrie, J. E., Hemingway, H., & Pentti, J. (2000). Factors underlying the effect of organisational downsizing on health of employees: Longitudinal cohort study. *British Medical Journal, 320*(7240), 971-975.

Kleim, R. (2004). Managing the risks of offshore IT development projects. *Information Systems Management, 21*(3), 22-27. Retrieved from http://www.ism-journal.com

Klein, K. J., Tosi, H., & Cannella, A. A. (1999). Multilevel theory building: Benefits, barriers, and new developments. *Academy of Management Review, 24*(2), 243-248.

Kobayashi-Hillary, M. (2004). *Outsourcing to India: The offshore advantage.* Heidelberg, Germany: Springer.

Kobayashi-Hillary, M. (2005). A passage to India. *Queue, 3*(1), 54-60.

Lacity, M., & Willcocks, L. (1998). An empirical investigation of information technology sourcing practices: Lessons from experience. *MIS Quarterly—Executive, 22*(3), 363-409.

Lacity, M., & Willcocks, L. (2000). Survey of IT outsourcing experiences in US and UK organizations. *Journal of Global Information Management, 8*(2), 5-23.

Laribee, J. F., & Michaels-Barr, L. (1994). Dealing with personnel concerns in outsourcing. *Journal of Systems Management, 45*(1), 6-12.

Lev, B. (2004). Sharpening the intangibles edge. *Harvard Business Review, 82*(6), 109.

Matloff, N. (2004). Globalization and the American IT worker. *Communications of the ACM, 47*(11), 27-29.

McGee, M. K. (2004). Behind the numbers: I.T. workers' morale mired in a slump. *InformationWeek,* (994), 86.

Mishra, A. K., & Spreitzer, G. M. (1998). Explaining how survivors respond to downsizing: The role of trust, empowerment, justice, and work redesign. *Academy of Management Review, 23*(3), 567.

Mishra, K. E., Spreitzer, G. M., & Mishra, A. K. (1998). Preserving employee morale during downsizing. *Sloan Management Review, 39*(2), 83.

Morck, R., & Yeung, B. (1992). Internalization: An event study test. *Journal of International Economics, 33*(1-2), 41.

Murray, J. Y., & Kotabe, M. (1999). Sourcing strategies of U.S. service companies: A modified transaction-cost analysis. *Strategic Management Journal, 20*(9), 791.

Niederman, F. (2004). IT personnel prospects for 2004: A mixed bag. *IEEE Computer, 37*(1), 69-77.

Overby, S. (2003). Offshore outsourcing the money: Moving jobs overseas can be a much more expensive proposition than you may think. *CIO, 16*(22), 1.

Pepper, L., Messinger, M., Weinberg, J., & Campbell, R. (2003). Downsizing and health at the United States Department of Energy. *American Journal of Industrial Medicine, 44*(5), 481-491.

Porter, M. E. (1990). *The competitive advantage of nations.* New York: The Free Press.

Pries-Heje, J., Baskerville, R., & Hansen, G. I. (2005). Strategy models for enabling offshore outsourcing: Russian short-cycle-time software development. *Information Technology for Development, 11*(1), 1-26.

Rao, M. T. (2004). Key issues for global IT sourcing: Country and individual factors. *Information Systems Management, 21*(3), 16.

Robinson, M., & Kalakota, R. (2004). *Offshore outsourcing: Business models, ROI, and best practices.* Alpharetta, GA: Milvar Press.

Sethi, V., King, R. C., & Quick, J. C. (2004). What causes stress in information system professionals? *Communications of the ACM, 47*(3), 99-102.

Tan, Z. A., Foster, W., & Goodman, S. (1999). China's state-coordinated Internet infrastructure. *Communications of the ACM, 42*(6), 44.

Teece, D. J. (2000). *Managing intellectual capital: Organizational, strategic, and policy dimensions.* Oxford: Oxford University Press.

Tirpak, T. M. (2005). Five steps to effective knowledge management. *Research Technology Management, 48*(3), 15.

Watson, R., & Myers, M. D. (2001). IT industry success in small countries: The cases of Finland and New Zealand. *Journal of Global Information Management, 9*(2), 4-14.

Wiesenfeld, B. M., Brockner, J., & Thibault, V. (2000). Procedural fairness, Managers' self-esteem, and managerial behaviors following a layoff. *Organizational Behavior and Human Decision Processes, 83*(1), 1.

Worthen, B. (2003). The radicalization of Mike Emmons: Until he was laid off by a company moving jobs offshore, Mike Emmons rarely voted. Now the computer programmer is considering a run for Congress. *CIO, 16*(22), 1.

Zaheer, S., & Mosakowski, E. (1997). The dynamics of the liability of foreignness: A global study of survival in financial services. *Strategic Management Journal, 18*(6), 439.

This work was previously published in the Journal of Global Information Management, 14(2), 52-74, April-June 2006.

Chapter IV

Experiences Conducting Cross-Cultural Research

M. Gordon Hunter, University of Lethbridge, Canada

Abstract

When conducting cross-cultural investigations, it is incumbent upon the information systems researcher to be prepared to reflect upon the differences between the frameworks of the researcher and the research participants. Three cross-cultural projects are discussed in this article. The first project, investigating systems analysts, employs the Repertory Grid from personal construct theory (Kelly, 1955, 1963). The second and third projects both employ narrative inquiry (Bruner, 1990). The second project investigates the use of information systems by small business and relies upon multiple regional researchers. The third project, which is currently on-going, investigates the emerging role of chief information officers and is a single researcher venture. These projects have contributed to the information systems field of study and are presented here to provide researchers with ideas for further qualitative cross-cultural investigations.

Introduction

Many businesses have established global operations. Large corporations may build processing operations close to natural resources or markets. Some large corporations may rely on access to skilled personnel to help make location decisions. This is shown by the creation of many versions of Silicon Valley around the globe. Also, it is now relatively easy for small businesses to establish a global presence. The development of a Web site allows small businesses to present their products and services to a global market. Thus, anyone anywhere (given Internet access) may avail themselves of the offerings of either small or large businesses. This internationalization of business leads to research that includes a cultural perspective. The investigation of international operations entails a scope beyond one specific country and includes individuals from different countries. Thus, the adopted research methods must address the inherent diversity or similarity of cultures.

It has been suggested some time ago (Klein & Lyytinen, 1985) that information systems researchers should adopt approaches to their investigations that will advance the discipline. Further, Galliers and Land (1987) have suggested that information systems research "methods must take account of the nature of the subject and the complexity of the real world" (p. 901). Galliers (1992) supported this comment, proposing that the adopted research method reflect the research objectives. Hirschheim (1992) expanded upon this idea, suggesting that information systems fundamentally are social systems. An approach to conducting investigations with objectives of taking account of the complexities of the real world of social systems may be found in qualitative research.

Now there is a growing community of information systems researchers employing a qualitative perspective to their investigations (Benbasat & Zmud, 1999; Trauth, 2001). Recently, Gallupe and Tan (1999) have challenged information systems researchers to use alternative qualitative approaches, such as ethnography, interpretive epistemology, and grounded theory. They suggest that these approaches are especially appropriate for international information systems researchers, who will inevitably become involved in cross-cultural research.

This article presents a perspective on conducting cross-cultural research. The next section discusses the consideration of taking a qualitative approach to cross-cultural research. Then, some examples of this type of research are presented. A discussion of implications follows. Conclusions finally are drawn regarding the use of qualitative methods when conducting cross-cultural research.

Applying Qualitative Approaches
to Cross-Cultural Research

Qualitative researchers work very closely with research participants. The researchers spend a lot of time in the field attempting to document research participant's interpretations of personally experienced events. It is incumbent upon the researcher to approach these investigations with an open mind. It is also very important that the researcher be prepared to reflect upon the differences between the frameworks of the researcher and the research participants. This is true especially when the research project is international and research participants from different cultures are involved. The research approach must allow the research participants to provide their own interpretations. The approach must facilitate grounding the data within the personal experiences and the culture of the research participants. Subsequent data analysis also should be based upon the elicited comments of the research participants.

Issues relating to diversity and similarity should be addressed when conducting cross-cultural research. One issue relates to the individual development of constructs upon which the research will be carried out. That is, when conducting cross-cultural research, it is important to identify if the research method takes an emic or an etic approach. These concepts originated within linguistic research (Pike, 1954; Berry, 1990; Headland, Pike & Harris, 1990). Essentially, an emic approach is based upon constructs developed in one culture. Conversely, an etic approach is based upon universal constructs developed by comparing data from many cultures. A complicating factor is the introduction of a third term: pseudo-etic (Triandis, 1972). This term suggests that the research constructs are developed from a limited number of cultures. The researcher must identify clearly which approach has been adopted. Cross-cultural researchers may replicate emic studies in different cultures and attempt to develop an etic model based upon universal constructs identified from the differences and similarities that emerge from the emic data. It has been suggested that "the most useful approach ... is to focus on the pseudo etic approach to develop quasi-universal constructs which may be subsequently challenged to more universal tests of validity" (Early & Mosakowski, 1995, p. 9).

Another issue in conducting cross-cultural research involves the competing hypotheses of convergence and divergence (Ronen, 1986; Webber, 1969; Yang, 1986). The convergence hypothesis suggests that cultures throughout the world are becoming similar. One explanation in support of the convergence hypothesis is the development and use of common technologies such as the Internet, which facilitates cross-cultural communication. Another explanation relates to the internationalization of education and the consequent influencing of common attitudes and values. Alternatively, the divergence hypothesis suggests that societies tend to resist changes to their culture and strive to retain their distinctiveness. This chapter will not attempt to present a resolution to this issue. It is important, however, that researchers conducting cross-cultural investigations indicate and support the perspective they propose to adopt.

Cross-cultural research also may include research participants from different cultures. An interesting perspective that may be employed to compare cultures has been presented by Hofstede (1980, 1983, 1993), Hofstede and Bond (1988), and Hofstede, Neuijen, Ohayv, and Sanders (1990), who present culture as the collective programming of the mind. Thus, as individuals grow up in a culture, they adopt rarely questioned assumptions about how to act. These assumptions, consequently, are inculcated into management practices. Hofstede (1980) proposed to differentiate culture based upon the following four dimensions:

- **Individualism-collectivism:** Individualistic cultures emphasize independence, while collectivist cultures emphasize mutual dependence and obligations.

- **Power distance:** High-power distance cultures accept an unequal distribution of power, while low-power distance cultures strive for an equal distribution.

- **Uncertainty avoidance:** Strong uncertainty avoidance cultures have formal codes of behavior, while weak uncertainty avoidance cultures are less controlled.

- **Masculinity-femininity:** Masculine cultures emphasize achievement, while feminine cultures emphasize caring.

The implications that these dimensions have for cultural differences are very important. Successful system development will be dependent in part upon user acceptance, which, in turn, may be affected by the relationship between the system developer and the functional user. While the vast divide between system developer and functional user is being addressed through common experiences and training, the consequences of this divide are exacerbated through the introduction of a cultural component to the system development process.

Some Example Project

The approach employed for the following investigations was based on grounded theory (Glaser & Strauss, 1967), which suggests that categories and their properties should emerge from the data rather than being influenced by the a priori adoption of a theoretical framework. The approach allows the identification of both similarities and differences to emerge from the data.

The remainder of this section discusses three projects that employed a qualitative approach to the cross-cultural research of some aspect of the subject area of information systems. The first project (Hunter, 1997; Hunter & Beck, 1996, 2000) presented the perceptions of what constitutes the characteristics of excellent systems analysts. Interviews were conducted in Canada and Singapore. The second project (Hunter, Burgess, & Wenn, 2005a, 2005b) relates to the use of information systems by small business. For this project, interviews were conducted in Canada, Portugal, and the U.S. The third project (Hunter, 2005a) is still in progress. It involves the investigation of the emerging role of chief information officers. Interviews have been conducted in Taiwan, the USA, and New Zealand. Further interviews are planned. For each of these projects described in the following, emphasis of the discussion will be on the process followed to conduct the investigations within the context of cross-cultural research. The presentation of the three projects will culminate with a discussion that reflects upon the lessons learned from the experience of conducting each investigation.

Systems Analysts

The internationalization of business has facilitated a growing need for a global approach to information systems. This project investigated the effects of cultural differences on the development of information systems (Hunter, 1997; Hunter & Beck, 1996, 2000). More specifically, the project elicited research participants' interpretations of what constitutes an excellent systems analyst participating in the development process. The research attempted to compare the differing perceptions of research participants of the role of excellent systems analysts between Canada and Singapore.

The objective of this project was to explore the differences in the way systems analysts perform their roles. The concept and interpretation of excellent may differ from one culture to another. Thus, excellent systems analysts may not only possess superior technical skills but will perform their roles in ways that accommodate the local culture.

In terms of Hofstede's (1980) dimensions, Singapore and Canada are societies that are different in a number of important ways. Canada is a highly individualistic society, where individuals are expected to act independently. Singapore is much more collectivist in social relationships, forming tightly knit, mutually beneficial social obligations. Further, in terms of power distance, Canada is a small power distance country, preferring equal distribution of power among individuals. Singaporeans are more comfortable with a relatively unequal distribution of power.

There are two dimensions in which Canada and Singapore are similar. Singapore is the society that had the weakest uncertainty avoidance score, and Canada is also a society that is relatively comfortable with uncertainty and ambiguity. That is, both cultures tend to be less control-oriented. Also, there is very little difference between the two cultures on the masculinity–femininity dimension. Masculine cultures emphasize achievement and assertiveness, while feminine cultures are identified more with close relationships and harmony.

The research used the Repertory Grid technique from Kelly's Theory of Personal Constructs (Kelly, 1955, 1963), which brings structure to the interview while allowing flexibility and reducing researcher bias. This is an important aspect of the technique when conducting cross-cultural research. Repertory Grids (Tan & Hunter, 2002) may be used to gather a large amount of rich, detailed, qualitative, and narrative data relating to a research participant's explanation of an elicited construct.

Seventy research participants from three companies in Canada and 17 from one company in Singapore were interviewed using the Repertory Grid technique. Within each of the four companies research participants were categorized into five audiences. Two of the audiences—systems analysts and their supervisors—represented information systems professionals. Three of the audiences—direct users, their supervisors, and knowledge workers—represented business professionals.

The results of this project suggest that there is support for both the convergence and divergence hypotheses, based upon the study of systems analysts. This is not as paradoxical as it might seem at first. The evidence in support of convergence relates to the overall consideration, identified in both cultures, of the importance of certain characteristics such as attitude, knowledge, and communication. This may be the result of the common education and training of systems analysts and may support further the identification of an international information systems profession. There also was evidence of divergence based upon a difference in the relative importance of the emerging characteristics. The excellent systems analysts in Singapore were viewed as more likely to rely upon expertise in order to fulfill their roles. In Canada, the excellent systems analysts were interpreted more as encouraging participation from the users. These differences are reflected in the culture based upon Hofstede's (1980) perspective. In Singapore, high power distance is more acceptable, leading to a more technocratic style and display of expert knowledge. Canada, however, is a lower power distance society and would tend to encourage an equal sharing of duties and participation in work efforts. In sum, excellent systems analysts in Singapore may be viewed as experts, while in Canada, they would be viewed as partners.

As a first foray into conducting cross-cultural research, the lessons learned in this project relate to titles and organization structures, incorporating other audiences, and audiotaping the interviews.

The project focused on obtaining interpretations about systems analysts. In many organizations, especially international ones, this title may not exist. Thus, it may be more appropriate to identify information systems professionals and then to document emerging themes or roles that may relate to the various generic stages of the system development life cycle.

Further, as more organizational structures become flatter and with the advent of outsourcing, reporting relationships vary significantly. That is, the relationship may be different from one culture to another. Thus, the person performing the role of the information system professional may report to an information system manager, a chief information officer, or a business manager. Also, in some large international organizations, the reporting relationship may involve individuals from different cultures.

Another aspect to consider when conducting this project across different cultures is the consideration for incorporating other audiences. As described previously, the project involved two audiences from the information systems profession and three from the business profession. The following is a list of audiences that also could have been included:

- **Information system profession:**
  - Project manager
  - Chief information officer
  - Programmer
  - Database administrator
  - Telecommunication specialist
- **Business profession:**
  - Senior management
  - Service division manager
- **External:**
  - Government regulators and administrators
  - Information systems societies representative
  - Academics
  - Consultants

The opinions and interpretations of these other audiences may vary from one culture to another and may be incorporated in order to provide valuable insights.

Finally, audiotaping the interviews should be incorporated. When this project was carried out, it was felt that the introduction of a tape recorder, especially when the research participant was from a different culture, would negatively affect the atmosphere within the interview. In turn, it was anticipated that the research participant responses may be conservative, and that the research participant would be less forthright in expressing his or her opinions. In hindsight and with the experience of taping subsequent cross-cultural interviews (see the following), it is now considered that this would not have been the case. In deed, not only would the audiotaping not have significantly affected the interview process, it would have provided the ability to more thoroughly review and support the analysis of the research participant's interpretations through the use of the verbatim transcripts.

Small Business

An essential component of any country's economy is the small business sector (Balderson, 2000; Curran & Blackburn, 2001). A core function of any business is the process by which information is acquired and presented in support of necessary decision making. This investigation (Hunter et al., 2005a, 2005b) adopted an international perspective to document the use of information systems by small business.

There were two objectives for conducting this project. The first objective was to investigate further the unique aspects of the use of information systems by small business. It has been identified previously that small business is unique from large business (Belich & Dubinsky, 1999; Pollard & Hayne, 1998). Small business is affected by resource poverty (Thong, Yap, & Raman, 1994). Small business managers lack time, finances, and human resource skills. Consequently, their approach to managing is to make minimum commitments with an emphasis on immediately addressing opportunities or resolving problems (Stevenson, 1999).

The second objective (Hunter, 2005b) was to try to identify if there is an international difference in how information systems are being used by small business. The plan was to incorporate experiences from a wide variety of geographical areas. This international perspective was taken in order to try to identify any variation in the use of information systems by small business.

Potential regional researchers were asked to adopt and to follow an interview protocol. The first part of the interview related to obtaining demographic data for the small business. The second part of the interview attempted to focus the discussion on the small business use of information systems. Questions in this part of the interview were developed in order to try to identify how information systems were employed to support the small business. Also, the regional researchers were encouraged to include any data gathering that they thought might be appropriate for their specific region. It was anticipated that regional data would be consolidated into a large international database. The regional data and the consolidated data then could be used for comparative purposes. The construction of the database allowed easy sharing of the consolidated data with the regional researchers, so they could then conduct any further data analysis that they felt might be necessary.

The first objective, gathering data from as geographically diverse sources as possible, was not as successful as had been hoped. While a number of researchers had expressed interest in the project at the beginning, for various reasons, several were unable to participate fully in the project. In the end, five researchers participated fully in the project. There was one from Canada, one from Portugal, and three from the USA total of 33 interviews were conducted.

The second objective, to obtain a better picture of the use of information systems by small businesses around the globe, was more successful. It was very interesting to find that there was not much variability based upon geography. There was, however, more variability relative to business type and size. Typically, most of the responses to the earlier questions about what information systems meant and how they were employed led to responses addressing the functional and support nature of information systems. As anticipated, most of the applications of information systems were accounting- or administrative-related functions used to support daily operations. Most of the small businesses did not have a strategic plan. However, for those that did, it typically was related to an annual review of their information systems budget. Most of the research participants felt that their information systems were delivering according to expectations and that the organization had been helped in the functional area. Where they identified obstacles, they were mainly about skill deficiencies or time constraints. This supports the concept of resource poverty (Thong et al., 1994) outlined earlier. Surprisingly, the cost of information systems was not considered by many research participants as an obstacle.

The lessons learned for this project relate to commitment, coordination, and communication. This project involved multiple researchers from different cultures. Thus, it is important that the perspectives adopted by each researcher are considered and addressed in the overall approach to conducting the investigation.

Group theory (McGrath, Arrow, & Berdahl, 2000) has been used to explain how this project may have been improved. The major comment here is that while the overall project may be considered a success, aspects such as team member interaction, commitment, and communication could have been coordinated and facilitated better through more specific adherence to the concepts of leadership of diverse research teams.

It is now recognized that it is very important to ensure that team member commitment is recognized and developed as early as possible in the project. It is also important to understand the different cultural perspectives regarding an individual's acknowledgment of a commitment.

Further, there could have been more extensive coordination. This could have been accomplished through more communication among the project director and the individual team members.

Finally, this project represents the first of its kind that has attempted to conduct simultaneous and joint investigations into the use of information systems by small businesses across a broad geographical area. The lessons learned both about conducting these types of projects and from the data gathered will prove valuable in subsequent, more extensive replications. Thus, this project represents the first step in the long journey of taking an international perspective to investigate the use of information systems by small business.

Chief Information Officers (CIOs)

As firms formally recognize the value of information to the organization, the role of the CIO emerges. The level of importance of this role is being elevated. While the CIO remains responsible for a firm's information technology function, it is now expected that the CIO also will understand the business and will contribute to the firm's competitive advantage, along with other members of senior management.

This currently ongoing project (Hunter, 2005a) is investigating the emerging and evolving roles of CIOs in New Zealand, Taiwan, and the U.S. In-depth interviews are being conducted to develop a better understanding of this role. Involvement of CIOs from other parts of the world currently is being investigated.

This exploratory investigation will document CIO comments about their roles within their firms. Thus, a qualitative approach has been adopted, employing narrative inquiry to document research participants' recitals of facts relating to the specific domain of discourse. Narrative inquiry has been defined as research that documents and analyzes "a segment of one's life that is of interest to the narrator and researcher" (Girden, 2001, p. 49). Bruner (1990) determined the narrative inquiry approach to conduct research included documenting stories that are contextually rich and temporally bounded. The first aspect, contextually rich, suggests that events that are directly experienced are remembered vividly by narrators (Tulving, 1972). A narrative is bounded temporally, the second aspect, when there is a beginning and an end, along with a sequential account of intervening events (Czariawska-Joerges, 1995).

Narrative inquiry has been employed extensively in other academic disciplines, such as: behavioral science (Rappaport, 1993), fiction and film (Chatman, 1978), and strategic management (Barry & Elmes, 1997). In the information systems area, narrative inquiry has been employed to investigate systems designers' interpretations of the structures involved in the design process (Boland & Day, 1989; Hirschheim & Newman, 1991). The results of these investigations have provided an improved understanding of the social interactions between information systems developers and users.

Through one-on-one interviews, research participants are asked to recount their experiences. Each interview follows a protocol developed to provide consistency across a number of interviews. The structure of the interview follows a chronological sequence, including a discussion of the relevant history of the firm and the CIO, issues surrounding initial assignment, major accomplishments, and the current situation. The research participants also are asked to provide their interpretation of the issues that will have to be addressed in the foreseeable future. Each interview is taped, and a transcript is prepared for the research participant's review. Emerging themes will be identified for subsequent analysis.

Currently, two CIOs have been interviewed in New Zealand, and six interviews have been conducted in Taiwan. Further, seven interviews in the U.S. have been conducted or are in various stages of completion. The results of these interviews and the identification of emerging themes are in progress. So, there will be ample opportunity for cross-cultural investigations of the emerging role of the CIO.

The lessons learned to date for this project relate to contacts and interviews.

With regard to contacts, sometimes a lesson may be learned by doing something right. In this case, two initial contact individuals proved to be extremely valuable assets for conducting the project. First, the contact in Taiwan was a very high-ranking and powerful outsider—a bank chairman, not a chief information officer. This person was able to make contacts at the highest level in very large organizations and to obtain commitment for an interview with the company's chief information officer. He was also valuable in making the necessary local travel and schedule arrangements. Second, the U.S. contact was a highly respected chief information officer within the local community. This person was able to deal directly with other chief information officers and to convince them of the benefits of their involvement in the project.

Various approaches were taken to conduct the interviews. First, in Taiwan, the interviews were audiotaped in face-to-face situations. An interview protocol was submitted sufficiently ahead of the interview date so that the CIO could prepare a response. This approach seemed to work well, although some of the Taiwan CIOs asked that an interpreter from within their organization to attend the interview. While the CIOs may have felt more comfortable expressing themselves in their first language, a concern about the translator's interpretation of words and phrases arose, which may have slightly altered the meanings of comments by the CIO. It is noted that it was beneficial to have the audiotapes and the transcripts of the conversations. This permitted subsequent analysis of the discussions.

Second, with the CIOs in the U.S., two approaches to conducting the interviews were used. To begin, the interview protocol was sent to those CIOs who agreed to participate in the project. The CIOs were asked to respond to the questions and to submit a Word file attached to an e-mail. This approach worked initially for two of the CIOs. However, for the remainder, it was not successful. Invariably, it seemed that the remaining CIOs encountered other items that required a higher priority than completing the interview protocol. In order to complete these interviews, the protocol was divided into three parts that represented about a one-hour discussion on the telephone. Each CIO was asked to commit to these sessions in advance and to be prepared to discuss the corresponding section of the interview protocol. These discussions were audiotaped for subsequent analysis. This approach has been very successful in completing the interviews and in providing feedback to the research participants. This latter approach also has been adopted for conducting the interviews with the New Zealand CIOs.

This project represents an in-depth investigation of the emerging role of the CIO. The management of information technology relates directly to an organization's bottom line. The results of this research project will provide a more thorough understanding of this role. This project also will contribute to the further understanding of how the role of the CIO is emerging in various corporate and national contexts. Subsequent cross-cultural investigations will provide comparative data at the international level.

Discussion

The examples described previously represent three very different projects. The first investigated interpretations of excellent systems analysts. Using the Repertory Grid technique, this project documented various audience members' interpretations based upon their experience working with systems analysts. Many people within different organizations participated. The second project investigated how small businesses use information technology. There were multiple researchers in different regions. One person in each company was involved in the project. The third project involved a single researcher conducting in-depth interviews with one individual within very large companies.

These projects also have some similarities. They all adopted a qualitative perspective and involved one-on-one interviews. The projects involved more than one culture. They all investigated roles, such as the role of excellent systems analysts, the role information technology plays in support of small business, and the emerging role of chief information officers.

A retrospective review of these projects allows the consideration of issues related to conducting qualitative cross-cultural research. These issues relate to perspectives, data gathering, and involvement of co-researchers.

One issue, as described earlier in this article, relates to the source of the development of the research constructs. Recall the discussion of an emic (single-culture) vs. an etic (multi-culture) perspective. The projects described here principally have adopted an emic perspective. Each researcher has carried out an investigation within one culture. Attempts were made in each project to draw etic or, at least, pseudo-etic conclusions based upon a comparison of the cultures involved in the investigation. A truly etic study would require conducting an international investigation on a very large scale. This exciting challenge would require participation of a large number of researchers or a very long time for one researcher. The issue of whether to involve more than one researcher is addressed later in this section.

Another issue introduced earlier in this article relates to the competing hypotheses of cultural convergence and divergence. The results of the projects described here suggest that cultures are converging regarding the consideration for roles and use of information technology. It is proposed that this convergence is supported by common education and experiences facilitated by the use of information technology. However, it must be noted that the research presented here represents a very narrow perspective on culture. Indeed, there may be many other areas where the hypothesis of cultural divergence may be supported.

When conducting qualitative interviews, researchers continually must be aware of whether the participants are attempting to respond by giving their interpretation of what they think the researcher wants to hear. They strive to provide the "right" answer. These types of responses can arise in any situation. They may occur when the researcher and participant are from the same culture. But they seem to have arisen more often when the two are from different cultures. Thus, the researchers should strive to reinforce the importance of the participant's comments and that there is neither a right nor a wrong answer.

Another issue about research participants relates to their desire only to tell the good news. It is difficult to encourage participants to discuss any negative aspects of their current situations or past experiences. One approach that has helped here is the development of a trusting relationship with the research participant over a long period of time. Eventually, as the research participants become more comfortable, it may be easier for them to discuss some of the negative issues.

A further issue relates to whether or not to involve co-researchers. If one researcher is involved, then a cross-cultural qualitative project will take a very long time. Establishing contacts and obtaining participant commitment will be very difficult, especially when trying to make these arrangements from afar and from a different culture. Alternatively, if many researchers are involved, concern arises about project coordination and researcher commitment. When more than one researcher is involved in a project, it becomes important to ensure a coordinated approach. This is especially the case when conducting qualitative cross-cultural research. All researchers must understand and agree with the research objectives. It is also important that an interview protocol be developed and employed consistently throughout the project. This will facilitate subsequent data comparisons. One of the major concerns originating from group theory (McGrath et al., 2000) is member coordination. This concern becomes even more important when the members are separated geographically. Researcher commitment is imperative when more than one researcher is involved. If priorities change during a project, valuable data may be lost, if a researcher does not complete the project. Employing the concepts of team building early in the project may contribute to resolving this issue. It is important to ensure that all researchers are able to identify the benefits of sharing the data and completing the project.

When considered at a more detailed level, adopting a qualitative perspective to conducting cross-cultural research will have consequences for the way projects may be carried out. For instance, this type of research usually involves conducting one-on-one interviews. Because of the distance involved in cross-cultural research, the logistics become much more complex. It becomes more complicated to make contacts, organize travel arrangements, and schedule interviews. Perhaps the most difficult of these three items is making contacts. Beyond involving a local co-researcher, a knowledgeable facilitator with the appropriate contacts will be helpful. In either case, it will take a long time to develop a relationship with this initial contact. Developing this initial relationship with the co-researcher for the systems analysts project took over one year. Friendship with the local facilitator in Taiwan goes back many years. Organizing travel and interviews is less complex but requires some planning to fit the schedule commitments of the individuals involved in both the home and visiting countries.

Another complicating factor relates to language. If research is being conducted in another culture, in all likelihood, another language will be involved. Thus, it may be necessary for either the researcher or the participant to speak a language that is not their first language. This may make expressing one's interpretations or understanding an explanation more difficult. Alternatively, a translator may be employed. However, this will increase the logistical complexity. Also, a translator may be less familiar with the content of the conversation, and word selection may affect the meaning of the participant's comments.

A more positive aspect of conducting qualitative cross-cultural research is the opportunity to gain new insights. Beyond the issues previously discussed, the in-depth interviews will be a source of rich data. Research participants' comments will give the researcher a valuable perspective on the subject under investigation from another culture. Comments in the interview will provide further elucidation and perhaps a new understanding of how a situation may be perceived in a different culture. Research participants' interpretations will be a valuable supply of data for subsequent analysis.

Finally, and this is the reason for conducting cross-cultural research, data will be gathered that will support the comparison of how different cultures perceive or interpret events or circumstances. Comments from interviews with research participants may be compared and contrasted. Identifying similarities and differences will expand understanding of the subject area being investigated.

Conclusion

This article has presented a perspective for conducting cross-cultural research in information systems. Qualitative research was proposed within the context of responding to employing innovative approaches. Examples of three projects have been presented to demonstrate the application of a qualitative approach.

Qualitative researchers become involved closely in research situations and with research participants. It is important that the cross-cultural researcher recognize and be prepared to reflect upon the differences between their own frameworks and those of the research participants that may exist as a result of cultural variability. That is, in an interview, questions may be posed in a certain way, or certain aspects of the discussion may be pursued more or less intensively. Some researchers would consider this flexibility to be beneficial, allowing the researcher to obtain relevant data. As Reason and Rowan (1981) suggest, "it is much better to be deeply interesting than accurately boring" (p. xiv). In the end, emphasis should be placed on the research method. Therefore, when conducting cross-cultural qualitative research, it is incumbent upon the investigator to gather data in a systematic way.

These techniques allow the research participants to determine their responses and to provide their own comment elaborations. The techniques lend structure to the qualitative data-gathering process, while allowing flexibility in the research participants' responses. Incorporating these techniques will support the grounding of interview data within the environment, as interpreted by the research participant. Finally, these approaches will support the qualitative researcher when conducting cross-cultural investigations.

References

Balderson, D. W. (2000). *Canadian entrepreneurship and small business management.* Toronto: McGraw-Hill Ryerson.

Barry, D., & Elmes, M. (1997). Strategy retold: Towards a narrative view of strategic discourse. *Academy of Management Review, 22*(2), 429-452.

Belich, T. J., & Dubinsky. A. J. (1999). Information processing among exporters: An empirical examination of small firms. *Journal of Marketing Theory and Practice, 7*(4), 45-58.

Benbasat, I., & Zmud, R. W. (1999). Empirical research in information systems: The practice of relevance. *MIS Quarterly, 23*(1), 3-16.

Berry, J. W. (1990). Imposed-etics, emics, and derived-etics: Their conceptual and operational status in cross-cultural psychology. In T. N. Headland, K. L. Pike,

& M. Harris (Eds.), *Emics and etics: The insider/outsider debate*. Newbury Park, CA: Sage Publications.

Boland, R. J., Jr., & Day, W. F. (1989). The experience of systems design: A hermeneutic of organizational action. *Scandinavian Journal of Management, 5*(2), 87-104.

Bruner, J. (1990). *Acts of meaning*. Cambridge, MA: Harvard University Press.

Chatman, S. (1978). *Story and discourse: Narrative structure in fiction and film*. Ithaca, NY: Cornell University Press.

Curran, J., & Blackburn, R. A. (2001). *Researching the small enterprise*. London: Sage Publications.

Czarniawska-Joerges, B. (1995). Narration or science? Collapsing the division in organization studies. *Organization, 2*(1), 11-33.

Earley, P. C., & Mosakowski, E. (1995). A framework for understanding experimental research in an international and intercultural context. In B. J. Punnett & O. Shenkar (Eds.), *Handbook of international management research*. Oxford, UK: Blackwell Publishers.

Galliers, R. D. (Ed.). (1992). *Information systems research: Issues, methods, and practical guidelines*. Henley-on-Thames, UK: Alfred Waller.

Galliers, R. D., & Land, F. F. (1987). Choosing appropriate information systems research methodologies. *Communications of the ACM, 30*(11), 900-902.

Gallupe, R. B., & Tan, F. B. (1999). A research manifesto for global information management. *Journal of Global Information Management, 7*(3), 5-19.

Girden, E. R. (2001). *Evaluating research articles* (2nd ed.). Thousand Oaks, CA: Sage Publications.

Glaser, B. G., & Strauss, A. L. (1967). *The discovery of grounded theory: Strategies for qualitative research*. New York: Aldine De Gruyter.

Headland, T. N., Pike, K. L., & Harris, M. (1990). *Emics and etics: The onsider/outsider debate*. Newbury Park, CA: Sage Publications.

Hirschheim, R. (1992). Information systems epistemology: An historical perspective. In R. D. Galliers (Ed.), *Information systems research—Issues, methods, and practical guidelines* (pp. 61-88). Henley-on-Thames, UK: Alfred Waller.

Hirschheim, R., & Newman, M. (1991). Symbolism and information systems development: Myth, metaphor and magic. *Information Systems Research, 2*(1), 29-62.

Hofstede, G. (1980). *Culture's consequences: International differences in work-related values*. Beverly Hills, CA: Sage Publications.

Hofstede, G. (1983, Fall). The cultural relativity of organizational practices and theories. *Journal of International Business Studies*, 75-89.

Hofstede, G. (1993). Cultural constraints in management theories. *Academy of Management Executive, 7*(1), 81-94.

Hofstede, G., & Bond, M. H. (1988). The Confucius connection: From cultural roots to economic growth. *Organizational Dynamics, 16*(4), 4-21.

Hofstede, G., Neuijen, B., Ohayv, D. D., & Sanders, G. (1990). Measuring organizational cultures: A qualitative and quantitative study across twenty cases. *Administrative Science Quarterly, 35*, 286-316.

Hunter, M. G. (1997). The use of RepGrids to gather interview data about information systems analysts. *Information Systems Journal, 7*(1), 67-81.

Hunter, M. G. (2005a, May 15-18). Chief information officers in Taiwan: An exploratory investigation. In M. Khosrow-Pour (Ed.), *Managing Modern Organizations with Information Technology: Proceedings of the 2005 International Conference of the Information Resources Management Association*, San Diego, CA (Vol. 2, pp. 1098-1100). Hershey, PA: Idea Group Publishing.

Hunter, M. G. (2005b). International multi-researcher qualitative investigations. In *Proceedings of the European Conference on Research Methods for Business and Management Studies,* Paris (pp. 177-184).

Hunter, M. G., & Beck, J. E. (1996). A cross-cultural comparison of "excellent" systems analysts. *Information Systems Journal, 6*(4), 261-281.

Hunter, M. G., & Beck, J. E. (2000). Using repertory grids to conduct cross-cultural information systems research. *Information Systems Research, 11*(1), 93-101.

Hunter, M. G., Burgess, S., & Wenn, A. (Eds.). (2005a). *Small business and information technology: Research issues and international cases*. Melbourne, Australia: Heidelberg Press.

Hunter, M. G., Burgess, S., & Wenn, A. (2005b). The use of information systems by small business: An international perspective. In M. G. Hunter, S. Burgess, & A. Wenn (Eds.), *Small business and information technology: Research issues and international cases* (pp. 3-14). Melbourne, Australia: Heidelberg Press.

Kelly, G. A. (1955). *The psychology of personal constructs*. New York: Norton.

Kelly, G. A. (1963). *A theory of personality.* New York: Norton.

Klein, H. K., & Lyytinen, K. (1985). The poverty of scientism in information systems. In E. Mumford et al. (Eds.), *Research methods in information systems* (pp. 131-161). Amsterdam: North-Holland.

McGrath, J. E., Arrow, H., & Berdahl, J. L. (2000). The study of groups: Past, present, and future. *Personality and Social Psychology Review, 4*(1), 95-105.

Pike, R. (1954). *Language in relation to a united theory of the structure of human behavior.* Glendale, AZ: Summer Institute of Linguistics.

Pollard, C., & Hayne, S. (1998). The changing faces of information systems issues in small firms. *International Small Business Journal, 16*(3), 70-87.

Rappaport, J. (1993). Narrative studies, personal stories and identity transformation in the mutual help context. *Journal of Applied Behavioral Science, 29*(2), 239-256.

Reason, P., & Rowan, J. (Eds.). (1981). *Human inquiry: A sourcebook of new paradigm research.* Chichester, UK: John Wiley & Sons.

Ronen, S. (1986). *Comparative and multinational management.* New York: John Wiley.

Stevenson, H. H. (1999). A perspective of entrepreneurship. In H. H. Stevenson, I. Grousebeck, M. J. Roberts, & A. Bhide (Eds.), *New business ventures and the entrepreneur* (pp. 3-17). Boston: Irwin McGraw-Hill.

Tan, F., & Hunter, M. G. (2002). The repertory grid technique: A method for the study of cognition in information systems. *MIS Quarterly, 26*(1), 39-57.

Thong, J., Yap, C., & Raman, K. (1994). Engagement of external expertise in information systems implementation. *Journal of Management Information Systems, 11*(2), 209-223.

Trauth, E. M. (2001). *Qualitative research in IS: Issues and trends.* Hershey, PA: Idea Group Publishing.

Triandis, H. C. (1972). *Analysis of subjective culture.* New York: Wiley Interscience.

Tulving, E. (1972). Episodic and semantic memory. In E. Tulving & W. Donaldson (Eds.), *Organization of memory* (pp. 381-404). New York: Academic Press.

Webber, R. H. (1969). Convergence and divergence. *Columbia Journal of World Business, 4*(3), 75-83.

Yang, K. S. (1986). Will societal modernization eventually eliminate cross-cultural psychological differences. In M. H. Bond (Ed.), *The cross-cultural challenge to social psychology* (pp. 67-85). Newbury Park, CA: Sage.

This work was previously published in the Journal of Global Information Management, 14(2), 75-89, April-June 2006.

Chapter V

The Challenge of Web Site Design for Global Organizations

Dianne Cyr, Simon Fraser University, Canada

Carole Bonanni, University College of the Fraser Valley, Canada

John Bowes, School of Interactive Arts and Technology, Canada

Joe Ilsever, Douglas College, Canada

Abstract

The growth of Internet shopping motivates a better understanding of how e-loyalty is built online between businesses and consumers. In this study, Web site design and culture are advanced as important to Web site trust, Web site satisfaction, and e-loyalty in online business relationships. Based on data collected in Canada, the U.S., Germany, and Japan, the research considers (1) examining, within culture, preferences for design elements of a local vs. a foreign Web site, and subsequent participant perceptions of trust, satisfaction, and e-loyalty, and (2) comparisons between cultures for design preferences of local and foreign Web sites, and subsequent participant perceptions of trust, satisfaction, and e-loyalty. As predicted, similarities were greatest among Americans, Canadians, and Germans, with the Japanese representing a different and unique case. The results are discussed against hypothesized expectations. Implications for future research are outlined.

Introduction

The origin of online shoppers is progressively more global and represents a multicultural community. In 2006, there are more than one billion Internet users with access to online consumer products (Internet Usage Statistics, 2006). Of those Internet users, the primary language is English (35.6%), followed by Chinese (12.2%), Japanese (9.5%), Spanish (8%), and German (7%). Understanding how to build trust, satisfaction, and ultimately loyalty for diverse consumers in electronic markets is a central imperative (Grewal, Munger, Iyer, & Levy, 2003; Jarvenpaa, Tractinsky, Saarinen, & Vitale, 1999; McKnight, Choudhury, & Kacmar 2002; Rattanawicha & Esichaikul, 2005; Schlosser, Barnett White, & Lloyd, 2006; Urban, Sultan, & Qualls, 2000; Yoon, 2002).

Despite an anticipated large number of consumers from multiple cultures, few studies have systematically examined Web preferences of users related to design characteristics across cultures. This appears an omission in the literature, considering Chen and Dhillon (2003, pp. 310-311) who note:

In the case of an Internet vendor, the Web site is perhaps the only way a firm communicates with its customers. Therefore, its appearance and structure encourage or discourage a consumer's purchase intentions. In the marketing literature Web site features such as layout, appeal, graphics, readability, and ease-of-use have been considered to affect consumers' clicking frequency.

Some researchers have done work in the area of culture and design (Barber & Badre, 2001; Del Galdo & Nielsen, 1996; Marcus & Gould, 2000), but results have been either inconclusive or unrelated to developing loyal online customers. Issues of interest extend beyond consideration of language to also include color, product information, and use of images.

With increased prevalence of the Internet for shopping, research has been focused on how to develop trust online. As with the literature on trust prior to the Internet, the elements contributing to online trust are diverse and include quality, customer support, on-time delivery, compelling product presentations, convenient and reasonably priced shipping and handling, clear and trustworthy privacy policies (Reichheld & Schefter, 2000), company reputation (Egger, 2000; Jarvenpaa et al., 1999; Lohse

& Spiller, 1998; Quelch & Klein, 1996; Resnick & Zeckhauser, 2002; Yoon, 2002), online transaction security (Palmer, Bailey, Faraj, & Smith, 2000), or information privacy (Hoffman & Novak, 1996) among other considerations. Overall shopping satisfaction has been used to predict subsequent purchases and loyalty to Internet shopping sites, (Anderson & Srinivasan, 2003; Devaraj, Fan, & Kohli, 2002; Flavián, Guinaliu, & Gurrea, 2005; Laurn & Lin, 2003; Szymanski & Hise, 2000; Yoon, 2002). In particular, Yoon tested both trust and satisfaction related to Web site design and security, and found trust related to security, while ease of navigation (generally accepted as a design characteristic of Web sites) tied to satisfaction. This is an interesting distinction, and suggests satisfaction merits further investigation related to various design features of Web sites.

Although trust and satisfaction are expected to be predictive of e-loyalty, few studies have systematically examined these elements linked to design preferences. More specifically, design preferences contributing to the development of trust, satisfaction, and e-loyalty have not been examined across cultures. This investigation addresses this gap by examining *within* culture preferences for design features of a local vs. a foreign Web site, and participants' consequent perceptions of trust, satisfaction, and e-loyalty. The research also examines comparisons *between* cultures for design preferences of the local Web site, and subsequent participant perceptions of trust, satisfaction, and e-loyalty. In other words, the investigation addresses whether some cultures are more sensitive than others to culturally biased Web design. The implications of this research are important as Internet commerce increasingly bridges national frontiers.

This chapter presents a literature review with emphasis on cultural implications of design, trust, satisfaction, and e-loyalty. Results of a four-nation study conducted onsite in Canada, the U.S., Germany, and Japan are reported. Data were collected using questionnaires, online user tasks, and follow-up interviews. The paper concludes with a discussion of Web design and culture with implications for future research.

Considerations of Culture

A definition of culture is complex. According to Matsumoto (1994), culture is characterized as the degree to which people share attributes, values, beliefs, and behaviors. Hofstede defines culture as "the collective programming of the mind which distinguishes the members of one group from another" (1984, p. 21). Doney et al. (Doney, Cannon, & Mullen, 1998) note culture is "a system of values and norms that are shared among a group of people and that when taken together constitute a design for living" (1998, p. 67). Although one definition of culture is not possible, various researchers have used nation-state as a loose categorization for culture (Doney et al., 1998). In fact, for more than 20 years, researchers have relied

Table 1. Country cultural dimensions

Country Dimension	U.S.	Canada	Germany	Japan
Power Distance	Low (40)	Low (39)	Low (35)	Med (54)
Uncertainty Avoidance	Low (46)	Low (48)	Med (65)	Very high (92)
Masculine	Med (62)	Med (52)	Med (66)	Very high (95)
Individualism	Very high (91)	High (80)	Med (67)	Low (46)

on the work by Hofstede (1984) in order to make meaningful comparisons between national groups. While it is recognized these categorizations are not perfect, they do provide a readily identifiable basis for contrast.

To understand how national culture is related to social psychological phenomena such as trust, several researchers (Dawar, Parker, & Price, 1996; Jarvenpaa et al., 1999; Simon, 2001; Yamagishi & Yamagishi, 1994) refer to Hofstede's (1984) cultural dimensions of individualism-collectivism, uncertainty avoidance, power distance, and femininity-masculinity.[1] Individualism-collectivism focuses on an individual's relationships with others. In an individualist society such as the U.S., Canada, or Germany, individuals are expected to consider personal interests over interests of the group and individual decision-making is valued. Uncertainty avoidance characterizes how societies accommodate high levels of uncertainty and ambiguity in the environment. Members of high uncertainty-avoidance societies, such as Japan, seek to reduce personal risk and to augment security. Power distance addresses the extent to which a society accepts unequal distributions of power in organizations and institutions. In low-power distance cultures such as Canada, the U.S., or Germany, there is a tendency to maintain a philosophy of equal rights for all, without acquiescence to those in power. Finally, in feminine societies there is emphasis on quality of life and relationships. Cultures that focus on material success and assertiveness are considered more masculine in orientation (Hofstede, 1984). Relevant to the cultures studied in this investigation: Canada, the U.S., Germany, and Japan, differences on each of Hofstede's dimensions are noted in Table 1.

Culture or ethnicity has been related to a wide range of consumer preferences in non-Internet settings including attitudes toward advertising (Alden, Hoyer, & Lee, 1993; de Mooij, 1998; Durvasula, Andrews, Lysonski, & Netemeyer, 1993), brand loyalty (Deshpande, Hoyer, & Donthu, 1986), consumer values (Valencia, 1989), consumption patterns (Wallendorf & Reilly, 1983), and perceived risk (Hoover, Green, & Saegert, 1978). The results of the studies suggest culture does have a large potential influence on consumption behavior, although most of the work has been descriptive in nature.

Culture has implications in Internet settings as well, and is proposed to affect marketing (Tian & Emery, 2002), consumer trust (Jarvenpaa et al., 1999), Internet diffusion (Ferle, Edwards, & Mizuno, 2002), Internet marketing (Tian & Emery, 2002), and Web site development (Kang & Corbitt, 2001; Sun, 2001). Differences in online communication strategies for target markets were detected between Japan, Spain, and the U.S. (Okayazaki & Rivas, 2002). In other work, Evers and Day (1997) demonstrate differences between cultures exist concerning Web interface acceptance and preferences for design features. However, how consumer preferences relate to culture and e-loyalty is not well understood. Further, research does not examine systematic preferences for a local Web site over a foreign Web site.

Web Site Trust, Web Site Satisfaction, and E-Loyalty

"Since transactions [on the Internet] occur without personal contact, consumers are generally concerned with legitimacy of the vendor and authenticity of products or services" (Chen & Dhillon, 2003, p. 1). Trust focuses on consumer confidence in the Web site as part of a buyer-seller transactional exchange, and consumer's "willingness to rely on the seller and take actions in circumstances where such action makes the consumer vulnerable to the seller" (Jarvenpaa et al., 1999, p. 4). In contrast, Web site satisfaction refers to a positive navigation experience and perception of a well-designed Web site (Balasubramanian, Konana, & Menon, 2003). A generally accepted definition of e-loyalty (and adopted in this research) is that loyalty in online environments refers to repeat purchase intention or intended return visits to a Web site (Corstjens & Lal, 2000; Flavián et al., 2005; Gommans, Krishan, & Scheddold, 2001).

Web Site Trust and Culture

Prior to the advent of the Internet, trust was examined in multiple disciplines in multiple ways. Traditionally, trust has been difficult to define and measure (Rousseau, Sitkin, Burt, & Camerer, 1998). Other researchers have called the state of trust definitions confusing (Lewis & Weigert, 1985; McKnight et al., 2002), a "conceptual morass" (Barber, 1983, p. 1; Carnevale & Wechsler, 1992, p. 473), and multidimensional (Chen & Dhillon, 2003; Mayer, Davis, & Schoorman, 1995; Rousseau et al., 1998). Others believe trust is a single dimension (Selnes, 1998). Bhattacherjee (2002) conducted an extensive review of trust based on previous research and concludes ability, benevolence, and integrity are conceptually distinct and reflect "different elements of cognitive and affective abstractions of trust" (p. 219).[2]

Disposition to trust is an enduring and personal characteristic that may also be embodied in culture. According to McKnight et al. (McKnight, Cummings, & Chervany, 1998, p. 473-490), "Disposition to trust is a general, i.e., not situation specific, inclination to display faith in humanity or to adopt a trusting stance toward others." Further, "[T]rust is determined by a general trusting disposition that is the product of a lifelong socialization process. This disposition is especially influential when the trusting party has not had extensive personal interaction with the specific organization or person in question. Therefore, also a trusting disposition should influence people's trust in a vendor" (Gefen, 2000, p. 729).

"Lack of trust is one of the most frequently cited reasons for consumers not purchasing from Internet vendors" (Grabner-Krauter & Kaluscha, 2003[3]). Despite the importance of the concept, a definition of trust in online environments remains as elusive as does a definition of trust when conducting traditional shopping. In general, online trust is a multifaceted concept, and supports earlier research on trust in traditional settings. Further, Grabner-Krautner and Kaluscha (2003) herald a call for future research on "cross-cultural effects on consumers' trust..." and suggest "there may be a relationship between trust and culture which needs to be further investigated" (2003, p. 807).

Cultural norms dictate a higher propensity to trust in collectivist than individualist cultures (Doney et al., 1998; Parks & Vu, 1994; Triandis, 1990). Collectivists rarely move in and out of groups, and levels of trust and cooperation are high among collectivist group members. Weber and Hsee (1998) found that Chinese collectivists are least risk averse when selecting risky financial options than participants from the U.S., Germany, or Poland. The authors suggest that in collectivist countries like China, collectivism acts like "a cushion" when other members in the family or society assist in bearing possible negative consequences of a decision.

Individualistic societies have commonly less trust and cooperation in relationships that are transitory. Between cultures, the tendency to trust is reversed. Individualists are more optimistic than collectivists concerning benevolence from strangers (Inglehart, Basanez, & Moreno, 1998; Yamagishi & Yamagishi, 1994). Kim and Son (1998) measured levels of distrust between Americans (highly individualist) and Koreans (highly collectivist) and found for Americans, 59% trust members of a different ethnic group in their society, and 57% trust people from a different country. For Koreans, the average responses were 23% and 18%, respectively. According to Yamagishi and Yamagishi (1994), exchange relationships outside a cultural group only occur when there are strong institutional safeguards (such as strong cultural norms or legal sanctions). In the evolving Internet environment, no strong legal structures prevail; thus, collectivists may see the risks of buying online as more pervasive than do members of individualist cultures (Jarvenpaa et al., 1999). This would be especially true when purchasing from a foreign Web site.

With reference to culture and the Internet, few studies focus on trust, and those that do often have inconclusive results. Lui et al. (Liu, Marchewka, & Ku, 2004) examined privacy and trust on electronic commerce between American and Taiwanese participants. The authors found systematic differences in Web site perceptions concerning privacy, but no differences were evident related to culture. Jarvenpaa et al. (1999) used Hofstede's dimensions to compare Internet trust in collectivist and individualist cultures. The researchers expected consumers from individualist cultures would exhibit higher trust in an Internet store than consumers from collectivist cultures (similar to Yamagishi & Yamagishi, 1994, noted above). Contrary to this hypothesis, no strong cultural effects were found regarding antecedents to trust. Similarly, Badre (2000) conducted research on consumer trust in an Internet environment in individualist vs. collectivist cultures with mixed outcomes. Simon (2001) found differences in trusting stance toward Web sites.[4] Asians were most trusting of information provided across American and European Web sites (83% positive), counter to the earlier findings of Yamagishi and Yamagishi (1994) and Inglehart et al. (1998). In Simon's study, Europeans (46% positive) and North Americans (42% positive) exhibited substantially lower levels of trust toward the Web sites. This finding supports research by Doney et al. (1998) and others who found that within a group, Americans would be unlikely to trust (i.e., American Web sites).

Of interest in this investigation is whether local Web sites will engender higher levels of trust for Web users than will a foreign site of the same vendor. Related to earlier work by Yamagishi and Yamagishi (1994) and others, the investigation will test whether Web users from individualistic cultures, such as Canada or the U.S., are least likely to trust the local Web site, and most likely to trust the foreign Web site than are moderately individualistic users as in Germany, and collectivist Japanese users.

Hypothesis 1: Within a cultural group, local Web site trust will be higher than foreign Web site trust.

Hypothesis 2a: Among cultural groups, American and Canadian participants are least likely to trust the local Web site, followed by Germans, and then the Japanese.

Hypothesis 2b: Among cultural groups, American and Canadian participants are more likely to trust the foreign Web site, followed by Germans, and then the Japanese.

Web Site Satisfaction and Culture

Web site satisfaction relates to "stickiness" and "the sum of all the Web site qualities that induce visitors to remain at the Web site rather than move to another site" (Holland & Menzel-Baker, 2001, p. 37). According to Anderson and Srivanan (2003), e-satisfaction is defined as the contentment of the customer with respect to his or her prior purchasing experience with a given electronic firm. Relating e-satisfaction to e-loyalty, Devaraj et al. (2003) claim "repeated satisfaction with purchases eventually leads to customer loyalty" (p. 185). Further, Szymanski and Hise (2000, p. 318) found "positive perceptions of site design are important to e-satisfaction assessments."

In concert with the usability literature, it is expected online consumers will be more satisfied with Web sites that are localized[5] to their particular cultural preferences. The goal of localizing user interfaces is to provide a "technologically, linguistically and culturally neutral platform from which to launch global e-commerce initiatives while allowing a framework that incorporates local content and functionality" (Shannon, 2000). More simply put, this involves "enhancing the site to fit the target users at different locales" (Alvarez, Kasday, & Todd, 1998; Lagon, 2000).

Few studies examine Web site satisfaction across cultures. Notable exceptions are Evers and Day (1997), who considered Web site satisfaction between a group of Asian students (from collectivist cultures including Indonesia, China, Hong Kong, Taiwan, Singapore, and Japan) and a group of Australian students (who represent an individualistic culture orientation). They found 87% of the Australian sample would be satisfied using technology adapted to their culture, compared to 70% of the Asian group. This finding appears to indicate Australians were most interested in localization of the Web site contents, and would be more satisfied with the outcome.

In other work relevant to the current investigation, Simon (2001) likewise examined Web site satisfaction across cultures. His findings are counter to those of Evers and Day (1997). Asians were slightly more satisfied with sites presented in the study than the Europeans and North Americans; although it should be noted different sites may contribute to this discrepancy. Simon concludes, "The creation of a single universally appealing global site does not appear feasible given the differences between some cultures/consumers, and that a preferable strategy might be to instead create culturally and consumer specific sites" (p. 32). In short, Web sites merit localization to appeal to diverse cultural constituents.

Based on the premise that Web site users will be more satisfied with a localized site that matches their cultural needs and preferences, the following hypothesis is outlined.

Hypothesis 3: *Within a cultural group, local Web site satisfaction will be higher than foreign Web site satisfaction.*

To date, there appears little if any sound theory to support Web site preferences between cultures related to satisfaction. Further, existing work (Evers & Day, 1997;

Simon, 2001) provides no consistent outcomes to inform future research. However, following Simon, who found Asians were more satisfied with a sample of sites than Europeans and North Americans, the following exploratory hypotheses are suggested.

Hypothesis 4a: *Among cultural groups, American and Canadian participants are least likely to be satisfied with the local Web site, followed by Germans, and then the Japanese.*

Hypothesis 4b: *Among cultural groups, American and Canadian participants are least likely to be satisfied with the foreign Web site, followed by Germans, and then the Japanese.*

E-Loyalty and Culture

In online environments, "understanding how or why a sense of loyalty develops in customers remains one of the crucial management issues of our day" (Laurn & Lin, 2003, p. 156). Providing services that are perceived as value-added to customers, such as easily accessible capabilities related to information access or navigation, allows online vendors to build successful relationships with customers (de Ruyter, Wetzels, & Lkeijnen, 2001). Online shoppers are more likely to revisit a Web site if they like its design and capabilities (Flavián et al., 2005; Mithas, Ramasubbu, Krishnan, & Fornell, 2003; Rosen & Purinton, 2004).

Little research has been conducted in which loyalty has been considered across cultures. In one study, Cyr (2006) modeled the relationships of Web site design to trust, satisfaction, and ultimately, to e-loyalty for Canadian, American, German, and Japanese participants. In this instance, loyalty was considered as two separate constructs: intent to revisit the Web site again (Loyalty1), and whether users would consider purchasing from it in the future (Loyalty2). Partial least squares (PLS) analysis demonstrated that Web site satisfaction is a strong predictor of e-loyalty, and more so than trust. Further, between country differences were uncovered. For example, satisfaction leading to Loyalty1 and Loyalty2 occurred for Canadians, Americans, and Germans, but not for Loyalty2 (purchasing from the site) for Japanese. Concerning trust, only Americans would trust the Web site sufficiently to purchase from it in the future.

To best knowledge, no other work has been conducted to study Web users' loyalty to a local and foreign Web site and to compare Web users loyalty across cultures.

Hypothesis 5: *Within a cultural group, loyalty to the local Web site will be higher than loyalty to the foreign Web site.*

Hypothesis 6a: *Among cultural groups, American and Canadian participants are most likely to express e-loyalty for the local Web site, followed by Germans, and then Japanese.*

Hypothesis 6b: *Among cultural groups, American and Canadian participants are most likely to express e-loyalty for the foreign Web site, followed by Germans, and then Japanese.*

Web Site Design and Culture

Effective Web site design engages and attracts online consumers (Agarwal & Venkatesh, 2002; Fogg & Tseng, 1999; 2002; Hoffman & Novak, 1996; Hu, Shima, Oehlmann, Zhao, Takemura, & Matsumoto, 2004; Nielsen, 2001; Rattanawicha & Esichaikul, 2005; Schlosser, Barnett White, & Lloyd, 2006; Venkatesh & Ramesh, 2006). Design elements often considered include architecture of the information, familiarity of metaphors, transparency of terminology, ease of access, and level to which the site is customer-centric (Egger, 2001).

According to Gommans et al. (2001, p. 51), "A Web site has to be designed for a targeted customer segment…Local adaptation should be based on a complete understanding of a customer group's culture." Barber and Badre (2001) refer to the merging of culture and usability as "culturability," when cultural elements are considered in Web site design and are expected to directly affect the way a user interacts with the site. In this regard Singh et al. (Singh, Xhao, & Hu, 2003) employed content analysis of 40 American-based companies to compare their domestic and Chinese Web sites. Significant differences in cultural characteristics were found for all major categories tested. The authors conclude, "the Web is not a culturally neutral medium" (p. 63).

Some research, in which design characteristics, such as color or screen images, were considered across cultures, did find different user preferences (Del Galdo & Nielsen, 1996; Marcus & Gould, 2000). In other research, results have been mixed, with no systematic design preferences determined across cultures (Barber & Badre, 2001). Badre (2000) tested Italian participants using Italian designs and found preferences for navigation, but not for color. In the same study, there were no significant differences uncovered as a result of varying cultural characteristics for Americans. Cyr and Trevor-Smith (2004) examined design elements using 30 municipal Web sites in each of Germany, Japan, and the U.S. Design elements considered were use of symbols and graphics, color preferences, site features (links, maps, search functions, page layout), language, and content. Significant modal differences were found in each of the listed categories, and suggest distinctive design preferences across cultures.

Relevant to the current research, and in alignment with the work outlined, it is expected Web users will perceive design elements of a local Web site as more culturally appropriate and therefore preferred over design elements of a foreign Web site. This gives rise to the following hypotheses concerning Web site design.

Hypothesis 7: *Within a cultural group, the design elements of the local site will be preferred rather than the design elements of the foreign site of the same online vendor.*

Further, building on the work by Hofstede (1984) outlined previously, it is expected there is general cultural similarity between Americans and Canadians. In turn, this may result in similar preferences concerning Web site design of either a local or foreign Web site. Germans represent a midrange position in Hofstede's work, and the Japanese are most dissimilar from Americans and Canadians. These reported cultural differences among these groups suggest the following hypotheses.

Hypothesis 8a: *Among cultural groups, Web site design preferences for the local site will be most similar between Americans and Canadians.*

Hypothesis 8b: *Among cultural groups, Web site design preferences for the foreign site will be most similar between Americans and Canadians.*

Hypothesis 9a: *Among cultural groups, Web site design preferences for the local site will be moderately similar among Americans, Canadians, and Germans.*

Hypothesis 9b: *Among cultural groups, Web site design preferences for the foreign site will be moderately similar among Americans, Canadians, and Germans.*

Hypothesis 10a: *Among cultural groups, Web site design preferences for the local site will be most dissimilar among Americans, Canadians, or Germans with the Japanese.*

Hypothesis 10b: *Among cultural groups, Web site design preferences for the foreign site will be most dissimilar between Americans, Canadians, or Germans with the Japanese.*

Methodology for the Study

Survey Development

A survey instrument was constructed to test several user reactions including design, trust, satisfaction, and e-loyalty. Design items relate to work by Marcus and Gould (1999), Egger (2001), Badre (2000), and Cheskin (1999; 2000). Items on trust and satisfaction are drawn from Yoon (2002) and Gefen (2000). All items are constructed as agree-disagree statements on five-point Likert scales. Once the survey was finalized, it was pretested with 62 undergraduate students. Categories were evaluated for item validity and reliability, and several items were revised for better fit and comprehension. A copy of the final survey items appears in the Appendix. Final versions of the survey were created in two versions (one with the foreign Web site experience first; the other with the local Web site experience first). In each country, one-half the respondents received each version. The survey was translated and back translated for each language required.

Research Task

After extensive search for a Web site that appeared well localized, the Samsung site was chosen. For the research treatments, participants responded to a local version of the Samsung Web site (represented in their native language), and a foreign version (which was the English version of the Hong Kong site in each case).[6] The Hong Kong site was specifically chosen since it was foreign and yet offered a language with which most respondents have either total proficiency, or at least some familiarity. In fact, this was the case. Initially, participants viewed the home page, and then were requested to navigate the site to choose a cell phone they would hypothetically purchase. Once participants completed the survey questions within a category, each was asked parallel interview questions to obtain further information about the Web site experience. Interviews were digitally recorded. An interpreter was used when necessary.

Participant Selection

Participants were selected and interviewed on site in the U.S., Canada, Germany, and Japan. These countries were chosen to represent diverse cultural characteristics as determined by Hofstede (1984) (cf. Table 1). Those interviewed comprised a stratified sample of employees from different levels in a multinational high-technology company. The original sample of 30 participants in each country ($4 \times 30 = 120$) was reduced to 114 respondents in the final analysis, and was equally distributed. Respondents included 41.5% females and 58.5% males, with an average age of 35 years.

Analysis

Mean scores and t-tests were calculated for survey items to test significance between country differences. Established theory was used for the categorization of interview data. Key participant responses were recorded by category and relevant quotes were produced verbatim. Once all individual responses had been extracted, a within-group analysis was carried out for each country. At the country level of analysis, responses were likewise coded and categorized. As the analysis proceeded, further segmentation of the data was required for emerging codes, themes, and categories. The final stage of the analysis consisted of a between-group analysis for all countries. This part of the process used the codes, themes, and categories developed in the previous stage. Once content analysis was completed, an independent reviewer considered the data from a different perspective in order to validate the findings. The second reviewer's examination of the data revealed virtually identical results.

Results

In this exploratory study, the objective was to examine differences within and between countries regarding preferred Web site design elements, Web site trust, Web site satisfaction, and Web site loyalty. To determine differences, t-tests were performed on the individual observed variables for the design elements, and on the factor scored variables for the trust, satisfaction, and e-loyalty variables.

Reliability measures for local trust, local satisfaction, local loyalty, foreign trust, foreign satisfaction, and foreign loyalty were assessed by using Cronbach's alpha. In Table 2, acceptable alpha scores are shown for these factors.

For each of the factors in Table 2, principal component analysis using varimax rotation was used to compute the factor score. Each factor is represented by only

Table 2. Cronbach alpha values

Factors	Mean	Std Dev	Alphas
Local Trust	3.90	0.87	.93
Local Satisfaction	2.97	1.10	.92
Local Loyalty	2.75	1.20	.85
Foreign Trust	3.77	0.80	.88
Foreign Satisfaction	3.03	0.93	.89
Foreign Loyalty	2.60	1.10	.78

one variable, which is the weighted sum of each of the observed variables included in the factor.

Web Site Trust, Satisfaction and Loyalty within Cultures

One objective was to test whether local Web sites will engender higher levels of trust, satisfaction, and loyalty for Web users than a foreign site of the same vendor. In addition, the investigation will test whether Web users from individualist cultures, such as Canada or the U.S., are less likely to trust, be satisfied, and be loyal to the local Web site, and most likely to trust, be satisfied, and be loyal to the foreign Web site than are moderately individualist users as in Germany, and collectivist Japanese users.

No statistically significant differences were found to indicate respondents in any of the countries trusted the local Samsung Web site more than the foreign site, rejecting hypothesis 1. Respondents trusted the foreign Hong Kong site as much as their local Samsung site. On average, the level of trust was higher than 3 on a scale from 1 to 5 for the respondents in each of the four countries for both conditions. Germans were overall most trusting (4.3 local site; 4.09 foreign site), and the Japanese were least trusting (3.3 local site; 3.45 foreign site).

Based on the interview data, all four cultural groups identify *vendor familiarity,* and *security signs* as important factors influencing their trust in online purchasing. Vendor familiarity refers to previous experience purchasing from a vendor, the popularity of the vendor's name, and the vendor's reputation. Such issues of security are particularly important to the Japanese and less so for Canadians, Americans, and Germans. On average, the Japanese indicate less trust for Internet stores, more concern about security when buying online, and more concern about the legitimacy of online sales contact.

The name of the company and its popularity are identified as important elements of trust. One Japanese participant observed, "What is important is…if the supplier

Table 3. Local vs. foreign Web site trust, satisfaction, and e-loyalty

	US	CAN	GER	JAPN
Local/Foreign Trust	-	-	-	-
Local/Foreign satisfaction	-	-	-	-3.12***
Local/Foreign E-loyalty	1.71*	-	-	-2.73**

*Note: *significant at 0.1, ** significant at 0.05, ***significant at 0.01 (2-tailed)*

Hypothesis 1: *Within a cultural group, local Web site trust will be higher than foreign Web site trust.*

Hypothesis 3: *Within a cultural group, local Web site satisfaction will be higher than foreign Web site satisfaction.*

Hypothesis 5: *Within a cultural group, loyalty to the local Web site will be higher than the loyalty to the foreign Web site.*

is very famous, very popular. Well, I can trust them." Another Japanese participant noted, "I don't buy anything from a company that I never heard about."

German participants emphasized personal experience with online purchasing, or friend's opinions, as an element that affected their trust in online purchasing. As noted in the following: "I really trust if I had good experience. Even if I hear from friends…good things [about the company], normally I trust more than, let's say, if it's the first time I'm on the site."

Within each country, as shown in Table 3, no statistically significant differences were found for level of satisfaction between foreign and local Web sites for the Canadians, Americans, and Germans. For Japanese respondents the differences are statistically significant, although *opposite* to expected. The Japanese are more satisfied with and more loyal to the foreign Web site than the local Web site. In particular, the Japanese reported they liked the brighter colors of the foreign site, and found the colors on the local site "cold," and that images are badly designed.

American respondents are the only group to express loyalty to the local Web site over the foreign Web site. This is the case even though the local and foreign Web sites provide them with equal satisfaction. Consequently, hypothesis 3 is rejected and hypothesis 5 is valid only for U.S. respondents.

In conclusion, Canadian and German participants report similar levels of satisfaction, trust, and loyalty for the foreign and local Web sites. American respondents are more loyal to the local Web site, even though they report equivalent levels of trust and satisfaction for the local and foreign Web sites. Japanese respondents equally trust the foreign and local version of the Samsung Web site. However, they are more satisfied with the foreign Web site and would be more likely to revisit or purchase from it.

Web Site Trust, Satisfaction, and Loyalty Across Cultures

The preceding section examined Web site trust, satisfaction, and e-loyalty *within* each country comparing the foreign and local Web sites. In this section, trust, satisfaction, and loyalty are investigated *across* countries to determine if there are systematic differences related to culture for (1) the local Web site, and (2) the foreign Web site. In keeping with the arguments of Yamagishi and Yamagishi (1994), Web users from individualistic cultures, such as Canada or the U.S., are expected to express less trust, satisfaction, and loyalty with the local Web site, and more trust, satisfaction, and loyalty with the foreign Web site than moderately individualistic German users, and collectivist Japanese users.

When comparing the level of trust, satisfaction, and loyalty between countries, for the *local* Web site, almost no differences are reported between the Canadians, Americans, and Germans. However, Table 4 records large differences between the Japanese and the

Americans, Canadians, or Germans. Similar to the within culture results, Japanese respondents (rather than Americans or Canadians) trust least, are least satisfied, and least loyal to their local Web site. Germans trust their local site most. As such, hypotheses 2a, 4a, and 6a are rejected.

Table 4. Web site trust, satisfaction, and e-loyalty across countries for the local Web site

	CDN/US	CDN/G	CDN/J	US/G	US/J	G/J
Local Trust	-	-	2.8***	-1.9*	2.8***	5.2***
Local Satisfaction	-	-	2.8***	-	3.4***	4.8***
Local Loyalty	-	-	3.6***	-	3.6***	3.8***

*Note: * significant at 0.1, ** significant at 0.05, ***significant at 0.01 (2-tailed)*

Hypothesis 2a: *Between cultural groups, American and Canadian participants are least likely to trust the local Web site, followed by Germans, and then the Japanese.*

Hypothesis 4a: *Between cultural groups, American and Canadian participants are least likely to be satisfied with the local Web site, followed by Germans, and then the Japanese.*

Hypothesis 6a: *Between cultural groups, American and Canadian participants are most likely to express e-loyalty for the local Web site, followed by Germans, and then the Japanese.*

Table 5. Web site trust, satisfaction, and e-loyalty across countries for the foreign Web site

	CDN/US	CDN/G	CDN/J	US/G	US/J	G/J
Foreign Trust	-	-	-	-1.8*	-	3.3***
Foreign Satisfaction	-	-2.4**	-	-1.8*	-	-
Foreign Loyalty	-	-	-	-3.0**	-	-

*Note: *significant at 0.1, ** significant at 0.05, ***significant at 0.01 (2-tailed)*

Hypothesis 2b: *Between cultural groups, American and Canadian participants are more likely to trust the foreign Web site, followed by Germans, and then the Japanese.*

Hypothesis 4b: *Between cultural groups, American and Canadian participants are least likely to be satisfied with the foreign Web site, followed by Germans, and then the Japanese.*

Hypothesis 6b: *Between cultural groups, American and Canadian participants are most likely to express e-loyalty for the foreign Web site, followed by Germans, and then the Japanese.*

Hypotheses 2b, 4b, and 6b are likewise rejected. When comparing trust, satisfaction, and loyalty between countries for the same *foreign* (Hong Kong) Samsung site, no statistically significant differences are reported in Table 5 between the American, Canadians, and Japanese. However, on average, Germans are more satisfied with the *foreign* Web site than Canadians and Americans. Germans are also more trusting and intend to be more loyal to the foreign Web site than Americans. Contrary to expectations, American and Canadian participants are neither least likely to be satisfied nor most likely to express e-loyalty for the foreign Web site. Neither are Americans or Canadians more likely to trust the foreign Web site.

Web Site Design Preferences within Cultures

The purpose of looking at Web users' preferences for design elements is twofold. One objective is to measure if differences in preferences for design elements exist between local and foreign Web sites. The expectation is that design elements of a local Web site should be preferred to those of a foreign Web site, thus supporting localization of Web sites. The second objective is to report differences across cultures regarding specific design elements. The survey included nine questions pertaining to preferences for design elements (in the Appendix).

Table 6 reports mean scores by country for each of these items for the local and foreign Samsung sites. On a scale of 1 to 5, mean values for the Americans, Germans, and Canadians are mostly between 3 and 4, suggesting they somewhat like the design of the foreign and local Web sites. Japanese participants report values less than 3 for 8 out of the 9 design elements of the local Web site, indicating moderate dislike of the local Web site.

To test for statistical differences in design preferences for the local vs. foreign Web site, t-tests were used. Counter to hypothesis 7, Table 7 indicates there are no statistically significant, clear preferences for the local site over the foreign Web site for Americans, Canadians, or Germans. Further, Japanese have a strong preference for the (Hong Kong) foreign Web site. Sentiments about the Japanese site are captured by this Japanese respondent: "I say…use more pictures, more drawings to appeal to Japanese people…Japanese people like the emotional approach." Japanese seemed to prefer the brighter colors and animation present on the Hong Kong site.

Web Site Design Preferences Across Cultures

The preceding analysis compared respondents' preference *within* each country for the local and foreign Web site designs. The following analysis compares the preferences *between* countries for the local and then the foreign Web sites.

Table 6. Mean values for design elements (local and foreign)

	US	CAN	GER	JPN
Menu layout	3.48	3.30	3.93	2.28
	3.48	3.67	4.03	3.82
Access to product information	3.79	3.70	4.07	2.39
	3.41	3.89	4.10	4.03
Professional design	4.03	3.85	3.80	2.82
	4.03	3.78	3.83	3.50
Logical presentation of product info	3.45	3.48	3.87	2.75
	3.55	3.33	4.10	3.42
Screen design	3.51	3.67	3.63	3.10
	3.86	3.48	3.57	3.57
Navigation	3.55	3.33	3.90	2.32
	3.45	3.59	3.93	3.61
Sequencing	3.21	3.63	3.87	2.29
	3.48	3.59	3.90	3.64
Presentation of product attributes	3.24	3.37	3.77	2.54
	3.21	3.07	3.83	3.71
Product availability	3.00	2.89	3.13	2.61
	3.03	2.78	2.67	3.11

Note: Unshaded values represent local Web site data, shaded values represent foreign Web site data

Table 7. Design preference within countries: Statistically significant t-tests

	Canada	U.S.	Germany	Japan
	Local vs. foreign	Local vs. foreign	Local vs. foreign	Local vs. foreign
Menu layout	-	-	-	-5.1***
Access to product information	-	-	-	-6.0***
Professional design	-	-	-	-2.4**
Logical presentation of product info	-	-	-	-2.8***
Screen design	-	-	-	-1.8***
Navigation	-	-	-	-4.8***
Sequencing	-	-	-	-5.3***
Presentation of product attributes	-	-	-	-5.0***
Description of product availability	-	-	-	-2.0*

*Note: * significant at 0.1, ** significant at 0.05, ***significant at 0.01 (2-tailed)*

Hypothesis 7: *Within a cultural group, design elements of the local site preferred rather than design elements of the foreign site of the same online vendor.*

In Table 8, t-test results are reported when comparing *local* Web site design preferences between countries. No differences are found between the U.S. and Canada, who each view their native Web sites similarly. Few differences exist between the U.S. or Canada, and Germany. The majority of significant differences are between Japan and the other three countries in the study. Largest differences are between Germany and Japan concerning menu layout, access to product information, navigation, and sequencing of the Web sites. The item not significant in any of the cases addresses description of product availability and variety. For almost every item related to design, Japanese mean scores are significantly lower than for other groups. The Japanese least liked the design of their local Samsung Web site. Therefore, hypotheses 8a, 9a, and 10a are confirmed.

Refer to Table 9 where respondents' preferences for design elements are compared by country for the same foreign (Hong Kong) Web site. Fewer differences between countries are reported for the foreign than for the local Web site. However, preferences for the presentation of the product attributes and preferences for the presentation of the product information are still statistically different across countries. Based on these results, hypotheses 8b is partially confirmed. Hypothesis 9b is partially confirmed with respect to comparisons of Canadians and Germans, and

Table 8. T-tests comparing mean preference between countries for local Web site design elements

	CDN/ US	CDN/G	CDN/J	US/G	US/J	G/J
Menu layout	-	-2.48**	3.8***	-	4.3***	6.8***
Access to product information	-	-	4.3***	-	4.8***	6.1***
Professional design	-	-	4.0***	-	4.6***	3.7***
Logical presentation of product info	-	-	2.90***	-	2.4**	4.8***
Screen design	-	-	2.20**	-	-	1.9*
Navigation	-	-2.6**	3.8***	-	4.1***	7.0***
Sequencing	-	-	5.0***	-2.47**	3.4***	6.2***
Presentation of product attributes	-	-	3.2***	-1.68*	2.5**	4.5***
Description of product availability	-	-	-	-	-	-

*Note: * significant at 0.1, ** significant at 0.05, ***significant at 0.01 (2-tailed)*

Hypothesis 8a: *Between cultural groups, Web site design preferences for the local site will be most similar between Americans and Canadians.*

Hypothesis 9a: *Between cultural groups, Web site design preferences for the local site will be moderately similar between Americans or Canadians, and Germans.*

Hypothesis 10a: *Between cultural groups, Web site design preferences for the local site will be most dissimilar between Americans, Canadians, or Germans with the Japanese.*

rejected with respect to comparisons of Americans and Germans. Hypothesis 10b is not confirmed in that in most instances, comparisons between the Japanese and other countries were not significant.

In conclusion, Table 8 and Table 9 illustrate that many design elements are statistically different between Germany or Japan and the other countries when comparing two countries at a time. Some of the broad perceptions of the Web sites are captured in the following quotes representing each country:

I would say, it (the Web site) doesn't have to be exciting. I just want to buy a handy item, I don't want to go on an exciting shopping tour…I just search the site where I can buy it, so I don't have to look at impressive animations, sounds, and multimedia. (German respondent)

... Banners drive me crazy, they are very distracting actually, when I got deeper into the site, there was a flashy thing over here, it is very distracting. (U.S. respondent)

There are two different kinds of home pages. There is the one with every possible link like the Yahoo home page...it turns me off. So this one I find a little simpler in the sense that it is broken into a few sections, there are pictures to break things off...It does a fairly good job. (Canadian respondent)

Table 9. T-tests comparing mean preference between countries for foreign Web site design elements

	CDN/ US	CDN/G	CDN/J	US/G	US/J	G/J
Menu layout	-	-	-	-2.0**	-	-
Access to product information	1.7*	-	-	-2.4**	-2.1**	-
Professional design	-	-	-	-	2.25**	-
Logical presentation of product info	-	-3.6***	-	-2.3**	-	3.0***
Screen design	-	-	-	-	-	-
Navigation	-	-	-	-1.9*	-	-
Sequencing	-					
Presentation of product attributes	-	-3.0***	-2.3**	-2.3**	-1.7*	-
Description of product availability	-	-	-	-	-	-

*Note: * significant at 0.1, ** significant at 0.05, ***significant at 0.01 (2-tailed)*

Hypothesis 8b: *Between cultural groups, Web site design preferences for the foreign site will be most similar between Americans and Canadians.*

Hypothesis 9b: *Between cultural groups, Web site design preferences for the foreign site will be moderately similar between Americans or Canadians and Germans.*

Hypothesis 10b: *Between cultural groups, Web site design preferences for the foreign site will be most dissimilar between Americans, Canadians, or Germans with the Japanese.*

In particular, results in Table 9 indicate, when looking at the same Web site, different cultural groups have different preferences regarding the presentation of product attributes, the presentation of product information, and access to product information. Also of interest are differences between Canada and the U.S. regarding access to product information. Based on the interview data, generally, participants across all groups noted they prefer to have few product details upon first entering a site, and like more details if they chose to investigate the product further. All national groups believe it is important online product information is complete and detailed. A Canadian states:

For a first glance I like the first ten bullet points, the ten most important things. But if I'm looking for detail information I want it to be there. For example, the sizes and dimensions or something like that.

Results Summary and Discussion

Although it was expected that participants would be more trusting, more satisfied, and more loyal to the local Web site than to the foreign Web site, this was not the case. Table 10 summarizes outcomes from testing the research hypotheses for *within* culture comparisons. No statistical differences are reported. Americans, Canadians, Germans, and Japanese all report the same level of satisfaction, trust, loyalty, and preference for Web site design for the foreign (Hong Kong) site as for their respective local Web sites. The only exception is for Americans who seem to display more loyalty for their local Web site than for the foreign Samsung Web site.

Further, Japanese participants reported higher satisfaction and loyalty to the foreign site over the local site. This may have been related to a strong preference on the

Table 10. Summary of hypotheses: Within cultural group comparisons

Within a cultural group:	
H1: Local Web site trust > foreign Web site trust	Rejected
H3: Local Web site satisfaction > foreign Web site satisfaction	Rejected
H5: Loyalty to the local Web site > than loyalty to the foreign Web site	Valid for Americans
H7: Design elements of the local site preferred rather than design elements of the foreign site of the same online vendor	Rejected

Table 11. Summary of hypotheses: Between cultural group comparisons

Between cultural groups:

H2a: American and Canadian participants are *least* likely to trust the *local* Web site, followed by Germans, and then Japanese.	Rejected
H2b: American and Canadian participants are *more* likely to trust the *foreign* Web site, followed by Germans, and then Japanese.	Rejected
H4a: American and Canadian participants are least likely to be satisfied with the *local* Web site, followed by Germans, and then Japanese.	Rejected
H4b: American and Canadian participants are least likely to be satisfied with the *foreign* Web site, followed by Germans, and then Japanese.	Rejected
H6a: American and Canadian participants are most likely to express e-loyalty for the *local* Web site, followed by Germans, and then Japanese.	Rejected
H6b: American and Canadian participants are most likely to express e-loyalty for the *foreign* Web site, followed by Germans, and then Japanese.	Rejected
H8a: Web site design preferences for the *local* site will be most similar between Americans and Canadians.	Accepted
H8b: Web site design preferences for the *foreign* site will be most similar between Americans and Canadians.	Partially Accepted
H9a: Web site design preferences for the *local* site will be moderately similar between Americans or Canadians, and Germans.	Accepted
H9b: Web site design preferences for the *foreign* site will be moderately similar between Americans or Canadians, and Germans.	Partially Accepted
H10a: Web site design preferences for the *local* site will be most dissimilar between Americans, Canadians, or Germans with Japanese.	Accepted
H10b: Web site design preferences for the *foreign* site will be most dissimilar between Americans, Canadians, or Germans with Japanese.	Rejected

part of Japanese participants for the design elements of the foreign Hong Kong site. However, from interview data, there are some common elements across the cultures investigated related to trust. All groups identify security signs and vendor familiarity as important. Overall, Japanese participants are less trusting of Internet stores, and are concerned about security when making purchases on the Internet.

For comparisons *between* cultural groups, Table 11 reports that contrary to expectations, no differences were recorded for trust, satisfaction, and loyalty. The only accepted hypotheses relate to design preferences. Specific design differences were already illustrated in Tables 8 and 9.

More specifically, Americans and Canadians were predicted to be least likely to trust and be satisfied with the local and foreign Web sites, followed by Germans, and then the Japanese (hypotheses 2a, 2b, 4a, 4b). Alternately, Americans and Canadians were predicted to be most loyal to either the local or foreign Web site, followed by the Germans, and then the Japanese (hypotheses 6a, 6b). These directional comparisons were all rejected, failing to support the work by Yamagishi and Yamagishi (1994).

For between country comparisons for the local and foreign Web sites, hypotheses 8a, 9a, and 10a are confirmed. That is, design preferences were most similar for Americans and Canadians, moderately similar for Canadians and Americans with Germans, and most dissimilar between these three countries with the Japanese. For the foreign site, results are less well defined, with only partial confirmation of hypothesis 8b and 9b. While there was only one design element that was viewed differently between Canadians and Americans, the same case occurred between Canadians and the Japanese. Further, there were many design elements where significant differences were found between Americans and Germans who were considered to be only moderately dissimilar. Hypothesis 10b was rejected in that greatest differences were not found with the Japanese where preferences for only a few design elements were significantly different between Japan and the other countries. Exactly why this occurred remains unknown, and bears further investigation.

Conclusion and Implications

Despite increasing numbers of online shoppers around the globe, very little research has examined the important concepts of trust, satisfaction, and e-loyalty and their relation to design preferences of differing national cultures.

Various researchers (Jarvenpaa et al., 1999; Kim and Son, 1998; Yamagishi and Yamagishi, 1994) have suggested members in individualist cultures such as Canada or the U.S. are less likely to trust a local Web site than Germans or Japanese, and more likely to trust a foreign Web site than Germans or Japanese. This suggestion was not supported in the current investigation. Thus, these results join the ranks of other inconclusive studies, such as those by Lui et al. (2004) or Jarvenpaa et al. (1999), in which other elements, such as privacy or reputation, may be better related to systematic differences across cultures than trust.

Within cultural groups, satisfaction and loyalty was not greater for the local rather than the foreign site. Americans were the only group to express greater loyalty for the local site. Counter to expectations, Japanese were more satisfied and loyal to the foreign site. Why would a cultural group not prefer their local Web site over a foreign site? Are these results a function of inadequate localization and cultural adaptation of Web sites? Indeed, Japanese respondents were quite specific in noting why they preferred the Hong Kong site. Or is the challenge to researchers deeper, with a requirement to more fully examine the underpinnings of what constitutes trust, satisfaction, or loyalty in an Internet based environment? Given the mixed results and inconsistencies in the literature to date, there appears much scope for additional investigation in this area. Could it be the "foreignness" of the Internet is dissipating for international users and becoming itself an internationalized common culture? Do e-loyalty intentions only occur when trust is implicit, and enhanced by other characteristics such as design? These prospects perhaps suggest a multifaceted and multidisciplinary model to uncover a better picture of preferences across diverse cultures. Further, is the identification of culture by country a valid differentiator of preferences? Might ethnicity, income, age, or even level of Internet literacy of respondents be equally or more relevant to determine design preferences resulting in trust, satisfaction, or e-loyalty?

In prior design research, Barber and Badre (2001) had mixed results in identifying stable design preferences across cultures. In this investigation, design elements elicit several statistically significant preferences between countries. This suggests that localization of Web content is important for diverse users, although it may not result in greater trust, satisfaction, or e-loyalty. When examining the local Web sites, there are many differences in design preferences. Further, comparing cultural preferences on the same foreign Web site, different cultural groups have different preferences regarding presentation of product attributes, presentation of product information, and access to product information. These findings are consonant with prior work (Cyr & Trevor Smith, 2004; Del Galdo & Nielsen, 1996; Marcus & Gould, 2000) that found significant differences in Web site design elements across Japanese, German, and American cultures.

The uniqueness of this research and its multidisciplinary roots is both a contribution and a challenge. As previously noted, there exists no study, to our knowledge, that examines e-loyalty related to design across cultures. As a first step in the investigation, the current work is focused on both within country and between country comparisons of a local and foreign Web site. However, there is no predictive power as to which elements of design result in greater trust, satisfaction, or e-loyalty. To this end, development and testing of a model for e-loyalty across cultures has been undertaken (Cyr, 2006). The model refines the concept of Web site design to consider navigation design, visual design, and information, and validates relationships between these design constructs with trust, satisfaction, and e-loyalty. Promising results from this secondary stage in this research stream suggest that additional work in this area is merited.

Methodologically, on-site data collection in each nation is a strength of this investigation. A limitation of the research is in the relatively small sample of participants who are drawn from constrained populations (e.g., a single technology company in developed nation-states). Also noteworthy, Web sites used in the present study are Samsung sites. While one would expect this choice to provide greater consistency in Web site design and localization features, response biasing may occur due to overriding participant knowledge of the company and its reputation. Replication with more diverse groups and Web sites within nations is the answer to these present constraints on the generalizability of our findings. Additional research may alternately focus on how e-loyalty is built through Web site design for developing or newly industrialized nations.

The present research may be usefully extended through more controlled laboratory-based research in assessing the human-computer interface. Cultural or national preferences could be systematically examined using specialized eye tracking or other usability equipment. This future work could both widen the selection of Web sites presented, and use eye tracking and subject's self-reports to identify profiles or patterns of preference for design characteristics by national groups. Further, it is of interest to determine how design elements resulting in e-loyalty may be applied beyond PC-based electronic commerce. With the evolution of M-commerce and ubiquitous computing, applications of this work may find a new home in emerging markets.

References

Agarwal, R., & Venkatesh, V. (2002). Assessing a firm's Web presence: A heuristic evaluation procedure for measurement of usability. *Information Management Research, 13*(2), 168-121.

Alden, D., Hoyer, W., & Lee, C. (1993). Identifying global and culture specific dimensions of humor. *Journal of Marketing, 57*(2), 64-76.

Alvarez, M. G., Kasday, L., & Todd, S. (1998). How we made the Web site international and accessible: A case study. In *Proceedings 4th Conference on Human Factors and the Web*. Basking Ridge, NJ. Retrieved April 15, 2004, from http://www.research.att.com/conf/hfweb/proceedings/alvarez/

Anderson, R. E., & Srivanan, S. S. (2003). E-satisfaction and e-loyalty: A contingency framework. *Psychology and Marketing, 20*, 123-138.

Badre, A. N. (2000). The effects of cross cultural interface design orientation on World Wide Web user performance. *GVE Research Technical Reports*. Retrieved April 20, 2004, from http://www.cc.gatech.edu/gvu/reports/2001/abstracts/01-03.html

Balasubramanian, S., Konana, P., & Menon, N. M. (2003). Customer satisfaction in virtual environments: A study of online investing. *Management Science 49*(7), 871-889.

Barber, W., & Badre, A. N. (2001). Culturability: The merging of culture and usability. In *Proceedings of the 4th Conference on Human Factors and the Web*. Basking Ridge, NJ.

Bhattacherjee, A. (2002). Individual trust in online firms: Scale development and initial test. *Journal of Management Information Systems, 19*(1), 211-241.

Carnevale, D. G., & Wechler, B. (1992). Trust in the public sector: Individual and organizational determinants. *Administrative Sociology, 23*, 471-494.

Chen, S. C., & Dhillon, G. S. (2003). Interpreting dimensions of consumer trust in e-commerce. *Information Management and Technology, 4*.

Cheskin Research Group. (1999). e-Commerce trust study. Retrieved April 24, 2004, from http://www.cheskin.com/think/studies/ecomtrust.html

Cheskin Research Group. (2000). Trust in the wired Americas. Retrieved April 24, 2004, from http://www.cheskin.com/think/studies/trust2.html

Corritore, C. L., Kracher, B., & Wiedenbeck, S. (2001). Trust in online environment. In M. J. Smith, G. Salvenjy, D. Harris, & R. J. Koubek (Eds.), *Usability evaluation and interface design: Cognitive engineering, intelligent agents and virtual reality* (pp. 1548-1552). Mahway, NJ: Erlbaum.

Corstjens, M., & Lal, R. (2000). Building store loyalty through store brands. *Journal of Marketing Research, 37*(3), 281-292.

Cyr, D. (2006). Modeling website design across cultures: Relationships to trust, satisfaction and e-loyalty. *Simon Fraser University Working Paper*, 1-53.

Cyr, D., & Trevor-Smith, H. (2004). Localization of Web design: An empirical comparison of German, Japanese, and U.S. website characteristics. *Journal of the American Society for Information Science and Technology, 55*(13), 1-10.

Dawar, N., Parker, P., & Price, L. (1996). A cross-cultural study of interpersonal information exchange. *Journal of International Business Studies,* Third quarter, 497-516.

Del Galdo, E., & Neilson, J. (1996). *International user interfaces.* New York: John Wiley & Sons.

de Mooij, M. (1998). Global marketing and advertising: Understanding cultural paradoxes. *Journal of Macro Marketing, 18*(1), 70-71.

de Ruyter, K., Wetzels, M., & Kleijnen, M. (2001). Customer adoption of e-service: An experimental study. *International Journal of Service Industry Management, 12*(2), 184–207.

Deshpande, R., Hoyer, W. D., & Donthu, N. (1986). The intensity of ethnic affiliations: A study of the sociology of Hispanic consumption. *Journal of Consumer Research, 13*, 214-220.

Devaraj, S., Fan, M., & Kohli, R. (2002, September). Antecedents of B2C channel satisfaction and preference: Validating e-commerce metrics. *Information Systems Research*, 1-32.

Doney, P. M., Cannon, J. P., & Mullen, M. R. (1998). Understanding the influence of national culture on the development of trust. *Academy of Management Review, 23*(3), 601-20.

Durvasula, S., Andrews, C. J., Lysonski, S., & Netemeyer, R. G. (1993). Assessing cross-national applicability of consumer behavior models: A model of attitude toward advertising in general. *Journal of Consumer Research, 19*, 626-36.

Egger, F. N. (2001). Affective design of e-commerce user interfaces: How to maximize perceived trustworthiness. *Proceedings of the International Conference on Affective Human Factors Design*. London: Academic Press.

Evers, V., & Day, D. (1997). The role of culture in interface acceptance. In Howard, Hammond, & Lindegaard (Eds.), *Human Computer Interaction*, INTERACT '97. London: Chapman and Hall.

Ferle, C., Edwards, S., & Mizuno, Y. (2002, March-April). Internet diffusion in Japan: Cultural consideration. *Journal of Advertising Research*, 65-79.

Flavián, C., Guinalíu, M., & Gurrea, R. (2005). The role played by perceived usability, satisfaction and consumer trust on website loyalty. *Information & Management*, 1–14.

Fogg, B. J., Soohoo, C., & Danielson, D. (2002). *How people evaluate a web site's credibility? Results from a larger study*. Persuasive Technology Lab, Stanford University.

Fogg, B. J., & Tseng, S. (1999). Credibility and computing technology. *Communications of the ACM, 14*(5), 39-87.

Gefen, D. (2000). E-commerce: the role of familiarity and trust. *The International Journal of Management Science, 28*, 725-737.

Gommans, M., Krishan, K. S., & Scheddold, K. B. (2001). From brand loyalty to e-loyalty: A conceptual framework. *Journal of Economic and Social Research, 3* (1), 43-58.

Grabner-Krauter, S., & Kaluscha, E. (2003). Empirical research in online trust: A review and critical assessment. *International Journal of Human-Computer Studies, 58*, 783-812.

Grewal, G., Munger, J. L.,Iyer, G. R., & Levy, J. (2003). The influence of Internet retailing factors on price expectations. *Psychology and Marketing, 20*(6), 477-493.

Hoffman, D. L., & Novak, T. P. (1996). Marketing in hypermedia computer-mediated environments: Conceptual foundations. *Journal of Marketing, 60*, 50-68.

Hofstede, G. H. (1984). *Culture's consequences: International differences in work-related values*. Beverly Hills, CA: Sage Publications.

Holland, J., & Baker, S. M. (2001). Customer participation in creating site brand loyalty. *Journal of Interactive Marketing, 15*(4), 34-45.

Hoover, R. J., Green, R. T., & Saegert, J. (1978). A cross-national study of perceived risk. *Journal of Marketing, 42*,102-8.

Hu, J., Shima, K., Oehlmann, R., Zhao, J., Takemura, Y., & Matsumoto, K. (2004). An empirical study of audience impressions of B2C Web pages in Japan, China and the U.K. *Electronic Commerce Research and Applications, 3*, 176-189.

Inglehart, R., Basanez, M., & Moreno, A. (1998). *Human values and beliefs: A cross- cultural sourcebook.* Ann Arbor: University of Michigan Press.

Internet Usage Statistics. (2006). Retrieved May 1, 2006, from http://www.inter-networldstats.com/stats.htm

Jarvenpaa, S. L., Tractinsky, N., Saarinen, L., & Vitale, M. (1999). Consumer trust in an Internet store: A cross-cultural validation. *Journal of Computer Mediated Communication, 5*(2). Retrieved April 20, 2004, from http://www.ascusc.org/jcmc/vol5/issue2/jarvenpaa.html

Kang, K. S., & Corbitt, B. (2001). Effectiveness of graphical components in web site e-commerce application: A cultural perspective. *The Electronic Journal Systems in Developing Countries.* Retrieved April 20, 2004, from http://www.ejisdc.org

Kim, Y. H., & Son, J. (1998). Trust, cooperation and social risk: A cross-cultural comparison. *Korean Journal, 38*(spring), 131-153.

Koufaris, M. (2002). Applying the technology acceptance model and flow theory to online consumer behavior. *Information Systems Research, 13*(2), 205-223.

Lagon, O. (2000). Culturally correct site design. *Web Techniques, 5* (9), 49-51.

Laurn, P., & Lin, H. H. (2003). A customer loyalty model for e-Service context. *Journal of Electronic Commerce Research, 4*(4), 156–167.

Lewicki, R., & Bunker, B. (1995). Trust in relationships: A model of development and decline. In B. B. Bunkler & J. Z. Rubin (Eds.), *Conflict, cooperation, and justice* (pp. 133-173). San Francisco: Jossey Bass.

Lewis, D. J., & Weigert, A. (1985). Trust as a social reality. *Social Forces, 63*, 967-85.

Lohse, G., & Spiller, P. (1999). Internet retail store design: How the user interface influences traffic and sales. *Journal of Computational Mediated Communication, 5*.

Lui, C., Marchewka, J, & Ku, C. (2004). American and Taiwanese perceptions concerning privacy, trust, and behavioral intentions in electronic commerce. *Journal of Global Information Management, 12*(1), 18-40.

Marcus, A., & Gould, E. W. (2000, July/August). Cultural dimensions and global web user interface design. *Interactions*, 33-46.

Matsumoto, D. (1994). *Psychology from a cultural perspective.* CA: Brookes/ Cole.

Mayer, R. C., Davis, J. H., & Schoorman, F. D. (1995). An integrative model of organizational trust. *Academy of Management Review, 20*(3), 709-34.

McKnight, D. H., Choudhury, V. C., & Kacmar, C. (2002). Developing and validating trust measures for e-Commerce: An integrative typology. *Information Management Research, 13*(3), 334-359.

McKnight, D. H., Cummings, L. L., & Chervany, N. M. (1998). Initial trust formation in new organizational relationships. *Academy of Management Review, 23*(3), 473-490.

Mithas, S., Ramasubbu, N., Krishnan, M. S., & Fornell, C. (2003). Effect of website characteristics on consumer loyalty: A multilevel analysis. *Proceedings of the Twenty-Fourth International Conference on Information Systems.*

Moorman, C., Deshpandé, R., & Zaltman, G. (1993). Factors affecting trust in market research relationships. *Journal of Marketing, 57*, 81-101.

Morgan, R. M., & Hunt, S. D. (1994). The commitment-trust theory of relationship marketing. *Journal of Marketing, 58*, 20-38.

Nielsen, J. (2001). *Designing for Web usability.* Indianapolis: New Riders Publications.

Okayazaki, S., & Rivas, J. A. (2002). A content analysis of multinationals' Web communication strategies: Cross-cultural research framework and pre-testing. *Internet Research: Electronic Networking Applications and Policy, 12*(5), 380-390.

Palmer, J. W., Bailey, J. P., Faraj, S., & Smith, R. H. (2000). The role of intermediaries in the development of trust on the WWW: The use and prominence of trusted third parties and privacy statements. *Journal of Computer Mediated Communication, 5*(3). Retrieved from http://www.ascusc.org/jcmc/vol5/issue3/palmer.html

Parks, C. D., & Vu, A. D. (1994). Social dilemma behaviour of individuals from highly individualist and collectivist cultures, *Journal of Conflict Resolution, 38*(4), 708-718.

Quelch, J. A., & Klein, L. R. (1996). The Internet and international marketing. *Sloan Management Review, Spring*, 60-74.

Rattanawicha, P., & Esichaikul, V. (2005). What makes websites trustworthy? A two-phase empirical study. *International Journal of Electronic Business, 3*(2), 110-136.

Reichheld, F. F., & Schefter, P. (2000). E-loyalty: Your secret weapon on the web. *Harvard Business Review, 78*(4), 105-14.

Resnick, P., & Zechauser, R. (2002). Trust among strangers in Internet transactions: Empirical analysis of eBay reputation system. In Baye (Ed.), *The Economics of the Internet and E-commerce: Advances in Applied Economics, 11,* 127-158. London: Elsevier Science.

Rosen, D. E., & Purinton, E. (2004). Website design: Viewing the Web as a cognitive landscape. *Journal of Business Research, 57*(7), 787.

Rousseau, D. M., Sitkin, S. M., Burt, R. S., & Camerer, C. (1998). Not so different after all: A cross-discipline view of trust. *Academy of Management Review, 23*(3), 393-404.

Schlosser, A. E., Barnett White, T., & Lloyd, S. M. (2006). Converting Web site visitors into buyers: How Web site investment increases consumer trusting beliefs and online purchase intentions. *Journal of Marketing, 70,* 133-148.

Selnes, F. (1998). Antecedents and consequences of trust and satisfaction in buyer-seller relationships. *European Journal of Marketing, 32,* 305-322.

Shannon, P. (2000). Including language in your global strategy for B2B e-commerce. *World Trade, 13*(9), 66-68.

Simon, S. J. (2001). The impact of culture and gender on web sites: An empirical study. *The Data Base for Advances in Information Systems, 32*(1), 18-37.

Singh, N., Xhao, H., & Hu, X. (2003). Cultural adaptation on the Web: A study of American companies' domestic and Chinese websites. *Journal of Global Information Management, 11*(3), 63-80.

Srinivasan, S. S., Anderson, R., & Ponnavolu, K. (2002). Customer loyalty in e-commerce: An exploration of its antecedents. *Journal of Retailing, 78,* 41-50.

Sun, H. (2001, October 21-24). Building a culturally-competent corporate web site: An explanatory study of cultural markers in multilingual Web design. In *Proceedings of SIGDOC '01* (pp. 95-102).

Szymanski, D. A., & Hise, R. T. (2000). E-satisfaction: An initial examination. *Journal of Retailing, 76*(3), 309-322.

Tian, R.G. & Emery, C. (2002, March). Cross-cultural issues in Internet marketing. *The Journal of American Academy of Business,* 217-224.

Triandis, H. C. (1990). Cross-cultural studies of individualism and collectivism. In J. J. Berman (Ed.), *Nebraska Symposium on Motivation, 37,* 41-133.

Urban, G. L., Sultan, F., & Qualls, W. J. (2000, Fall). Placing trust at the center of your Internet strategy. *Sloan Management Review,* 39-48.

Valencia, H. (1989). Hispanic values and subcultural research. *Journal of the Academy of Marketing Science, 17*(1), 23-28.

Venkatesh, V., & Ramesh, V. (2006). Web and wireless site usability: Understanding differences and modeling use. *MIS Quarterly, 30*(1), 181-206.

Wallendorf, M., & Reilly, M. D. (1983). Ethnic migration, assimilation, and consumption. *Journal of Consumer Research, 10*, 292-302.

Weber, E. U., & Hsee, C. (1998). Cross-cultural differences in risk perception, but cross-cultural similarities in attitudes towards perceived risk. *Management Science, 44*, 1205-1217.

Yamagishi, T., & Yamagishi, J. (1994). Trust and commitment in the United States and Japan. *Motivation and Emotion, 18*, 129-165.

Yoon, S.-J. (2002). The antecedents and consequences of trust in online-purchase decisions. *Journal of Interactive Marketing, 16*(2), 47-63.

Endnotes

[1]   It is expected most readers are familiar with Hofstede's cultural categorizations and, therefore, details of this work will not be elaborated here. However, for more information on this topic refer to Hofstede (1980), Dawar et al. (1996), or to Simon (2001), who provide an excellent overview of Hofstede's dimensions in a compressed format.

[2]   A thorough review of trust in nononline settings is not feasible within the scope of the present paper. However, the reader may wish to refer to the authors cited in this paragraph, as well as to Doney and Cannon (1997), Lewicki and Bunker (1995), Moorman et al. (Moorman, Deshpande, & Zaltman, 1993), or Morgan and Hunt (1994). In particular, Rousseau et al. (1998) presents a comprehensive and cross-disciplinary critique of trust.

[3]   These authors provide a recent and comprehensive review of empirical research conducted in online trust, although no singular definition of trust can be ascribed from this work.

[4]   The four Web sites viewed by participants included Reebok Shoes (American), CapEx Investments (American), British Airways (British), and Godiva Chocolates (Belgium).

[5]   Localization is the process of adapting a product or service to a particular language, culture, and desired local "look-and-feel." In localizing a product, in addition to idiomatic language translation, such details as time zones, currency, local color sensitivities, product or service names, gender roles, and geographic examples must all be considered. A successfully localized service or product is one that appears to have been developed within the local culture.

6   The local sites are Canada (http://www.samsung.ca/cgi-in/nasecabc/init_seca. jsp),

USA (http://www.samsungusa.com/cgi-in/nabc/home/b2c_home_samsungusa. jsp),

Germany (http://www.samsung.de/), and Japan (http://www.samsung.co.jp/)

The Hong Kong site can be found at http://www.samsungelectronics.com. hk/

Appendix

Survey (answered by each participant for both the local and the foreign Samsung site separately)

Web site design elements
1. The user menus are clearly categorized and are well laid out on the screen.
2. I can easily recognize and find where product information is located.
3. The Web site looks professionally designed and well   presented.
4. The product information provided on the Web site is presented consistently and logically.
5. The screen design on the Web site (i.e., colors, boxes, menus, navigation tools, etc.) is harmonious and well presented.
6. The Web site can be easily navigated.
7. The organization, sequencing, and overall arrangements of the site are understandable and easy to use.
8. All product options, product attributes, and product information are well designed and presented.
9. Site product availability and product variety are well explained.
Trust
10. I can trust the online vendor.
11. The Web site is credible to me.
12. I can trust information presented on the Web site.

continued on following page

Satisfaction
13. The Web site completely fulfills my needs and expectations.
14. This Web site satisfies my particular needs well.
15. Using this site/service is satisfactory overall.
E-loyalty
16. I would visit this Web site again.
17. I would consider purchasing from this Web site in the future.

Chapter VI

Understanding E-Government Development:
A Global Perspective

Keng Siau, University of Nebraska – Lincoln, USA

Yuan Long, Colorado State University – Pueblo, USA

Abstract

Information and communication technologies (ICT) have been used to enhance services and improve the efficiency of government operations. To further improve the e-government operations, understanding e-government development and studying factors that affect e-government development are important research topics. The purpose of this research is to investigate factors influencing e-government development through a social development lens. Based on growth and regional development theories, this chapter hypothesizes that income level, development status, and region are three factors that differentiate e-government development in various countries. Group comparison tests are conducted using secondary data from the United Nations and the United Nations Development Programme. The results support the hypotheses that significant differences in e-government development exist between countries with respect to the three categorical variables mentioned. In addition, the paper applies planned post hoc tests to further investigate the differences in e-government development between different groups of countries (e.g., countries with low income vs. countries with high income). The results of this research are valuable to e-government scholars and practitioners. As the research involves data from countries all over the world, it contributes to understanding e-government development factors on a global scale.

Introduction

With the advancement of computer and communication technologies (which include both wired and wireless) in recent years, e-government has attracted increasing interests from both practitioners and researchers (Huang, Siau, & Wei, 2005). By utilizing information and communication technologies, e-government provides an efficient and effective channel for governments to facilitate their internal administration and to improve their external services. In addition, the emergence of e-government provides extensive opportunities for citizens to participate in democratic institutions and political processes.

E-government development can be classified into four major areas: government-to-customer (G2C), government-to-business (G2B), government-to-government (G2G), and government-to-employee (G2E). Figure 1 (Siau & Long, 2004, 2005) lists the objectives and activities (possible projects or functionalities) of each of the four areas.

Within these four areas, G2C and G2E involve interaction between both governments and individuals, while G2B and G2G focus on the interaction and cooperation between governments and organizations. Furthermore, G2C and G2B represent the external interaction and collaboration between governments and their surrounding institutions, while G2E and G2G involve the internal interaction and cooperation between governments and their employees, as well as between governments at different levels and locations. Figure 2 features the overall e-government framework.

With successful implementation, e-government has the potential to make valuable and highly effective connections between governments and citizens (G2C), businesses (G2B), employees (G2E), and other governments (G2G).

Prior research studied e-government development from various perspectives, such as e-government security (Smith & Jamieson, 2006), knowledge management in e-government (Koh, Ryan, & Prybutok, 2006), e-government growth (Reddick, 2004; Siau & Long, 2005), and assessment and evaluation of e-government development (Janssen, Rotthier, & Snijkers, 2004; Kunstelj & Vintar, 2004). However, the concept of e-government and research on e-government development are still in their infancies. Little research had been conducted with regards to viewing the development of e-government from a cross-national perspective. Based on the secondary data provided by the United Nations (2003) and the United Nations Development

Figure 1. E-government portfolios

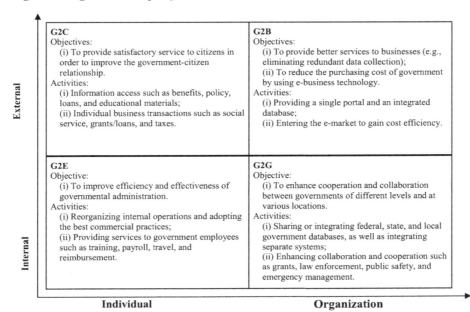

Figure 2. E-government framework

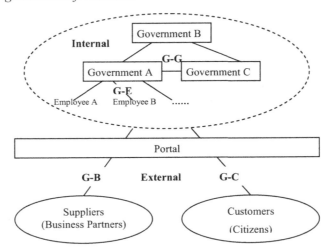

Programme (2003), this chapter investigates the impact of three potential factors—income level, development status, and region—on e-government evolvement.

The rest of the chapter is organized as follows: First, theoretical foundation is discussed and research hypotheses are presented. Following that, research method is described and research results are reported. Finally, limitations and contributions of this research, as well as future research directions are presented.

Theoretical Foundation and Hypotheses

Theory of Growth and Development

Growth theory is an economic theory that investigates determinants of actual growth, differences in growth rates over time and space, and policies for raising growth rates (Hacche, 1979). Since Adam Smith, the theory has been developed for over 200 years. Growth theory can be differentiated into three categories: classical growth theory, neoclassical growth theory, and new growth theory. Classical growth theory regards the increases in capital and labor as the main reasons for growth, while new growth theory extends the reasons to technological progress and creativity (Lucas, 1988; Romer, 1986, 1990). New growth theory believes that technology is an endogenous rather than an exogenous variable (as also believed in neoclassical growth theory). It attributes the growth to three key elements: increase in human capital, increase in research and development, and formulation of progrowth trade policies. The new growth theory supports the notion of knowledge-based economy, and emphasizes the role of information and computer technology in growth.

Growth theory suggests that aggregate factors lead to social growth. Growth of labor force could occur through either enlarged labor market or increased immigration. Investment in human capital renders the labor units more productive. Investment in physical capital, such as factories, machines, plants, leads to a growth in capital. Technology, especially information and computer technology, brings innovations in the production process and leads to technical progress. All these factors are important aspects of economics performance that positively affect the multidimensional socioeconomic environment associated with growth and development, such as investment, policy-making, strategies, and so on. Economists (e.g., Delong, 2002) believe that long-run growth depends on the performance of economy.

E-government development, as a comprehensive social phenomenon, is an aggregate performance of technology, policy-making, and national strategy. The development of e-government, in general, depends on the economic performance of a specific country as argued by the growth theory. Therefore, we hypothesize that economy plays an important role in e-government development. Specifically, e-government development will be different between countries with various income levels. The null hypothesis is:

Hypothesis 1: *There is no difference in e-government development between low-income, medium-income, and high-income countries.*

Development Status

Besides income level, the developmental status of a specific country is also a potential factor associated with e-government development. The definition of a developed vs. a developing country depends on both the claim of the country itself and the comprehensive capability of that country. Comprehensive capability includes politics, economics, and other environmental factors. These factors may affect the decision-making, investment, and technology application of e-government. Therefore, we hypothesize that e-government development is different between countries with different development status. The null hypothesis is:

Hypothesis 2: *There is no difference in e-government development between least developed, developing, and developed countries.*

Regional Development Theory

The regional development theory explains the reasons for regional growth and the different growth rates across the space (Dawkins, 2003). The increasing interest in regional development is due to the recognition that national growth and innovation are fundamentally spatial in nature. In other words, "space matters" (Dawkins, 2003).

The growth rates are different due to multidimensional reasons such as politics, economics, technology, culture, and environment. Scientists, especially economists, develop models to investigate the regional growth problems. Therefore, region is potentially a determining factor for the development and progress of countries.

Many researchers have examined the use of e-government within specific areas. For example, they investigated e-government development in various regions such as Scotland, Africa, and Australia (Heeks, 2002; Huang, D'Ambra, & Bhalla, 2002; Li, 2003; Teicher & Dow, 2002), and in different locations within one specific country, such as the states and municipalities of the U.S. (Holzer & Melistski, 2003; Kaylor, Deshazo, & Van Eck, 2001; McNeal, Tolbert, Mossberger, & Dotterweich, 2003; The Public Sphere Information group, 2002). However, few researchers have studied regional differences of e-government development on a global context.

Based on the regional development theory, we hypothesize that differences exist between countries of various regions of the world in terms of e-government development. The null hypothesis is:

Hypothesis 3: *There is no difference in e-government development among countries in different regions of the world*

Research Method

Secondary Data

The data used in this study is secondary data obtained from two sources. Secondary data, as argued by some researchers (e.g., Jarvenpaa, 1990), presents a variety of untapped opportunities in information systems research.

One source of the data is the Web measure index, which is used as an indicator of e-governments development. It can be extracted from the United Nations' (UN) report, Global Survey of E-Government (2003). The other source of the data is country classification, which is taken from the United Nations Development Programme's (subsequently refer to as UNDP in this paper) report, Human Development Report (2003). The former report (i.e., E-Government Report, 2003) is a comprehensive report based on the UN global e-government survey in 2003, which is the most extensive global survey of e-governments to date. The latter report (i.e., Human Development Report, 2003) addresses human developmental issues, and provides valuable country-level data such as human development index (HDI), income level, and country classification.

The report from the UN (2003) covers 191 UN members, while the one from the UNDP (2003) covers 173 countries. Combining the data sets from these two reports, a sample size of 173 countries is used for this research.

Dependent Variable

Web measure index (WMI), an indicator of e-government development provided by the UN (2003) report, serves as the dependent variable in this research. WMI aims to evaluate the services and facilities provided by government Web sites. WMI is a quantitative index that measures the generic capability of e-government. Since Web presence directly reflects the e-services provided to the public, WMI is a straightforward assessment to indicate the progress of e-government development of that country.

According to the UN report, the survey procedure utilizes a questionnaire for researchers to assign a binary number to the index based on the presence or absence of the information or services available. The questionnaire was revised and improved from the earlier (since 2001) UN research. It integrates multiple areas of e-government development that are introduced in Figure 1 (i.e., G2B, G2C, G2E, and G2G).

The national portal or the official homepage of a government has been chosen in the UN survey. The survey limited itself to a predetermined set of five additional Web sites that are closely related to people-centric departments/ministries. These five governmental Web sites include health, education, social welfare, labor, and finance. The same questionnaires were used for each Web site. In summary, the same or similar functional Web sites were selected for each country, and each Web site was assessed with the same questionnaire.

There are three major reasons to choose WMI as the indicator of e-government development of a specific country. First, the measurement is based on a theoretical e-government stage model developed by the UN. The model depicts the generic e-government development across nations. Assessing services provided by official government Web sites is a direct and succinct way to measure the e-government development situation of a country. Second, the measurement is an extension and improvement of earlier UN's assessment. It was revised by a group of researchers through feedback from earlier usage. Therefore, the instrument is relatively reliable. Third, WMI provided by the UN is by far the most authentic and comprehensive index depicting the e-government development across the world. It is difficult for individual researchers or institutes to conduct such a comprehensive and costly survey. Secondary data from the UN makes this research possible.

Categorical Variables

Three categorical variables have been chosen in this research. They are income level, development status, and region. Country classification, as shown in Table 1, relies on region/income classifications from the UNDP report (UNDP, 2003). The overall sample covers 173 countries in the world.

Statistical Analysis

Since the sample size of each group is different and there is no guarantee of normal distribution, nonparametric statistics methods, such as Kruskal-wallis test, were used. The dependent variable is Web measure index (WMI), which is an indicator

Table 1. Number of the countries in each classification

Categorical variables	Groups	Examples of countries	Number of countries (173 countries in total)
Income classification	Low income	Angola, Congo, India, Pakistan, Sudan, Vietnam	55
	Middle income	Brazil, China, Cuba, Mexico, Russian Federation, Turkey	80
	High income	Australia, Canada, France, Germany, Japan, United States	38
Development status	Least developed countries	Angola, Congo, Haiti, Mali, Rwanda, Sudan	35
	Developing countries	Brazil, Chile, China, India, Mexico	115
	Developed countries	Australia, Canada, Germany, Finland, Sweden, United Kingdom	23
Regional classification	Arab states	Algeria, Egypt, Iraq	16
	East Asian and Pacific	China, Indonesia, Mongolia	26
	South and Central Asian	Afghanistan, India, Pakistan	12
	Latin America and Caribbean	Argentina, Brazil, Mexico	30
	Europe	France, Italy, United Kingdom	44
	Africa	Angola, Congo, Zambia	41
	North America and Australia	Australia, Canada, United States	4

Note: In this table, income classification is based on gross national income (GNI) per capita: Low income (<$755), middle income ($755~$9265), and high income (>$9266).

of e-government development. The three categorical variables, as discussed, are income level, development status, and region.

Research Results

Testing of Hypotheses

Table 2 depicts the results of the three hypotheses. The Appendix shows the rank difference between the groups for each categorical variable.

The results of the statistical tests suggest that significant differences exist between the various country groups for the three categorical variables. In other words, income level, development status, and region do affect the e-government development.

Planned post hoc tests were then conducted to further investigate the location of the differences. First, confidence interval was checked to achieve a straightforward observation. Within each category, the confidence intervals illustrate an obvious trend and distinct differences between the groups. Second, planned post hoc tests were conducted to test the differences observed in the confidence interval chart.

Post Hoc Test on Income (GNI per capita)

Figure 3 shows the confidence interval chart of e-government development for the countries at three different income levels. The height of each bar indicates the range of the dependent variable (i.e., WMI in this case), and the middle point of each bar represents the mean of WMI. The confidence interval chart illustrates differences between each pair; there are significant differences between countries of low and middle incomes, middle and high incomes, and low and high incomes.

To test whether significant statistical differences exist between each pair, we applied planned post hoc nonparametric tests. Table 3 presents the comparison results for each pair, indicating that significant differences on e-government development ex-

Table 2. Group difference between countries with respect to the three categorical variables

	Income	Development Status	Region
Chi-Square	55.762**	69.161**	50.883**

*Note: ** P<.001*

Figure 3. Confidence interval between country groups on income

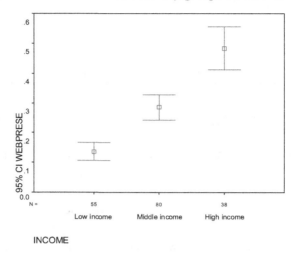

Table 3. Post-hoc comparison tests

Comparison	M-W U[1]	Sig. [2,3]
Low income—Middle income	1142	<.0001**
Middle income—High income	759	<.0001**
Low income—High income	168	<.0001**

*Note: (1) M-W U refers to the score of Mann-Whitney test; (2) ** P<.001; (3) Bonferoni a is used to control Type I Error.*

ist between countries with low and middle income, middle and high income, and low and high income. In summary, the finding of these statistical tests suggests that income is an important factor in e-government development.

Post Hoc Test on Development Status

Figure 4 shows the confidence interval chart of e-government development for the countries at three development statuses: least developed, developing, and developed. Table 4 presents the results of the planned post hoc tests for each pair.

Figure 4. Confidence interval between country groups on development status

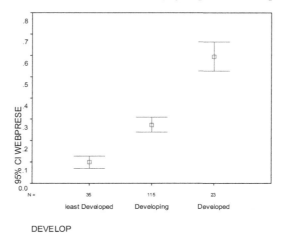

DEVELOP

Table 4. Post-hoc comparison tests

Comparison	M-W U[1]	Sig. [2,3]
Least developed—developing	732.5	<.0001**
Developing—developed	270	<.0001**
Least developed—developed	0.00	<.0001**

*Note: (1) M-W U refers to the score of Mann-Whitney test; (2) ** P<.001; (3) Bonferoni a is used to control Type I Error.*

The confidence interval chart shows obvious differences between each pair (i.e., least developed vs. developing countries, developing vs. developed countries, and least developed vs. developed countries) on e-government development. The post hoc tests show that the differences are statistically significant.

Two observations should be noted here. First, the test score shows a wider distance between developed countries and developing countries in comparison to the distance between developing countries and least developed countries. This suggests that

Figure 5. Confidence interval between different regions

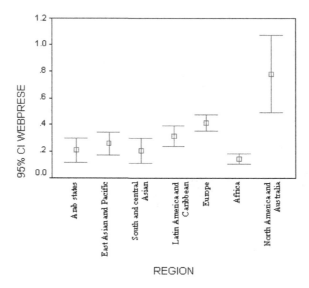

developing countries and least developed countries are still far behind compared to the developed countries in terms of e-government development.

Second, the confidence interval chart shows that the range of WMI (i.e., the height of the bars) of developed countries is larger than those of the least developed and developing countries. This indicates a relatively larger variance on e-government development within developed countries than the other two groups, which suggests the existence of different levels of e-government development within the group of developed countries.

Post Hoc Test on Regional Classification

Because sample sizes vary greatly in this category (i.e., only four countries in the region of North America and Australia, compared to over 40 European countries), statistical tests are not appropriate and too risky to rely on. In this case, the use of the confidence interval is probably the most efficient way to examine group differences. Figure 5 shows the confidence interval between different regions on e-government development.

Three observations can be obtained from the confidence interval chart. First, the chart indicates two extreme cases: the highest case found in Australia and North

America vs. the lowest case found in Africa. The large variance of Web measurement of Australia and North America might be due to the small sample size. The lowest case, comprising African countries, indicates that they are the least advanced in terms of e-government development. Second, the figure suggests that e-government development in European countries is more advanced than the other five groups (except Australia and North America countries). Finally, the confidence interval implies a fairly similar level of e-government development among countries of Arab states, East Asia and Pacific, South and Central Asia, and Latin America and the Caribbean.

Discussion and Future Research Directions

Based on the growth theory and regional development theory, we hypothesize that income level, development status, and region are three factors differentiating countries on e-government development. The results of nonparametric statistical analyses support our hypotheses. In terms of the planned post hoc test on development status, the e-government development level is more advanced in developed countries than in developing countries. However, there is a larger variance in the group of developed countries in comparison to that of developing and least developed countries. Similar observations are found in terms of the planned post hoc test on income level. E-government development of high-income countries is generally more advanced than that of middle-level and low-level income countries. With respect to region, African countries are the least advanced in terms of e-government development when compared to countries in other regions.

The general high level but relatively large variance on e-government development among the group of developed countries indicates a possible lag of e-government development in some countries within this group. Certain developed countries may not have paid sufficient attention to the fast development of online governing. On the contrary, some developing countries, such as Singapore (Ke & Wei, 2004), receive essential support from their governments to improve their information and computer technology as well as online governing. Based on an integrated e-government strategy, these countries achieved rapid progress in providing government services through the Internet (Ke & Wei, 2004).

Our research also indicates that there are significant differences between countries with different income level, with different development status, and in different regions. As such, e-government should not be studied as if it is the same issue for all countries/regions in the world. Successful experience on e-government development and implementation in a developed country may not be directly applicable to a developing country without careful considerations and adaptations.

Limited research had studied e-government development, and even fewer studies had looked at e-government development on a global scale. This research contributes to the literature from two aspects. First, it empirically investigates factors affecting e-government development. Second, it statistically tests the hypotheses using data from 173 countries. The large number of countries involved in this research enables us to provide an overview of e-government development on a global scale.

This study, like any others, has its limitations. First, the data used in this study is secondary data from two main sources. One potential issue with secondary data is the reliability and validity of the data. Also, the use of Web presence as a measure of e-government development is debatable. However, as the data collection was conducted by the United Nations, which is probably one of the most authorized organizations to conduct government research around the world, we have faith that the data was consistently and scientifically collected, and the use of Web presence as a measure of e-government development had been fully researched.

Second, the classification of a country can be somewhat fuzzy. For example, the development status of one country can be determined based on a number of factors. There are no authoritative definitions on developed and developing countries. Typically, developing countries refer to countries characterized as low industrialization, low levels of living, high population growth, low income per capita, and general economic and technological dependence on developed economies. On the contrary, developed countries are characterized as wealthy, highly industrialized, and technologically advanced, and those that have generally evolved through both economic and demographic transitions. Due to its comprehensive nature, the development status of a country is typically influenced by a large variety of variables, such as human development status and economic development. In this research, we followed the classification provided by the UN.

Future research may focus on several directions. First, there is a need to construct a comprehensive research framework. Besides the factors studied in this research, other factors such as knowledge, technology, culture, government policies, and leadership are also interesting factors that need to be investigated. Second, developing and validating instruments that measure e-government development is critical for future research on e-government. Third, in-depth studies that focus on certain aspects or factors of e-government development via qualitative research methods (such as case studies or grounded theories) will contribute to the field of e-government development.

References

Dawkins, C. J. (2003). Regional development theory: Conceptual foundations, classic works, and recent developments. *Journal of Planning Literature*, CPL Bibliography 370.

Delong, J. B. (2002). *Macroeconomics* (updated ed.). McGraw-Hill.

Hacche, G. (1979). *The theory of economic growth: An introduction.* New York: St. Martins Press.

Heeks, R. (2002). E-government in Africa: Promise and practice. *Information Polity, 7,* 97-114.

Holzer, M., & Melistski, J. (2003). *A comparative e-government analysis of New Jersey's 10 largest municipalities.* Retrieved November 2003, from http://www.cornwall.rutgers.edu/pdf/Holzer.pdf

Huang, W., D'Ambra, J., & Bhalla, V. (2002). An empirical investigation of the adoption of eGovernment in Australian citizens: Some unexpected research findings. *Journal of Computer Information Systems, XXXXIII*(1), 15-22.

Huang, W., Siau, K., & Wei, K. K. (Eds.). (2005). *Electronic government: Strategic and implementations.* Idea Group Publishing.

Janssen, D., Rotthier, S., & Snijkers, K. (2004). If you measure it they will score: An assessment of international eGovernment benchmarking. Information Polity: *The International Journal of Government & Democracy in the Information Age, 9*(3/4), 121-130.

Jarvenpaa, S. (1990, December 14-16). Panning for gold in information systems research: Second-hand data. In Hans-Erik Nissen et al. (Eds.), *ISRA-90 Proceedings—Vol. 1, The IFIP TC WG 8.2 Working Conference on The Information Systems Research Arena of the 90's: Challenges, Perceptions and Alternative Approaches,* Copenhagen, Denmark.

Kaylor, C., Deshazo, R., & Van Eck, D. (2001). Gauging e-government: A report on implementing services among American cities. *Government Information Quarterly, 18,* 293-307.

Ke, W., & Wei, K. K. (2004). Successful e-government in Singapore. *Communications of the ACM, 47*(6), 95-99.

Koh, C. E., Ryan, S., & Prybutok, V. R. (2005). Creating value through managing knowledge in an e-government constituency (G2C) environment. *Journal of Computer Information Systems, 45*(4), 32-41.

Kunstelj, M., & Vintar, M. (2004). Evaluating the progress of e-government development: A critical analysis. *Information Polity: The International Journal of Government & Democracy in the Information Age, 9*(3/4), 131-148.

Levis, W. A. (1995). *The theory of economic growth.* Homewood, IL: Irwin.

Li, F. (2003). Implementing e-government strategy in Scotland: Current situation and emerging issues. *Journal of Electronic Commerce in Organizations, 1*(2), 44-65.

Lucas, R. E. (1988). On the mechanics of economic development. *Journal of Monetary Economics, 22,* 3-42.

McNeal, R. S., Tolbert, C. J., Mossberger, K., & Dotterweich, L. J. (2003). Innovation in digital government in the American states. *Social Science Quarterly, 84*(1), 52-70.

The Public Sphere Information Group. (2002). *What all communities can learn from the learning edge: Best practices emerging from the municipality eGovernment assessment project.* Retrieved November 2003, from http://www.psigroup.biz/resources/PSI-Supp-Content-UGLETI.pdf

Reddick, C. G. (2004). Empirical models of e-government growth in local governments. *e-Service Journal, 3*(2), 59-74.

Romer, P. M. (1986). Increasing returns and long run growth. *Journal of Political Economy, 94,* 1002-1037.

Romer, P. M. (1990). Endogenous technological change. *Journal of Political Economy, 98,* 71-102.

Schultz, T. W. (1959). Human wealth and economic growth. *The Humanist, 2,* 71-81.

Schultz, T. W. (1961). Investment in human capital. *American Economic Review, 51*(1), 1-17.

Siau, K., & Long, Y. (2004). Factors impacting e-government development. *International Conference on Information Systems 2004* (pp. 221-234). Washington DC.

Siau, K., & Long, Y. (2005). Synthesizing e-government stage models: A meta-synthesis based on meta-ethnography approach. *Industrial Management and Data System (IMDS), 105*(4), 443-458.

Siau, K., & Long, Y. (2006). Using social development lenses to understand e-government development. *Journal of Global Information Management, 14*(1), 47-62.

Smith, S., & Jamieson, R. (2006). Determining key factors in e-government information system security. *Information Systems Management, 23*(2), 23-32.

Teicher, J., & Dow, N. (2002). E-government in Australia: Promise and progress. *Information Polity, 7,* 231-246.

The United Nations and American Society for Public Administration. (2001). *Global survey of e-government.* Retrieved October 5, 2003, from http://www.unpan.org/egovernment2.asp

The United Nations and American Society for Public Administration. (2003). *The United Nations world public sector report 2003: E-government at the cross-roads*. Retrieved November 2003, from http://unpan1.un.org/intradoc/groups/public/documents/un/unpan012733.pdf

The United Nations Development Programme. (2003). *Human development report 2003-millennium development goals: A compact among nations to end human poverty*. Retrieved November 2003, from http://www.undp.org/hdr2003/pdf/hdr03_complete.pdf

Appendix

Rank difference between groups within each category (Kruskal-wallis test)

1.   Rank difference between groups classified by income (GDP per capita)

Ranks

WEBPRESE	Low income	55	51.82
	Middle income	80	90.71
	High income	38	130.11
	Total	173	

2.   Rank difference between groups classified by development status

Ranks

WEBPRESE	Least Developed	35	38.93
	Developing	115	88.98
	Developed	23	150.26
	Total	173	

3.   Rank difference between groups classified by region

Ranks

WEBPRESE			
WEBPRESE	Arab states	16	70.97
	East Asian and Pacific	26	80.90
	South and Central Asian	12	71.75
	Latin America and Carribbean	30	97.22
	Europe	44	118.53
	Africa	41	52.65
	Australia and North America	4	165.13
	Total	173	

Section II

Regional Themes

Chapter VII

Strategic Alliances and E-Commerce Adoption in Regional SMEs:
A Comparative Study of Swedish and Australian Regional SMEs

R. C. MacGregor, University of Wollongong, Australia

L. Vrazalic, University of Wollongong, Australia

Abstract

This chapter examines the role of strategic alliance membership on the adoption and nonadoption of e-commerce in regional SMEs. The study was conducted in Karlstad, Sweden and Wollongong, Australia. The study specifically examined whether members of a strategic alliance rated e-commerce adoption factors (criteria for adoption, barriers to adoption, benefits derived from adoption, or disadvantages caused by the adoption of e-commerce) differently to nonmembers. The results showed that membership in a strategic alliance was associated with the rating of importance of e-commerce adoption factors, but only for specific sections of the SME population. The results also showed that these associations are not "universal," but differ from location to location.

Introduction

In the late 1990s, a number of western governments (see Blair, 2000; European Commission, 2000; NOIE, 1998) realised that e-commerce might be a mechanism whereby SMEs might gain a larger share of the marketplace. Motivated by the possibility of increasing employment and reducing trade deficits, government bodies developed a number of initiatives to encourage small businesses to become "wired to the marketplace." These initiatives consisted of a series of stepwise strategies through which a small business might move in order to achieve e-commerce adoption and use. Together with these steps were a set of benefits deemed achievable through the adoption of e-commerce. To manage the proposed changes, SMEs were encouraged to pool their limited skills into strategic alliances (Miles, Preece, & Baetz, 1999).

There are many studies that advocate the importance of strategic alliances in the early adoption of e-commerce, particularly by SMEs (see for example Donckels & Lambrecht, 1997; Jarratt, 1998; Overby & Min, 2001). These studies note that as SMEs confront an environment that is increasingly complex, technologically uncertain, and globally focussed, there is a growing need to be flexible and proactive in business dealings, and they conclude that SME strategic alliances often provide a ready source of technical information, market expertise, and business know how, and a more flexible business structure for dealing with environmental turbulence.

As might be expected, along with those that advocate the role of strategic alliances, there are those that have criticised its development and use. Much of the criticism centres on the apparent belief that small businesses are considered to be "small large businesses." Under such assumptions, business characteristics such as business size, business age, business sector, geographic location, and level of internationalisation are simply removed and replaced by the simplistic notion that all SMEs are intent on gaining a proportion of global market share (Culkin & Smith, 2000; Martin & Matlay, 2001).

Given the debate that surrounds the role of small business strategic alliances, it is interesting to note that little research has been carried out to determine whether these structures have an impact on an SME's decision to adopt e-commerce. Furthermore, there has been a lack of research into comparing e-commerce adoption in those SMEs that are members of a strategic alliance to those that have opted to remain outside such arrangements.

This chapter examines four aspects of e-commerce adoption: the criteria for adoption, the barriers resulting in nonadoption, the benefits derived from adoption, and the disadvantages incurred through adoption of e-commerce. The four aspects were applied to two regional locations, Karlstad, Sweden and Wollongong, Australia. The aim of the studies was to determine whether there were differences in the perception of importance of any of the four aspects between respondents that were members of a small business strategic alliance and respondents that were not.

The chapter begins by examining the nature of SMEs. This is followed by a brief overview of the adoption of e-commerce by SMEs. The chapter then examines the criteria for adoption of e-commerce, the barriers that lead to nonadoption, the benefits derived from e-commerce adoption and use and the disadvantages incurred through the adoption of e-commerce. The chapter then examines the nature and role of strategic alliances as they apply to the SME sector. Finally, the chapter presents a study of 313 Swedish regional SMEs and 161 Australian regional SMEs. The study compares the rating of criteria for adoption, barriers precluding adoption, benefits derived from adoption, and disadvantages incurred through the adoption between those SMEs that are part of a small business strategic alliance and those that are not. Finally, the limitations of the study are presented along with the conclusions and future research directions.

The Nature of SMEs

There are a variety of definitions pertaining to what constitutes a small to medium enterprise. Some of these definitions are based on quantitative measures such as staffing levels, turnover or assets, while others tend to employ a qualitative approach. Meredith (1994) suggests that any description or definition must include a quantitative component that takes into account staff levels, turnover, assets together with financial and nonfinancial measurements, but that the description must also include a qualitative component that reflects how the business is organised and how it operates.

Not only is there a myriad of views concerning the nature of SMEs, but from a governmental standpoint, there are a variety of definitions of an SME. As this study was conducted in both Sweden and Australia, the joint definition of having less than 50 employees (see Gustaffson, Klefsjo, Berggren, & Granfors-Wellemets, 2001; Meredith, 1994) was used.

Not only do the definitions of SME vary, there are wide-ranging views on the characteristics of SMEs.

There have been many studies in the literature that have attempted to demonstrate the characteristics of SMEs. Central to all of these studies is the underlying realization that many of the processes and techniques that have been successfully applied to large businesses do not necessarily provide similar outcomes when applied to SMEs. This is perhaps best summed up by two separate articles in the literature (see Barnet & Mackness, 1983; Wynarczyk, Watson, Storey, Short, & Keasey, 1993) that stated that SMEs are not small large businesses, but are unique in their own right.

Table 1. Features unique to small to medium enterprises (SMEs)

ID	FEATURES UNIQUE TO SMEs	REPORTED BY	
	Features Related to Management, Decision Making and Planning Processes		INTERNAL FEATURES
INT 1	SMEs have small and centralised management with a short range perspective	Markland (1974) Reynolds et al. (1994) Bunker & MacGregor (2000) Welsh & White (1981)	
INT 2	SMEs have poor management skills	Blili & Raymond (1993)	
INT 3	SMEs exhibit a strong desire for independence and avoid business ventures which impinge on their independence	Dennis (2000) Reynolds et al. (1994)	
INT 4	SME Owner(s) often withhold information from colleagues	Dennis (2000)	
INT 5	The decision making process in SMEs is intuitive, rather than based on detailed planning and exhaustive study	Reynolds et al. (1994) Bunker & MacGregor (2000)	
INT 6	The SME Owner(s) has/have a strong influence in the decision making process	Reynolds et al. (1994) Murphy (1996) Bunker & MacGregor (2000)	
INT 7	Intrusion of family values and concerns in decision making processes	Dennis (2000) Bunker & MacGregor (2000) Reynolds et al. (1994)	
INT 8	SMEs have informal and inadequate planning and record keeping processes	Reynolds et al. (1994) Tetteh & Burn (2001) Miller & Besser (2000) Markland (1974) Rotch (1981)	
INT 9	SMEs are more intent on improving day-to-day procedures	MacGregor et al. 1998	
	Features Related to Resource Acquisition		
INT 9	SMEs face difficulties obtaining finance and other resources, and as a result have fewer resources	Cragg & King (1993) Welsh & White (1981) Gaskill & Gibbs (1994) Reynolds et al. (1994) Blili & Raymond (1993)	
INT 10	SMEs are more reluctant to spend on information technology and therefore have limited use of technology	Walczuch et al. (2000) Dennis (2000) MacGregor & Bunker (1996) Poon & Swatman (1997) Abell & Limm (1996) Brigham & Smith 1967	

continued on following page

Table 1. continued

ID	FEATURES UNIQUE TO SMEs	REPORTED BY	
	Features Related to Management, Decision Making and Planning Processes		INTERNAL FEATURES
INT 11	SMEs have a lack of technical knowledge and specialist staff and provide little IT training for staff	Martin & Matlay (2001)	
		Cragg & King (1993)	
		Bunker & MacGregor (2000)	
		Reynolds et al. (1994)	
		Welsh & White (1981)	
		Blili & Raymond (1993)	
	Features Related to Products/Services and Markets		EXTERNAL FEATURES
EXT 1	SMEs have a narrow product/service range	Bunker & MacGregor (2000)	
		Reynolds et al. (1994)	
EXT 2	SMEs have a limited share of the market (often confined towards a niche market) and therefore heavily rely on few customers	Hadjimonolis (1999)	
		Lawrence (1997)	
		Quayle (2002)	
		Reynolds et al. (1994)	
EXT 3	SMEs are product oriented, while large businesses are more customer oriented	Reynolds et al. (1994)	
		Bunker & MacGregor (2000)	
		MacGregor et al. (1998)	
EXT 4	SMEs are not interested in large shares of the market	Reynolds et al. (1994)	
		MacGregor et al. (1998)	
EXT 5	SMEs are unable to compete with their larger counterparts	Lawrence (1997)	
	Features Related to Risk Taking and Dealing with Uncertainty		
EXT 6	SMEs have lower control over their external environment than larger businesses, and therefore face more uncertainty	Westhead & Storey (1996)	
		Hill & Stewart (2000)	
EXT 7	SMEs face more risks than large businesses because the failure rates of SMEs are higher	Brigham & Smith (1967)	
		DeLone (1988)	
		Cochran (1981)	
EXT 8	SMEs are more reluctant to take risks	Walczuch et al. (2000)	
		Dennis (2000)	

Although size is a major distinguishing factor, SMEs have a number of other unique features that set them apart from large businesses. There have been various studies carried out in order to isolate these features. Brigham and Smith (1967) found that SMEs tended to be more risky than their larger counterparts. This view is supported in later studies (Delone,1988; Walker, 1975). Cochran (1981) found that SMEs tended to be subject to higher failure rates while Rotch (1987) suggested that SMEs had inadequate records of transactions. Welsh and White (1981), in a comparison of SMEs with their larger counterparts, found that SMEs suffered from a lack of trained staff and had a short-range management perspective. They termed these traits "resource poverty," and suggested that their net effect was to magnify the effect of environmental impact, particularly when information systems were involved.

These early suggestions have been supported by more recent studies that have found most SMEs lack technical expertise (Barry & Milner, 2002), most lack adequate capital to undertake technical enhancements (Gaskill, Van Auken, & Kim, 1993, Raymond, 2001), most SMEs suffer from inadequate organisational planning (Miller & Besser, 2000; Tetteh & Burn, 2001) and many SMEs differ from their larger counterparts in the extent of the product/service range available to customer (Reynolds, Savage, & Williams, 1994).

A number of recent studies (see Bunker & MacGregor, 2000; Murphy, 1996; Reynolds et al., 1994) have examined the differences in management style between large businesses and SMEs. These studies have shown that among other characteristics, SMEs tend to have a small management team (often one or two individuals), they are strongly influenced by the owner and the owner's personal idiosyncrasies, they have little control over their environment (this is supported by the studies of Westhead & Storey, 1996 and Hill & Stewart, 2000) and they have a strong desire to remain independent (this is supported by the findings of Dennis, 2000 and Drakopolou-Dodd, Jack, & Anderson, 2002).

An extensive review of the available literature was undertaken to identify the features and create a context for the study. Following this process, an analysis of the features identified revealed that they could be classified as being internal or external to the business. Internal features include management, decision making, and planning processes within the organisation, and the availability of resources, while external features are related to the market (products/services and customers) and the external environment (risk taking and uncertainty). These are presented in Table 1.

Small Business in Regional Locations

SMEs located in regional areas are affected by circumstances inherent to their location. Regional areas are defined as geographical areas located outside metropolitan centres and major cities. The Australian Bureau of Statistics (2001) classifies regional areas into inner and outer regions, and remote and very remote areas. Determining the classification of a region is based on a formula that primarily relies on the measures of proximity to services. Rather than remote and rural areas (which are sparsely populated), the research presented in this chapter focuses on inner and outer regional areas (which are more urbanised).

Regional areas are of particular interest to governments because they are character-
ised by high unemployment rates (Larsson, Hedelin, & Gärling, 2003), a shortage
of skilled people, limited access to resources, and a lack of infrastructure (Keniry,
Blums, Notter, Radford, & Thomson, 2003). Yet, at the same time, businesses located in regional areas in Australia contribute 50% of the national export income
(Keniry et al., 2003). This implies that small businesses have the potential to play
a major role in developing regional areas. The European Union views small businesses as a catalyst for regional development (Europa, 2003). In 2001, the Swedish
Parliament passed legislation that resulted in the creation of Regional Development
Councils (Johansson, 2003). The Councils have a mandate to promote a positive
business climate and sustainable growth in their respective regions. SMEs have been
earmarked as playing an important role in promoting this growth because they are
seen as a key source of jobs and employment prospects (Keniry et al., 2003; Lars-
sen et al., 2003). To encourage growth and development in regional areas, government organisations have been heavily promoting the adoption of information and
communication technology by small business, including e-commerce. However, a
number of studies have found that following e-commerce adoption, small businesses
have experienced a variety of problems or disadvantages brought about as a result
of implementing this type of technology.

E-Commerce

There are nearly as many definitions of e-commerce as there are contributions to
the literature. Turban et al. (Turban, King, Warkentin, & Chung, 2002) define e-
commerce as:

*an emerging concept that describes the process of buying, selling or exchanging
services and information via computer networks.* (p. 4)

Choi et al. (1997, cited in Turban et al., 2002) draw a distinction between what they
term pure e-commerce and partial e-commerce. According to Choi et al., "pure
e-commerce" has a digital product, a digital process, and a digital agent. All other
interactions (including those that might have one or two of the three nominated by
Choi et al.) are termed "partial e-commerce."

Raymond (2001) defines e-commerce as:

*functions of information exchange and commercial transaction support that operate
on telecommunications networks linking business partners (typically customers and
suppliers).* (Raymond, 2001, p. 411)

Damanpour (2001), by comparison, defines e-commerce as:

any 'net' business activity that transforms internal and external relationships to create value and exploit market opportunities driven by new rules of the connected economy. (Damanpour, 2001, p. 18)

For the purposes of this study, which examines changes to the organisation brought about by involvement in e-commerce, the definition provided by Damanpour is used. While it may be argued that other definitions do not preclude organisational transformation, only the definition of Damanpour "demands" those transformations and it is consistent with the concept in the literature, generally.

As already stated, e-commerce is not just another technology that sustains and enhances business practice; it is an innovation that has disrupted traditional ways of doing business (Lee, 2001). Indeed, Treacy and Wiersema (1997) suggest e-commerce transforms a company from one geared towards "production excellence" to one geared towards "customer intimacy." Thus, a traditional management focus, which included total quality management, lean manufacturing, and business process reengineering (collectively termed economics of scarcity by Lee, 2001), are replaced by gathering, synthesis and distribution of information (collectively termed economics of abundance by Lee). Similarly, output from the organisation is no longer simply the finished goods, but must include information and information services, bundled for customer use.

E-Commerce and SMEs

Studies carried out at the onset of e-commerce (Acs, Morck, Shaver, & Yeung, 1997; Auger & Gallaugher, 1997; Gessin, 1996; McRea, 1996; Murphy, 1996; Nooteboom, 1994) predicted that, since SMEs had always operated in an externally uncertain environment, they were more likely to benefit from e-commerce. Other authors, while agreeing in principle with this viewpoint, did so with a degree of caution. Hutt and Speh (1998) felt that most areas of the SME sector, with the exception of those SMEs involved in the industrial market, would benefit from e-commerce. They suggest that the industrial SMEs already concentrated on an established base of customers and product offerings. Swartz and Iacobucci (2000) felt that the service industries would benefit far more than other areas of the SME community. Other studies (Donckels & Lambrecht, 1997; Reuber & Fischer, 1999) felt that the business age was a strong predictor of relative benefit of e-commerce adoption, suggesting that older businesses would not adopt as easily as newer ones. Among the predicted benefits available to SMEs were:

- A global presence presenting customers with a global choice (Barry & Milner, 2002)

- Improved competitiveness (Auger & Gallaugher, 1997)

- Mass customisation and "customerisation," presenting customers with personalised products and services (Fuller, 2000)

- Shortening of supply chains, providing rapid response to customer needs (Barry & Milner, 2002)

Recent studies have found that these predictions have not eventuated and that it has been the larger businesses that have been more active with respect to e-commerce (see Barry & Milner, 2002; Riquelme, 2002; Roberts & Wood, 2002). A number of reasons have been put forward, including poor security, high costs, and lack of requisite skills. However, some researchers have begun to examine how decisions concerning IT adoption and use are made in the SME sector.

There have been many governmental as well as privately funded projects attempting to further the cause of adoption of e-commerce by SMEs. Unfortunately, many of these projects relied on pre-e-commerce criteria, and focussed on internal systems within the SME rather than interorganisational interaction (Fallon & Moran, 2000; Martin & Matlay, 2001; Poon & Swatman, 1997). The resulting models were stepwise or linear, beginning with e-mail, progressing through website, to e-commerce adoption, and finally organisational transformation. Not only are these models based on inappropriate or oversimplified criteria (Kai-Uwe Brock, 2000), but they recommend the adoption of e-commerce prior to, or without any consideration of any form of organisational change.

E-commerce brings with it changes in communication (Chellappa, Barua, & Whinston, 1996), business method (Henning, 1998), market structure and approach to marketing (Giaglis, Klein, & O'Keefe, 1999) as well as changes in day-to-day activities (Doukidis, Poulymenakou, Terpsidis, Themisticleous, & Miliotis, 1998). These changes are exacerbated in the SME sector as many SMEs have no overall plan and, for the most part, fail to understand the need for competitive strategies (Jeffcoate, Chappel, & Feindt, 2002).

Unlike previous technological innovations, e-commerce brings with it changes to both procedures within the organisation as well as changes to the structure of the organisation itself. These changes include the way businesses interact, their approaches to marketing, products and customers, and the way decisions are made and disseminated, particularly decisions concerning technology adoption and use. For SMEs, these changes can have both positive and negative effects. Those SME owners/managers who have developed an organisation-wide strategy for e-commerce adoption, report increases in efficiency. Those who have not, often find that the changes reduce flexibility within their business. As this study is examining both

SME adopters as well as nonadopters, it is appropriate to briefly consider the criteria for adoption, the barriers to adoption, the benefits derived from adoption, and the disadvantages incurred through adoption. These will be considered separately.

Criteria for the Adoption of E-Commerce by SMEs

In their study of 146 SMEs, Poon and Swatman (1997) provided five "drivers" or criteria for e-commerce adoption by respondents. These were: new modes of direct or indirect marketing, strengthening of relationships with business partners, the ability to reach new customers, improvement to customer services, and the reduction of costs in communication. Similar studies have been carried out in a variety of SME communities. Some of the criteria for adoption and use have been similar to those found by Poon and Swatman, others have provided alternative responses. Abell and Limm (1996) found that reduction in communication costs, improvement in customer services, improvement in lead time, and improvement in sales were the major criteria for e-commerce adoption and use, adding that external technical support was considered vital to any adoption and use strategies.

Lawrence (1997), in an examination of Tasmanian SMEs, noted that improved marketing and the ability to reach new customers were the most common incentives for adopting and using e-commerce. Lawrence also noted that decisions concerning e-commerce adoption were often forced onto SMEs by their larger trading partners. This is supported by studies carried out MacGregor and Bunker (1996), MacGregor et al. (1998), Reimenschneider and Mykytyn (2000), and Raymond (2001). Auger and Gallaugher (1997) noted that improvement in customer services and improvement to internal control of the business were strong criteria for e-commerce adoption in SMEs. The strong desire for control was also noted in studies carried out by Reimenschneider and Mykytyn (2000), Poon and Joseph (2001), and Domke-Damonte and Levsen (2002).

A number of studies (Power & Sohal, 2002; Price-Waterhouse Cooper 1999; Reimenschneider & Mykytyn 2000) have found that some SMEs have adopted e-commerce nominating pressure from customers as one of the motivating criteria.

Table 2 provides a summary of the findings related to the criteria used by SMEs in their decision to adopt e-commerce.

Benefits and Disadvantages of E-Commerce in SMEs

For SMEs, the changes associated with e-commerce have produced both positive and negative effects. Studies by Raymond (2001) and Ritchie and Brindley (2000)

Table 2. Summary of research on criteria used by SMEs in the decisions to adopt and use electronic commerce

Criteria	Researcher
Demand/pressure from customers	Reimenschneider & Mykytyn (2000) Price Waterhouse Coopers (1999) Power & Sohal (2002)
Pressure of competition	Raisch (2001) Poon & Strom (1997)
Pressure from suppliers	Reimenschneider & Mykytyn (2000) MacGregor & Bunker (1996b) Lawrence (1997) Raymond (2001)
Reduction of costs	Abell & Limm (1996) Raisch (2001) Auger & Gallaugher (1997)
Improvement to customer service	Abell & Limm (1996) Senn (1996) Auger & Gallaugher (1997) Power & Sohal (2002)
Improvement in lead time	Power & Sohal (2002) Reimenschneider & Mykytyn (2000) Abell & Limm (1996)
Increased sales	Abell & Limm (1996) Lee (2001) Phan (2001)
Improvement to internal efficiency	Porter (2001)
Strengthen relations with business partners	Raymond (2001) Evans & Wurster (1997) Poon & Swatman (1997)
Reach new customers/markets	Poon & Swatman (1997) Lawrence (1997) Power & Sohal (2002) Reimenschneider & Mykytyn (2000)
Improve competitiveness	Turban et al. (2000) Raymond (2001) Reimenschneider & Mykytyn (2000)
External technical support	Abell & Limm (1996)
Improve marketing	Poon & Swatman (1997) Lawrence (1997) Power & Sohal (2002) Reimenschneider & Mykytyn (2000)
Improve control and follow-up	Reimenschneider & Mykytyn (2000) Domke-Damonte & Levsen (2002) Poon & Joseph (2001) Auger & Gallaugher (1997)

found that, while e-commerce adoption has eroded trading barriers for SMEs, this has often come at the price of altering or eliminating commercial relationships and exposing the business to external risks. Lawrence (1997), Tetteh and Burn (2001) and Lee (2001) contend that e-commerce adoption fundamentally alters the internal procedures within SMEs. Indeed, Lee (2001) adds that the biggest challenge to SMEs is not to find the best e-commerce model, but to change the mindset of the owners/managers themselves. For those who have developed an organisation-wide strategy (in anticipation of e-commerce), these changes can lead to an increase in efficiency in the business for those who have not; this can reduce the flexibility of the business (Tetteh & Burn, 2001), and often leads to a duplication of the work effort (MacGregor et al., 1998).

E-Commerce Benefits

Many of the substantial benefits of e-commerce adoption fall into the category of intangible benefits, and are often not realised by SMEs at the time of adoption. However, SMEs have reported various benefits in the long term following e-commerce implementation. A number of studies have examined both the tangible and intangible benefits achieved by SMEs from the adoption of e-commerce. Studies by Abell and Limm (1996), Poon and Swatman (1997) and Quayle (2002) found that the tangible benefits (such as reduced administration costs, reduced production costs, reduced lead time, increased sales) derived from e-commerce were marginal in terms of direct earnings. These same studies found that the intangible benefits (such as improvement in the quality of information, improved internal control of the business, improved relations with business partners) were of far greater value to SMEs. Poon and Swatman (1997) also found that e-commerce had led to an improved relationship with customers.

It is interesting to note that various authors (Abell & Limm, 1996; Martin & Matlay, 2001; Poon & Swatman, 1997) all suggest that tangible benefits are marginal in the short term, contrary to the expectations of SME owners/managers, and that, at best, these may be more fruitful in the longer term. This is supported in a recent article by Vrazalic, Bunker, MacGregor, Carlsson, and Magnusson (2002). For summary purposes, the actual benefits of e-commerce derived from a comprehensive review of the literature are listed in Table 3.

Table 3. Summary of e-commerce adoption benefits reported by previous studies

E-commerce Benefits	Related Literature
E-commerce had led to increased sales	Abell & Limm (1996)
E-commerce has given us access to new customers and markets	Quayle (2002) Ritchie & Brindley (2001) Raymond (2001) Sparkes & Thomas (2001)
E-commerce has improved our competitiveness	Vescovi (2000)
E-commerce has lowered our administration costs	Quayle (2002) Poon & Swatman (1997) Abell & Limm (1996)
E-commerce has lowered our production costs	Quayle (2002) Poon & Swatman (1997) Abell & Limm (1996)
E-commerce has reduced the lead time from order to delivery	Quayle (2002) Poon & Swatman (1997) Abell & Limm (1996)
E-commerce has reduced the stock levels	Quayle (2002)
E-commerce has increased internal efficiency	Tetteh & Burn (2001) MacGregor et al. (1998)
E-commerce has improved our relations with business partners	Poon & Swatman (1997)
E-commerce has improved the quality of information in our organisation	Quayle (2002) Poon & Swatman (1997) Abell & Limm (1996)

Disadvantages Encountered Through the Adoption and Use of E-Commerce by SMEs

E-commerce has always carried the stigma of poor security. Innumerable studies have pointed to the perceived lack of visible security as a reason for nonacceptance of the technology, both by businesses and customers (see as examples Lawrence, 1997; MacGregor et al., 1998). Recent studies, however, have identified a number of other disadvantages incurred by SME operators in their day-to-day use of e-commerce technologies.

Raymond (2001), in examining the removal of business intermediaries by e-commerce, noted a deterioration of relationships with business partners and customers. He termed this effect as "disintermediation." Similar findings have been presented by Stauber (2000). Stauber also found that many SME operators complained of increasing costs in their business dealings attributable to e-commerce use.

Table 4. Disadvantages found by SME's in their use of e-commerce technology

Disadvantage	Researcher
Deterioration of relations with business partners	Raymond (2001) Stauber (2000)
Higher costs	Stauber (2000) MacGregor et al. (1998)
Increased computer maintenance	MacGregor et al. (1998)
Doubling of work	MacGregor et al. (1998)
Reduced flexibility of work	MacGregor et al. (1998) Lawrence (1997) Lee (2001)
Monotonous work	MacGregor et al. (1998) Lawrence (1997) Lee (2001)
Security risks	Ritchie & Brindley (2001)
Dependence on e-commerce (non-e-commerce proce-dures having to be done through e-commerce formats)	Sparkes & Thomas (2001) MacGregor et al. (1998) Lawrence (1997)
Greater demand for "on-time" service	Lee (2001)

Lawrence (1997) found that e-commerce, particularly, but not exclusively EDI, resulted in reduced flexibility of work practices and heavier reliance on the technology. Her findings are supported in studies by MacGregor et al. (1998), Lee (2001), and Sparkes and Thomas (2001).

MacGregor et al. (1998), in a study of 131 regional SMEs in Australia, found that many respondents complained that they were doubling their work effort, this, in part, being due to the e-commerce systems not being fully integrated into the existing business systems in the organisation. They also found that many respondents complained that the technology had resulted in higher computer maintenance costs.

Again, for convenience, these studies are summarised in Table 4.

Nonadopters: Barriers to E-Commerce Adoption

There have been many studies examining the barriers to e-commerce adoption in SMEs. Some studies have simply reported these barriers, others have attempted to categorise them. Hadjiminolis (1999), in a study of e-commerce adoption in Cyprus, categorized barriers as either internal or external. She suggested that external barriers could be further categorised into supply barriers (difficulties obtaining finance and

Table 5. Summary of e-commerce adoption barriers in SMEs

Barriers to e-commerce adoption	Reported by
High cost of e-commerce implementation; Internet technologies too expensive to implement	Iacovou, Benbasat, & Dexter, (1995); Lawrence (1997); Purao & Campbell (1998); Van Akkeren & Cavaye (1999); Riquelme (2002); Quayle (2002)
E-commerce too complex to implement	Quayle (2002)
Low level of existing hardware technology incorporated into the business	Lawrence (1997)
SMEs need to see immediate ROI and e-commerce is a long-term investment	Lawrence (1997)
Organisational resistance to change because of the fear of new technology amongst employees	Lawrence (1997); Van Akkeren & Cavaye (1999)
Preference for and satisfaction with traditional manual methods, such as phone, fax, and face-to-face	Lawrence (1997); Poon & Swatman (1999); Venkatesan & Fink (2002)
Lack of technical skills and IT knowledge amongst employees; lack of computer literate/specialised staff	Iacovou et al. (1995); Lawrence (1997); Van Akkeren & Cavaye (1999); Quayle (2002); Riquelme (2002)
Lack of time to implement e-commerce	Lawrence (1997); Van Akkeren & Cavaye (1999); Walczuch et al. (2000)
E-commerce is not deemed to be suited to the way the SME does business	Iacovou et al. (1995); Abell & Limm (1996); Poon & Swatman (1997); Hadjimanolis (1999);
E-commerce is not deemed to be suited to the products/services offered by the SME	Hadjimanolis (1999); Walczuch et al. (2000); Kendall & Kendall (2001)
E-commerce is perceived as a technology lacking direction	Lawrence (1997)
Lack of awareness about business opportunities/benefits that e-commerce can provide	Iacovou et al. (1995); Quayle (2002)
Lack of available information about e-commerce	Lawrence (1997)
Concern about security of e-commerce	Abell & Limm (1996); Purao & Campbell (1998); Hadjimanolis (1999); Van Akkeren & Cavaye (1999); Poon & Swatman (1999); Quayle (2002); Riquelme (2002)
Lack of critical mass among customers, suppliers and business partners to implement e-commerce	Abell & Limm (1996); Hadjimanolis (1999)
Heavy reliance on external consultants (who are considered by SMEs to be inadequate) to provide necessary expertise	Lawrence (1997); Van Akkeren & Cavaye (1999)
Lack of e-commerce standards	Robertson & Gatignon (1986)

technical information), demand barriers (e-commerce not fitting with the products/ services or not fitting with the way clients did business), and environmental barriers (security concerns). Internal barriers were further divided into resource barriers (lack of management and technical expertise) and system barriers (e-commerce not fitting with the current business practices). While it is not within the scope of the current study to investigate the validity of these categories, a detailed list of findings and related studies is presented in Table 5.

Strategic Alliances and SMEs

Frequently, it has been argued that multilevel hierarchical structures no longer fit the marketplace (Overby & Min 2000, Tikkanen 1998). Not only has this meant a reexamination of organisational structure, but many factors previously considered "informal procedures," such as sharing expertise and advice, have now become prominent in day-to-day organisational procedures. This reduction in hierarchical structure, together with the increasing importance of informal interorganisational links, has meant that organisations are not only interacting economically, but are tied together by factors that Storper (1995) describes as "untraded interdependencies." These links, which include sharing of practical experience, sharing of technical expertise, collective learning, and market knowledge (see Keeble, Lawson, Moore, & Wilkinson, 1999; O'Donnell, Gilmore, Cummins, & Carson, 2001; Overby & Min, 2001; Tikkanen, 1998) have been termed strategic alliances or networks and are based on relationships of trust and reciprocity.

There are a variety of reasons in the literature as to why strategic alliances have developed. Black and Porter (2000) argue that the more complex and dynamic the environment, the more need there is for some structure to coordinate disparate groups. Christopher (1999) suggests that businesses need to achieve greater agility with supply chain partners. Gilliland and Bello (1997) point to market volatility and technological uncertainty as a source of need for some form of controlling structure, while Tikkanen (1998) suggests a need to realign organisational structure to market structure.

It could be argued that by the very nature of business, all organisations relate to others and are thus part of some form of strategic alliance. On the surface these relationships may appear to be nothing more than exchanges of goods and payments, but relationships with customers, suppliers, and competitors can never be simply described in terms of financial transactions. Dennis (2000) suggests that any dealing with other organisations must impinge on the decision-making process, even if these decisions only involve the strengthening or relaxing of the relationships themselves. Nalebuff and Brandenburg (1996) state that for a relationship to be truly a strategic alliance it must be conscious, interdependent, and cooperating towards a predetermined set of goals.

There are many definitions of strategic alliances in the literature. Dennis (2000) suggests that SME strategic alliances:

... are dynamic arrangement(sic) that are constantly evolving and adjusting in order to accommodate changes in the business environment. Member companies have interconnected linkages that allow them to move more efficiently towards set objectives than those operating as a separate entity. (p. 287)

She adds that while all companies form relationships with suppliers, customers, and business partners, it is the extent of the closeness, interdependence, and consciousness of these relationships that determines whether they are truly part of an SME strategic alliance. This definition implies that only those interorganisational links that have formal governance can be termed SME strategic alliances. By comparison, Yeung (1994) defines an SME strategic alliance as:

... an integrated and coordinated set of ongoing economic and non-economic relations embedded within, among and outside business firms. (p. 476)

Thus for Yeung, an SME strategic alliance is not only a structure, but embodies processes between organisations. These processes may be formal economic processes or may be informal cooperative relationships, sharing expertise and know-how. Indeed, Dahlstrand (1999) suggests that informal links may be conscious or unconscious mechanisms.

While recent studies (O'Donnell et al., 2001; Overby & Min, 2001) stress the importance of informal interorganisational links, the definition of these links in SMEs varies widely. As this study has as its focus SME strategic alliances with some form of governance (be they organisationally linked SMEs or firms that have made use of SME associations), the definition provided by Achrol and Kotler (1999) will be adopted, viz.:

... an independent coalition of task- or skill-specialised economic entities (independent firms or autonomous organisational units) that operates without hierarchical control but is embedded by dense lateral connections, mutuality, and reciprocity, in a shared value system that defines 'membership' roles and responsibilities. (p.148)

Achrol and Kotler (1999) suggest that by developing and organising functional components, alliances provide a better mechanism to learn and adapt to changes in their environment.

For the SME, strategic alliances can provide a number of advantages over stand-alone organisations. These include the sharing of financial risk (Jorde & Teece, 1989) and technical knowledge (Marchewka & Towell, 2000), market penetration (Achrol & Kotler, 1999), and internal efficiencies (Datta, 1988). In addition to providing much needed information, SME strategic alliances often provide legitimacy to their members. For businesses that provide a service and whose products are intangible, company image and reputation become crucial, since customers can rarely test or inspect the service before purchase. Cropper (1996) suggests that membership of an SME strategic alliance very often supplies this image to potential customers. However, the question of whether belonging to a strategic alliance has an impact on an SME's decision to adopt e-commerce remains unexplored. The study described in the following section attempts to extend our knowledge about e-commerce adoption criteria in SMEs that are members of a strategic alliance and those that are not.

Methodology

As can be seen in Tables 2 to 5, previous studies have given rise to 14 criteria, 14 benefits, 9 disadvantages, and 10 barriers to e-commerce adoption. A series of six interviews, three of the interviews were with SMEs that had adopted e-commerce and three with SMEs that had rejected the adoption of e-commerce, were under-taken. For the three SMEs that had adopted e-commerce, owners/managers were asked whether the criteria in Table 2, benefits in Table 3, and disadvantages in Table 4 were pertinent to their experience with e-commerce adoption and postadoption. Owners/managers were also asked whether any other criteria, benefits, or disadvantages should be added to those in the tables. All three owners/managers indicated that the criteria, benefits, and disadvantages were pertinent to their experience and that there were no others that need to be added. For the SMEs that had rejected adoption of e-commerce, a similar set of interviews was carried out to determine the appropriateness and completeness of the list of barriers (see Table 5). Again, all three owners/managers indicated that the barriers in Table 5 were pertinent to their decision-making and that no other barriers needed to be added to the existing list.

Based on the findings of the six in-depth interviews, a survey instrument was developed for SME managers. The survey was used to collect data about criteria for adoption of e-commerce, benefits derived from adoption of e-commerce, disadvantages incurred through adoption of e-commerce and barriers to adoption of e-commerce. Respondents that had adopted e-commerce were asked to rate the criteria for adoption, the benefits derived from adoption, and the disadvantages incurred through adoption of e-commerce across a 5-point Likert scale (with anchors 1 – very unimportant, 5 very important). Respondents that had not adopted e-commerce were asked to rate the barriers to e-commerce adoption across a 5-point Likert scale (with anchors 1 – very unimportant, 5 very important). All respondents were asked whether they were part of a small business strategic alliance or not.

Previous research has also shown that various organisational factors also appear to impinge on e-commerce adoption. Fallon and Moran (2000), for example, found significant links between the size of the small business in terms of the number of employees and the level of Internet adoption. Matlay (2000) showed that the business sector was significantly associated with e-commerce adoption. This was supported by Riquelme (2002) who, in a study of 75 Chinese small businesses, found that those involved in the service sector tended to adopt e-commerce far more than their counterparts in the manufacturing sector. The studies clearly suggest that when examining e-commerce adoption, organisational factors, such as business age, business size, business sector, and market focus, need to be considered.

Many studies have simply categorised business age in sets of five (e.g., 0 to 5, 6 to 10, etc.). The results of the in-depth interviews showed that within the first of these groups (0 to 5), three subsets existed. The first was the very new business (in business for less than a year), the second was those businesses (including the dot.com businesses) that were 1- to 2-years old, while the third was businesses that were between 3- and 5-years old. The interviews showed that the three of these acted very differently where e-commerce adoption and use was concerned. The interviews also showed that the other ranges should be 6-10 years, 11-20 years, and >20 years.

In relation to business size, a number of authors have arbitrarily categorised small businesses with less than five employees as micro businesses. Studies by Fallon and Moran (2000) and Matlay (2000) suggest that businesses with fewer than 10 employees are a far more significant subdivision than simply small or micro businesses. The in-depth interviews added a separate category for the sole-operated business (0 employees). The interviews also showed that businesses with between 20 and 50 employees were sufficiently similar to consider them as a single business size group. Thus, the four categories for business size were 0 employees, 1-9 employees, 10-19 employees, and 20-50 employees.

A number of studies (Achrol & Kotler, 1999; Blackburn & Athayde, 2000) suggested that market focus was associated with the level of adoption of e-commerce. Based on the findings of the interviews, four market focus groups were considered: local businesses (5-10 km radius), regional businesses (up to 50 km radius), national businesses, and international businesses.

Based on the findings of the interviews, four categories of business sector were determined. These were industrial (including manufacturing, engineering, transport), service (including professional small businesses such as medical and legal providers), retail (including business to business and business to customer), and finance (including insurance, banking, and accountancy).

As the survey was intended to examine the criteria, benefits, disadvantages, and barriers of e-commerce adoption in regional SMEs, the location of the respondents needed to be considered. A set of location guidelines was developed. These were:

- The location must be a large regional centre rather than a capital city.

- A viable government initiated Chamber of Commerce for SMEs must exist and be well patronised by the SME community.

- The location should have the full range of educational facilities.

- The business community represented a cross-section of business ages, sizes, sectors, and market foci.

- The SME community included those that had adopted as well as not adopted e-commerce.

Two locations were chosen: Karlstad, Sweden and Wollongong, Australia. The locations met all of the location guidelines, and contained personnel who could assist with the distribution and regathering of the survey materials.

A total of 1,170 surveys were distributed by post in four regional areas of Sweden: Karlstad, Filipstad, Saffle and Arvika. A total of 250 surveys was conducted by phone in Wollongong. The small businesses were selected randomly from government lists. The mode of data collection was chosen based on previous research by de Heer (1999), which indicated that Scandinavian countries had historically high survey response rates, while Australia had a higher nonresponse rate.

Results

Responses were obtained from 350 SMEs in Sweden, giving a response rate of 29.9%. From these, 313 responses were considered valid and usable. The total number of adopters was 189, representing 60.4% of the valid responses. One hundred and fifteen respondents that had adopted e-commerce indicated that they were not members of any form of alliance. Sixty three (50%) of the respondents that had not adopted e-commerce indicated that they were not part of any form of alliance. An inspection of the frequencies indicated that the full range of the scale was utilised by respondents for all four of the measures (criteria for adoption of e-commerce, benefits derived from adoption of e-commerce, disadvantages incurred through adoption of e-commerce, and barriers to adoption of e-commerce). These will each be presented separately.

One hundred and sixty responses were obtained from the study in Wollongong, giving a higher response rate of 65.5%, which is consistent with phone surveys (Frazer & Lawley, 2000). Of these, 25 (15.6%) indicated that they had adopted e-commerce. Ten of the 25 respondents indicated that they were part of an alliance. Thirty four (25.2%) of the respondents that had not adopted e-commerce indicated that they were part of some form of alliance. An inspection of the frequencies indicated that the full range of the scale was utilised by respondents for all four of the measures (criteria for adoption of e-commerce, benefits derived from adoption of e-commerce, disadvantages incurred through adoption of e-commerce, and barriers to adoption of e-commerce). These will each be presented separately.

A profile of the respondents is shown in Tables 6 and 7. It is interesting to note that the adoption rate in Sweden is far higher than that of Australia.

For each of the four measures (criteria for adoption of e-commerce, benefits derived from adoption of e-commerce, disadvantages incurred through adoption of e-commerce, and barriers to adoption of e-commerce) a series of two-tailed t-tests was applied to determine whether there were any significant differences between the ratings of member respondents and nonmember respondents.

Sweden

Table 8 provides the results of the two-tailed t-tests for criteria to adopt e-commerce.

An examination of Table 8 shows that for the Swedish regional SME respondents, there were no statistically significant differences between member and nonmember respondents for any criteria of adoption of e-commerce.

Table 9 provides the data for the barriers to e-commerce adoption.

A number of previous studies (Cirillo, 2000; Daniel & Wilson, 2002; Terziovski, 2003) suggest that membership of a small business strategic alliance reduces barriers to e-commerce adoption by providing the necessary organisational and technical expertise to the members. However, an examination of Table 9 shows that 9 of the 10 barriers are rated higher by member respondents than they are by nonmembers. One possible explanation is that through membership of a small business strategic alliance, respondents are better placed to fully appreciate e-commerce and the potential barriers to its adoption than stand-alone businesses.

Two barriers, "e-commerce does not fit with our products and services" and "we do not see any advantage in using e-commerce," showed a statistically significant difference in rating of importance between member respondents and nonmember respondents.

Table 6. (Sweden)

Adoption/nonadoption of electronic commerce

		Frequency	Percent
Valid	Adopted EC	188	60.4
	Not adopted	125	39.6
Total		313	100.0

Membership/nonmembership of a small business strategic alliance

		Frequency	Percent
Valid	Nonmembers	163	52.1
	Members	140	44.7
	Total	303	96.8
Missing		10	3.2
Total		313	100.0

Age of the business

		Frequency	Percent
Valid	< 1 year	4	1.3
	1-2 years	14	4.5
	3-5 years	42	13.4
	6-10 years	62	19.8
	11-20 years	79	25.2
	> 20 years	111	35.5
	Total	312	99.7
Missing		1	.3
Total		313	100.0

continued on following page

Table 6. continued

Size of business

		Frequency	Percent
Valid	Sole trader	56	17.9
	1-9 employees	164	52.4
	10-19 employees	49	15.7
	20-50 employees	40	12.8
	Total	309	98.7
Missing		4	1.3
Total		313	100.0

Business sector

		Frequency	Percent
Valid	Industrial	62	19.8
	Service	114	36.4
	Retail/trading	65	20.8
	Financial	6	1.9
	Total	247	78.9
Other	Total	66	21.1
Total		313	100.0

Market focus

		Frequency	Percent
Valid	Local business	171	54.6
	Regional business	29	9.3
	National	82	26.2
	International	31	9.9
	Total	313	100.0

Table 7. (Australia)

Adoption/nonadoption of electronic commerce

		Frequency	Percent
Valid	Adopted EC	25	15.6
	Not adopted	135	84.4
	Total	160	100.0

Membership/nonmembership of a small business strategic alliance

		Frequency	Percent
Valid	Nonmembers	112	70.0
	Members	48	30.0
	Total	160	100.0

Age of the business

		Frequency	Percent
Valid	< 1 year	11	6.9
	1-2 years	16	10.0
	3-5 years	25	15.6
	6-10 years	27	16.9
	11-20 years	40	25.0
	> 20 years	41	25.6
	Total	160	100.0

Size of business

		Frequency	Percent
Valid	Sole trader	30	18.8
	1-9 employees	112	70.0
	10-19 employees	9	5.6
	20-50 employees	9	5.6
	Total	160	100.0

continued on following page

Table 7. continued

Business sector

		Frequency	Percent
Valid	Industrial	10	6.3
	Service	79	49.8
	Retail/trading	67	41.9
	Financial	1	0.1
	Other	3	1.9
	Total	160	100.0

Market focus

		Frequency	Percent
Valid	Local business	44	27.5
	Regional business	95	59.4
	National	20	12.5
	International	1	0.6
	Total	313	100.0

Table 8. A comparison of the rating of importance of criteria to adopt e-commerce between respondents that were members of a small business strategic alliance and respondents that were not

Criteria	Mean members	Mean nonmembers	t value
A	1.82	2.10	1.241
B	2.10	2.34	1.011
C	1.61	1.71	.522
D	3.03	3.00	-.126
E	3.64	3.64	.016
F	2.44	2.59	.549
G	2.70	2.98	1.040
H	3.38	3.71	1.316
I	2.69	2.98	1.169
J	2.84	2.91	.283
K	2.97	3.42	1.587
L	1.16	1.42	1.555
M	2.72	3.01	1.027
N	2.25	2.72	1.884

Legend: (A) Demand and/or pressure from customers. (B) The pressure from competition in the line of business. (C) Pressure from the suppliers. (D) To reduce costs. (E) To improve customer service. (F) To shorten lead time and to reduce stock. (G) To increase sales. (H) To improve internal efficiency. (I) To strengthen relations with business partners. (J) The possibility to reach new customers/markets. (K) To improve our competitiveness. (L) External support. (M) To improve our marketing. (N) To improve possibilities of control and follow-ups.

Table 9. A comparison of the rating of importance of barriers to adopting e-commerce between respondents that were members of a small business strategic alliance and respondents that were not

	Mean members	Mean nonmembers	t value
A	3.14	2.27	-2.597*
B	2.92	2.27	-1.949
C	2.65	2.47	.542
D	2.86	1.81	3.408***
E	2.84	2.21	-1.937
F	2.11	1.77	-1.169
G	2.29	1.84	-1.541
H	2.38	2.05	-1.069
I	2.33	2.52	.557
J	2.41	2.11	-.907

*Note: * significant to .05 ; *** significant to .001*

Legend: (A) E-commerce is not suited to our products/services. (B) E-commerce is not suited to our way of doing business. (C) E-commerce is not suited to the ways our clients (customers and/or suppliers) do business. (D) E-commerce does not offer any advantages to our organisation. (E) We do not have the technical knowledge in the organisation to implement e-commerce. (F) E-commerce is too complicated to implement. (G) E-commerce is not secure. (H) The financial investment required to implement e-commerce is too high for us. (I) We do not have time to implement e-commerce. (J) It is difficult to choose the most suitable e-commerce standard with so many different options available.

Table 10. A comparison of the rating of importance of benefits derived from adopting e-commerce between respondents that were members of a small business strategic alliance and respondents that were not

	Mean members	Mean nonmembers	t value
A	2.85	2.76	-.384
B	2.64	2.80	.300
C	2.15	2.11	-.148
D	2.82	2.75	-.271
E	1.85	2.06	.847
F	2.51	2.43	-.341
G	2.57	2.87	1.208
H	2.56	2.50	-.244
I	2.67	2.95	1.106
J	2.00	1.97	-.154
K	2.92	2.90	-.082

Legend: (A) Lower administration costs. (B) Lower production costs. (C) Reduced lead time. (D) Reduced stock. (E) Increased sales. (F) Increased internal efficiency. (G) Improved relations with business partners. (H) New customers and markets. (I) Improved competitiveness. (J) Improved marketing. (K) Improved quality of information.

Table 11. A comparison of the rating of importance of disadvantages incurred through the adoption of e-commerce between respondents that were members of a small business strategic alliance and respondents that were not

	Mean members	Mean nonmembers	t value
A	1.16	1.29	.912
B	1.59	1.98	1.923*
C	1.89	2.24	1.728*
D	1.59	1.94	2.146**
E	1.44	1.83	1.650*
F	1.05	1.25	2.642*
G	1.16	1.41	1.110

*Note: * significant to .05 ; ** significant to .01*

Legend: (A) Deterioration of relations with business partners. (B) Higher costs. (C) Increased computer maintenance. (D) Doubling of work. (E) Reduced flexibility of work. (F) Security risks. (G) Dependence on e-commerce.

Table 10 provides the data for the perception of importance of benefits derived from e-commerce adoption and use.

A number of studies (Ciappei & Simoni, 2005; Daniel & Wilson, 2002; Daniel, Wilson, & Myers, 2002; Singh & Gilchrist, 2002) have shown that SMEs that are part of some form of strategic alliance benefit more from the adoption and use of e-commerce than those that stand-alone. An examination of Table 10 shows that for the regional Swedish SME respondents, this appears not to be the case.

Table 11 provides the data for the perception of disadvantages incurred through the adoption and use of e-commerce.

An examination of Table 11 shows that five disadvantages showed a statistically significant difference between member and nonmember respondents. While both sets of respondents rated the disadvantage as fairly unimportant, respondents that were not members of a small business strategic alliance perceived these disadvantages as being more important than member respondents. A number of studies (Dennis, 2000; Overby & Min, 2000) have suggested that membership of a strategic alliance dissipates difficulties and disadvantages for their members. The data in Table 11 seems to support this view.

As already indicated, a number of authors (Blackburn & Athayde, 2000; Fallon & Moran, 2000; MacGregor & Vrazalic, 2005; Matlay, 2000; Riquelme, 2000) have shown that factors such as business size, business age, business sector, and market focus appear to impinge on measures of e-commerce adoption. As such, those barriers and disadvantages that showed a statistical significant difference between member and nonmember respondents were examined to determine whether these differences were specific to particular subgroups of the sample. The data was sepa-

Table 12. Comparison of means of e-commerce barriers in small business subdivided by business size, business age, business sector, and market focus

Barrier	Member of an alliance mean	Nonmember mean	t-value
Business age (10-20 yrs) E-com. not suited to prod/servs	2.40	3.55	2.129*
Business size (0 employees) E-com. not suited to prod/servs E-com shows no advantage	1.13 1.00	2.94 3.35	2.274* 3.499**
Business sector (service) E-com shows no advantage	1.78	2.90	2.146*
Business sector (retail) E-com. not suited to prod/servs E-com shows no advantage	1.40 1.20	3.00 3.29	2.553* 3.715***
Market focus (local) E-com shows no advantage	2.65	3.46	2.219*

*Note: * significant to .05 ; ** significant to .01 ; *** significant to .001*

Table 13. Comparison of means of e-commerce disadvantages in small business subdivided by business size, business age, business sector, and market focus

Disadvantage	Member of an alliance mean	Nonmember Mean	t-value
Business size (10-19 employees) Reduced flexibility	1.61	1.00	3.275***
Business sector (service) Security	1.40	1.00	2.246*
Business sector (retail) Doubled work	2.89	1.45	2.103*
Market focus (local) Security	1.70	1.22	2.086*
Market focus (national) Doubled work	1.91	1.30	2.289*

*Note: * significant to .05 ; ** significant to .01 ; *** significant to .001*

rately subdivided by business size, business age, business sector, and market focus, and a series of two-tailed t-tests was applied to determine whether the perception of those barriers and disadvantages differed significantly between respondents that were members of an alliance and those respondents that were not. Tables 12 and 13 provide the overall findings.

Australia

Table 14 provides the results of the two-tailed t-tests for criteria to adopt e-commerce.

An examination of Table 14 shows that, for the Australian respondents, there was a statistically significant difference in the rating of importance of four criteria (pressure from competition, the possibility of reaching new customers and markets, improvement to competitiveness, and the offer of external support) between respondents that were members of a small business strategic alliance and respondents that were not. In all cases, those that were not members of a small business strategic alliance rated these higher in importance than those that were members. One possible explanation, supported by previous studies (Jorde & Teece, 1989; Marchewka & Towell, 2000)

Table 14. A comparison of the rating of importance of criteria to adopt e-commerce between respondents that were members of a small business strategic alliance and respondents that were not

Criteria	Mean members	Mean nonmembers	t value
A	1.90	3.20	-1.983
B	1.40	3.53	-4.290***
C	1.80	1.73	.096
D	3.50	3.47	.047
E	3.20	4.00	-1.362
F	2.10	2.93	-1.255
G	2.70	4.13	-2.135
H	3.20	4.13	-1.352
I	1.00	1.00	0
J	2.50	4.13	-2.349*
K	2.60	4.20	-2.238*
L	1.40	2.07	-2.991**
M	2.90	3.73	-1.310
N	2.80	3.73	-1.415

*Note: * significant to .05 ; ** significant to .01; *** significant to .001*

Legend: (A) Demand and/or pressure from customers. (B) The pressure from competition in the line of business. (C) Pressure from the suppliers. (D) To reduce costs. (E) To improve customer service. (F) To shorten lead time and to reduce stock. (G) To increase sales. (H) To improve internal efficiency. (I) To strengthen relations with business partners. (J) The possibility to reach new customers/markets. (K) To improve our competitiveness. (L) External support. (M) To improve our marketing. (N) To improve possibilities of control and follow-ups.

Table 15. A comparison of the rating of importance of barriers to adopting e-commerce between respondents that were members of a small business strategic alliance and respondents that were not

	Mean members	Mean nonmembers	t value
A	3.26	3.26	0
B	3.39	3.45	-.201
C	4.12	3.25	1.864
D	2.91	3.42	-1.707
E	2.76	3.20	-1.292
F	2.71	3.14	-1.346
G	2.79	2.86	-.218
H	2.24	3.09	-2.719**
I	2.82	3.06	-.735
J	2.50	2.77	-.843

*Note: * significant to .05 ; ** significant to .01 ; *** significant to .001*

Legend: (A) E-commerce is not suited to our products/services. (B) E-commerce is not suited to our way of doing business. (C) E-commerce is not suited to the ways our clients (customers and/or suppliers) do business. (D) E-commerce does not offer any advantages to our organisation. (E) We do not have the technical knowledge in the organisation to implement e-commerce. (F) E-commerce is too complicated to implement. (G) E-commerce is not secure. (H) The financial investment required to implement e-commerce is too high for us. (I) We do not have time to implement e-commerce. (J) It is difficult to choose the most suitable e-commerce standard with so many different options available.

is that many of the criteria for e-commerce adoption had been achieved through membership of the alliance. This, however, raises the question as to why other criteria failed to show any statistically significant differences.

Table 15 provides the data for barriers to e-commerce adoption.

An examination of Table 15 shows that the perception of importance of one barrier, "cost too high," showed a statistically significant difference between respondents that were members of an alliance and respondents that were not. The data shows that nonmember respondents felt that this was a more important barrier than member respondents. Again, one possible explanation is that membership reduces the importance of this barrier. This is in line with the findings of Jorde and Teece (1989) and Marchewka and Towell (2000). Again, however, this raises the question as to why only one barrier showed any significant difference. It also raises the question as to why the barrier "e-commerce is not suited to the way our customers do business," while not statistically significant, has a higher rating of importance by the member respondents.

Table 16 provides the data for the benefits derived from e-commerce adoption and use.

Before examining the data in Table 16 in detail, a number of comments should be made. Firstly, the low response rate due to the low adoption rates in Australia

Table 16. A comparison of the rating of importance of benefits derived from adopting e-commerce between respondents that were members of a small business strategic alliance and respondents that were not

	Mean members	Mean nonmembers	t value	Significance
A	3.30	3.13	.257	.799
B	1.50	2.53	-1.428	.167
C	1.60	2.67	-1.742	.095
D	2.10	2.47	-.499	.623
E	1.00	2.40	-2.095*	.047
F	1.80	3.33	-2.815**	.010
G	3.30	3.87	-.963	.346
H	#	#	#	#
I	2.20	3.33	-1.604	.122
J	2.10	3.93	-3.051**	.006
K	2.50	3.80	-2.100*	.047

*Note: # insufficient data ; * significant to .05 ; ** significant to .01 ; *** significant to .001*

Legend: (A) Lower administration costs. (B) Lower production costs. (C) Reduced lead time. (D) Reduced stock. (E) Increased sales. (F) Increased internal efficiency. (G) Improved relations with business partners. (H) New customers and markets. (I) Improved competitiveness. (J) Improved marketing. (K) Improved quality of information.

needs to be noted when considering the data in Table 16. While statistically these low figures have been accounted for procedurally, the use of the data in terms of wider inferences needs to be done with caution. Secondly, with the exception of the benefit "reduced administration costs," the perception of benefits is higher for the nonmember respondents than the member respondents. At first glance this appears to refute the earlier studies (Ciappei & Simoni, 2005; Cirillo, 2000; Daniel & Wilson, 2002; Daniel et al., 2002; Terziovski 2003,), however, one possible explanation is that many of the benefits tested in this study have been achieved through membership of a small business strategic alliance, and are, thus, less perceptibly important in e-commerce adoption and use.

An examination of Table 16 shows that four benefits (increased sales, improvement to marketing, improved internal efficiency, and improved quality of information) showed a statistically significant difference between member and nonmember respondents.

Table 17 provides the details for the disadvantages incurred through the adoption and use of e-commerce.

Again, the low response rate due to the low adoption rates in Australia needs to be noted when considering the data in Table 17. While statistically these low figures

Table 17. A comparison of the rating of importance of disadvantages incurred through the adoption of e-commerce between respondents that were members of a small business strategic alliance and respondents that were not

	Mean members	Mean nonmembers	t value
A	1.00	2.00	0.647
B	1.10	2.07	-1.897
C	2.30	4.13	-2.935**
D	1.10	2.87	-3.750***
E	1.50	2.07	-1.187
F	2.10	3.27	-1.715
G	1.00	2.27	-1.715

*Note: * significant to .05 ; ** significant to .01 ; *** significant to .001*

Legend: (A) Deterioration of relations with business partners. (B) Higher costs. (C) Increased computer maintenance. (D) Doubling of work. (E) Reduced flexibility of work. (F) Security risks. (G) Dependence on e-commerce.

have been accounted for procedurally, the use of the data in terms of wider inferences needs to be done with caution.

Two disadvantages, "increased maintenance" and "doubling of work," showed a statistically significant difference between respondents that were members of a small business strategic alliance and respondents that were not. Nonmember respondents rated both of these disadvantages as significantly higher than member respondents. A number of studies have suggested that membership of some form of alliance "dampens" the effect of disadvantages. This appears to be the case with the disadvantages "increased maintenance" and "doubling of work," but is not in evidence with any of the other disadvantages tested for.

As with the Swedish responses, those measures that showed a statistically significant difference (member − nonmember) were examined to determine whether these differences were specific to particular subgroups of the sample. Again, the data was separately subdivided by business size, business age, business sector, and market focus, and a series of two-tailed t-tests was applied to determine whether the perception of those barriers and disadvantages differed significantly between respondents that were members of an alliance and those respondents that were not. Unfortunately, there was insufficient data to examine the criteria, benefits, or disadvantages (due to the low adoption levels in the Australian sample). Table 18 provides the data for the barriers to e-commerce.

Table 18. Comparison of means of e-commerce barriers in small business subdivided by business size, business age, business sector, and market focus

Barrier	Member of an alliance mean	Nonmember mean	t-value
Business sector (retail) Cost too high	4.00	2.67	3.218**

*Note: * significant to .05 ; ** significant to .01 ; *** significant to .001*

Discussion

As the results for the Swedish and Australian studies have been presented separately, it is appropriate to firstly consider each of them separately, and then to provide a more general discussion.

Sweden

An examination of Tables 8 and 10 indicate that there are no differences between strategic alliance members and nonmembers when it comes to criteria and benefits. This suggests that being a member of a small business strategic alliance does not necessarily imply a different set of drivers, or criteria would replace those criteria already established when considering e-commerce adoption. Indeed, the level of importance of those criteria appears not to be affected by membership of a small business strategic alliance. Similarly, membership does not imply greater benefits through the use of e-commerce.

An examination of Table 9 shows that two barriers, "e-commerce is not suited to our products/services" and "e-commerce does not offer any advantages to our organisation," showed a statistically significant difference between member and nonmember respondents. The mean rating for the barriers was higher for member respondents than for nonmembers. At first glance, it may be argued that the results refute the notion that strategic alliances reduce the effect of barriers to e-commerce; however, an alternative view might be that alliance members are better placed to judge the value of e-commerce to their particular situation.

The data was subdivided by business size, business age, business sector, and market focus to determine whether differences (member – nonmember) were specific to particular subgroups of the sample. An examination of Table 12 shows that the barrier "e-commerce is not suited to our products/services" appeared to be specific to businesses that were 10- 20-years old, sole traders, and the retail sector. One possibility is that these businesses are perhaps less flexible to change than other small business groups. The barrier "e-commerce does not offer any advantages to our organisation" was specific to sole traders, both the retail and service sectors, and small businesses trading locally. Again, as small businesses trading locally would be more likely to deal with customers face-to-face, compared to regional, national, or international businesses, e-commerce might not offer the same advantages as to the other groups. Similarly, as service-oriented businesses are less likely to provide specific products, e-commerce may not be a viable option.

An examination of Table 13 shows that three disadvantages, "reduced flexibility," "security, and "doubling of work," appeared to be more specific to one or more subgroups of the sample. Security was rated higher by nonmember respondents from the service sector and also by those that traded locally, compared to member respondents. Two different groups, retailers and those businesses that traded nationally, showed a significant difference in the rating of doubling of work between the two groups, while nonmember respondents that had between 10 and 19 employees rated flexibility higher than member respondents. While membership in a small business strategic alliance appears to "soften" the disadvantages for its members, this "softening" appears to be only specific to particular disadvantages and particular sections of the overall small business sector.

Australia

The Australian sample differs from the Swedish findings. In Australian small businesses, several e-commerce criteria, barriers, benefits, and disadvantages show significant differences between alliance members and nonmembers. Where adoption criteria are concerned, four criteria were different between the two groups, with nonmembers consistently rating the criteria higher than members. Particularly surprising was that nonmembers rated "external support" higher than members, since one of the benefits of membership of an alliance is the access to resources and support.

The e-commerce barriers show a different picture, although nonmembers, as expected, rated barriers higher than member respondents. However, this difference was significant in only one instance related to the cost of adoption.

E-commerce benefits indicated an unexpected result in that alliance members generally rated these lower than nonmembers. Four benefits relating to sales, marketing, quality of information, and internal efficiency showed significant differences. In the case of the increased sales, members gave the benefit a mean rating of 1. One possibility is that members had already achieved a number of these benefits through alliance membership, rather than e-commerce adoption.

Finally, in relation to disadvantages of e-commerce adoption, security risks were rated highly by nonmembers. Indeed, this was the only disadvantage that showed a significant difference between the two groups. Considering one of the roles of an alliance is to dissipate the impact of disadvantages, it is interesting to note that only one disadvantage showed any significant difference.

As with the Swedish study, the data was separated by business age, business size, business sector, and market focus. Table 18 shows that only one subgroup (retail) showed any significant difference.

A Comparison of the Two Studies

A comparison of the results across the two locations shows a number of divergent views. In Sweden, there were no significant differences between members and nonmembers for any of the adoption criteria. This is in contrast to the Australian respondents who had four criteria showing significant differences. This would appear to suggest that in the Swedish context, belonging to an alliance is not an incentive to adopt e-commerce. However, in Australia, small businesses that belong to an alliance showed a difference in four criteria. These criteria are mainly related to competition/competitiveness, new customer and markets, and the availability of external support. All the nonmembers rated these higher than members, suggesting that belonging to an alliance may already afford access to these.

In Sweden, all but one of the barriers was rated higher by members than nonmembers, however, only two showed a significant difference (member – nonmember). By contrast, only one barrier, "high costs," surfaced in the Australian study. Indeed, the studies show that while member respondents found the barriers more important in Sweden, the opposite was the case in the Australian situation.

In relation to benefits, the Swedish data showed that there were no significant differences between members and nonmembers. In Australia, four benefits differed between the two groups. These were related to sales, marketing, internal efficiency, and quality of information. In all four cases, the nonmember respondents rated these higher than the member respondents.

Five disadvantages (increased costs, increased computer maintenance, doubling of work, flexibility of work, and security) showed a significant difference in the Swedish study. The Australians were in agreement with their Swedish counterparts on two of the disadvantages (increased computer maintenance and doubling of work). In both studies, nonmembers rated the disadvantages higher, which would tend to support the findings of Achrol and Kotler (1999) and Overby and Min (2001), who suggest that difficulties are dissipated by strategic alliances.

Since this is the first time this type of research has been undertaken, it is difficult to support the results through previous studies. However, the current study indicates that factors such as business size, business age, business sector, and market focus appear to impinge on the role of the strategic alliance. These findings provide a direction for further in-depth research to determine the role of these factors on strategic alliances.

Limitations

It should be noted that the study presented here has several limitations. Firstly, the membership/nonmembership of some type of SME strategic alliance may be biased by the lack of geographic proximity to other SMEs needed to form and maintain some type of viable alliance. It may also be biased by the perception of the respondent as to what constitutes an SME strategic alliance. Secondly, the choice of variables selected for the study is somewhat problematic because of the complex nature of e-commerce criteria, which change over time. Furthermore, according to Sohal and Ng (1998), the views expressed in the surveys are of a single individual from the responding organisation, and only those interested in the study are likely to complete and return the survey. However, previous empirical studies (Raymond, 2001) have demonstrated this methodology to be valid. Finally, this is a quantitative study, and further qualitative research is required to gain a better understanding of the key issues.

Conclusion

Unlike previous studies that have focussed on SMEs that are part of a strategic alliance, the data presented in this paper has attempted to compare and contrast those SMEs that are part of a strategic alliance with those that are not in relation to the reasons they have adopted e-commerce. The results of the study show that the role of the small business strategic alliance in the adoption of e-commerce cannot be generalised across all measures of the adoption process. Nor, indeed, can they be generalised across all locations. For example, while four criteria and four benefits differed in the Australian study, no such differences were found in the Swedish study. The results also showed that differences (member – nonmember) appeared only to exist in certain subgroupings of the entire small business sector.

The results of this study are significant for several reasons. This has been the first attempt at understanding the relationship between strategic alliance membership and e-commerce. The research presented here indicates that this relationship is worthy of further examination because by formally explicating it, researchers and government organisations engaged in promoting e-commerce adoption will have more comprehensive knowledge about the organisational factors that have an effect on the relationship, and will be able to provide better advice to regional SMEs on e-commerce adoption.

However, a number of questions still remain unanswered. Firstly, are small business strategic alliances more applicable to specific sections of the entire small business sector? Secondly, are small business strategic alliances only applicable to certain measures of e-commerce adoption? Finally, are small business strategic alliances "unique" to particular locations?

Acknowledgment

The authors would like to acknowledge the assistance of Professor Sten Carlsson and Monika Magnusson from Karlstad University in collecting the data in Sweden.

References

Abell, W., & Limm, L. (1996). *Business use of the Internet in New Zealand: An exploratory study*. Retrieved from http//www.scu.edu.au/sponsored/ausweb96

Achrol, R. S., & Kotler, P. (1999). Marketing in the network economy. *Journal of Marketing, 63*(special issue), 146-163.

Acs, Z. J., Morck, R., Shaver, J. M., & Yeung, B. (1997). The internationalisation of small and medium sized enterprises: A policy perspective. *Small Business Economics ,9*(1), 7-20.

Auger, P., & Gallaugher, J. M. (1997). Factors affecting adoption of an Internet-based sales presence for small businesses. *The Information Society, 13*(1), 55-74.

Australian Bureau of Statistics. (2001). Retrieved December 10, 2005, from http://www.abs.gov.au

Barnett, R. R., & Mackness, J. R. (1983). An action research study of small firm management. *Journal of Applied Systems, 10,* 63-83.

Barry, H., & Milner, B. (2002). SME's and electronic commerce: A departure from the traditional prioritisation of training? *Journal of European Industrial Training, 25*(7), 316-326.

Black, J. S., & Porter, L. W. (2000). *Management: Meeting new challenges*. Englewood, NJ: Prentice Hall.

Blackburn, R., & Athayde, R. (2000). Making the connection: The effectiveness of Internet training in small businesses. *Education and Training, 42*(4/5).

Blair, T. (2000). UK prime minister. Press release regarding the launch of UK Online opengov site 11th September.

Blili, S., & Raymond, L. (1993). Threats and opportunities for small and medium-sized enterprises. *International J. of Information Management, 13*, 439-448.

Brigham, E. F., & Smith, K. V. (1967). The cost of capital to the small firm. *The Engineering Economist, 13*(1), 1-26.

Bunker, D. J., & MacGregor, R. C. (2000). Successful generation of information technology (IT) requirements for small/medium enterprises (SMEs). In *Proceedings of SMEs in a Global Economy* (pp. 72-84). Wollongong, Australia.

Chellappa, R., Barua, A., & Whinston, A. (1996). Looking beyond internal corporate Web servers. In R. Kalakota & A. Whinston (Eds.), *Readings in electronic commerce* (pp. 311-321). Reading, MA: Addison Wesley.

Christopher, M. L. (1999). Creating the agile supply chain. In D. L. Anderson (Ed.), *Achieving supply chain excellence through technology* (pp. 28-32). San Francisco: Montgomery Research Inc.

Ciappei, C., & Simoni, C. (2005). Drivers of new product success in the Italian sport show cluster of Montebelluna. *Journal of Fashion Marketing and Management, 9*(1), 20-42.

Cirillo, R., (2000). The new rules: Move beyond 'E' ... and eight other strategies for competing in the new economy—A new generation of e-business consultants is playing by a different set of rules. Nine of them to be exact. Are you up to speed? *Varbusiness, 1612*, 26.

Cochran, A. B. (1981). Small business mortality rates: A review of the literature. *Journal of Small Business Management, 19*(4), 50-59.

Cragg, P. B., & King, M. (1993). Small firm computing: Motivators and inhibitors. *MIS Quarterly, 17*(1), 47-60.

Cropper, S. (1996). Collaborative working and the issue of sustainability. In C. Huxham (Ed.), *Creating collaborative advantage* (pp. 80-100). London: Sage.

Culkin, N., & Smith, D. (2000). An emotional business: A guide to understanding the motivations of small business decision takers. *Qualitative Market Research: An International Journal, 3*(3), 145-157.

Dahlstrand, A. L. (1999). Technology-based SMEs in the Goteborg region: Their origin and interaction with universities and large firms. *Regional Studies, 33*(4), 379-389.

Damanpour, F. (2001). E-business e-commerce evolution: Perspective and strategy. *Managerial Finance, 27*(7), 16-33.

Daniel, E., & Wilson, H. (2002). Adoption intentions and benefits realised: A study of e-commerce in UK SMEs. *Journal of Small Business and Enterprise Development, 9*(4), 331-348.

Daniel, E., Wilson, H., & Myers, A. (2002). Adoption of e-commerce by SMEs in the UK. *International Small Business Journal, 20*(3), 253-268.

Datta, D. (1988). International joint ventures: A framework for analysis. *Journal of General Management, 14*, 78-91.

Delone, W. H. (1988). Determinants for success for computer usage in small business. *MIS Quarterly,* 51-61.

Dennis, C. (2000). Networking for marketing advantage. *Management Decision, 38*(4), 287-292.

Domke-Damonte, D., & Levsen, V. B. (2002). The effect of Internet usage on cooperation and performance in small hotels. *SAM Advanced Management Journal,* 31-38.

Donckels, R., & Lambrecht, J. (1997). The network position of small businesses: An explanatory model. *Journal of Small Business Management, 35*(2), 13-28.

Doukidis, G., Poulymenakou, A., Terpsidis, I, Themisticleous, M., & Miliotis, P. (1998). *The impact of the development of electronic commerce on the employment situation in European commerce.* Athens University of Economics and Business.

Doukidis, G. I., Smithson, S., & Naoum, G. (1992). Information systems management in Greece: Issues and perceptions. *Journal of Strategic Information Systems, 1*, 139-148.

Drakopoulou-Dodd, S., Jack S., & Anderson, A. R. (2002). Scottish entrepreneurial networks in the international context. *International Small Business Journal, 20*(2), 213-219.

Europa—The European Commission. (2003). *SME Definition.* Retrieved December 15, 2003, from http://europa.eu.int/comm/enterprise/enterprise_policy/sme_definition /index_en.htm

Evans, P. B., & Wurster, T. S. (1997). Strategy and the new economics of information. *Harvard Business Review,* 70-82.

Fallon, M., & Moran, P. (2000). Information communications technology (ICT) and manufacturing SMEs. *2000 Small Business and Enterprise Development Conference* (pp. 100-109). University of Manchester.

Frazer, L., & Lawley, M. (2000). *Questionnaire design and administration.* Wiley.

Fuller T. (2000). The small business guide to the Internet: A practical approach to going online. *International Small Business Journal, 19*(1), 105-107.

Gaskill, L. R., & Gibbs, R. M. (1994). Going away to college and wider urban job opportunities take highly educated youth away from rural areas. *Rural Development Perspectives, 10* (3), 35-44.

Gaskill, L. R., Van Auken, H. E., & Kim, H. (1993). The impact of operational planning on small business retail performance. *Journal of Small Business Strategy, 5*(1), 21-35.

Gessin, J. (1996). Impact of electronic commerce on small and medium sized enterprises. *Management,* 11-12.

Giaglas, G., Klein S., & O'Keefe, R. (1999). Disintermediation, reintermediation, or cybermediation? The future of intermediaries in electronic marketplaces. *12ᵗʰ Bled Electronic Commerce Conference.*

Gilliland, D. I., & Bello, D. C. (1997). The effect of output controls, process controls, and flexibility on export channel performance. *Journal of Marketing, 6*(1), 22-38.

Gustafsson, R., Klefsjo, B., Berggren, E., & Granfors-Wellemets, U. (2001). Experiences from implementing ISO 9000 in small enterprises: A study of Swedish experiences. *The TQM Magazine, 13*(4), 232-246.

Hadjimonolis, A. (1999). Barriers to innovation for SMEs in a small less developed country (Cyprus). *Technovation, 19*(9), 561-570.

Henning, K. (1998). *The digital enterprise. How digitisation is redefining business.* New York: Random House Business Books.

Hill, R., & Stewart, J. (2000). Human resource development in small organisations. *Journal of European Industrial Training, 24*(2/3/4), 105-117.

Hutt, M. D., & Speh, T. W. (1998). *Business marketing management: A strategic view of industrial and organisational markets.* Fort Worth, TX: Dryden Press.

Iacovou, C. L., Benbasat, I., & Dexter, A. S. (1995). Electronic data interchange and small organisations: Adoption and impact of technology. *MIS Quarterly, 19*(4), 465-485.

Jarratt, D. G. (1998). A strategic classifiaction of business alliances: A qualitative perspective built from a study of small and medium-sized enterprises. *Qualitative Market Research: An International Journal, 1*(1), 39-49.

Jeffcoate, J., Chappell, C., & Feindt, S. (2002). Best practice in SME adoption of e-commerce. *Benchmarking: An International Journal, 9*(2), 122-132.

Johannisson, B., Ramirez-Pasillas, M., & Karlsson, G. (2002, August). Theoretical and methodological challenges bridging firm strategies and contextual tetworking. *Entrepreneurship and Innovation,* 165-174.

Jorde, T., & Teece, D. (1989). Competition and cooperation: Striking the right balance. *Californian Management Review, 31,* 25-38.

Kai-Uwe Brock, J. (2000). Information and technology in the small firm. In S. Carter & Jones-Evans (Eds.), *Enterprise and the Small Business* (pp. 384-408). Prentice Hall, Pearson Education.

Keeble, D., Lawson, C., Moore, B., & Wilkinson, F. (1999). Collective learning processes, networking and 'institutional thickness' in the Cambridge region. *Regional Studies, 33*(4), 319-332.

Kendall, J. E., & Kendall, K.E. (2001). A paradoxically peaceful coexistence between commerce and e-commerce. *Journal of Information Technology, Theory and Application, 3*(4), 1-6.

Keniry, J., Blums, A., Notter, E., Radford, E., & Thomson, S. (2003). *Regional business: A plan for action.* Department of Transport and Regional Services. Retrieved December 13, 2003, from http://www.rbda.gov.au/action_plan

Larsson, E., Hedelin, L., & Gärling, T. (2003). Influence of expert advice on expansion goals of small businesses in rural Sweden. *Journal of Small Business Management, 41*(2), 205-212.

Lawrence, K. L. (1997). Factors inhibiting the utilisation of electronic commerce facilities in Tasmanian small-to-medium sized enterprises. *8th Australasian Conference on Information Systems* (pp. 587-597).

Lee, C. S. (2001). An analytical framework for evaluating e-commerce business models and strategies. *Internet Research: Electronic Network Applications and Policy, 11*(4), 349-359.

MacGregor, R. C., & Bunker, D.J. (1996a). Does experience with IT vendors/consultants influence small business computer education requirements. In *Association of Information Systems Proceedings of the Americas Conference on Information Systems* (pp. 31-33). Phoenix, AZ.

MacGregor, R. C., & Bunker, D. J.(1996b), The effect of priorities introduced during computer acquisition on continuing success with IT in small business environments. *Information Resource Management Association International Conference* (pp. 271-277). Washington.

MacGregor, R. C., Bunker, D. J., & Waugh, P. (1998, June). Electronic commerce and small/medium enterprises (SMEs) in Australia: An electronic data interchange (EDI) pilot study. In *Proceedings of the 11th International Bled Electronic Commerce Conference*, Slovenia.

MacGregor, R. C., & Vrazalic, L. (2005). The effects of strategic alliance membership on the disadvantages of electronic commerce adoption: A comparative study of Swedish and Australian regional small business. *Journal of Global Information Management, 139*(3), 1-19.

Marchewka, J. T., & Towell, E. R. (2000). A comparison of structure and strategy in electronic commerce. *Information Technology and People, 13*2, 137-149.

Markland, R. E. (1974). The role of the computer in small business management. *Journal of Small Business Management, 12*(1), 21-26.

Martin, L. M., & Matlay, H. (2001). "Blanket" approaches to promoting ICT in small dirms: Some lessons from the DTI ladder adoption model in the UK. *Internet Research: Electronic Networking Applications and Policy, 11*(5), 399-410.

Matlay, H. (2000). Training in the small business sector of the British economy. In S. Carter & D. Jones (Eds.), *Enterprise and small business: Principles, policy and practice.* London: Addison Wesley Longman.

McRea, P. (1996). Reshaping industry with the Internet. *Management,* 7-10.

Meredith, G. G. (1994). *Small business management in Australia* (4th ed.).

McGraw Hill, Miles, G., Preece, S., & Baetz, M. C. (1999). Dangers of dependence: The impact of strategic alliance use by small technology based firms. *Journal of Small Business Management,* 20-29.

Miller, N. L., & Besser, T. L. (2000). The importance of community values in small business strategy formation: Evidence from rural Iowa. *Journal of Small Business Management, 38*(1), 68-85.

Murphy, J. (1996). *Small business management.* London: Pitman.

Nalebuff, B. J., & Brandenburg, A. M. (1996). *Co-operation.* Philadelphia: Harper Collins Business.

National Office of the Information Economy. (1998). *A strategic framework for the information economy: Identifying priorities for action.* Australian Commonwealth Government

Nooteboom, B. (1994). Innovation and diffusion in small firms: Theory and evidence. *Small Business Economics, 6*(5), 327-347.

O'Donnell, A., Gilmore, A., Cummins, D., & Carson, D. (2001). The network construct in entrepreneurship research: A review and critique. *Management Decision, 39*(9), 749-760.

Overby, J. W., & Min, S. (2001). International supply chain management in an Internet environment: A network-oriented approach to internationalisation. *International Marketing Review, 18*(4), 392-420.

Phan, D. D. (2003). E-business development for competitive advantages: A case study. *Information & Management, 40,* 581-590.

Poon, S., & Joseph, M. (2001). A preliminary study of product nature and electronic commerce. *Marketing Intelligence & Planning, 19*(7), 493-499.

Poon, S., & Strom, J. (1997). Small business use of the Internet: Some realities. *Association for Information Systems Americas Conference,* Indianapolis.

Poon, S., & Swatman, P. (1997). The Internet for small businesses: An enabling infrastructure. *Fifth Internet Society Conference* (pp. 221-231).

Porter, M. (2001). Strategy and the Internet. *Harvard Business Review,* 63-78.

Power, D. J., & Sohal, A. S. (2002). Implementation and usage of electronic commerce in managing the supply chain: A comparative study of ten Australian companies. *Benchmarking: An International Journal, 92*, 190-208.

Price Waterhouse and Coopers. (1999). *SME electronic commerce study final report, 37.*

Purao, S., & Campbell, B. (1998, August 14-16). Critical concerns for small business electronic commerce: Some reflections based on interviews of small business owners. In *Proceedings of the Association for Information Systems Americas Conference* (pp. 325-327). Baltimore.

Quayle, M. (2002). E-commerce: The challenge for UK SMEs in the twenty-first century. *International Journal of Operations and Production Management, 22*10, 1148-1161.

Raisch, W. D. (2001). *The e-marketplace: Strategies for success in B2B.* New York: McGraw-Hill.

Raymond, L. (2001). Determinants of Web site implementation in small business. *Internet Research: Electronic Network Applications and Policy, 11*(5), 411-422.

Reimenschneider, C. K., & McKinney, V. R. (2001). Assessing beliefs in small business adopters and non-adopters of Web-based e-commerce. *Journal of Computer Information Systems, 42*2, 101-107.

Reimenschneider, C. K., & Mykytyn, P. P., Jr. (2000). What small business executives have learned about managing information technology. *Information & Management, 37,* 257-267.

Reuber, A. R., & Fischer, E. (1999). Understanding the consequences of founders' experience. *Journal of Small Business Management, 3*(2), 30-45.

Reynolds, W., Savage, W., & Williams, A. (1994). *Your own business: A practical guide to success.* ITP.

Riquelme, H. (2002). Commercial Internet adoption in China: Comparing the experience of small, medium and large business. *Internet Research: Electronic Networking Applications and Policy, 12*(3), 276-286.

Ritchie, R., & Brindley, C. (2000). Disintermediation, disintegration and risk in the SME global supply chain. *Management Decision, 38*8, 575-583.

Roberts, M., & Wood, M. (2002). The strategic use of computerised information systems by a micro enterprise. *Logistics Information Management, 15*(2), 115-125.

Robertson, T., & Gatignon, H. (1986). Competitive effects on technology diffusion. *Journal of Marketing, 50.*

Rotch, W. (1967). *Management of small enterprises: Cases and readings.* University of Virginia Press

Senn, J. A. (1996). Capitalisation on electronic commerce. *Information Systems Management.*

Singh, J. P., & Gilchrist, S. M. (2002). Three layers of the electronic commerce network: Challenges for the developed and developing worlds. *Info, 42*, 31-41.

Sparkes, A.. & Thomas, B. (2001). The use of the Internet as a critical success factor for the marketing of Welsh agri-food SMEs in the twenty first century. *British Food Journal, 103*(4), 331-347.

Sohal, A. S., & Ng, L. (1998). The role and impact of information technology in Australian business. *Journal of Information Technology, 13*(3), 201-217.

Stauber, A. (2000). *A survey of the incorporation of electronic commerce in Tasmanian small and medium sized enterprises.* Tasmanian Electronic Commerce Centre.Storper, M. (1995). The resurgence of regional economies, ten years later: The region as a nexus of untraded interdependencies. *European Urban and Regional Studies, 2*(3), 191-221.

Swartz, T. A., & Iacobucci, D. (Eds.). *Handbook of services marketing and management.* CA: Sage.

Terziovski, M. (2003). The relationship between networking practices and business excellence: A study of small to medium enterprises (SMEs). *Measuring Business Excellence, 7*(2), 78-92.

Tetteh, E., & Burn, J. (2001). Global strategies for SME-business: Applying the SMALL framework. *Logistics Information Management, 14*(1-2), 171-180.

Tikkanen, H. (1998). The network approach in analysing international marketing and purchasing operations: A case study of a European SME's focal net 1992 -95. *Journal of Business and Industrial Marketing, 13*(2), 109-131.

Treacy, M., & Wiersema, F. (1997). *The discipline of market leaders.* Cambridge MA: Perseus Press.

Turban, E., King, D., Lee, J.. Warkentin, M., & Chung, H. M. (2002). *Electronic commerce.* Englewood, NJ: Prentice Hall.

Turban, E., Lee, J., King, D., & Chung, H. (2000). *Electronic commerce: A managerial perspective.* Englewood, NJ: Prentice Hall.

Van Akkeren, J., & Cavaye, A. L. M. (1999, December 1-3). Factors affecting entry-level Internet technology adoption by small business in Australia: An empirical study. In *Proceedings of the 10th Australasian Conference on Information Systems*, Wellington, New Zealand.

Venkatesan, V. S., & Fink, D. (2002). Adoption of Internet technologies and e-commerce by small and medium enterprises (SMEs) in Western Australia. In *Proceedings of the Information Resource Management Association International Conference* (pp. 1136-1137).

Vescovi, T. (2000). Internet communication: The Italian SME case. *Corporate Communications: An International Journal, 5*(2), 107-112.

Vrazalic, L., Bunker, D., MacGregor, R. C., Carlsson, S.. & Magnusson, M. (2002). Electronic commerce and market focus: Some findings from a study of Swedish small to medium enterprises. *Australian Journal of Information Systems, 10*(1), 110-119.

Walczuch, R., Van Braven, G., & Lundgren, H. (2000). Internet adoption barriers for small firms in the Netherlands. *European Management Journal, 18*(5), 561-572.

Walker, E. W. (1975). Investment and capital structure decision making in small business. In E. W. Walker (Ed.), *The dynamic small firm: Selected readings.* Austin, TX: Austin Press.

Welsh, J. A., & White, J. F. (1981). A small business is not a little big business. *Harvard Business Review.*

Westhead, P., & Storey, D. J. (1996). Management training and small firm performance: Why is the link so weak? *International Small Business Journal, 14*(4), 13-24.

Wynarczyk, P., Watson, R., Storey, D. J., Short, H., & Keasey, K. (1993). *The managerial labour market in small and medium sized enterprises.* Routledge.

Yeung, H. W. (1994). Critical reviews of geographical perspectives on business organisations and the organisation of production: Towards a network approach. *Progressive Human Geography, 18*(4), 460-490.

Chapter VIII

E-Business Integration by SMEs in the Manufacturing Sector:
A Data Envelopment Analysis Approach

Roman Beck, Johann Wolfgang Goethe University, Germany

Rolf T. Wigand, University of Arkansas at Little Rock, USA

Wolfgang Koenig, Johann Wolfgang Goethe University, Germany

Abstract

SMEs in the manufacturing industry are impacted by enormous changes in their business processes. E-business-related developments have reduced the importance of physical branches and moved towards more sophisticated, e-business-enabled supply chains for products and services. This contribution analyzes the differences in adoption behavior and actual use of e-business applications among 152 investigated SMEs in the manufacturing sector from four countries. Best practice cases of efficient e-business performance, such as in Denmark or the U.S., are identified by deploying a data envelopment analysis (DEA). Leading SMEs in the sample are characterized by a wide range of thoroughly implemented and integrated e-business applications, resulting in higher satisfaction rates.

Introduction

The diffusion of IT and e-business applications has received broad attention among practitioners as well as academicians (Cooper & Zmud, 1990; Dekleva, 2000; Kiiski & Pohjola, 2002), especially in the context of supply chain management, interorganizational cooperation, and the integration of heterogeneous partners including small- to medium-sized enterprises (SMEs) (Beck, Weitzel, & König, 2002; Beck, Wigand, & König, 2005). Apart from theoretical deficiencies in the field of standardization theory and resulting network effects, there is a lack of comparable empirical data on business networks, especially at the international level. One of the most challenging tasks within and, even more, across industries is the electronic, seamless integration of SMEs within supply chains. This is largely due to the still insufficient diffusion of commonly accepted communication standards and solutions that are capable to provide benefits even to SMEs. In many developed countries, SMEs are regarded as the economic backbone that adds to the relevance of their adoption and usage behavior of e-business standards for economies.

At the same time, SMEs have to cope with a variety of difficulties that usually impede the successful integration of e-business solutions, for example, the existence of an inadequate ERP system, lack of IT know-how, or not-yet-automated internal business processes as a prerequisite to gaining benefits from exchanging business messages electronically (Willems, Hampton, & Ketler, 1997). In the pre-Internet and e-business era, SMEs were often forced by larger business partners to implement certain exchange standards, such as EDI, to communicate with them, disregarding if the SME can also benefit from such efforts or not. Since SMEs are playing a vital role in most supply networks, even large business partners have recognized now that it is important to cooperate with SMEs in a way allowing them to also benefit from supply chain management (George, Wood, & Khan, 2001).

Otherwise, SMEs are often predicted to be more flexible and innovation friendly than large firms when it comes to using new applications to conduct their business more efficiently, for example, in the manufacturing sector. At the same time, SMEs are more restricted in their budget than large firms, and are often not able to vie with large competitors due to the high setup costs of, for example, Web-enabled materials management systems or Web-based shopping systems. Moreover, SMEs have more difficulties in attracting IT specialists for their business. Due to their size, SMEs often cannot benefit from economies of scale; nor do they deploy sophisticated distribution systems in comparison to large enterprises (König, Wigand, & Beck, 2003).

Therefore, SMEs are focusing and evaluating the return on investment of IT spending more carefully and conservatively. In order to convince them to adopt a new e-business solution, it is even more important then for large firms to demonstrate the successful integration and likely success upfront. The systematic difference in perceived usefulness between SMEs and large firms when regarding the same e-business application makes it necessary to research SME-specific drivers and barriers of e-business adoption and usage. In order to gain the most out of the implementation of e-business applications, it is pivotal for SMEs to adopt the right set, which has to be integrated thoroughly into the existing IT infrastructure. Only if this condition is fulfilled, e-business has a strong positive impact on both the improvement of processes and the expansion of markets in a satisfying way, especially when operating on an international level.

This contribution provides empirical results based on a survey conducted during the summer of 2002 by International Data Corporation (IDC) on behalf of the underlying research project. We have researched SMEs that are defined as enterprises with 25 to 249 employees that used at least a material management or ERP system and had a connection to the Internet. The research analyzes the implementation and usage differences in the manufacturing industry in three European countries (Denmark, France, and Germany) as well as the U.S. Although European countries have different demand drivers (industry structure, information infrastructure, financial and human resources, and social and cultural factors), they have to cope with the same productivity gap (Farrell, Fassbender, Kneip, Kriesel, & Labaye, 2003), the same EU regulations of the common market, and nearly the same e-business readiness and historical diffusion paths (Kraemer & Dedrick, 2000; Kraemer, Dedrick, & Dunkle, 2000). These analogies, but also differences investigated among those mid-European SMEs in the survey, are analysed against the results of the survey from the U.S. Due to these national and industrial path dependencies in the diffusion of e-business applications, a comparison of the two largest economies on continental Europe (France and Germany), with innovative and e-business-leading countries such as the U.S. and Denmark, was chosen to identify differences and best practice cases in the manufacturing industry.

In what follows, this chapter provides a short description of innovation diffusion theories and their limitations. Next, important results of the empirical survey are presented, together with a data envelopment analysis (DEA) to identify efficient SMEs in each country as an international benchmark. We conclude with a summary about SMEs' behavior in adopting of innovative technologies and the related impact on operational process efficiency.

Diffusion of Innovations

The term diffusion is generally defined as "the process by which an innovation is communicated through certain channels over time among the members of a social system" (Rogers, 1983, p. 5). The traditional economic analysis of diffusion focuses on describing and forecasting the adoption of products in markets. In particular, the question of which factors (drivers and barriers) influence the speed and specific course of diffusion processes arises (Weiber, 1993). Traditional diffusion models are based on similar assumptions: generally, the number of new adopters in a certain period of time is modeled as the proportion of the group of market participants that have not yet adopted the innovation. Based on this fundamental structure, three different types of diffusion models are most common (Lilien & Kotler, 1983, pp. 706-740; Mahajan & Peterson, 1985, pp. 12-26; Weiber, 1993): The exponential diffusion model (also external influence model or pure innovative model) assumes that the number of new adopters is determined by influences from outside the system, for example, mass communication. The logistic diffusion model (also internal influence model or pure imitative model) assumes that the decision to become a new adopter is determined solely by the positive influence of existing adopters (e.g., word of mouth). The semilogistic diffusion model (also mixed influence model) considers both internal and external influences.

Although these theories are able to explain the process of diffusion, in general, they fail in the area of explaining the impact of innovation on existing organization structures or the measuring of improvements that will hopefully result in increased efficiency, as a result of insufficiently installed accounting or measuring methods. If the increased usage of innovations has impact on intermediary goods that exist but cannot be measured, then the impact should be visible at least on the output side. But even measuring these spillover effects seems to be difficult, although PCs and the Internet have doubtless created additional consumer surplus (Gordon, 2000). Furthermore, these models do not explain the real-world phenomena of different adoption decisions for SMEs and large enterprises at the same time, nor do they give any information about the role of "gun-to-the-head" adoption pressures of large business partners on small enterprises. Although the nature of e-business applications is more or less the same in the manufacturing industry, each country is following its own diffusion path, based on national differences in competition, IT infrastructure, business concentration, governmental regulations, or even mentality. Consequently, this chapter provides an inside view of the different drivers and barriers resulting in the various paths of diffusion in the four countries.

Identifying Efficient SMEs: A DEA Description

For a better understanding of the national differences in e-business diffusion among SMEs in the countries studied, the underlying empirical questionnaire comprised 50 questions to globalization, use of e-business technologies, use of the Internet, drivers, and barriers to e-business adoption, and to online sales, procurement, and services. The survey itself was conducted via telephone interviews by IDC during the period of February 18, 2002 to April 5, 2002. A predetermined number of interviews were completed to ensure an adequate sample to report on at the 95% confidence level. The survey was successfully conducted in four countries with altogether 152 SMEs from the manufacturing industry in Denmark (35 firms), Germany (33 firms), France (34 firms), and the United States (50 firms). The sample was stratified by size (SMEs) and by industry (manufacturing SIC 20-39). The survey included only SMEs that used the Internet to buy, sell, or support products or services. All 152 firms studied belonged to this category.

For analyzing the relative efficiency of e-business-deploying SMEs in the manufacturing sector, a data envelopment analysis (DEA) is used (Charnes, Cooper, & Rhodes, 1978). Efficiency in this context is defined as the perceived impact on business processes, aggregated as satisfaction indicator on a five-point scale, ranging from a level of e-business impact of "not at all" (1) to "a great deal" (5) and based on the individual set of IT and e-business implementations. SMEs with a high satisfaction index based on the IT and e-business infrastructure in place may be defined as *efficient* in comparison to the rest of SMEs in the four-country sample.

The focal object of interest in a DEA model is the decision-making unit (DMU), which is here equivalent to a firm. A DMU is a flexible unit responsible for the in- and output variables. DEA compares each DMU with the "most efficient" DMUs of the sample. Efficient DMUs characterized by combinations of input and output relations form the so-called "efficient frontier line". In a multidimensional room, the efficient frontier is equivalent to an imaginary "cloak" at the top of the entire data sample, including all efficient DMUs and representing all theoretically possible combinations of efficient combinations or virtual DMUs. The DEA model calculates the relative position inside the data sample for each DMU, based on its set of inputs and set of outputs. Using a linear programming procedure for the frontier analysis of inputs and outputs, DEA here evaluates the "best-practice" users of e-business technologies. The basic idea of DEA is the multi-input and multi-output-oriented efficiency evaluation without any further assumptions about the structure of the data sample (e.g., normal distribution). Unlike parametric methods, DEA can use all kinds of input and output data to analyze the productivity or efficiency level of each data set within the sample. The DEA model used was neither input- nor output-oriented because neither an input-minimizing (input-oriented) nor an output-maximizing (output-oriented) analysis was necessary to evaluate the observed, actual input/output relation identified in the survey. Moreover, the model assumes varying returns of scale for each DMU depending on the size and a concave function of decreasing returns. The software used for the data analysis, together with a detailed description, is available in Scheel (2004).

In comparison to traditional methods, the DEA model needs no assumptions about the productivity function of a company, with the exception of the given assumption that productivity is following a monotonely increasing and concave curve. A further difference between DEA and traditional analysis methods, such as regression analysis, is that DEA derives the efficient frontier line from the combination of in- and output relations, while regression functions use a maximum-likelihood approach to identify the average input-output curve with a general tendency. This may be useful to compare the average e-business efficiency impact with other countries, but it can hardly be used to identify best practice cases and benchmarks within the national data set. Different kinds of DEA models were used in diverse ways to measure the impacts of IT, for example, in the banking industry (Barr, Killgo, Siems, & Zimmel, 1999) or in the distribution industry (Beck, König, & Wigand, 2003).

Here the DEA was used as follows: as input variables for the DEA model, the results of seven questions about the set of e-business applications used are utilized (cf., Table 2), measuring the number of adopted technologies necessary to conduct e-business as a binary variable. Variables are coded as 0 when an establishment uses the asked for technology and 1 if it does not. The coding is equivalent to more input costs when e-business is not available or vice-versa, that is, firms using e-business gain benefits by reducing their processing costs.

Input variables (Internet usage indicator) = u (online advertising, online sales, online procurement ..., same formal business processes along supply chain)

s. t. $u_i \in \{0;1\}$

The 10 output variables—aggregated to an e-business satisfaction index—of the model are measured on a five-point scale with 1 ("no impact at all") to 5 ("a great deal") and comprise the results of the following questions: internal processes more efficient, staff productivity increased, sales and national/international sales area increased, customer service improvement, procurement and inventory costs decreased, coordination with suppliers improved and competitive position improved (cf., Table 4).

Output variables (E-commerce satisfaction index) = v (internal process more efficient, staff productivity increased ..., competitive position improved)

s. t. $v_j \in \{1;2;3;4;5\}$

The basic formula of the chosen model is similar to the CCR model (Charnes et al., 1978):

$$\max \theta = \frac{\displaystyle\sum_{j=1}^{s} v_j y_j}{\displaystyle\sum_{i=1}^{t} u_i x_i}$$

The previous formulation cannot be solved by linear programming tools and therefore has to be transformed in the following equation, which is an output-oriented maximization example:

$$\max = \sum_{j=1}^{s} v_j y_j \text{ with constant input } \sum_{i=1}^{t} u_i x_i = 1$$

$$\sum_{i=1}^{t} u_i x_i \leq \sum_{j=1}^{s} v_j y_j$$

with s. t. $u_i \geq 0, v_j \geq 0$

Efficiency in this context is the benefit gained, based on the e-business application used improving efficiency or productivity. SMEs with a high satisfaction index based on the installed e-business-enabling infrastructure may be defined as efficient in comparison to other SMEs of the sample. DEA identifies the best practice cases or the efficient establishments within the sample. Firms that are investigated as being part of the "efficient frontier line" are relatively more efficient than the rest of the firms below the frontier line. For a better explanation of the results, the average of "efficient" and "inefficient" establishments are calculated and therefore, the efficient frontier line is not shown in Figure 3. The 7 input variables are aggregated to an Internet usage indicator, while the 10 output variables resemble an average e-business satisfaction index. For simplicity's sake, the input variables are used unweighted so that each e-business-enabling technology has the same explanatory weight or loading for the efficiency of DMUs.

Results of the Four Country SMEs Survey in the Manufacturing Sector

E-Business Readiness and Usage in the Manufacturing Sector

In most developed countries, the manufacturing industry (as part of the industry sector) is the second-largest economic sector after the service sector. Due to market globalization, manufacturers and their suppliers are increasingly forced to intensify and improve their business relations within their internationalized supply chain in order to stay competitive. Therefore, one possible solution to meet this challenge is to increase the level of interorganizational integration or cooperation respectively (Oliver & Webber, 1992). For SMEs, this implies more than just being "EDI-ready" for larger business partners; it is not unusual that they have to reorganize their internal business processes first before they can start thinking about e-business-based supply chain management. Moreover, it is not sufficient to simply adopt e-business-enabling technologies, but to master and integrate them to efficiently use these e-business applications. Very often, the most challenging task is not the handling of the new technology, but the organizational willingness to change existing business processes and to cooperate on an interorganizational level (Swaminathan, Smith, & Sadeh, 1998). This involves the sharing of information and knowledge that was originally considered as being proprietary or even of strategic importance. Since a supply chain cannot be optimized as long as one or more players are not able to share important information with their business partners, especially the integration of SMEs, and their information technology (IT) into supply chains has been focused on lately to perform joint procurement, shipping, and production decisions (Beck & Weitzel, 2005; Lee, 1998). For this reason, the first step towards a sound supply chain is the investigation of the available IT technologies among SMEs within an industry such as in manufacturing.

In fact, our research on the overall diffusion and adoption of e-business applications has revealed that a high level of diffusion was reached already in 2002 within the countries surveyed. As Table 1 indicates, the use of e-mail has become a common tool in everyday work. In the underlying data sample, Danish SMEs, in particular, are at the forefront in the field of Internet-based services in comparison to other countries or manufacturing sectors investigated. The differences in the diffusion of e-business technologies among SMEs in each country have various reasons. Market size, for instance, has a major impact on diffusion. Feeling the competitive pressure from abroad is, consequently, an important factor for Danish SMEs to adopt international e-business standards faster, in contrast to U.S. SMEs that mainly serve the enormous national market. Similar to Danish SMEs, German SMEs have a long

Table 1. SMEs e-business readiness in the manufacturing sector by country (Source: Own survey, conducted by IDC, 2002)

	Denmark	France	Germany	USA
Use of e-mail	100.0%	94.1%	100.0%	98.0%
Public Web site	91.4%	61.8%	90.9%	84.0%
Use of intranet	74.3%	67.6%	69.7%	44.0%
Use of extranet	40.0%	38.2%	36.4%	26.0%
Use of EDI	48.6%	64.7%	51.5%	54.0%
Use of electronic funds transfer	82.9%	23.5%	90.9%	50.0%
Use of call centers	31.4%	20.6%	21.2%	50.0%

Table 2. SMEs e-business usage in the manufacturing sector by country (Source: Own survey, conducted by IDC, 2002)

	Online Sales	After sales customer services	Online procurement	EDI with suppliers	EDI with customers	Internet-based supply chain management
Denmark	65.7%	31.4%	45.7%	74.3%	54.3%	54.3%	25.7%
France	32.4%	8.8%	17.6%	20.6%	44.1%	52.9%	23.5%
Germany	75.8%	27.3%	42.4%	51.5%	51.5%	57.6%	21.2%
USA	72.0%	26.0%	60.0%	76.0%	44.0%	64.0%	34.0%

Average Increasing Complexity of Integration →

tradition in exporting all kinds of machinery and equipment, and have also adopted quickly. Apart from globalization, further important factors influencing national adoption behavior are technological path dependency and differences in mentality. Only to give one example, according to our survey, French SMEs deploying sophisticated EDI technologies could hardly find any additional benefit in switching to Internet-based solutions and, moreover, they have been reluctant to adopt foreign technologies as long as national industry champions do not use them.

Based on the large installed base of established e-business-enabling technologies in the manufacturing sectors, e-business is used to improve all kinds of internal and external business processes (cf., Table 2).

While in Table 1, Danish enterprises reported the highest availability of e-business technologies on average, in the field of e-business use, U.S. SMEs are leading, especially in the field of more sophisticated and complex applications such as electronic data exchange with customers (64.0%) or Internet-based supply chain management (34.0%). While German SMEs use, with 75.8%, online advertising more often than any other manufacturing sector, only 32.4% of French SMEs used these technologies at the same time. Online sales services are more often provided in Denmark than anywhere else (31.4%), together with EDI with suppliers (54.3%). SMEs in the U.S. use the facilities more often by deploying after sales customer services (60.0%) and online procurement (76.0%).

E-Business Drivers and Barriers in the Manufacturing Sector

The reasons for implementing e-business technologies also vary among the countries surveyed, depending on the time lag in innovation diffusion behavior in each country, as well as on the different drivers and inhibitors, which are also closely related to national tradition and mentality.

Figure 1 depicts the drivers of e-business yielded by the survey, using a five-point scale, where 1 corresponds to "not a factor at all" and 5 to "a very significant factor." Alphabetically ordered by country, important drivers for SMEs to adopt e-business technologies are provided. Although online procurement has more importance than

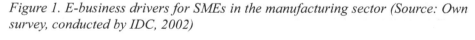

Figure 1. E-business drivers for SMEs in the manufacturing sector (Source: Own survey, conducted by IDC, 2002)

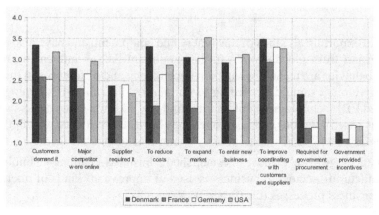

Figure 2. E-business impeding reasons for SMEs in the manufacturing sector (Source: Own survey, conducted by IDC, 2002)

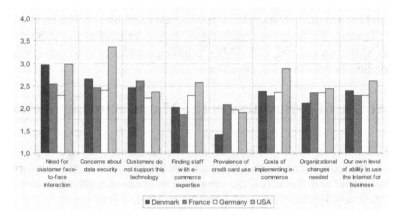

online sales (cf., Table 2), more pressure to implement e-business-enabling technologies seems to be exercised by the customer side than by the supplier side. The most important drivers in Denmark, Germany, and the U.S. are the possibility of reducing costs by implementing e-business solutions, the expansion of markets, together with the ability to improve coordination with customers and suppliers. The latter reason is also of importance in France, while on average France reported the lowest level of rated drivers. The government's contribution to the diffusion of e-business seems to be rather unimportant in all countries surveyed. With the exception of Denmark, where online business with government seems to require some kind of e-business applications, SMEs in the manufacturing sector do not regard the impact of the government as a driving factor.

Conversely, and apart from the e-business drivers, the questionnaire also investigated the most important factors impeding SMEs doing business online (cf., Figure 2). Analogous to Figure 1, a five-point scale was used where 1 corresponded to "not an obstacle" and 5 to "a very significant obstacle." The sequence of results in Figure 2 is randomly ordered. Interestingly, SMEs in the U.S. rated the highest obstacles on average. While the need for customer face-to-face interaction is not as important in Germany or France, U.S. or Danish SMEs rate this obstacle as an important hindering factor. U.S. SMEs, followed by Danish and French ones, regard security reasons as important obstacles. While the obstacles in the field of technology support on the customer side, or the bottleneck of e-business-skilled staff is more of a problem in France and the U.S., the prevalence of credit cards for online shopping is not seen as an important impeding factor in all countries, especially not in Denmark. An often-mentioned barrier for SMEs is the high cost of integrating e-business applications into an existing in-house IT infrastructure. U.S. SMEs regard this as an important barrier. With regard to mandatory organizational changes, U.S. SMEs, followed by German and French ones, responded at the highest rated levels. The level of ability to use the Internet for their own business is seen as critical in the U.S., followed by Danish SMEs. In general, U.S. SMEs believe themselves to be confronted with more impeding factors than European ones.

Efficient Use of E-Business in the Manufacturing Sector

After the descriptive, empirical insights into the manufacturing sector provided in the previous section, here the DEA is used to gain some more detailed information. E-business output and, therefore, the impact of e-business application on business process efficiency depend directly on a consistent implementation and a high degree of intensity.

In order to analyze the impact of e-business on business efficiency, the DEA approach, as described in the following, uses the 152 data sets, which are our decision-making units (DMU). The results of the DEA analysis are used to select the efficient (marked by *) from the inefficient DMUs. A DMU is "efficient" if there is no other comparable data set that performs better according to its multi-input and multi-output coordinates. Vice versa, "inefficient" DMUs are characterized by input and output relations that are dominated by efficient DMUs generating higher output with the same input, or needing less input for the same output. In Figure 3, the results of the DEA are provided. On average, efficient SMEs in the U.S. use 67.5%, in Denmark 81.8%, in France 46.4%, and in Germany 64.3% of the seven e-business applications used as input for the Internet-usage indicator (cf., Table 2). The impact on business improvement is measured by the satisfaction index for efficient SMEs, with an index of 3.0 in Germany, 3.1 in France, and 3.2 each for Denmark and the U.S. As output variables for the DEA, we have used the data that are provided in aggregated form in Table 4 for each DMU.

The largest differences between efficient and inefficient SMEs in the availability of e-business applications, as well as the resulting satisfaction, are observable in Denmark. While inefficient French SMEs deploy only 18.4% fewer e-business applications, the differences between efficient and inefficient SMEs in Denmark are, with 47.5%, or in the U.S., with 23.6%, quite large. There seems to be a larger divide between strong and effectively e-business-applying SMEs on the one side and SMEs with, in fact, many e-business applications in place, but insufficient use.

Interestingly, efficient French SMEs derive a higher satisfaction from e-business in contrast to German ones with only 46.4% of all available e-business technologies. One possible explanation might be the innovative character of e-business, which is embraced more enthusiastically in France. Another explanation might be

Figure 3. Results of the DEA analyses (Source: Own survey, conducted by IDC, 2002)

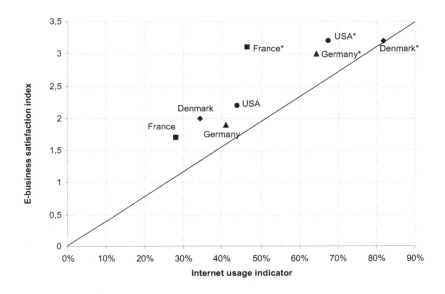

Table 3. Percentage of efficient SMEs in the sample per country (Source: IDC, 2002)

	Denmark	France	Germany	USA
Efficient	31.4%	13.3%	31.3%	44.9%

larger efficiency potentials of even fewer e-business technologies in France than in Germany.

While Figure 3 only indicates the percentage of e-business applications and the resulting satisfaction among efficient and inefficient firms, it provides no information about the percentage of inefficient and efficient SMEs in each country. The percentage of efficient SMEs per country, identified by the DEA method, is provided in Table 3.

Only 13.3% of French and 31.3% of German SMEs are efficient users of e-business at the international level, gaining nearly as much process improvement and satisfaction from these applications as efficient Danish or U.S. SMEs. While, with 31.4%, Danish SMEs are equal to German ones (31.3%), the efficiency ratio in the U.S. is, with 44.9%, quite high.

Table 4. Impact of doing business online, that is, percent indicating impact is a great deal (Source: Own survey, conducted IDC, 2002)

	Denmark	France	Germany	USA
Internal processes more efficient	31.4%	26.5%	36.4%	32.0%
Staff productivity increased	28.6%	11.8%	12.1%	24.0%
Sales increased	22.9%	2.9%	12.1%	22.0%
Sales area widened	20.0%	8.8%	18.2%	40.0%
Customer service improved	48.6%	20.6%	18.2%	34.0%
International sales increased	17.1%	5.9%	12.1%	14.0%
Procurement costs decreased	20.0%	11.8%	0.0%	18.0%
Inventory costs decreased	11.4%	8.8%	3.0%	4.0%
Coordination with suppliers improved	28.6%	23.5%	27.3%	28.0%
Competitive position improved	28.6%	2.9%	18.2%	34.0%

Drivers and barriers, as well as the efficient use of e-business, have impacts on internal and external business processes. Detailed information on the resulting process improvements are provided in Table 4, where SMEs in the manufacturing sector per country are provided who responded "a great deal (4 or 5 on a five-point scale)" as the impact of employing e-business technologies on their business.

Overall, the highest impact, in comparison to other countries, is reported in Denmark. Only in three e-business areas are other countries leading, such as internal process improvements, where Germany leads with 36.4%, or in the areas of widening sales (40%) and improvement of competitive position (34%), where U.S. SMEs are leading.

Conclusion

SMEs in the manufacturing industry have been impacted by enormous changes in their business processes. The diffusion of e-business technologies and related developments have reduced the importance of physical branches and reengineered and improved supply chains by using more sophisticated e-business applications for the necessary information flows.

While German SMEs in the manufacturing industry invested heavily in the development of their IT and e-business infrastructure, it seems that the targeted efficiency gains had not yet been completely achieved. Nevertheless, IT innovation, or the fast adoption of innovative techniques and technologies in Denmark, Germany, and the U.S., is a critical factor in order to be successful today and in the future. It appears that French SMEs still have quite a substantial growth potential in the field of e-business implementation and usage.

France and Germany, however, have different demand drivers (industry structure, information infrastructure, financial and human resources, as well as social and cultural factors), but are united in experiencing an increased productivity gap and a time lag in the diffusion of e-business in comparison to the U.S. and Denmark. From the U.S. perspective, one might expect a common SMEs landscape all over Europe due to EU common market regulations. While this—to some extent—is true, there are also very different national business environments for SMEs, such as the strong dependency of SMEs on large so-called business champions in France, which has resulted in an awaiting and innovation-preventing climate in the manufacturing sector. SMEs in small countries such as Denmark benefit from their long export tradition and international market relations, which had promoted an early adoption and diffusion of e-business accompanied by supportive governmental initiatives. SMEs in the German manufacturing industry have also benefited, to a small extent, from governmental programs and funding, but definitely more from industry associations coordinating e-business standards, marketplaces, and knowledge transfer. The heterogeneities investigated in the diffusion of e-business technologies and use confirmed the authors' opinion that it is important to understand industrial and national differences better to learn from best practice cases.

Although the nature of e-business applications is more or less the same, each manufacturing sector or country is following its own diffusion path, based on national differences in competition, IT infrastructure, business concentration, governmental regulations, or even mentality. Consequently, this work provides an inside view of the different drivers and barriers leading to various paths of e-business diffusion among SMEs in four different industrialized countries.

Acknowledgment

This research is supported by a grant from the German National Science Foundation ("IT-Standards and Network Effects," Grant No. 220352). This research is also part of the Globalization and E-Commerce Project of the Center for Research on Information Technology and Organizations (CRITO) at the University of California, Irvine. This material is based upon work supported by the National Science Foundation under Grant No. 0085852. Any opinions, findings, and conclusions or recommendations expressed in this material are those of the authors and do not necessarily reflect the views of the National Science Foundation.

References

Barr, R. S., Killgo, K. A., Siems, T. F., & Zimmel, S. (1999). *Evaluating the productive efficiency and performance of U.S. commercial banks.* (Working Paper 99-3). Federal Reserve Bank of Dallas.

Beck, R., König, W., &Wigand, R. T. (2003). The efficient usage of e-commerce applications by SMEs in the retail/wholesale industry: A four-nation comparison. In *Proceedings of the Americas Conference on Information Systems* (pp. 697-706). Tampa, FL.

Beck, R., & Weitzel, T. (2005). Some economics of vertical standards: Integrating SMEs in EDI supply chains. *International Journal of Electronic Markets, 15*(4), 313-322.

Beck, R., Weitzel, T., & König, W. (2002). The myth of WebEDI. In J. Monteiro, P. M. C. Swatman, & L. Valadares Tavares (Eds.), *Towards the knowledge society, eCommerce, eBusiness and eGovernment* (pp. 585-599). Norwell, MA: Kluwer Academic Publishers.

Beck, R., Wigand, R. T., & König, W. (2005). The diffusion and efficient use of electronic commerce in small and medium-sized enterprises: An international three-industry survey. *International Journal of Electronic Markets, 15*(1), 38-52.

Charnes, A. W., Cooper, W., & Rhodes, E. (1978). Measuring the efficiency of decision making units. *European Journal of Operations Research, 2*, 429-444.

Cooper, R. B., & Zmud, R. W. (1990). Information technology implementation research: A technological diffusion approach. *Management Science, 36*(2), 123-139.

Dekleva, S. (2000). Electronic commerce: A half-empty glass? *Communications of the AIS, 3*, 2-99.

Farrell, D., Fassbender, H., Kneip, T., Kriesel, S., & Labaye, E. (2003). Reviving French and German productivity. *The McKinsey Quarterly,* (1), 40-47.

George, G., Wood, D. R., & Khan, R. (2001). Networking strategy of boards: Implications for small and medium-sized enterprises. *Entrepreneurship & Regional Development, 13*, 269-285.

Gordon, R. J. (2000). Does the new economy measure up to the great inventions of the past? *Journal of Economic Perspectives, 14*(4), 49-74.

Kiiski, S., & Pohjola, M. (2002). Cross-country diffusion of the Internet. Information. *Economics and Policy, 14*, 297-310.

König, W., Wigand, R. T. & Beck, R. (2003). Globalization and e-commerce: Environment and policy in Germany. *Communications of the Association for Information Systems, 10*, 33-72.

Kraemer, K. L., & Dedrick, J. (2000). *European EC report*, Center for Research on Information Technology and Organizations, University of California, Irvine. Retrieved May 1, 2003, from http://www.crito.uci.edu/git/publications/pdf/european-EC-report2.pdf

Kraemer, K. L., Dedrick, J., & Dunkle, D. (2000). *EC in the United States: Leader or one of the pack?* Center for Research on Information Technology and Organizations, University of California, Irvine. Retrieved July 24, 2006, from http://www.crito.uci.edu/publications/pdf/GIT/GEC/ USsnapshot.pdf

Lee, H. L. (1998). Postponement of mass customization. In J. Gattorna (Ed.), *Strategic supply chain alignment. Best practice in supply chain management* (pp. 77-91). Aldershot, Hampshire, UK: Gower Publishing Limited.

Lilien, G. L., & Kotler, P. (1983). *Marketing decision making. A model building approach*. New York: Harper & Row.

Mahajan, V., & Peterson, A. P. (1985). *Models for innovation diffusion*. Thousand Oaks, CA: Sage Publications.

Oliver, R. K., & Webber, M. D. (1992). Supply chain management: Logistics catches up with strategy. In M. Christopher (Ed.), *Logistics: The strategic issue* (pp. 63-75). London: Chapman & Hall, London.

Rogers, E. M. (1983). *Diffusion of innovations* (3rd ed.). New York: Free Press.

Scheel, H. (2004). EMS: Efficiency measurement system. Retrieved July 24, 2006, from http://www.wiso.uni-dortmund.de/lsfg/or/scheel/ems/

Swaminathan, J. M., Smith, S. F., & Sadeh, N. M. (1998). Modelling supply chain dynamics: A multiagent approach. *Decision Sciences, 29*(3), 607-632.

Weiber, R. (1993). Chaos: Das Ende der klassischen Diffusionsforschung? *Marketing ZFP, 1,* 35-46.

Willems, J. R., Hampton, V., & Ketler, K. (1997). The EDI implementation decision: A small business perspective. In *Proceedings of the Association for Computing Machinery* (pp. 70-76).

Chapter IX

Small Firms and Offshore Software Outsourcing:
High Transaction Costs and Their Mitigation

Erran Carmel, American University, USA

Brian Nicholson, Manchester Business School, UK

Abstract

It seems surprising that small firms engage in offshore outsourcing given that they lack the resources that large firms possess to overcome the difficulties involved. We examine these factors using transaction cost theory's three stages: contact costs, contract costs, and control costs. Then, using our field data from small client firms (in the United States and the United Kingdom), intermediaries, and offshore vendors, we analyze the mitigation approaches that reduce transaction costs for small firms. We identify nine such approaches: three for client firms and six for suppliers. For the small client firm, they are liaisons of knowledge flows, gaining experience, and overcoming opportunism; and, for the service providers, they are onshore presence, reducing contact costs, simplifying contracting, providing control channels, expert intermediaries, and standardization of services.

Introduction

Over the last decade, many firms in the U.S. and Western Europe have outsourced software development tasks to offshore sites in countries such as India, Russia, and the Philippines. More than 50% of the American Fortune 500 firms and an increasing proportion of Western European and Japanese firms are users of offshore software sourcing (Carmel & Agarwal, 2002; Sahay, Nicholson, & Krishna, 2003). Research on onshore or domestic information-systems outsourcing has significantly enhanced our understanding of why such firms outsource software development (Lacity & Hirschheim, 1993) and how relationships may be effectively managed with appropriate risk mitigation, coordination, and control strategies (for example, Kern & Willcocks, 2000; Lacity & Willcocks, 2001; Levina & Ross, 2003; Sabherwal, 1999, 2003). Other scholars and practitioners have drawn attention to the particular difficulties presented by offshore software outsourcing (Apte, 1990; Kumar & Willcocks, 1999; Nicholson & Sahay, 2001). Communication may be impacted by technical issues such as telecommunications infrastructure, cultural differences, accents, and language ability (Walsham, 2001). Time-zone differences may lead to coordination difficulties (Carmel, 1999). Often the offshore team lacks domain knowledge in the business application in question, and transferring this knowledge is hampered by distance (Sahay et al., 2003).

This prior research in onshore and offshore software sourcing has improved our understanding of the management of software outsourcing and the additional complexities presented in offshore relationships. However, most of this research has centered on large organizations that have the internal resources to address the problems of managing across time and space. Therefore, in this chapter our approach is to focus on the issues faced by small companies when sourcing[1] software offshore.

We have noticed in the course of our related research, fieldwork, conference attendance, and consultancy that an increasing amount of offshore sourcing of software development work is taking place between small client firms and offshore vendors in India and other countries. This trend looks set to continue. Small and large firms have chosen to outsource for a number of reasons such as skills shortages, cost, capacity, flexibility, and a "bandwagon effect" (Heeks, 1995; Lacity & Hirschheim, 1993). We have encountered cases of small U.S. and UK technology firms engaging in offshore software development since the late 1990s. At that time, the growth of the Indian IT industry was closely linked to the demand for skills from Europe and the U.S. for Y2K (year 2000) alleviation and subsequently the demand for development skills in dot-com companies. During the late 1990s, small UK and American technology firms faced a recruitment crisis due to the high cost of IT skills and the inability to provide the perks and career paths that large companies could offer. Access to scarce skills was shown to be a major driver in the cases of Sierra (Nicholson & Sahay, 2004; Nicholson, Sahay, & Krishna, 2000; Sahay et al.,

2003) and Harlequin Solutions (Ballard, 2003), which are both small technology firms that sourced software development in India during the late 1990s. After the dot-com bust and U.S. economic downturn post-2001, the Indian IT industry has continued to grow despite recession in the UK and the U.S. ("Nasscom Indian IT Industry: A Success Story," 2004). This is largely because the highly competitive American and British IT services market compelled technology firms into sourcing software offshore in order to cut production costs.

Our sample of small firms is comprised of American and British firms, so we note these two nations' propensity to source offshore. First, small American and British firms are more likely to source offshore than small firms from other nations (Aepple, 2004; Sonwalkar, 2004). The second point is inferential; since, as is repeatedly stated in the media, a greater proportion of U.S. firms have been outsourcing than firms in Europe, it is likely that a greater proportion of small American firms have been outsourcing than in the U.K. Nevertheless, the forecasts for the UK suggest growth. According to Datamonitor, IT spending by UK smaller firms is estimated to rise from \$76 billion in 2002 to \$109 billion by 2006 (Mortleman, 2003). Inevitably, as outsourcing increases from small companies and becomes common practice, offshore firms will be striving to compete.

Defining "small firm"[2] is controversial (D'Amboise & Muldowney, 1988; Nooteboom, 1993) as there is no single definition mainly because of the wide diversity of sectors and business types, and different treatments in different nations. We use as our guideline the definition from Section 248 of the UK Companies Act (1985)[3] that a small firm employs 50 or less employees. Even though the vast majority of firms of all sizes are small firms, little is known about the magnitude of offshore software outsourcing by small firms[4], although Ansberry (2003) found that 60% of companies with fewer than 500 employees were planning expenditures of more than \$1 million in the following 12 months on all types of outsourcing including IT, manufacturing, and logistics—both domestic and offshore.

In this article, we posit that small firms face relatively high transaction (coordination) costs when undertaking offshore software sourcing. This is because small firms are disadvantaged relative to large firms in a wide range of resources crucial to coordination (DeLone, 1981; Pollard & Hayne, 1998). Resources for travel, research, and control are tight. Small firms must deal with the relative shortage of management staff and with personnel-recruitment disadvantages. In small firms, the entrepreneur is often involved in operational and managerial tasks and therefore his or her time is scarce. Usually small firms have no specialized staff for finance, legal affairs, or information technology, and thus are less likely to have the resources in-house for strategic software development projects. Communications improvements commonly used in large firms such as videoconferencing or other collaborative technologies may be financially prohibitive for the small firm. When outsourcing, small firms have higher search costs due to limited staff support, and they incur relatively high set-up costs relative to the transaction size. Furthermore, small firms tend to have fewer documented sources of information, and this results in them being more inscrutable to transaction partners (Nooteboom, 1993).

As we noted, the majority of research on software outsourcing, whether on- or offshore, does not make distinctions between constructs as they apply to small or large firms. However, the case of Sierra (Nicholson & Sahay, 2004; Nicholson et al., 2000; Sahay et al., 2003) describes the difficulties facing such ventures. This case involved a small software firm that attempted to set up and sustain an offshore software development subsidiary in India. The failure resulted from a lack of resources typical to small firms: capital to sustain the growing offshore center, capital for the travel costs of expatriates with India-specific context knowledge, and resources (such as reputation and dedicated staff) to attract and retain the best offshore staff.

Therefore, sourcing software development offshore is an enormously difficult undertaking for a small firm. We set out to examine whether small firms can mitigate offshore transaction costs at least as well as large firms. Transaction cost economics (TCE; Williamson, 1975) and Nooteboom's (1993) differentiation of relative transaction costs incurred by small and large firms respectively provide the theoretical framework through which we analyze the following questions.

- What are the transaction costs facing small firms engaging in offshore software outsourcing relative to large firms?
- What transaction cost mitigating strategies are small companies adopting to manage the process of offshore software development?

The article is organized as follows. In the next section we present a summary of the theoretical frame and present the argument that small and large firms incur different levels of transaction costs when sourcing offshore. Then, we present the research methodology and sample description. Next, we present our empirical findings of small-firm mitigation strategies for relatively high transaction costs. We also discuss the special case of small technology firms. Finally, we present our conclusions, contribution, and implications.

Theoretical Frame

Literature from strategic management (Chen & Hambrick, 1995; D'Amboise & Muldowney, 1988; Dean, Brown, & Bamford, 1998) has demonstrated that small and large firms require different theories and models to explain their behavior, strategy, and performance.

One distinction is that small firms cannot rely on economies of scale to gain advantage (Fiegenbaum & Karnani, 1991). They are restrained by limited resources in terms of staffing with reliance on fewer generalists and less structural formalism (Borch & Arthur, 1995). Smaller firms face relative limitations in raising financial resources in contrast to the "deep pockets" of large firms that enable them to weather financial losses or other difficulties and to be less negatively impacted by sunk costs (Dean et al., 1998). This prior research has advanced our understanding of small firms and has established the need for continued, serious theoretical and empirical consideration of the particularities of firm size.

Offshore software outsourcing presents communication and coordination difficulties that are highly challenging for small firms. To analyse the importance of firm size and offshore software outsourcing requires a framework that allows the analysis of such coordination costs and emphasizes the particularities of small firms. For this we draw on the work of Nooteboom (1993) and Nooteboom, Zwart, and Bijmolt (1992), who have utilized and extended transaction cost economics (Williamson, 1975, 1985) to take account of small- and large-firm differences. In the sections to follow, we summarize relevant TCE concepts and then proceed to discuss the relative differences in transaction costs between small and large firms when outsourcing offshore.

TCE explains where the firm boundary will be positioned based on the costs of various production and coordination mechanisms. We draw on TCE for two reasons. First, the theory has been used often as a basis for examining outsourcing (Ang & Straub, 1998; Aubert, Rivard, & Patry, 1996; Lacity & Hirschheim, 1993; Lacity & Willcocks, 1996; Wang 2002). Second, TCE is a framework through which many differences between small and large firms may be understood. TCE proposes that costs are comprised of production and transaction costs. Transaction costs, or coordination costs, are the costs of managing (controlling and coordinating). Units within the firm can be combined or split up depending on their production and transaction costs. Some units will split off or be outsourced if the costs of the internal units are higher than the market costs. In contrast, large governance units may be more efficient if units can be combined to reduce transaction costs. Firms acting rationally will adopt market-based strategies when their production cost savings of outsourced offshore work outweigh the additional transaction costs incurred. This may be depicted numerically:

production cost savings $> \Sigma$(transaction costs)

Much of the production cost savings in offshore outsourcing stem from the wages of the software staff in low-wage nations such as India. Indian wages, not including overhead, are 10% to 30% of comparably skilled staff in the U.S. or the UK. However, transaction costs incurred are the coordination costs due to such issues as the cost of monitoring the offshore vendor across time and space. These transaction costs, if calculated, may exceed the production cost savings due to lower wages. In such a case, the firm would more profitably organize production inside the organizational hierarchy, that is, in house. This "make or buy" decision is also related to the frequency of transactions, whether occasional or recurrent, and the degree of asset specificity or customization necessary for the transaction. Also of relevance is the threat of vendor opportunism, especially where there are small numbers of vendors. Finally, conditions of uncertainty present potentially high transaction costs as commensurate coordination and information-gathering mechanisms are required to be put in place to manage the uncertainty surrounding the transaction.

In particular, Nooteboom's (1993, p. 284) contribution has enhanced our understanding of how "smaller firms as both suppliers and buyers, incur higher transaction costs directly, and cause higher transaction costs for transaction partners" than large firms. In order to justify this, Nooteboom presents an extension to the TCE framework to include firm size, taking into account economies of scale, scope, experience, and learning. He states that "small firms generally produce small volumes (scale) of few products (scope). Often they have not been in business long and thereby have little benefit from economies of experience. Often they have limited capacity for the acquisition of knowledge [learning]" (p. 283). Nooteboom identifies how a transaction can be examined in three generic stages: contact, contract, and control. All three stages have threshold costs that are relatively higher for small firms. These threshold costs are the set-up costs: the costs of setting up a contract, judging an offer, and setting up channels of communication and governance mechanisms. These costs arise regardless of the transaction size and thus weigh heavily for smaller transactions.

In the following three subsections, we explain and expand on Nooteboom's (1993) work and examine the relative transaction costs incurred by small firms relative to large firms. These issues are presented in relation to the three generic stages—contact, contract, and control—focusing on the particularities of offshore outsourcing.

Contact

At the stage of contact, buyers incur search costs and the seller incurs costs of marketing. Small firms may be attracted by economies of scale and scope offered by offshore vendors. Economies of scale suggest that the small firm would benefit more than the large firm from outsourcing since small firms tend to have difficulties attracting and retaining the best personnel, generally cannot afford to maintain technical specialists in house in narrow areas, and cannot "ramp up" for one-time large projects. The process of vendor search and assessment is an example of a critical task where small firms are hindered by economies of learning. Nooteboom (1993) points to an increase in the ability to perceive, interpret, and evaluate when firms are larger due to, for example, the numbers of specialist staff, spread of personal networks, and propensity of access to technologies. In contrast, a small firm has fewer individuals in specialized information roles who tend to have relatively lower levels of education. For Nooteboom (p. 289), "the smaller firm rationality is more bounded along three dimensions: width (fewer functional areas in staff support), depth (lower level of education with the exception of firms in science based sectors), and variety (dominance of the personal perspective of the entrepreneur)."

The implications of these deficiencies are marked when engaging in sourcing software offshore. Small firms are unlikely to have competent internal expertise to conduct the search, evaluation, and implementation of offshore software sourcing. Contact costs for suppliers tend to be higher when marketing to small firms than to large firms because suppliers have more trouble in generating awareness. The small firm has a relatively limited number of individual staff members, many of whom act in generalist roles. For offshore software sourcing, these individuals must learn many new topics, such as the legal and cultural norms of the vendor's country. Small firms may mitigate this by hiring a variety of specialists such as outsourcing consultants and lawyers, for example. However, these specialists themselves bring about high threshold costs for small firms relative to large firms.

Contract

Nooteboom (1993, p. 285) identifies costs at the stage of contract as:

incurred in the preparation of an agreement to transact in which one tries to anticipate possible problems during execution. Costs include search of information on reliability of the transaction, possible contingencies in the future and degree to which investments will be sunk. They further include costs of negotiation, legal advice, set up of arbitration, design of safeguards and guarantees against misuse.

Small firms suffer higher relative contracting costs because of the relatively small transaction size. This includes the costs of negotiation, legal advice, set-up of any third-party procedures, and designing safeguards. Contracting across international legal regimes presents high threshold costs for small firms. Enforcing contractual clauses and penalties such as procedures for data transfer upon contract termination is more difficult and costly across different regulatory and judicial environments. Pursuing an offshore software vendor in Indian, Chinese, or Russian courts is not a task a small firm should undertake lightly. Contract law is different in each nation, so different enforcement and dispute-resolution approaches need to be considered and included in the contract. These are all daunting tasks for the small firm often without individuals experienced in global business. If the small firm chooses to open a subsidiary abroad (i.e., within the hierarchy), then the contracting and legal arrangements are significantly more complex and time consuming. This may be contrasted with the "red carpet" treatment that large firms often receive when outsourcing or opening subsidiaries offshore. Large firms are welcomed by a menu of incentives and matching investments. For example, Microsoft executives were received by national political and business elites when they visited India in recent years, particularly in Andhra Pradesh where promises of changes to educational curricula in colleges were made to facilitate the supply of skilled labor. Intel executives were solicited by the president of Costa Rica himself, who was closely involved in negotiations.

Control

Nooteboom (1993, p. 285) identifies the stage of control as comprising of "costs of monitoring, settling disputes ('haggling'), renegotiation, arbitration, litigation, loss of investments due to the relationship breaking up." When a firm sources software development offshore, it needs to have control beyond the boundaries of the firm and beyond the political, economic, social, and technological boundaries of the country. In order to control the software development process across this diverse environment, control measures need to be put in place. Appropriate measures include process measures (percent complete and number of bugs) as well as outcome measures (meeting functionality and performance). Small client firms often do not have the knowledge of how to put in place measurement systems such as these for global operations. Measurement systems are another form of threshold cost that impact small firms relatively more than large firms. Small companies are less likely to be accustomed to long-distance control. For instance, recent research on the use of information systems in small and large companies found that small firms tend to use computers more as tools and less as a communications medium (Pollard & Hayne, 1998). Prior research has shown how using computers as a communications medium is important in facilitating communication and monitoring distant suppliers of IT services (Sahay et al., 2003).

Offshore outsourcing is fraught with implementation failures. Prior outsourcing research has shown that it is common to find that firms fail on their first or second episode, and then give up on outsourcing or achieve success in subsequent attempts (Lacity & Wilcocks, 2001). Thus, success stems from experience, or in the language of transaction costs, economies of experience. However, Nooteboom (1993) points out that small firms are hindered by their size in achieving economies of experience. Economies of experience are the decline of average costs caused by the "increase of cumulate production over time, accumulation of knowledge and the ability to reduce errors and redundancies that occurred the first time that one performs a task." This experience effect, in essence, is the result of doing more of the same. Smaller firms lack the financial resources to absorb failures and learn from experience. According to Nooteboom (p. 290), knowledge in small firms tends to be "more craft-like and based more on experience (learning by doing) as opposed to procedural, formal explicit rules and procedures associated with the need to communicate more widely and therefore more formally." In essence, small firms cannot absorb the failures associated with learning from offshore outsourcing. Furthermore, they lack formalisms, stores of processes, practice guidelines, rules, or methodologies. This feature has the effect of making the small firm less able to adapt its processes over time as learning takes place. It also makes the firm more inscrutable to offshore vendors. Records or formalized documentation on coding and quality standards, for instance, may be lacking. This may be justified in a small firm because of the expense, or formal standards may be perceived as bureaucratic and unnecessary due to the reliance on informal oral communication. However, lack of client-side formalism will mean higher threshold costs at the start of outsourcing. Also, it may affect learning from experience and continuity, a problem that may become acute in small firms if key persons should leave.

Opportunism is concerned with the circumstances when one party to a transaction takes advantage of the other. The distance between the client and outsourcer accentuates the possibility for undisclosed, "behind the scenes" improvizations and unseen third-party subcontracting. We illustrate a case of opportunism that we learned of in the course of our study. While the end client was not a small firm, this incident illuminates opportunism in offshore outsourcing.

N is a well-known U.S. firm that contracted to an Irish vendor. The Irish firm contracted for the work to be done by a British firm. The British firm then contracted the work to be done by a Belarus firm. The Belarussian firm performed all the coding! The Irish firm (unashamedly) did not disclose to the American firm that it had passed on the software coding work to these other firms.

Small firms, by contrast, are more likely to purchase from a small number of other small firms due to the lower prices typically charged by smaller firms. However, such small suppliers are more likely to be opportunistic or "fly by night" and disappear more easily than large firms. There is also evidence that the largest suppliers in India selectively choose not to do business with small clients. Larger firms are relatively less sensitive to a single act of opportunism because the risk tends to be spread across many transaction partners. Doing business with large companies enhances the reputation of suppliers, and they may act as reference sites for other potential customers. We have heard many anecdotes of Indian outsourcing companies opportunistically moving their best staff unseen to new prestigious clients with high-value contracts. The relative size and prestige of large firms reduces the risk of opportunism, especially if there is a large contract and the possibility of high-value contracts in the future. By contrast, smaller firms tend not to have the "brand presence" of large firms or the contract size to guard against supplier opportunism.

Controlling the high levels of uncertainty in this environment forces small firms to incur high information costs. This can be examined at three levels. At the macro level, small and large firms face uncertain political and economic instabilities. For instance, India has been close to war with Pakistan on several occasions, most recently in 2002. Fiscal incentives to offshore to the Philippines may be eliminated because the national government has been under pressure to eliminate the generous tax incentives on offshore sourcing, which could push up prices. At the micro level, there is uncertainty over intellectual property in less developed countries; China, for example, has weak enforcement. At the operational level, there is uncertainty over such issues as vendor nonperformance, ineffective communication due to unreliable telecommunications, corruption, and access to recruitment networks. Large and small firms are, of course, affected by these uncertainties. However, large firms have the resources to overcome some of them more effectively than small firms can. Sahay et al. (2003) discuss how Globtel, a major North American telecommunications company, had the resources to standardize Indian operations by moving large numbers of expatriates, methods, standards, and training programs into their Indian offshore outsourcing partners. This had the effect of creating a piece of the U.S. in India in terms of the reduction of cross-cultural and communication problems, provision of a reliable infrastructure, standardized project management processes, accounting conventions, and due diligence procedures. In the 1980s and 1990s when offshore outsourcing began in India, large companies like Texas Instruments and Motorola had the technical and financial resources to install their own satellite links to overcome local telecommunications weaknesses, while smaller firms had to rely on unreliable, low-bandwidth public telecommunications or on transporting computer tapes on a daily or weekly basis by air freight (Carmel, 1999).

In summary, our theoretical frame is derived from TCE and in particular the work of Nooteboom (1993). A consideration of the relative differential in transaction costs between small and large firms at the three stages of contact, contract, and control will enable a discussion of the transaction cost mitigating strategies adopted by the firms in the sample.

Methodology

In order to study this topic and address our research questions, we sought out to understand offshore outsourcing practices by small firms. Therefore, we collected data from the small (client) firms, from the vendors that serve them, and from the emerging layer of intermediaries and specialized service providers. This approach

Table 1. Small-firm-sample key characteristics

Client firm	Location of client	Client firm no. of employees	Offshore location	Activity sourced offshore
C1	UK	25	India	Coding in Lotus Domino
C2	U.S.	25	India	Collaboration product
C3	UK	180	India	Web site in JAVA
C4	U.S.	20	India	E-Commerce platform
C5	UK	29	Oman (to Indian firm)	Web site with online shop
C6	U.S.	3	Russia	Module for a streaming product
C7	U.S.	12	Russia	Insurance system
C8	UK	25	Iran	Utilities billing
C9	U.S.	50	Pakistan	Health care
Median		25		

is consistent with recent work on IT sourcing by Hui and Beath (2002). During the period of 2000 to 2003, the authors collected data from 9 small client firms, 5 consultancies5, and 11 vendors. The principal thrust of our data collection was from the small client firms themselves, and we begin with a description of our approach for this segment.

Table 1 summarizes our sample of small firms. The client firms ranged from having 3 to 180 employees. (The firm with 180 employees was allowed into the sample because the client was a small unit of less than 25 employees that was largely independent from the larger company.) Most of the clients sourced from India, but other destinations included Russia and Pakistan. Because of the authors' location, the sample client firms are all in the U.S. and UK. Our sample was opportunistic: firms were identified from the authors' professional contacts and from articles in practitioner journals. We had no restrictions on the location of the offshore unit.

We conducted in-depth semi-structured interviews with key personnel. In all, there were 18 interviews. Interviews took place with the owner-entrepreneur in most cases, and in some (C1, C3, C8) we asked and were allowed to interview other staff such as project managers and analyst-developers. In one case (C8), interviews took place with the offshore unit in Iran as well as with the client side in the UK. Respondents were asked to reconstruct events from the inception of the offshore outsourcing project relationship as well as provide us with their perspectives on the relations and tensions within the projects over time. To ensure reliability, we used a standard format for data collection. Some firms provided us with additional data such as corporate information, reports, and specifications. We also attempted to obtain data from the trade press and from Web sites in a process of the triangulation of data sources. Interviews were taped if the interviewees agreed and were then transcribed verbatim. We offered anonymity to induce interviewees to share more sensitive aspects.

The cases we examined had varying relationship arrangements; some projects were short-term while others involved longer-term arrangements. Some clients worked directly with the offshore unit while others worked indirectly through onshore personnel or an onshore software house with offshore arrangements. The nature of the work included both custom and software package development. The unit of analysis was at the level of the project sourced to the offshore unit, but we also gathered background data on other projects.

We triangulated our data collection further by conducting interviews with vendors and intermediaries that are active in serving small client firms in the offshore context. Our approach here was to validate and complement our data from small client firms described above. We sought out vendors and consultants for interviews in which we focused on our two research questions regarding transaction costs for small client firms. For both communities, we probed for problems and solutions of selling IT services in the offshore context. We interviewed vendors in a number of regions including India, Central America, and Eastern Europe, as well as the vendor representatives in the U.S. and UK. We also sought out intermediaries (these reside in the client nations, e.g., the U.S. and UK).

We analyzed all our data first by performing an interview summary and a preliminary theoretical analysis of the interviews from each case. We then grouped together the themes and responses into categories organized around the dimensions of the theoretical framework by applying a data display method (Miles & Huberman, 1994). The resulting tables allowed us to compare and contrast the strategies and multiple perspectives in the case companies in subjective cross-case analysis. It also enabled patterns to be identified in the process of moving back and forward between the data and theory in a "hermeneutic circle" (Klein & Myers, 1999), enabling us to make sense of the large amount of qualitative data. This process was accompanied by reading and rereading the transcripts and summaries in relation to the theory, and discussion between the authors and with other colleagues and students in our respective institutions. With regard to the generalization potential of the findings, the aim of the qualitative analysis of the cases is concerned with making an analytical generalization (Walsham, 1995) offering deep insight into the transaction costs mitigating strategies employed by the vendor and client to enable offshore outsourcing.

Data and Discussion

In the previous section, we introduced and explored the relatively high transaction costs for small firms engaging in offshore sourcing relative to large firms. We turn now to a discussion of what small firms can and are doing to mitigate these costs. We illustrate our analysis with our field data. We present our observations in three parts. First, we examine what the small (client) firms can do to mitigate offshore costs. Then, we examine how the offshore marketplace (primarily the vendor firms) is evolving to mitigate offshore costs for their small client firms. Finally, we present our findings about the special case of small technology firms, which we find to have different characteristics than small non-technology firms vis-à-vis offshore sourcing.

Client-Side Mitigation Approaches

Liaisons of Knowledge Flows

Our findings suggest that it is the presence of one or two key individuals, or liaisons, that pivots the relationship between the client firm and offshore vendor and is critical to its success or failure. The role of these liaisons is critical since the IT teams in the small firms we interviewed had limited resources and thus placed greater responsibility on one or two individuals. This is consistent with recent research on the role of individuals and relationships within internationalizing service firms. Lindsay, Chadee, Mattsson, Johnston, and Millet (2003, p. 8) write that "services firms have not only a higher dependence on knowledge flows, but also on individuals within the firm that are relationship builders and creators and transmitters of knowledge." The cases demonstrated several instances of how these liaisons mitigated transaction costs. First we illustrate the importance of network ties and then the importance of individual skills and qualities. Then we demonstrate the importance of stakeholders as liaisons of knowledge flows.

Transaction cost theory is often criticized for ignoring the importance of embedded network ties (Granovetter, 1995) that may significantly reduce transaction costs. Firm C8 sourced software from Iran, which, due to many factors including a U.S. embargo, political instabilities, and corruption, seems an impossible place to source software. The high transaction costs of sourcing from Iran were mitigated because the vendor software company was owned by a close family with resultant high levels of trust and a reduced need for extensive control mechanisms. Other cases illustrate this importance of trust in the relationship and network ties to mitigate high transaction costs. Firm C4 is an American firm developing e-commerce software. C4's U.S.-based chief technology officer (CTO) is an Indian expatriate. The

CTO set up a small development unit in his home city in India staffed with some of the CTO's former schoolmates. He had nightly telephone calls with them, and the personal relationship reduced transaction costs considerably. The contact costs were reduced, and the contract costs were reduced because of the trust between the Indian expatriate and the offshore supplier. Finally, the control costs were lowered due to the reliance on the trust between friends.

We found that in many of the small firms in the sample, the skills, personal qualities, and even appearance of the liaison were seen to be crucial. In firm C3, the liaison between Britain and India was resident in Manchester, UK, and Caucasian in appearance. He had his upbringing in Burma (Myanmar) married an Indian woman with family residing in India. He had many years of experience in management consultancy in the UK and in offshore outsourcing management consultancy, and subsequently started his own business. He told us that he felt that his appearance, manner, family, and business ties in India and Britain coupled with his experience of living and working in both countries (and others) enabled him to sensitively "straddle" both the Indian and British cultures in terms of his understanding of the norms and constraints of doing business and the social structural environments in India and Britain. Thus, the resulting relationship had relatively low information and search costs, as well as a reduced requirement for consulting with intermediaries.

Another example of network ties mitigating transaction costs was found in Firm C5, a UK-based multimedia company contracted to a Dubai-based offshore outsourcing firm. The managing director of C5 was introduced by a venture capitalist to a Dubai-based software firm for which he was a director. Due to his stake in both sides of the business, the venture capitalist had strong influence over the service C5 received and became involved at several points to overcome problems.

With strong liaisons of knowledge flows, many of the disadvantages of small firms (relative to large ones) are mitigated through friendship and kinship, straddlers, and stakeholders. The case studies indicate that, in different ways, these liaisons can also mitigate opportunism on the part of the vendor, reduce or eliminate contact costs, and lower contract costs because of trust, which reduces the need for control (Sabherwal, 1999).

Firm C1, however, was a contrary case. The firm had no individual to play the key role of liaison. Instead, the firm experienced several failures and then instituted strict control, incurring high transaction costs. Over time, a liaison emerged, client staff identified with the key personality of the vendor's managing director (in Chennai, India), and thus control levels were reduced, leading mainly to larger batches of code sent offshore with less monitoring. However, the client-side developers said they were "stung when a large amount of code was sent by the vendor that was incomprehensible and had to be returned." This event led to a regression of trust in the role of the managing director as liaison, leading to a reinstatement of very small batches and high control.

Gaining Experience

The small firms in our sample were gaining experience in the area of offshore out-sourcing through trial and error, compensating for economies of experience present in larger firms but initially absent at the small firm. Put differently, some small firms chose to persevere through several expensive failures in order to see their projects through with offshore vendors. Thus, they were paying a high cost to utilize the low-cost services of offshore vendors.

Firm C1 failed twice in offshore outsourcing endeavors, but the intervention of the entrepreneur maintained the determination to succeed. The UK-based client outsourced to a small Indian vendor. Upon embarking on a third project, the project manager on the client side stated that "unless we found out otherwise, we were pessimistic about the competence of [the vendor]." This company was cognizant of the reasons for prior failures and instituted a control strategy that the project managers said "was a pain to make work." The client focused on the detailed control of outputs preceded by clear specifications. The contract included a bug-fixing warranty and payment on delivery. The client sent only clearly specifiable coding work offshore, and projects were broken into very small, manageable modules of around 300 lines of code, which were then subsequently broken into regular-staged releases and iterations. The small chunks facilitated output control and prevented intellectual property theft, which was also a concern. There were weekly checks on the telephone and regular increments for output progress. The client-side development staff in Britain double-checked Indian testing and quality control. In this case, the small firm was capable of overcoming scale and resources, and engaging in learning from experience without formalization. However, the transaction costs were never measured so it was not known how profitable offshore outsourcing was when taking into account the high cost of control considered necessary.

Evidence from prior studies helps shed light on this dynamic. The literature posits that some small firms have a number of behavioral advantages over large firms that may contribute to overcoming their relatively limited experience (Levy & Powell, 1998; Nooteboom, 1993; Pollard & Hayne, 1998). These studies indicate that small companies often have relatively greater entrepreneurial drive, a propensity to risk taking, perseverance, contain highly motivated people, lack burdensome bureau-cratic and political processes, and are fast and flexible. It is these advantages that we observed here.

Overcoming Opportunism

Opportunism takes place when one party of a transaction takes advantage of the other. The distance between the client and vendor accentuates the possibility for undisclosed behind-the-scenes behaviors. Opportunism is particularly costly for the small firm. We describe here the case of a small firm that responded reasonably to the discovery of opportunism, but incurred high control costs in the process.

Firm C2 is a small U.S.-based technology firm that contracted with a large, established Indian vendor that is certified at CMM Level 5. Such certification would mean that the vendor's processes are world-class. Nevertheless, the project ran into difficulties early on when the vendor staffed the project with staff who, in the client's view, were not able to execute the specifications properly. The small company manager told us:

[i]t turned out, they do keep all those processes carefully, on a hard drive database, where somebody can look at them if they want, but they do not actually follow them. So that was a bit of a surprise to us.

He was also disappointed with the level of the staff that were assigned to the project. The developers assigned to the project were essentially programmers who would write code that met the specification. C2 management had expected staff with project-management experience capable of analysis and design. In addition, as the life cycle progressed, the same manager told us how it was discovered that the Indian team was not doing any unit testing or bug tracking:

So, it's pretty clear with 30 programmers working on the project, some of them were very good, and others were rookies who didn't have a clue; the rookies didn't have enough supervision. And they turned out some real junk code. And they didn't have any way to track bugs, or discover bugs that were tracked, and no way to know whether they had been resolved or not. They had no way of projecting completion dates because they had no data collection going on. It was junk processes; there was nothing CMM Level 5.

Serious quality issues arose as a result of this, and in response, C2 management escalated control mechanisms significantly. This was in the form of improvised output controls using spreadsheets for bug tracking. The U.S. manager moved to shorter development cycles of 4 weeks. He also began to travel to India regularly, and when he was not in India, he introduced twice-daily telephone calls at the start and end of the Indian working day despite the time difference. He also complained bitterly to the Indian company. As with the case of Firm C1, these high levels of control were time consuming and costly for the client, although no formal evaluation of this cost was made to justify the "make vs. buy" decision. The project completion stretched to years. C2's management justified their continued involvement for two reasons: the firm did not have internal resources (could not do it in the hierarchy) and, in spite of the difficulties, they felt it was still inexpensive compared with American outsourcing rates.

Marketplace Mitigation Approaches

For the software vendor, selling services to small firms is more expensive than selling to large firms due to scale and setup costs. Nevertheless, we present some evidence from our sample that point to some transaction cost mitigation approaches. The marketplace has adapted to the potential market for offshore work by small firms.

Onshore Presence

Perhaps the most important approach that offshore vendors have adopted and refined is onshore presence. Since undertaking software development tasks tends to be more successful with proximate work of the client and vendor, vendors situate some development and management staff close to the client or even at the client's site. Thus, the offshore vendor maintains an onshore site staffed with various relationship functions such as sales, contracting, systems analysis, and some client support. The local vendor conducts nearly all relationship functions via the onshore staff.

Onshore presence has been common for vendors providing services to large client firms. But this relationship structure is now prevalent for vendors providing services to small firms. For example, there are now 260 Indian IT service firms with at least one office abroad, and many of these vendors are small. Numerous offshore firms from dozens of nations now maintain some representation in the U.S. The number of Indian IT companies with UK offices has grown from 10 in 1994 to 150 in 2003 (Ballard, 2003). For small vendors, the onshore presence is often one individual who wears the "dual hats" of sales person and relationship manager.

Onshore vendor presence addresses many of the offshore sourcing transaction costs. Contact costs are reduced because vendors are close by, contracting costs are reduced because vendors have domicile in the country, and control costs are reduced because of proximity (e.g., legal presence and low telephone costs). Resources are better utilized because the difficult phase of requirements specification, for which the client firm may be ill-equipped, can be done via face-to-face contact.

We emphasize that the converse is to have no onshore presence, which is the case for some smaller offshore vendors. Thus, since they have no proximity between the client and vendor, most communication is conducted via IT. This keeps production costs low because there are no expensive onshore staff. Thus, firms offering services using this approach tend to be able to offer lower prices. To take advantage of this, Firm C5, which began offshore work with the vendor's onshore presence, has slowly shifted a greater proportion of work to the Indian subsidiary center. Its plan was to move toward removing the onshore presence altogether and deal wholly with the offshore operation.

Reducing Contact Costs

In practice, we found that contact costs for small companies are lower than might be expected. First, information search costs have been reduced by the Internet, particularly by online marketplaces. Online marketplaces expose firms to hundreds of vendors in many countries. Numerous online marketplaces have emerged to provide match-making and thus provide the small client firm with relatively low search costs[6]. Some of these marketplaces also provide basic project advice. Information search costs have been reduced by attendance at specialist offshore outsourcing symposia or conferences. Before 2000 there were few of these events in North America or Europe. At the time of this writing, these conferences were numerous in major U.S. and Western European cities. For example, a manager at a small client firm just embarking on offshore sourcing, when told about these conferences in an interview, said, "Oh, yes, we already went to one of these."

In addition, creative approaches have emerged to address the small firm's need to conduct due diligence. For example, we learned in our interviews of quality-certification schemes that will produce a database of accredited small offshore vendors that can be provided to clients for a fee.

Simplifying Contracting

Crafting an offshore contract is becoming less expensive partly because a greater population of lawyers now specializes in the offshore niche. These lawyers now advertise their specialized expertise of offshore outsourcing and meet their prospective clients at various specialized workshops and conferences. As offshore vendors mature, they are also standardizing their contracts. This reduces the transaction costs of contracts for small firms. An offshore vendor we interviewed has created a standardized, phase-based contract and a standardized contracting process.

Separately, the increased prevalence of onshore presence, which we noted above, implies that many of the vendor firms present a legal entity in their client's home country, thus removing contractual uncertainties for dispute resolution and the complexity of foreign legal norms. Local contracts reduce the risk of vendor opportunism since poor performance may be penalized and enforced in the client's home country.

Providing Control Channels

Small client firms need a "control environment" for offshore sourcing similar to those typically employed by large firms. This includes agreeing on a methodology, mandating frequent reporting, regular product increments (e.g., interim deliverables and pilots), and payments at milestones. This process should be made visible and measurable to the small client. Most small firms find it too expensive to design and implement such control mechanisms themselves.

Vendors in our sample are providing these control channels and reducing transaction costs for their small clients. We interviewed one U.S.-based vendor with offshore IT work in India that is phasing in a Web-based project-management system or "dashboard" that will give its small clients a more detailed and accurate view of the process. This firm is following the lead of larger offshore vendors that began to provide such online mechanisms to their large clients several years ago.

The vendor-provided control channel reduces transaction costs in other ways: it allows the small firm to assess uncertainty, offers the potential to reduce opportunism, and reduces contract costs since fewer safeguards need to be in place.

Expertise Intermediaries

In recent years we have observed growth in a variety of third parties that provide expertise and services to firms seeking offshore work. Such intermediaries have become expert at educating and preparing the small clients for outsourcing. We illustrate with two examples of intermediaries: I1 and I2. I1 is an American consultancy that helps small companies outsource offshore by selecting partners and guiding them through contracting. One of the methods the firm implements before the client outsources is referred to as "clean house." This is a process by which the consultancy brings the client's IT function to such a stage that the firm can construct robust measures for contracting and control. I2 is an Indian consultancy that specializes in setting up small development subsidiaries for small U.K. companies in India. The service includes renting buildings, dealing with local "officialdom," handling the copious bureaucracy, interviewing, employing staff, and, if required, facilitating the ongoing incubation of the firm. This company has already had several successful implementations.

Standardization of Services

Standardizing the software sourcing service lowers transaction costs in all three of the stages: contact, contract, and control. These lower costs can raise profitability for the vendor to be passed on to the client. The standardization of services reduces asset specificity, meaning that a transaction is less expensive if the asset is less specific to one of the transaction parties.

We observed that offshore vendors are reducing asset specificity by standardizing the software development methodology. This results in reduced transaction costs for the vendor. We interviewed one offshore vendor that developed its own methodology derived from the well-accepted rational methodology augmented with distributed development techniques. The firm's process to support the small firm begins with a standard four-page template to collect data from the client. This template is then immediately e-mailed to the offshore staff for comments.

Many of the firms in our study reported that they had been (or are planning on) improving their life-cycle methodologies. These were especially noticeable in the small firms that maintained their own subsidiaries offshore. While the initial stage was characterized by ad hoc development, typically within a year the firms were instituting "CMM-like" process improvements.

There are some indications that vendors are attempting to reduce their production costs. As the crop of vendors that serve the small-client market mature, they have implemented factory-like processes and moved away from the ad hoc production processes that characterized their operations in their early years. For example, the previously mentioned offshore vendor, which has many projects that involve Web sites, is increasing code reuse in FLASH.

The Special Case of Small Technology Firms

Our case studies and secondary sources suggest that small technology[7] firms behave much differently than small nontechnology firms. Specifically, our data suggest that they are far more likely to source offshore than nontechnology small firms. We illustrate with four examples from our interviews with small vendors that provide offshore software outsourcing. From the first firm, we learned that 60% of the firm's clients are technology firms. At the second firm, the CEO expressed his frustration at the difference between selling to small technology firms and other small firms:

We don't have to educate IT firms about offshore—they already know about it.

A third firm is a small Swiss firm that does almost all its telephony software work in Russia. The fourth firm is an American firm, which upon start-up with only three staff, contracted with an Indian vendor to develop its software product.

In small business literature, Nooteboom (1993) and Nooteboom et al. (1992) note that small business staff are relatively less educated than in large businesses. However, they note that the exception in education is technology firms; in these cases, the level of education is higher than in the general population of smaller companies. Thus, the capacity for learning is high and may, indeed, be higher than in some large firms. This learning means that the firm can detect and absorb new information, making it more likely to be aware of offshore sourcing.

In the internationalization literature, we see that small technology firms have a global perspective relative to nontechnology firms (Jones, 1999). Jones summarizes the reasons for this: the orientation and perspective of the entrepreneurs, the short product life cycles (time-to-market pressures), and the drive for innovation. Since the 1990s, some of the literature referred to this class of firms as "born global" (Rennie, 1993). However, much of the literature is about small technology firms selling to international markets rather than sourcing from international markets.

It seems, based on our data, that quite a number of small technology firms "know about" offshore sourcing because of a key manager who is of Indian or other ethnic origin. Repeatedly, we have seen this to be a critical factor in the process of awareness and information. Importantly, this individual becomes one of the "liaisons of knowledge" that we noted earlier and thus mitigates the small firm's relatively higher offshore transaction costs.

In our fieldwork in India, we came across an Indian vendor that specializes in outsourcing for small technology firms. We asked the CEO (chief executive officer) why such small firms seek offshore outsourcing. He noted three reasons. First, small technology firms are very sensitive to the competitive pressures of time-to-market, and therefore hiring offshore resources reduces the time-to-market. Second, because they deal with inherently riskier business, small technology firms take bigger risks. Third, small technology firms are often encouraged, and sometimes even mandated, by their venture capital investors to develop offshore and are even given the name of the firm that they should work with. While we noted earlier that the large Indian firms turn down smaller clients, the exception is for technology clients. Working on leading-edge technologies with entrepreneurial clients, the large Indian firms can keep up with the latest innovations.

Conclusion

In this chapter, we delineated the offshore transaction cost categories that are relatively higher for small firms compared to large firms. We divided these into categories, as suggested in Nooteboom et al. (1992), into contact, contract, and control. We were then able to assemble the practices and approaches used in the small company cases to mitigate the transaction costs. We summarize all our findings and observations in Table 2.

Table 2. Summary of transaction cost mitigation findings for small firms engaging in offshore outsourcing

Source of mitigation	Mitigation approach	Brief description of mitigation approach	Impact on transaction costs
Client side	Liaisons of knowledge flows	Key individuals pivot the relationship between the client firm and offshore vendor.	Lowers transaction costs, primarily via control-cost reduction
	Gaining experience	Small firms use their strengths: motivated people, perseverance, and flexibility.	Expensive trial and error until economies of experience are gained
	Overcoming opportunism	Small firms use their relative strengths: motivated people, perseverance, and flexibility.	Expensive trial and error until opportunism is overcome
Vendor side	Onshore presence	Vendor has presence of staff close to client rather than offshore.	Reduces contact costs, contracting costs, and control costs, leading to an overall reduction in transaction costs for the client, but raises production and vendor transaction costs for the vendor that are passed onto client
	Reducing contact costs	Client has greater access to vendor firms primarily via Internet-enabled mechanisms.	Transaction costs are reduced.
	Simplifying contracting	Legal intermediaries specializing in offshore services have emerged.	Transaction costs are reduced.
	Providing control channels	Vendors are providing control channels for their clients' benefit.	Transaction costs are reduced for the client. Transaction costs increase somewhat for the vendor, which are passed onto the client.
	Expert intermediaries	Third-party consultants specialize in assisting firms in the offshore context.	Transaction costs are reduced
	Standardization of services	Standard development methodology. Introduction of reuse in software production	Lowers transaction costs for contract and control. Production costs are lowered.

We make several observations based on our summary analysis of Table 2. First, given that the landscape of offshore outsourcing is relatively new and that the involvement of small (client) firms is even newer, many of the transaction costs mitigation approaches are emerging and not fully diffused. Our data do not suggest that all small firms or their vendor-suppliers are using all the mitigation approaches listed in Table 2.

Second, two of the mitigation approaches that we found in small firms (on the client side in Table 2) are actually costly in the short term for the small firm. Gaining experience and overcoming opportunism are approaches that involve considerable resources for the small firm. It is questionable whether these small firms would have invested so much money, effort, and calendar time in these approaches if they could correctly anticipate them ahead of time.

Third, we restate a key predictive question about small firms sourcing offshore: Can small firms mitigate offshore costs at least as well as large firms? Based on our study, we suggest that small firms are not using their resources in unique ways relative to large firms in order to mitigate the offshore costs. The nine cost mitigation actions that we point to are not markedly different from the practices in large firms. It seems, at this stage, that the transaction cost mitigation approaches for small firms are simply lagging behind those for larger firms. We did find some weak evidence that some small firms find that their behavioral advantages can play a positive role in these mitigation approaches, namely, their flexibility, perseverance, and motivation. However, we did not find that these advantages played a key role in any of these transaction cost mitigation approaches.

Fourth, our most encouraging finding was the potential for the marketplace to reduce transaction costs rather than any behaviors or qualities of the small client firm. Small firms are benefiting from the marketplace, which is now offering lower offshore transaction costs. Both the vendors and an assortment of intermediaries are filling gaps and thus lowering the relative offshore costs for the small firms. Thus, our findings on mitigation approaches are consistent with recent theory of complementarity in IT vendors (Levina & Ross, 2003). Complementarity theory suggests that (vendor) firms improve productivity by engaging in complementary activities. These vendors' value proposition is enhanced with the complementarity of their three core competencies: methodology development and dissemination, client relationship management, and IT personnel career development. In our analysis, we noted evidence of increased competencies and the maturity of offshore vendors in the first two of these three activities, although we did not collect data relevant to the third.

In summary, we cautiously suggest that the most promising area may well be vendors' standardization of services and production. It is this trajectory that is the most fertile area for research (and practice) and will likely yield the most insight about how the global marketplace is narrowing the gap for offshore sourcing by small firms.

References

Aepple, T. (2004, January 7). Small firms outsource abroad by tapping offshore providers. *Wall Street Journal.*

Ang, S., & Straub, D.W. (1998). Production and transaction economies and IS outsourcing: A study of the U.S. banking industry. *MIS Quarterly, 22*(4).

Ansberry, C. (2003, July 14). Outsourcing abroad draws debate at home. *Wall Street Journal*, p. A2.

Apte, U. (1990). Global outsourcing of information systems and processing services. *The Information Society, 7*(4), 287-303.

Aubert, B., Rivard, S., & Patry, M. (1996). A transaction cost approach to outsourcing behaviour: Some empirical evidence. *Information and Management, 30*(2), 51-64.

Ballard, M. (2003, March 25). Outsourcing: East meets West. *Computer Weekly.*

Borch, O., & Arthur, M. (1995). Strategic networks among small firms: Implications for strategy research methodology. *Journal of Management Studies, 32*(4), 419-441.

Carmel, E. (1999). *Global software teams.* Englewood Cliffs, NJ: Prentice Hall.

Carmel, E., & Agarwal, R. (2002). The maturation of offshore sourcing of IT work. *MISQ-Executive, 1*(2), 65-78.

Chen, M., & Hambrick, D. (1995). Speed, stealth and selective attack: How small firms differ from large firms in competitive behaviour. *Academy of Management Journal, 38*(2), 453-482.

D'Amboise, G., & Muldowney, M. (1988). Management theory for small business: Attempts and requirements. *The Academy of Management Review, 13*(2), 226-240.

Dean, T., Brown, R., & Bamford, C. (1998). Differences in large and small firm responses to environmental context: Strategic implications from a comparative analysis of business formations. *Strategic Management Journal, 19*(8), 709-728.

DeLone, W.H. (1981). Firm size and the characteristics of computer use. *MIS Quarterly, 5*(4), 65-77.

Fiegenbaum, A., & Karnani, A. (1991). Output flexibility: A competitive advantage for small firms. *Strategic Management Journal, 12*(2), 101-114.

Granovetter, M. (1985). Economic action and social structure: The problem of embeddedness. *American Journal of Sociology, 91*(3), 481-510.

Heeks, R. (1995). Global software outsourcing to India by multinational corporations. In P. Palvia et al. (Eds.), *Global information technology and systems management: Key issues and trends* (pp. 364-389). Nashua: Ivy League Publishing.

Hui, P.P., & Beath, C.M. (2002). *The IT sourcing process: A framework for research* (Working paper). TX: University of Texas, McCombs School of Business.

Jones, M.V. (1999). The internationalization of small high-technology firms. *Journal of International Marketing, 7*(4).

Kern, T., & Wilcocks, L. (2000). Contracts, control and presentation in IT outsourcing: Research in 13 UK organizations. *Journal of Global Information Management, 8*(4).

Klein, H., & Myers, M. (1999). A set of principles for conducting and evaluating interpretive field studies in information systems. *MIS Quarterly, 23*(1), 67-93.

Kumar, K., & Wilcocks. (1999). A passage to India. In E. Carmel (Ed.), *Global software teams.* Englewood Cliffs, NJ: Prentice Hall.

Lacity, M., & Hirschheim, R. (1993). The information systems outsourcing bandwagon. *Sloan Management Review,* (Fall), 73-86.

Lacity, M., & Willcocks, L. (1996). Interpreting information technology sourcing decisions from a transaction cost perspective: Findings and critique. *Accounting, Management and Information Technology, 5*(3/4), 203-244.

Lacity, M., & Wilcocks, L. (2001). *Global information technology outsourcing.* Chichester: Wiley.

Levina, N., & Ross, J.W. (2003). From the vendor's perspective: Exploring the value proposition in information technology outsourcing. *Management Information Systems Quarterly, 27*(3).

Levy, M., & Powell, P. (1998). SME flexibility and the role of information systems. *Small Business Economics, 11*(2), 183-196.

Lindsay, V., Chadee, D., Mattsson, J., Johnston, R., & Millet, B. (2003). Relationships, the role of individuals and knowledge flows in the internationalisation of service firms. *International Journal of Service Industry Management, 14*(1), 7-35.

Miles, M., & Huberman, A. (1994). *Qualitative data analysis: An expanded sourcebook.* Thousand Oaks, CA: Sage.

Mortleman, J. (2003, June 17). Seeking out SME saviours. *Computer Weekly.*

Nasscom Indian IT industry: A success story. (n.d.). Retrieved January 19, 2004, from http://www.nasscom.org/download/it_industry_fact.doc

Nicholson, B., & Sahay, S. (2001). The political and cultural implications of the globalisation of software development: Case experience from UK and India. *Information and Organisation, 11*(1), 25-43.

Nicholson, B., & Sahay, S. (2004). Embedded knowledge and offshore software development. *Information and Organisation, 14,* 329-365.

Nicholson, B., Sahay, S., & Krishna, S. (2000). Work practices and local improvisations within global software teams: A case of a UK subsidiary in India. In *Proceedings of IFIP 9.4 Conference,* Cape Town, South Africa.

Nooteboom, B. (1993). Firm size effects on transaction costs. *Small Business Economics, 5,* 283-295.

Nooteboom, B., Zwart, P.S., & Bijmolt, T.H.A. (1992). Transaction costs and standardisation in professional services to small business. *Small Business Economics, 4*(2), 141-151.

Pollard, C., & Hayne, S. (1998). The changing face of information systems issues in small firms. *International Journal of Small Business, 16*(3), 70-89.

Rennie, M.W. (1993). Global competitiveness: Born global. *McKinsey Quarterly, 4*, 45-52.

Sabherwal, R. (1999). The role of trust in outsourced IS development projects. *Communications of the ACM, 42*(2), 80-86.

Sabherwal, R. (2003). The evolution of coordination in outsourced software development projects: A comparison of client and vendor perspectives. *Information and Organization, 13*, 153-202.

Sahay, S., Nicholson, B., & Krishna, S. (2003). *Global IT outsourcing*. Cambridge University Press.

Sobol, M.G., & Apte, U. (1995). Domestic and global outsourcing practices of America's most effective IS users. *Journal of Information Technology, 10*, 269-280.

Sonwalkar, P. (2004, January 10). Small and medium firms keen to outsource to India. The Economic Times.

Walsham, G. (1995). Interpretive case studies in IS research: Nature and method. *European Journal of Information Systems, 4*(2), 74-81.

Walsham, G. (2001). Making a world of difference. Chichester: Wiley.

Wang, E.T.G. (2002). Transaction attributes and software outsourcing success: An empirical investigation of transaction costs theory. *Information Systems Journal, 12*, 121-152.

Williamson, O.E. (1975). *Markets and hierarchies: Analysis and antitrust implications*. New York: Free Press.

Williamson, O.E. (1985). *The economic institutions of capitalism: Firms, markets, relational contracting*. New York: Free Press.

Endnotes

[1]   The term "sourcing" encompasses outsourcing and what is sometimes called insourcing. Some small firms do not perform offshore outsourcing, but rather offshore (in)sourcing.

[2]   Small- and medium-sized enterprises are often labeled SMEs in much of the European literature and small- and medium-sized businesses (SMBs) in current American literature.

[3]   More specifically, the act states that a firm is small if it satisfies at least two of the following criteria: a turnover of not more than £2.8 million, a balance-sheet total of not more than £1.4 million, and having no more than 50 employees.

[4]   We also note that Sobol and Apte (1995) found that firms with larger MIS budgets (a proxy for size) were more likely to outsource both domestically and offshore.

[5]   Third parties, intermediaries, or consultancies provide expertise and services to firms seeking offshore work.

[6]   We note several of these online marketplaces facilitating offshore software work: Elance (http://www.elance.com/), Freelancers (http://www.freelancers.com/), Guru, (http://www.guru.com/), and Rentacoder, (http://www.rentacoder.com/RentACoder/).

[7]   By technology firms we mean firms that develop either software products or are IT service firms (that may subcontract some of their work offshore).

This work was previously published in the Journal of Global Information Management, 13(3), 33-54, July-September 2005.

Chapter X

Information Systems Effectiveness in Small Businesses:
Extending a Singaporean Model in Canada

Ana Ortiz de Guinea, Queen's University, Canada

Helen Kelley, University of Lethbridge, Canada

M. Gordon Hunter, University of Lethbridge, Canada

Abstract

This study examines the applicability of the Thong, Yap, and Raman (1996) model of information systems (IS) effectiveness tested among Singaporean small businesses in a Canadian context. The model evaluates the importance of managerial support and external expertise (vendors and consultants) for IS effectiveness. This study extends the Thong et al. model by adding an intention of expansion construct. The sample included 105 small business users of IS in a small city in western Canada. The results show that both managerial and vendor support are essential for effective IS in Canadian small businesses, and supported part of the relations between IS effectiveness and intention of expansion. Overall, the results suggest that managers should engage quality vendors to obtain IS that contribute to the specific goals of the small business. The results of the Canadian study were, for the most part, similar to the results reported in the Singaporean study; however, a few notable differences appear to exist.

Introduction

The capacity of a country's economy to adapt to changing demands has been linked to and achieved by the flexibility and responsiveness of small businesses (Hunter & Long, 2003). Furthermore, governments and economists view small firms as the mechanism by which national growth is created (Pollard & Hayne, 1998). In 1997, Industry Canada reported that there were over 2.3 million small businesses with fewer than 100 employees, which accounted for over 50% of the private-sector employment and for 43% of the total economic output of the country (Hunter, Diochon, Pugsley, & Wright, 2002). One year later, the Canadian Federation of Independent Business estimated that between 84% and 87% of all Canadian businesses could be classified as small (Pollard & Hayne). These data demonstrate that small businesses are essential for the prosperity of Canada.

Furthermore, as an economy based on knowledge emerges, information is essential for any ongoing organization (Pugsley, Wright, Diochon, & Hunter, 2000). The globalization of products, services, markets, and competition has increased the need for flexibility, quality, cost effectiveness, and timeliness (Hunter et al., 2002). A key resource for attaining these requirements is information systems (IS)1. Consequently, IS has revolutionized business practices (Hunter et al.) and now plays a more central part of business strategies (Pollard & Hayne, 1998).

However, small businesses have unique characteristics and, in fact, researchers have found that firm size is directly associated with IS success (Choe, 1996; DeLone, 1981; Raymond, 1985). The concept of "resource poverty" (Thong, Yap, & Raman, 1994; Welsh & White, 1981) provides one explanation for this uniqueness. According to Thong et al. (1996), resource poverty refers to the lack of financial and human resources. The lack of financial resources forces small firms to make minimal commitments that are often spread out at different moments in time (Hunter & Long, 2002). For example, Duxbury, Decady, and Tse (2002) found that the main perceived barriers to the implementation of computer technologies among Canadian small businesses were the lack of financial resources and skilled personnel. Furthermore, small business managers tend to adopt a "promoter" role (Stevenson, 1999), responding to opportunities within a very short period of time (Hunter & Long). Hence, small businesses are flexible organizations that facilitate rapid and accurate assessments of their environments in order to respond to the goal of gaining opportunities (El Louadi, 1998). This leads to an absence of formal planning in the decision-making context of small firms (Lefebvre & Lefebvre, 1988). Consequently, results regarding large-business IS environments may not apply to small businesses (Ein-Dor & Segev, 1978; Raymond, 1985). Thus, Burgess (2002) suggests that there is a need to conduct additional IS research within the specific framework of small businesses.

This study has two main objectives. The first objective is to test the Thong et al. (1996) model of IS effectiveness in a Canadian small business environment and to compare the Canadian results to the Thong et al. results in Singapore. IS effectiveness refers to the IS contribution in the achievement of organizational goals (Raymond, 1990). There are two main reasons for choosing the Thong et al. study for the basis of this research project. First, the Thong et al. study uses Attewell's (1992) theory of technology diffusion to cumulate some of the factors identified by the literature as affecting the IS effectiveness of small businesses. These factors include managerial support (i.e., DeLone, 1988; Igbaria, Zinatelli, Cragg, & Cavaye, 1997) and external IS expertise (i.e., Thong, 2001; Thong et al., 1994; Yap, Soh, & Raman, 1992). The Thong et al. model tests the influence of managerial support and external IS expertise on IS effectiveness. Second, the Thong et al. model has not been tested within a Canadian environment. In terms of Hofstede's (1980) cultural dimensions, Singaporean and Canadian societies are different. Although the two cultures show little difference with respect to masculinity, Singapore tends to have lower uncertainty avoidance and lower individualism than Canada (Hofstede). In addition to this, Canada has a relatively more equal distribution of power than Singapore (Hofstede). Furthermore, there is empirical evidence of differences in how excellent systems analysts, and therefore IS experts, are seen by Canadian and Singaporean professionals (i.e., Hunter & Beck, 1996). Thus, according to Hofstede (1993), management theories developed within a specific culture cannot necessarily be applicable to other countries. Thong et al. (1996) concur with the previous statement and recommend future research to test the applicability of the IS effectiveness model in other cultural environments. Thus, the examination of the Thong et al. model in Canada will provide a better understanding of the situation of IS in Canadian small businesses, as well as identify potential factors that encourage IS effectiveness in Canada and the generalizability of the Thong et al. model.

The second aim is to expand the Thong et al. (1996) model by introducing the additional construct of intention of IS expansion. Harrison, Mykytyn, and Riemenschneider (1997) define intention as the strength of specific plans toward the accomplishment of the target behavior. The intention of IS expansion refers to the plans for new IS implementation by those businesses that already use computer technology. The Thong et al. study did not include this aspect, which is closely related to Attewell's (1992) theory of technology diffusion and the resource-based theory of the firm (Wernerfelt, 1984, 1995). Thus, this research will also analyze whether managerial support, external IS expertise, and IS effectiveness are factors that may influence the intention of IS expansion among Canadian small businesses.

Theoretical Background

The Thong et al. (1996) study stated that managerial support and external IS experts can overcome the lack of resources and knowledge that small businesses face in the implementation of IS and, therefore, can influence the effectiveness of their IS. The basis for their model was Attewell's (1992) theory of technology diffusion. In this article, we combine Attewell's theory with the resource-based theory of the firm (Wernerfelt, 1984, 1995). The reason for including the resource-based theory of the firm is that it has been used to study managerial support and external IS experts' influence on IS implementation success (i.e., Thong, 2001).

According to Attewell (1992), businesses tend to delay technology adoption due to the lack of knowledge about how to implement and operate IS. In these circumstances, mediating entities, such as consultants and IS vendors, play a vital role in the diffusion of IS. While the businesses provide the expertise in their areas of operation, the external experts (consultants and vendors) provide the knowledge regarding technical issues. Consequently, the support of external experts lowers the absence of technical knowledge regarding IS implementation that companies face (Attewell). Furthermore, the resource-based theory of the firm (Wernerfelt, 1984, 1995) states that businesses are collections of resources where the value of a resource is partially contingent upon the presence of other resources. As explained previously, small businesses operate under severe time, financial, and expertise constraints (Thong et al., 1994), and tend to control their limited funds for IS purposes (Yap, 1989). On the other hand, managers of small businesses have the power to commit resources toward the implementation of IS (Thong, 1999, 2001). Therefore, taking technology diffusion and resource-based theory into consideration, the conceptual model for this study (see Figure 1) theorizes that managerial support and external IS expertise are factors that can alleviate the knowledge barrier and resource poverty that small businesses face in their use and implementation of IS.

In addition, the Thong et al. (1996) model has been expanded to include the additional construct of intention of IS expansion. This construct is closely related to Attewell's (1992) theory of technology diffusion and the resource-based theory of the firm (Wernerfelt, 1984, 1995). Hence, external experts and managerial support play an important role not only in the effectiveness of IS, but also in the intention to expand IS (Attewell).

The importance of management support for IS effectiveness in small businesses has been recognized consistently in the IS literature (i.e., Cragg & King, 1993; DeLone, 1988; Igbaria et al., 1997; Thong, 1999, 2001; Thong et al., 1996; Yap et al., 1992). According to Yap (1989), there are two reasons why managers support IS implementation. First, managers are in the best position to identify business opportunities for the exploitation of IS. This is because managers are the ones who understand their business the best (Thong et al.). Thus, managers can bring IS into

Figure 1. Conceptual model

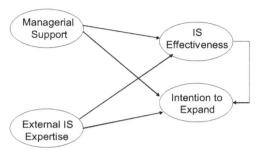

alignment with corporate objectives and strategies (Jarvenpaa & Ives, 1991). Second, IS implementation requires a substantial investment and has an impact on the whole organization (Yap). Managers have the authority to ensure sufficient allocation of resources and create a more conductive environment for IS implementation (Lucas, 1981). In addition, management support encourages users to develop positive attitudes towards the use of IS and contributes to a smoother transition in the way work is achieved between nonuse and use of IS (Thong et al.). Management support is also positively associated with the perceived ease of use and perceived usefulness of IS within small businesses (Igbaria et al.). Therefore, management commitment toward IS can make the difference between successful and unsuccessful IS implementation (Ginzberg, 1981).

Previous studies have identified other possible determinants of IS effectiveness among small businesses. One key factor critical to IS effectiveness is external IS expertise (Thong, 2001; Thong et al., 1994, 1996; Yap et al., 1992). However, there seems to be a lack of recent empirical studies investigating consultant and vendor support among small businesses and, therefore, there is a need for current research on the topic. For instance, the key references of Bode and Burn's (2002) study of consultant engagement for e-business development in small businesses are Gable (1991) and Thong et al. (1996). Also, prior research that evaluates the engagement of external IS experts in small businesses has been mainly descriptive surveys (i.e., Garris & Burch, 1983; Senn & Gibson, 1981) and case studies (i.e., Gable; Kole, 1983).

IS effectiveness is one of the most common dependant variables in the MIS literature (i.e., DeLone & McLean, 1992; Seddon, 1997; Thong, 2001; Thong et al., 1994, 1996). According to Raymond (1990), IS effectiveness is the extent to which IS actually contributes to achieving organizational goals. Nevertheless, a consensus on the definition and conceptualization of IS effectiveness appears not to exist among constituents (DeLone & McLean, 1992; Hwang, Windsor, & Pryor, 2000), and researchers are still wrestling with the problem of which construct has the greatest influence on IS (Rai, Lang, & Welker, 2002). Approaches to measure IS effectiveness in previous research include IS usage (Ein-Dor & Segev, 1978), user satisfaction (Bailey & Pearson, 1983), incremental performance in decision-making effectiveness (King & Rodriguez, 1978), cost-benefit analysis (King & Schrems, 1978), information economics (Maish, 1979), utility analysis (Kleijnen, 1980), and information attribute examination (Epstein & King, 1982). Furthermore, the complexity of the phenomenon includes multiple dimensions (DeLone & McLean). Due to these different approaches, it is unlikely that a single measure of IS effectiveness will emerge and, therefore, there is a need for multiple measures.

In this study, the domain IS effectiveness is assessed using three perceived effectiveness measurements: user satisfaction (i.e., Thong et al., 1996), organizational impact (i.e., Thong, 2001; Thong et al.), and overall IS effectiveness (i.e., Thong et al.). Overall IS effectiveness is included as it was used to complement IS effectiveness in the Thong et al. study. DeLone and McLean's (1992) model of IS effectiveness includes both user satisfaction and organizational impact as appropriate surrogates for IS effectiveness. In addition, Seddon's (1997) revision of DeLone and McLean's model maintains these two measures as representative of IS effectiveness. User satisfaction is the extent to which users believe that IS meets their information requirements (Ives, Olson, & Baroudi, 1983). Seddon and Kiew (1994) empirically supported the idea that user satisfaction is the best omnibus construct of IS success by testing it along with system quality, information quality, and usefulness. Furthermore, previous research states that user satisfaction provides the most useful assessment of IS success (Hamilton & Chervany, 1981). Organizational impact refers to the impact of IS on the performance of the small business (Thong). Thus, IS is only effective when it adds value to organizational effectiveness (Thong et al.). Overall IS effectiveness is included to capture the participants' conceptualization of IS effectiveness (Thong et al.). This conceptualization of IS effectiveness may vary, and therefore, the measure attempts to capture the meaning that IS effectiveness has among the participants.

Intention is defined as "the strength of conscious plans to perform the target behavior" (Harrison et al., 1997, p. 176). In this study, the target behavior refers to the expansion of IS. Researchers have suggested that intention models or behavioral decision theories from social psychology may provide a foundation for research investigating IS adoption by businesses (Swanson, 1982). Fishbein and Azjen's (1975) and Azjen and Fishbein's (1980) theory of reasoned action (TRA), and Azjen's (1991) theory of planned behavior (TPB) have been used in the IS literature to incorporate theoretical concepts and principles for predicting successful intentions of IS adoption (i.e., Harrison et al., 1997; Venkatesh & Brown, 2001). However, this study uses Attewell's (1992) theory of technology diffusion and the resource-based theory of the firm (Wernerfelt, 1984, 1995) to determine the predictors of the intention of IS expansion and intention of IS adoption. This is because the TRA and TPB do not include the antecedents that are used in this study for predicting intention. On the other hand, Attewell's theory of technology diffusion emphasizes the role of external expertise in the potential adoption of IS, and the resource-based theory of the firm (Wernerfelt) suggests the influence of managerial support in the expansion of IS.

Besides Attewell (1992), Kimberly and Evanisko (1981) identified three clusters of predictors of innovation adoption: the characteristics of organizational leaders, characteristics of organizations, and characteristics of the environmental context. This study focuses on the characteristics of organizational leaders and environmental contexts in order to predict intention. Relating this to Attewell's theory of technology diffusion, it is reasonable that the combination of the perception that small business managers get from vendors and consultants, and the characteristics of small business managers can compensate for small businesses' lack of technical knowledge and resources. Therefore, this facilitates IS expansion among small businesses. Hence, it is reasonable to expand the Thong et al. (1996) model due to the close associations between technology diffusion and the intention of IS expansion.

Research Model

Figure 2 depicts the research model. The hypotheses of this model are presented in the following discussion.

Figure 2. Research model

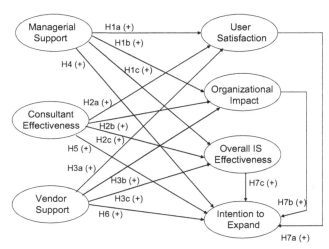

When the level of managerial support is low, the level of IS effectiveness is expected to be low due to a lack of information regarding business needs. Conversely, in environments with high levels of managerial support, managers are more likely to be involved in the implementation of IS (Thong et al., 1996), leading to greater levels of IS effectiveness (DeLone, 1988). Recent research has established a positive relation between the level of management support and the degree of IS effectiveness among small businesses (i.e., Igbaria et al., 1997; Thong, 2001; Yap et al., 1992).

Hypothesis 1: *Higher levels of managerial support will result in greater user satisfaction (1a), greater organizational impact (1b), and greater overall IS effectiveness (1c).*

In environments with a high level of consultant effectiveness (i.e., consultants conduct a correct information requirement analysis), the extent of IS effectiveness is expected to be high (Thong et al., 1996). Furthermore, several studies have reported that a supportive external expert network, such as consultants, is positively associated with the IS effectiveness among small businesses (i.e., Cragg & King, 1993; Thong, 2001; Thong et al., 1994, 1996; Yap et al., 1992).

Hypothesis 2: *Higher levels of consultant effectiveness will result in greater user satisfaction (2a), greater organizational impact (2b), and greater overall IS effectiveness (2c).*

When vendors provide poor technical support, the resultant IS may not satisfy user requirements and expected benefits (Thong et al., 1996; Yap et al., 1992). On the other hand, if vendors provide adequate service, the level of IS effectiveness is likely to be high (Thong et al.). Moreover, several studies have found a positive association between the level of vendor support and IS effectiveness (i.e., Cragg & King, 1993; Thong, 2001; Thong et al.; Yap et al.), which leads to the third hypothesis.

Hypothesis 3: *Higher levels of vendor support will result in greater user satisfaction (3a), greater organizational impact (3b), and greater overall IS effectiveness (3c).*

Thong et al. (1994) found that some managerial characteristics are determining factors of the likelihood of IS adoption among small businesses. In addition to this, Cragg and King's (1993) study showed that managerial support and effective external IS expertise are factors that encourage the growth of IS among small businesses.

Therefore, according to Thong (2001), a business that receives good managerial, consultant, and vendor support is more likely to implement new IS.

Hypothesis 4: *Higher levels of managerial support will result in greater intention of IS expansion.*

Hypothesis 5: *Higher levels of consultant effectiveness will result in greater intention of IS expansion.*

Hypothesis 6: *Higher levels of vendor support will result in greater intention of IS expansion.*

Seddon's (1997) revised model of DeLone and McLean (1992) suggests that an increase in the outcomes of IS use will lead to higher expectations about future benefits, and, therefore, to an increase in IS use. An increase in IS use means that more employees are using IS, and/or that IS is used more often or to a greater extent. Usually the growth of IS usage will lead to more IS implementations and IS updates for the business.

Hypothesis 7: *Higher levels of user satisfaction (7a), organizational impact (7b), and overall IS effectiveness (7c) will result in greater intention of IS expansion.*

Research Method

A cross-sectional field survey was used to collect empirical data from small businesses in a small city in western Canada. The survey instrument was directed to the individual in the small business who could answer questions regarding IS/IT issues: either the owners or managers of the small businesses or the employee primarily responsible for computer technology. The decision to limit data collection to one small city in western Canada controlled for the potential effects of macro-level regional differences (i.e., economic factors, markets, consultants, and vendors) on individual firm IS and IT activities, hence increasing the possibility of detecting the desired organizational-level effects of IS and IT outcomes.

The sample for this study consisted of 600 small businesses randomly selected from a 2002 business list, which contained the addresses of approximately 5,000 small businesses with valid business licenses. Each potential survey respondent was mailed a survey package, which included a self-addressed return envelope, during the spring of 2003. The design of the survey and data collection procedures followed Dillman's (2000) recommendations and guidelines.

The choice of a sample size of 600 small businesses was based on three factors. First, according to Zikmund (2000), sample size may be determined on the basis of a researcher's judgment by using a sample size similar to the sample sizes used in previous studies. Thong et al. (1996) distributed their questionnaire to 304 small businesses in Singapore with a response rate of 37.5%. In this Canadian study, the mailing list provided by the midsize city might have contained small businesses that were no longer operating or invalid addresses. Consequently, the sample size was increased to ensure that the number of potential responses was comparable to that in the Thong et al. Singaporean study. Second, Salmant and Dillman (1994) state that for a population of 5,000 members, a sample of 601 adequately estimates the population with a sampling error of $\pm 3\%$ at the 95% confidence level. Third, in order to satisfy the requirements for data analysis using a structural equation modeling technique (i.e., PLS [partial least squares]), responses from 60 small businesses were needed.

Instrument Construction

Seven constructs, as depicted in Figure 2, were measured in this study: managerial support, consultant effectiveness, vendor support, user satisfaction, organizational impact, overall IS effectiveness, and the intention to expand. The measurements used were adapted from previously validated measures (Harrison et al., 1997; Thong et al., 1996). Each construct was measured using multiple-item scales, which were reworded to relate specifically to the western Canadian context of IS and IT use. All the scale items except for intention were based on a seven-point Likert scale ranging from strongly agree to strongly disagree. The intention items were based on bipolar anchors with a seven-point scale anchored between extremely unlikely and extremely likely, extremely uncertain and extremely certain, and extremely weak and extremely strong. The operational definitions and sources of the seven constructs are presented in Table 1.

A systematic protocol was developed for pretesting the survey instrument. The purpose of the multi-step pretest process was to reduce the potential for cultural wording artifacts present in the adapted construct measurements developed for other countries such as Singapore. The pretest included two different techniques. In some cases, Dillman's (2000) think-aloud interview technique was used in order to determine when the pretester was confused or could not answer a question. This technique consisted of the investigators taking notes of comments, difficulties, concerns, and

Table 1.Operationalization of constructs

Construct	Operational Definition	Number of Items	Source
Managerial Support	Managers' behavioral support of IS in the firm	5	Adapted from Thong et al. (1996), original adapted from Yap et al. (1994)
Consultant Effectiveness	Consultant effectiveness during the IS implementation life cycle	4	Extended from Thong et al. (1996), original adapted from Thong et al. (1994)
Vendor Support	Vendor support of technology, training, and relationships	6	Extended from Thong et al. (1996), original adapted from Thong et al. (1994)
User Satisfaction	Affect with the use of the IS	7	Adapted from Thong et al. (1996), original adapted from Raymond (1987)
Organizational Impact	Perception of the impact of IS on the performance of the business	6	Adapted from Thong et al. (1996), original adapted from DeLone (1990)
Overall IS Effectiveness	Perception of the overall effectiveness of IS in the business	2	Extended from Thong et al. (1996)
Intention	Intention of the likelihood to adopt IS, certainty of business plans of IS adoption, and the level of the business commitment to adopt IS	3	Adapted from Harrison et al. (1997)

questions the tester had while he or she was completing the instrument. For the other pretests, the investigators used Dillman's retrospective technique with the testers. Following this technique, the tester was given the questionnaire and asked to review and complete the questions independently, and then return the questionnaire with his or her comments to the tester. After each pretest, the investigators studied the comments and decided how to address the concerns of the tester. Approximately 21 individuals from western Canada participated in the pretest, which included 10 owners or managers of small businesses who were subsequently excluded from the final sample. During pretesting, several testers expressed that they used different consultants and vendors for software and hardware, and that they would rank them differently. Consequently, the consultant-effectiveness and vendor support constructs developed by Thong et al. (1996) for the Singaporean study were extended to include two dimensions: software and hardware. In addition, some testers observed that sometimes they took advice from vendors rather than participating in training sessions. Based on this pretest finding, two items regarding the provision of advice from vendors were added to the vendor support measurement for the Canadian sample.

Data Analysis and Results

Demographic Data

Of the 600 survey packages mailed, 43 were returned because they did not reach the target businesses in western Canada. Completed questionnaires were received from 116 small businesses, a response rate of approximately 21%. However, only 105 completed questionnaires were usable for data analysis. The respondent Canadian small businesses employed, on average, 17.87 employees and operated approximately six days per week. Of the 105 small businesses that responded, 66 organizations reported that they had been operating for 10 years or more and only 15 of the small businesses operated franchises. The majority of the small businesses operated in the retail-trade (n = 23) and construction industries (n = 18). In addition, 28 small businesses reported that they offered a combination of different services. The geographic market for the majority of small businesses was local, with only 10 small businesses reporting an international market for their products.

At the time of the survey, the respondent Canadian small businesses reported that, on average, they had 7.41 computers, and the majority of the firms had been using computer technology for three years or more. This is an interesting finding as it suggests that most of these businesses were familiar with IS. The majority of these firms reported that they had both the resources and knowledge to purchase IS as well as the time to plan for IS. Of interest, 59 small businesses reported that they had an employee responsible for the firm's IS and IT, and 63 organizations had implemented computer technology in the past six months. These results suggested that the respondent small businesses viewed IS as important to the firm.

The majority of respondent Canadian small businesses reported that both their hardware and software were provided by a single vendor. Of interest, approximately 83% of the managers purchased the hardware and software themselves. In addition, approximately half of the small businesses reported that they did use consultants for the purchase of software and/or hardware.

Respondent small businesses reported that the software applications used the most were for accounting, word processing, Internet, and e-mail. Over half of the firms reported that they utilized applications for planning and budgeting. Overall, they used applications primarily for administrative purposes. These findings are consistent with the results reported in the Lefebvre and Lefebvre (1988) study and the Malone (1985) study. Lefebvre and Lefebvre reported that accounting applications were used the most by small businesses, followed by word-processing programs. Malone found that small businesses used IS for the achievement of operational tasks. Furthermore, Hunter et al. (2002) concurred with Malone's findings and stated that the majority of small businesses felt that the main benefit of IS was the reduction of the resources required to perform operational tasks.

Data Analysis

Partial least squares[2], a structural equation modeling technique, was used to assess the research model depicted in Figure 2. Chin (1998) stated that PLS is preferable to other structural equation modeling techniques in the earlier stages of theory development and a suitable tool for prediction-oriented research. PLS was preferred to other structural equation modeling techniques for this research project since the objectives of this study were to assess the predictive validity of the Thong et al. (1996) extended model and to compare the Canadian results to the Singaporean results. Following Chin's recommendations, both the measurement model and the structural model were assessed simultaneously and are discussed next.

Measurement Model

The manifest variables of each latent construct were modeled as reflective. Therefore, the individual item loadings, internal consistency, convergent validity, and discriminant validity of the manifest variables and their associated latent constructs were assessed. According to Fornell and Larcker (1981), individual item loadings and internal consistency values greater than 0.7 are considered adequate. Analysis of the initial factor structures of the measurement model showed that two manifest variables performed poorly. The loading of one of the statements ("I attend the meetings regarding computer technology in my business.") for the managerial-support construct loaded at 0.621. Similarly, one statement for user satisfaction ("I am satisfied with the ease of access to the information provided by our computers.") loaded at 0.586. Both of these items were dropped from further analysis for several reasons. The construct items were modified slightly during the pretest process. The original items were used in Singapore, and the testers indicated some difficulties with their applicability in a Canadian context. Apparently, the modified versions of the questions did not totally overcome the contextual problems. Specifically related to the problematic item for managerial support, 56% of the Canadian businesses that participated in the study had one employee responsible for the IS and IT implemented in their organizations. A secondary PLS analysis conducted only with businesses with an IS employee indicates that this item scored considerably lower in this case. This suggests that the IS and IT employee may be the one attending most of the meetings regarding computer technology in his or her business. Similar to the Canadian result, Thong et al. (1996) reported a 0.60 loading for this managerial-support item based on the Singaporean data.

After trimming the two problematic items, the majority of the other manifest variables loaded at 0.70 or greater (see Table 2) except for a few of the manifest variables that demonstrated weak (0.65 to 0.69) loadings. The internal consistency reliabilities of the related latent variables, however, were all greater than Fornell and Larcker's (1981) guideline of 0.70, so the decision was made not to drop any more items. Furthermore, the Cronbach's Alpha values for the constructs ranged from 0.86 for overall IS effectiveness to 0.97 for consultant effectiveness. The internal consistency reliabilities and Cronbach alpha values of the latent variables are reported in Table 3.

Convergent validity and discriminant validity of the latent variables were assessed using average variance extracted (AVE), correlations, and cross-loadings. AVE attempts to measure the extent of the variance that a measurement captures from its items relative to the amount due to measurement error (Chin, 1998). All the latent variables demonstrated convergent validity because their AVE scores were greater than the 0.50 guideline suggested by Chin (see Table 3). An examination of the square root of the AVE of each latent variable and the correlation between the constructs (see Table 4) showed that all the constructs were more strongly correlated with their own measures than they were with any of the other constructs. In addition, the cross-loadings of the manifest variables were lower than the loadings for the items of their related construct. These two findings showed that discriminant validity was observed for the constructs. Based on the results reported above, the reliability, convergent validity, and discriminant validity of all the latent variables were determined to be acceptable.

Structural Model

The evaluation of the structural model consisted of two assessments: an assessment for the significance of the path coefficients using a nonparametric technique called jackknifing (Fornell, 1982) and an examination of the explanatory power of the exogenous constructs (Fornell). Jackknifing generates standard errors and t-statistics. The results of the structural model are depicted in Figure 3, and the results of the jackknifing technique are presented in Table 5. The scale for the intention to expand was reversed for the analysis of the results in PLS. The rationale for this is to provide the intention of expansion with the same scale order as the rest of the latent variables in the model.

Hypotheses 1a, 1b, and 1c were supported. Higher levels of managerial support resulted in greater user satisfaction (H1a), greater organizational impact (H1b), and higher levels of overall IS effectiveness (H1c). Hypotheses 3a, 3b, and 3c were also supported. Greater vendor support resulted in greater user satisfaction (H3a), higher levels of organizational impact (H3b), and higher levels of overall IS effectiveness (H3c). Hypotheses 2a (positive relation between consultant effectiveness and user satisfaction), 2b (positive relation between consultant effectiveness and organizational impact), and 2c (positive relation between consultant effectiveness and overall IS effectiveness) were not supported. Hypotheses 4, 5, and 6, which hypothesized significant relationships between managerial support and the intention to expand, consultant effectiveness and the intention to expand, and vendor support and the intention to expand, were also not supported.

The final set of hypotheses predicted that higher levels of user satisfaction (7a), organizational impact (7b), and overall IS effectiveness (7c) would result in greater intention to expand IS. Only hypothesis 7b was supported (t-value = 4.0485; p = 0.001); organizational impact exerted a significant positive influence on the intention to expand. One possible explanation for the nonsignificant results regarding hypotheses 7a and 7c might be that the majority of respondents had implemented IS within the previous six months. Additional data analysis was performed to determine if firms' recent expansion of IS biased the results. The path coefficients of managerial support with IS effectiveness increased, whereas the path coefficients for consultant

Table 2. Loadings and cross-loadings for the measurement model (trimmed)

Measure	Construct						
	1	2	3	4	5	6	7
Managerial Support (MS; 1)							
Involvement in information requirement analysis (MS 2)	.897	.092	.030	.390	.289	.370	.033
Involvement in reviewing consultant's recommendations (MS 3)	.698	.378	.149	.274	.085	.089	.096
Involvement in decision-making (MS 4)	.957	.179	.002	.448	.186	.339	.030
Involvement in monitoring the project (MS 5)	.925	.211	.079	.370	.152	.317	.035
Consultant Effectiveness (CE; 2)							
Effectiveness in performing information requirements analysis (CE 1 HW)	.214	.914	.313	.160	.015	.057	.162
Effectiveness in performing information requirements analysis (CE 1 SW)	.181	.923	.240	.111	.122	.081	.173
Effectiveness in recommending suitable computer solution (CE 2 HW)	.229	.929	.295	.135	.022	.033	.120
Effectiveness in recommending suitable computer solution (CE 2 SW)	.195	.945	.257	.147	.050	.126	.093
Effectiveness in managing implementation (CE 3 HW)	.226	.935	.277	.187	.044	.108	.144
Effectiveness in managing implementation (CE 3 SW)	.179	.946	.284	.201	.034	.205	.121
Relationship with other parties in the project (CE 4 HW)	.169	.886	.307	.118	.022	.023	.031
Relationship with other parties in the project (CE 4 SW)	.162	.891	.291	.139	.040	.100	.043

continued on following page

Table 2. continued

Vendor Support (VS; 3)							
Adequacy of technical support during IS implementation (VS 1 HW)	.140	.203	.737	.200	.108	.242	.030
Adequacy of technical support during IS implementation (VS 1 SW)	.009	.118	.781	.154	.158	.244	.148
Adequacy of technical support after IS implementation (VS 2 HW)	.125	.195	.830	.270	.226	.236	.101
Adequacy of technical support after IS implementation (VS 2 SW)	.028	.141	.829	.226	.266	.246	.272
Quality of technical support (VS 3 HW)	.079	.091	.784	.114	.107	.169	.087
Quality of technical support (VS 3 SW)	.020	.089	.825	.092	.137	.157	.158
Adequacy of advice (VS 4 HW)	.023	.190	.837	.172	.232	.209	.093
Adequacy of advice (VS 4 SW)	.072	.206	.852	.143	.231	.194	.133
Adequacy of training (VS 5 HW)	.025	.303	.793	.204	.177	.185	.049
Adequacy of training (VS 5 SW)	.003	.338	.826	.218	.207	.232	.111
Quality of advice (VS 6 HW)	.087	.258	.672	.123	.070	.160	.029
Quality of advice (VS 6 SW)	.001	.294	.733	.125	.142	.109	.072
Quality of training (VS 7 HW)	.033	.403	.734	.111	.046	.070	.003
Quality of training (VS 7 SW)	.070	.429	.770	.133	.149	.120	.068
Relationship with other parties in the project (VS 8 HW)	.087	.347	.699	.202	.128	.124	.156
Relationship with other parties in the project (VS 8 SW)	.010	.365	.690	.182	.226	.115	.245
User Satisfaction (US; 4)							
Currency of reports (US 2)	.406	.175	.199	.911	.600	.657	.219
Timeliness of reports (US 3)	.397	.073	.228	.862	.586	.530	.248
Reliability of reports (US 4)	.287	.137	.153	.878	.628	.673	.305
Relevancy of reports (US 5)	.421	.158	.237	.886	.676	.647	.201
Accuracy of reports (US 6)	.426	.189	.228	.896	.528	.630	.149
Completeness of reports (US 7)	.317	.167	.129	.872	.566	.669	.107

continued on following page

effectiveness and vendor support with IS success decreased. Interestingly, the path coefficients for consultant effectiveness and vendor support with the intention to expand increased substantially but in a negative direction. Moreover, the path coefficients between IS effectiveness and the intention to expand decreased considerably. This suggests that businesses that had recently adopted IS were reluctant to expand their IS. Additional data analysis with those businesses that did not have a recent IS expansion showed the opposite effects. Therefore, it appears that the recent adoption of IS within the previous six months was affecting the results.

In this study, approximately 23% of the variance in user satisfaction was accounted for by the model (see Figure 3). The predicted power of the model was similar to that reported in other small business studies. For example, Thong (2001) reported

Table 2. continued

Measure	Construct						
	1	2	3	4	5	6	7
Organizational Impact (OI; 5)							
Pretax profit (OI 1)	.185	.005	.154	.619	.884	.524	.361
Sales revenue (OI 2)	.187	.093	.095	.542	.847	.414	.278
Staff productivity (OI 3)	.268	.041	.224	.484	.767	.450	.364
Competitive advantage (OI 4)	.086	.082	.148	.513	.834	.479	.382
Operating cost (OI 5)	.225	.016	.246	.584	.809	.529	.317
Quality of decision-making (OI 6)	.112	.029	.240	.605	.816	.422	.395
Overall IS Effectiveness (6)							
Satisfaction of needs (Overall IS Effect 1)	.371	.136	.215	.713	.572	.947	.080
Satisfaction with the overall IS effectiveness (Overall IS Effect 2)	.262	.066	.235	.614	.490	.923	.092
Intention To Expand (IE; 7)							
Likelihood of the intention of use (IE 1)	.033	.143	.116	.189	.354	.042	.899
Plans to use (IE 2)	.043	.140	.148	.244	.423	.111	.945
Commitment to use (IE 3)	.041	.075	.158	.255	.433	.142	.951

Table 3. Descriptive statistics, reliability, and convergent validity

Construct	Mean	Std. Dev.	Internal Consist.	Cronbach's Alpha	AVE
Managerial Support	3.39 1	.44 .	93 .	90 .	87
Consultant Effectiveness 3	.20	1.35 .	98 .	97 .	85
Vendor Support 4	.12	1.39 .	96 .	96 .	60
User Satisfaction	2.53 1	.14 .	96 .	94 .	78
Organizational Impact 3	.25	1.47	.93	.91	.68
Overall IS Effectiveness	2.47	1.16 .	93 .	86 .	87
Intention To Expand	4.16	2.03 .	95 .	94 .	87

Note: Managerial support, consultant effectiveness, vendor support, user satisfaction, organizational impact, and overall IS effectiveness were measured using a seven-point Likert scale, ranging from strongly agree (1) to strongly disagree (7). The intention to expand had bipolar anchors with a seven-point scale, ranging from extremely unlikely (1) to extremely likely (7).

Table 4. Correlation among constructs (square root of AVE extracted in bold font)

Construct	1	2	3	4	5	6	7
Managerial Support (1)	.94						
Consultant Effectiveness (2)	.21	.92					
Vendor Support (3) .	04 .	30 .	78				
User Satisfaction (4)	.43	.23	.17	.88			
Organizational Impact (5) .	22 .	23 .	02 .	68 .	83		
Overall IS Effectiveness (6)	.34	.24	.11	.71	.57	.94	
Intention To Expand (7)	.03	.16	.13	.24	.43	.09	.93

Figure 3. Results of the structural model

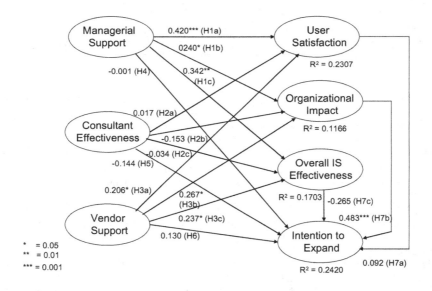

an R^2 of 0.26 for user satisfaction based on the Singaporean data. Approximately 12% of the variance in organizational impact was explained by management support, vendor support, and consultant effectiveness. Furthermore, 17% of the variance in overall IS effectiveness was accounted for by the exogenous variables. Finally, 24%

Table 5. Tests of hypotheses and research questions (trimmed)

Hypothesis	Path Coefficient (Direct Effect)	t-Value for Path	Indirect Effect	Total Effect
Managerial support → User satisfaction (H1a)	0.420	3.387*** -		0.420
Managerial support → Organizational impact (H1b)	0.240	1.652*	-	0.240
Managerial support → Overall IS effectiveness (H1c)	0.342	2.746**	-	0.342
Managerial support → Intention to expand (H4)	-0.001	0.028	0.258	0.259
Consultant effectiveness → User satisfaction (H2a)	0.017	0.285 -		0.017
Consultant effectiveness → Organizational impact (H2b)	-0.153	1.420 -		-0.153
Consultant effectiveness → Overall IS effectiveness (H2c)	-0.034	0.381 -		0.034
Consultant effectiveness → Intention to expand (H5)	-0.144	1.429 0	.082	0.226
Vendor support → User satisfaction (H3a)	0.206	1.944*	-	0.206
Vendor support → Organizational impact (H3b)	0.267	2.475**	-	0.267
Vendor support → Overall IS effectiveness (H3c)	0.237	2.047* -		0.237
Vendor support → Intention to expand (H6)	0.130	1.357 0	.205	0.335
User satisfaction → Intention to expand (H7a)	0.092	0.667	-	0.092
Organizational impact → Intention to expand (H7b)	0.483	4.048*** -		0.483
Overall IS effectiveness → Intention to expand (H7c)	-0.265	2.501 -		0.265

*Note: * = 0.05 ** = 0.01 *** = 0.001*

of the variance in the intention to expand was explained by the model. The amount of variance explained by extending the Thong et al. (1996) framework appears reasonable. For example, Harrison et al. (1997) reported that attitude, subjective norm, and perceived control explained approximately 27% of the variance in the intention to expand.

In summary, 7 of the 15 hypotheses tested by the structural model were significant (see Table 5). These results provide statistical evidence for the application of the

Thong et al. (1996) model, which was tested with data from Singapore, in a Canadian context for predicting small businesses' IS outcomes and the intention to expand IS.

Discussion

The objectives of this study were to test the Thong et al. (1996) model within a Canadian context, to extend the model to include the construct of the intention of IS expansion, and to compare the Canadian results to the Singaporean results. With regard to the expansion construct, it seems that although some of the directions in the relations between IS success, managerial support, and IS expertise with the intention of IS expansion are not clear, it is worthwhile to include this construct in the model since almost one quarter of its variance is explained by the independent variables in the model.

The Thong et al. (1996) model tested with Singaporean data is, for the most part, applicable to a Canadian context. Overall, managerial support is a predictor of IS effectiveness in both studies. IS effectiveness in both studies is conceptualized as user satisfaction, organizational impact, and overall IS effectiveness. The first difference was that while this study strongly supported the hypothesis regarding managerial support and user satisfaction (see Table 6), Thong et al. did not find a significant relation. The reason for this difference might be that Thong et al. distributed their survey instrument only to managers who used the IS, whereas this study did not differentiate between managers who used IS and those who did not directly interact with IS. Hence, in this study, managers who did not use IS often expressed their opinions regarding their satisfaction with the technology. Other studies have found that in fact managerial support and user satisfaction are positively associated (i.e., Thong, 2001; Yap et al., 1992), which is consistent with the results reported in this study. In contrast, the relations between managerial support, organizational impact, and overall IS effectiveness reported in this study were consistent with the Singaporean results of Thong et al. As a result, this study provides evidence that the commitment of managers in the implementation of IS for Canadian small businesses is essential for IS effectiveness.

Vendor support is positively associated with IS effectiveness. This is consistent with Thong et al. (1996) and Yap et al. (1992). This finding is also related to Attewell's (1992) notion of knowledge barriers. Although managerial support must provide business expertise to the implementation process, vendors bring the IS experience needed, thereby lowering the barrier of IS knowledge. Also, managerial support is more highly related to user satisfaction, organizational impact, and overall IS effectiveness than vendor support. Conversely, Thong et al. stated that vendor support

Table 6. Path coefficient comparison

Hypothesis	Path Coefficient	
	Singapore	Canada
Managerial support → User satisfaction	0.01 0	.420***
Managerial support → Organizational impact	0.09[a] 0	.240*
Managerial support → Overall IS effectiveness	0.13[a] 0	.342**
Consultant effectiveness → User satisfaction	0.19[a]	0.017
Consultant effectiveness → Organizational impact	0.05[a] -	0.153
Consultant effectiveness → Overall IS effectiveness	0.11[a] -	0.034
Vendor support → User satisfaction	0.33[a] 0	.206*
Vendor support → Organizational impact	0.20[a] 0	.267**
Vendor support → Overall IS effectiveness	0.23[a] 0	.237*

*Note: All the path coefficients in Thong et al. (1996) were significant at 0.05 or better, except for the path from managerial support to user satisfaction. * = 0.05 ** = 0.01 *** = 0.001*

was more important than managerial support for a successful IS implementation based on the Singaporean data. This difference may be due to a potential different cultural interaction between vendors and managers, and Canadian small business managers appear to support vendors more than consultants. Furthermore, Thong et al. found that vendor support was more closely related to IS effectiveness than consultant effectiveness. Moreover, Thong et al. (1994) empirically supported the adoption of vendor-only services to provide small business in Singapore with more effective IS than consulting services or any combination of both. The findings in this study support this statement. The vast majority of the Canadian small businesses adopted IS through vendors or a combination of them. Therefore, vendor support plays a key role for the success of IS among small businesses in western Canada.

The second difference was Thong et al. (1996) found that consultant effectiveness influenced user satisfaction, organizational impact, and overall IS effectiveness for the Singaporean data, whereas the relations between consultant effectiveness and the variables for IS effectiveness were not significant (see Table 6) in the Canadian study. An analysis of the means of the items for the consultant-effectiveness construct indicated that small businesses in Singapore were more satisfied with the effectiveness of consultants than the small businesses in Canada. It is possible that the quality and availability of consultants might vary between Singapore and a small city in western Canada and, therefore, this might have impacted the results.

It is important to acknowledge that there are potential cultural differences between small businesses operating in Singapore and western Canada. For example, during

Table 7. R² comparison

	R²	
Dependent Variable	Singapore	Canada
User satisfaction	0.31 0	.23
Organizational impact 0	.10	0.12
Overall IS effectiveness	0.19 0	.17

the pretesting of the survey instrument, it became obvious that small businesses in western Canada used different consultants and vendors for hardware and software acquisitions. In contrast, the Thong et al. (1996) study suggested that small businesses operating in Singapore may have used the same consultants and vendors for hardware and software purchases.

As in the previous discussion regarding the path coefficients, a comparison of the predictive power of the model between the Thong et al. (1996) study and this study is presented in Table 7. Interestingly, the predictive power of the model in both studies was similar for organizational impact and overall IS effectiveness (cf., 0.10 and 0.12, and 0.19 and 17, respectively). In contrast, the explained variance of user satisfaction in the Canadian study was lower (cf., 0.23 and 0.31, respectively) than that reported by the Thong et al. study.

Several reasons could explain the differences in the results reported in the two studies. For example, analyzing the model with only those businesses that had an employee in charge of IS increased the explained variance in user satisfaction in the Canadian model to 26%. This suggests that businesses with in-house IS employees obtained computer technology that better matched their business needs and, therefore, they were more satisfied with their systems. Furthermore, when three resource variables—resources to purchase IS, time to plan for IS, and knowledge to purchase IS—were included in the PLS model, each explained variance increased substantially to over 26%. In this case, the R^2 of user satisfaction reached 0.29, closer to the Thong et al. (1996) results.

The change in R^2 can be explored to see whether the influence of recently included exogenous variables on the endogenous variable is substantive. Based on Cohen's (1988) guideline, the results of the effect size f^2 indicated that the resource variables had a medium effect on organizational impact ($f^2 = 0.1957$) and overall IS effectiveness ($f^2 = 0.1305$), and a small effect on user satisfaction ($f^2 = 0.0900$).

In addition, analyzing the model for only those Canadian small businesses that did not have any adoptions during the six months before this study increased the explained variance of user satisfaction to 36%. In this case, the explained variance for organizational impact also increased to over 34%. Once again, this analysis suggests that the recent adoption of IS by Canadian firms was affecting the results.

Furthermore, the Thong et al. (1996) study provided a positive association between consultant effectiveness and user satisfaction, organizational impact, and overall IS effectiveness. However, the results of this study contradict the findings of Thong et al. There are two explanations for this difference. First, the data of this study indicate that of the 105 Canadian small businesses, only 57 used consultants to purchase hardware and/or software. The rest of the businesses obtained consulting services either through vendors or they did not employ consultants at all. Unfortunately, Thong et al. did not provide any information with respect to the number of small businesses in Singapore that used consulting services in their study.

Finally, another possible explanation for the different results with respect to consultant effectiveness is again related to the different characteristics of the two samples. Thus, while in Thong et al. (1996) 42 businesses out of a total of 114 Singaporean businesses (36.84% of the sample) had fewer than 25 employees, in this study, 79 of the adopter firms in Canada (76% of the sample) had fewer than 25 employees. In addition, in this study 95 Canadian businesses (91.3% of the total) had fewer than 50 employees, while in Thong et al. there were 72 Singaporean businesses (63.15% of the total) with fewer than 50 employees. Furthermore, only 9 Canadian businesses in this study employed between 50 and 100 employees, while in the Thong et al. study, there are 41 Singaporean organizations. These differences in the sizes of the small businesses may provide some insight into the different results regarding consultant effectiveness. Thus, when a business has fewer employees, their operational tasks are easier to coordinate, and communication may be more direct. Conversely, when a business has more employees, for example, more than 50, the coordination of the tasks becomes more complex, and communication may be indirect or multileveled. IS implementation for these two situations would be substantially different and may affect the use of consulting services.

Limitations

There are five limitations that should be noted when interpreting the findings of this study. First, in this cross-sectional study, only a single research methodology has been used. Other methodologies, such as a triangulation, may enrich the findings and complement the numerical results with a deeper understanding of the situation of IS among small businesses in western Canada. Second, the generalization of the results is limited. This study was conducted in a midsize city in western Canada. Thus, the results may not be applicable to larger Canadian cities such as Toronto or Vancouver. Furthermore, the findings may not apply to other midsize cities in Canada embedded in a different cultural environment, such as those in Quebec.

Third, this is a cross-sectional study and, therefore, the causality of results cannot be demonstrated. A longitudinal study could be used to determine the causal links more explicitly and to enhance the reliability of the results over time. Fourth, this study was carried out in Canada while the study of Thong et al. (1996) was conducted in Singapore. Canada and Singapore score differently in some of Hofstede's (1980) cultural dimensions, specifically in uncertainty avoidance, individualism, and power distance. Therefore, cultural characteristics may influence the association between the studied constructs in each country as well as the results. Finally, the measurement of overall IS effectiveness consists of only two items. The use of a measurement for overall IS effectiveness with more items may have been more reliable.

Implications

The findings of this study have implications for practice and research. With respect to practice, there are four main implications. First, small business managers in Canada need to get involved in the critical stages of the implementation process and decision-making with respect to IS, as well as monitor the project and the parties involved in it. Although demanding that managers in Canada supervise the implementation in detail on a daily basis would be impractical due to the constraints on their available time, managerial support is the most important factor for the successful implementation of IS, and their involvement in the implementation process is essential. Second, Canadian small businesses should engage qualified vendors who have experience, who understand the unique characteristics of small business, and who maintain good working relationships with all parties involved in the process. Third, managers in Canada need to be aware that qualified vendors can provide not only effective IS, but they can also help businesses overcome their lack of IS knowledge. Managers should be aware that vendors can also provide adequate expertise for increasing the IS knowledge of the business. Finally, vendors should be aware of the critical role they play in the IS implementation process of Canadian small businesses. They should direct efforts to understand the characteristics and needs of this type of business. Furthermore, vendors need to help small Canadian businesses in the acquisition of IS knowledge by providing them with quality and adequate training.

This chapter has four main implications for research. First, there is a positive association between vendor and managerial support, and IS effectiveness. Thus, this study complements previous research by having supported this association within a Canadian context. Further studies may replicate this study to enhance the external validity of the results. Second, there are contradictory findings between this study and previous literature with respect to the relation of consultant effectiveness and IS effectiveness. There are a number of potential phenomena, such as business size and the existence of an in-house IS employee, that may affect the results. Future research could include these potential sources of differences in order to provide an empirical explanation of the differences between these results and previous findings. Third, the intention of IS expansion is a construct that complements the model tested in Singapore. However, the relations of the intention of IS expansion and the model of IS success are not clear enough. Future research could study the extent of the relations between IS success and the intention of IS expansion. Finally, it would be interesting to expand the model by introducing constructs such as IS knowledge, resources to purchase IS, and time to plan for IS. The secondary results, based on the Canadian data, show the importance of these variables and the possibility that they could explain to a greater extent the variances of the dependent variables.

Conclusion

One of the objectives of this study was to examine the Thong et al. (1996) model of IS effectiveness, which was tested in Singapore, within a Canadian environment. This objective has been achieved, and the results showed that managerial support and vendor support are predictors of IS effectiveness among the small businesses in the small city in western Canada. In contrast to the Singapore findings of Thong et al., the positive relation between consultant effectiveness and IS effectiveness was not supported in this Canadian study.

The second objective of this project was to expand the Thong et al. (1996) model by including the construct of the intention of IS expansion for adopter small businesses. With respect to this objective, although the Canadian results supported only one of the hypotheses regarding the intention of IS expansion, there is evidence to support the idea that the model explains a substantial percentage of the variance of this construct.

Future studies should direct more research efforts to further investigate the expansion of the Thong et al. (1996) model and enhance the external validity of the results. In addition, researchers could introduce resource variables into the model to further investigate the resource constraints that small businesses face, and the extent to which these variables may influence the results.

Overall, the findings in this Canadian project call for the engagement of quality vendors by supportive managers in order to obtain effective IS. Moreover, vendors should provide small businesses in Canada with the necessary IS expertise to implement IS, as well as quality advice and training to increase small businesses' IS knowledge. On the other hand, small business managers in Canada need to get involved in the key stages of the IS implementation process as well as actively participate in the decision-making regarding IS.

References

Attewell, P. (1992). Technology diffusion and organizational learning: The case of business computing. *Organization Science, 3*(1), 1-19.

Azjen, I. (1991). The theory of planned behavior. *Organizational Behavior and Human Decision Processes, 50*(2), 179-211.

Azjen, I., & Fishbein, M. (1980). *Understanding attitudes and predicting social behavior.* Englewood Cliffs, NJ: Prentice-Hall.

Bailey, J.E., & Pearson, S.W. (1983). Development of a tool for measuring and analyzing computer user satisfaction. *Management Science, 29*(5), 530-545.

Bode, S., & Burn, J. (2002). Strategies for consultancy engagement for e-business development: A case analysis of Australian SMEs. In S. Burgess (Ed.), *Managing information technology in small business: Challenges and solutions* (pp. 98-117). Hershey, PA: Idea Group Publishing.

Burgess, S. (2002). Information technology in small business: Issues and challenges. In S. Burgess (Ed.), *Managing information technology in small business: Challenges and solutions* (pp. 1-17). Hershey, PA: Idea Group Publishing.

Chin, W.W. (1998). The partial least squares approach to structural equation modeling. In G.A. Marcoulides (Ed.), *Modern methods for business research* (pp. 295-336). Mahwah, NJ: Lawrence Erlbaum Associates.

Choe, J.M. (1996). The relationships among performance of accounting information systems, influence factors, and evolution level of information systems. *Journal of Management Information Systems, 12*(4), 215-239.

Cohen, J. (1988). *Statistical power analysis for the behavioral sciences* (2nd ed.). Hillsdale, NJ: Lawrence Erlbaum Associates.

Cragg, P.B., & King, M. (1993). Small-firm computing: Motivators and inhibitors. *MIS Quarterly, 17*(1), 47-60.

DeLone, W.H. (1981). Firm size and the characteristics of computer use. *MIS Quarterly, 5*(4), 65-77.

DeLone, W.H. (1988). Determinants of success for computer usage in small business. *MIS Quarterly, 12*(1), 51-61.

DeLone, W.H., & McLean, E.R. (1992). Information systems success: The quest for the dependent variable. *Information Systems Research, 3*(1), 60-95.

Dillman, D.A. (2000). *Mail and Internet surveys: The tailored design method.* New York: John Wiley & Sons.

Duxbury, L., Decady, Y., & Tse, A. (2002). Adoption and use of computer technology in Canadian small businesses: A comparative study. In S. Burgess (Ed.),

Managing information technology in small business: Challenges and solutions (pp. 19-47). Hershey, PA: Idea Group Publishing.

Ein-Dor, P., & Segev, E. (1978). Organizational context and the success of management information systems. *Management Science, 24*(10), 1064-1077.

El Louadi, M. (1998). The relationship among organization structure, information technology and information processing in small Canadian firms. *Canadian Journal of Administrative Sciences, 15*(2), 180-190.

Epstein, B.J., & King, W.R. (1982). An experimental study of the value of information. *Omega, 10*(3), 249-258.

Fishbein, M., & Azjen, I. (1975). *Belief, attitude, intention and behavior: An introduction to theory and research.* Reading, MA: Addison-Wesley.

Fornell, C. (Ed.). (1982). *A second generation of multivariate analysis* (Vol. 1). New York: Praeger.

Fornell, C., & Larcker, D. (1981). Evaluating structural equation models with unobservable variables and measurement error. *Journal of Marketing Research, 18,* 39-50.

Gable, G.G. (1991). Consultant engagement for computer system selection: A proactive client role in small businesses. *Information & Management, 20,* 83-93.

Garris, J.M., & Burch, E.E. (1983). Small businesses and computer panic. *Journal of Small Business Management, 21*(3), 19-24.

Ginzberg, M.J. (1981). Key recurrent issues in the MIS implementation process. *MIS Quarterly, 5*(2), 47-59.

Hamilton, S., & Chervany, N.L. (1981). Evaluation information system effectiveness part II: Comparing evaluator viewpoints. *MIS Quarterly, 5*(4), 79-86.

Harrison, D.A., Mykytyn, P.P., & Riemenschneider, C.R. (1997). Executive decisions about adoption of information technology in small business: Theory and empirical tests. *Information Systems Research, 8*(2), 171-193.

Hofstede, G. (1980). *Culture's consequences: International differences in work-related values.* Beverly Hills, CA: Sage Publications.

Hofstede, G. (1993). Cultural constraints in management theories (Electronic version). *The Executive, 7*(1).

Hunter, M.G., & Beck, J.E. (1996). A cross-cultural comparison of "excellent" systems analysts. *Information Systems Research, 6*(4), 261-281.

Hunter, M.G., Diochon, M., Pugsley, D., & Wright, B. (2002). Unique challenges for small business adoption of information technology: The case of the Nova Scotia ten. In S. Burgess (Ed.), *Managing information technology in small business: Challenges and solutions* (pp. 98-117). Hershey, PA: Idea Group Publishing.

Hunter, M.G., & Long, W.A. (2002). *Information technology and small business: Lessons from the entrepreneurial process*. Paper presented at the Information Resources Management Association International Conference (IRMA), Seattle, WA.

Hunter, M.G., & Long, W.A. (2003). Adopting the entrepreneurial process in the study of information systems and small business. In G. Gingrich (Ed.), *Managing IT in government, business, and communities*. Hershey, PA: IRM Press.

Hwang, M.I., Windsor, J.C., & Pryor, A. (2000). Building a knowledge base for MIS research: A meta-analysis of a systems success model. *Information Resources Management Journal, 13*(2), 26-32.

Igbaria, M., Zinatelli, N., Cragg, P., & Cavaye, L.M. (1997). Personal computing acceptance factors in small firms: A structural equation model. *MIS Quarterly, 21*(2), 279-302.

Ives, B., Olson, M.H., & Baroudi, J.J. (1983). The measurement of user information satisfaction. *Communications of the ACM, 26*(10), 785-793.

Jarvenpaa, S.L., & Ives, B. (1991). Executive involvement and participation in the management of information technology. *MIS Quarterly, 15*(2), 205-227.

Kimberly, J.R., & Evanisko, M.J. (1981). Organizational innovation: The influence of individual, organizational, and contextual factors on hospital adoption of technological and administrative innovations. *Academy of Management Research, 24*(4), 689-713.

King, J.L., & Schrems, E.L. (1978). Cost-benefits analysis in IS development and operation. *Computing Surveys, 10*(1), 19-34.

King, W.R., & Rodriguez, J.I. (1978). Evaluating management information systems. *MIS Quarterly, 2*(3), 43-51.

Kleijnen, J.P.C. (1980). *Computers and profits: Quantifying financial benefits of information*. Boston: Addison-Wesley.

Kole, M.A. (1983). Going outside for MIS implementation. *Information & Management, 6,* 261-268.

Lefebvre, L.A., & Lefebvre, E. (1988). Computerization of small firms: A study of the perceptions and expectations of managers. *Journal of Small Business and Entrepreneurship, 5*(5), 48-58.

Lucas, H.C., Jr. (1981). *Implementation: The key to successful information systems*. New York: McGraw-Hill.

Maish, A.M. (1979). A user's behavior towards his MIS. *MIS Quarterly, 3*(1), 39-52.

Malone, S.C. (1985). Computerizing small business information systems. *Journal of Small Business Management, 23*(2), 10-16.

Pollard, C.E., & Hayne, S.C. (1998). The changing faces of information system issues in small firms (Electronic version). *International Small Business Journal, 16*(3).

Pugsley, D., Wright, B., Diochon, M., & Hunter, M.G. (2000). *Information technology and small business: Listening to voices from the field.* Paper presented at the Administrative Sciences Association of Canada (ASAC) Conference, Montreal, Quebec.

Rai, A., Lang, S.S., & Welker, R. (2002). Assessing the validity of IS success models: An empirical test and theoretical analysis. *Information Systems Research, 13*(1), 50-59.

Raymond, L. (1985). Organizational characteristics and MIS success in the context of small business. *MIS Quarterly, 9*(1), 37-52.

Raymond, L. (1990). Organizational context and information systems success: A contingency approach. *Journal of Management Information Systems, 6*(4), 5-20.

Salmant, P., & Dillman, D.A. (1994). *How to conduct your own survey.* New York: John Wiley & Sons, Inc.

Seddon, P.B. (1997). A respecification and extension of the DeLone and McLean model of IS success. *Information Systems Research, 8*(3), 240-253.

Seddon, P., & Kiew, M.Y. (1994). A partial test and development of the DeLone and McLean model of IS success. *Proceedings of the 15th International Conference on Information Systems,* Vancouver, BC (pp. 99-110).

Senn, A., & Gibson, V.R. (1981). Risk of investment in microcomputers for small business management. *Journal of Small Business Management, 19*(3), 24-32.

Stevenson, H.H. (1999). A perspective of entrepreneurship. In H.I. Grousebeck, M.J. Roberts, & A. Bhide (Eds.), *New business ventures and the entrepreneur* (pp. 3-17). Boston: Irwin McGraw-Hill.

Swanson, E.B. (1982). Measuring user attitudes in MIS research: A review. *Omega, 10,* 157-165.

Thong, J.Y.L. (1999). An integrated model of information systems adoption in small businesses (Electronic version). *Journal of Management Information Systems, 15*(4).

Thong, J.Y.L. (2001). Resource constraints and information systems implementation in Singaporean small businesses. *Omega, 29*(2), 143-156.

Thong, J.Y.L., Yap, C.S., & Raman, K.S. (1994). Engagement of external expertise in information system implementation (Electronic version). *Journal of Management Information Systems, 11*(2).

Thong, J.Y.L., Yap, C.S., & Raman, K.S. (1996). Top management support, external expertise and information systems implementation in small business. *Information Systems Research, 7*(2), 248-267.

Venkatesh, V., & Brown, S.A. (2001). A longitudinal investigation of personal computers in homes: Adoption determinants and emerging challenges. *MIS Quarterly, 25*(1), 71-102.

Welsh, J.A., & White, J.F. (1981). A small business is not a little big business. *Harvard Business Review, 59*(4), 18-32.

Wernerfelt, B.A. (1984). A resource-based view of the firm. *Strategic Management Journal, 5*(2), 171-180.

Wernerfelt, B.A. (1995). The resource-based view of the firm: Ten years later. *Strategic Management Journal, 16*(3), 171-174.

Yap, C.S. (1989). Issues in managing information technology. *Journal of Operational Research Society, 40*(7), 649-658.

Yap, C.S., Soh, C.P.P., & Raman, K.S. (1992). Information systems success factors in small business. *Omega, 20*(5/6), 597-609.

Zikmund, W.G. (2000). Business research methods. In *South-Western* (6th ed.). Mason, OH: South-Western Thomson Learning.

Endnotes

[1]   For the purposes of the study executed in Canada, IS and IT were viewed as synonymous.

[2]   PLS is a regression-based technique that analyzes the structural models, both direct and indirect paths, and the measurement models of multiple-item constructs. PLS produces item loadings (similar to principal components analysis) for the manifest variables, standardized regression coefficients for the paths between constructs, and R2 values for the endogenous constructs.

This work was previously published in the Journal of Global Information Management, 13(3), 55-79, July-September 2005.

Chapter XI

E-Government Implementation Framework and Strategies in Developed vs. Developing Countries

Y. N. Chen, Western Kentucky University, USA

H. M. Chen, Shanghai Jiaotong University, China

W. Huang, Ohio University, USA

R. K. H. Ching, California State University, USA

Abstract

Given the fact that more and more governments invest heavily in its design and implementation, e-government has become an evolving and important research area in the IS field. Recent studies have shown an increase in the adoption of e-government by various countries (e.g., Archer, 2005; I-Ways, 2005; Janssen, rotthier, & Snijkers, 2004). Most, if not all, currently published e-government strategies are based on successful experience from developed countries, which may not be directly applicable to developing countries. Based on literature review, this study summarizes main differences between developed and developing countries in various aspects. In addition, this study identifies key factors for a successful e-government implementation and proposes an e-government implementation framework. As a demonstration, we follow the guidance of the proposed framework in conducting a case study to analyze the implementation strategies of e-government in developed and developing countries.

Introduction

With the Internet surging, governments at all levels are utilizing it to reinvent their structure and efficiency, coining the term "e-government" to describe this initiative. Bill Gates of Microsoft claims that e-government is one of the most exciting fields in electronic commerce in the near future. E-government is a cost-effective solution that improves communication between government agencies and their constituents by providing access to information and services online. *The Economist* magazine estimates that the potential savings of implementing e-government could be as much as $110 billion and 144 billion English pounds in the U.S. and Europe respectively (Symonds, 2000). Though a new subject, e-government has attracted more and more research interest and focus from industries, national governments, and universities (Carter & Belanger, 2005; Chen, Huang, Chen, & Ching, 2006; Chircu & Lee, 2003; Grönlund & Horan, 2004; Huang, Siau, & Wei, 2004; Jain & Patnayakuni, 2003; Moon & Norris, 2005; Navarra & Cornford, 2003), such as IBM's Institute for Electronic Government and various "e-government task forces" in different countries (Huang, D'Ambra, & Bhalla, 2002).

E-government is a permanent commitment made by government to improve the relationship between the private citizen and the public sector through enhanced, cost-effective, and efficient delivery of services, information, and knowledge. Broadly defined, e-government includes the use of all information and communication technologies, from fax machines to wireless palm pilots, to facilitate the daily administration of government, exclusively as an Internet driven activity that improves citizen's access to government information, services, and expertise to ensure citizen's participation in, and satisfaction with government process (UN & ASPA, 2001). Narrowly defined, e-government is the production and delivery of government services through IT applications; used to simplify and improve transactions between governments and constituents, businesses, and other government agencies (Sprecher, 2000).

The development and implementation of e-government brings about impacts and changes to the structure and functioning of the public administration (Snellen, 2000). Unlike the traditional bureaucratic model where information flows only vertically and rarely between departments, e-government links new technology with legacy systems internally and, in turn, links government information infrastructures externally with everything digital (Tapscott, 1995). Moreover, e-government will help in breaking down agency and jurisdictional barriers to allow more integrated whole-of-government services across the three tiers of government (federal, state, and local). Government in the offline environment can be difficult to access, which is especially problematic for people in regional and remote locations. E-government offers a potential to dramatically increase access to information and services. E-government makes it easier for citizens to participate in and contribute to governmental issues.

Various stages of e-government reflect the degree of technical sophistication and interaction with users (Hiller & Belanger, 2001). A broad model with a three-phase and dual-pronged strategy for implementing electronic democracy is proposed by Watson and Mundy (2000) (see Figure 1). The three phases draw on the principles of skill development (Quinn, Anderson, & Finkelstein, 1996), and the prongs echo the dual foundations of democratic government—effectiveness and efficiency. Note that we identify e-government and e-politics as elements of e-democracy. E-government informs citizens about their representatives and how they may be contacted, and it improves government efficiency by enabling citizens to pay transactions online; whereas e-politics is the use of Internet technology to improve the effectiveness of political decisions by making citizens aware of the how and why of political decision making and facilitating their participation in this process.

The *initiation phase* focuses on providing citizens with a single point of access to government information and Web-enabling government payments are the critical initial goals. For a minimum level of political involvement, citizens need to know who represents them and what is happening in the political scene.

Figure 1. Three-phases model

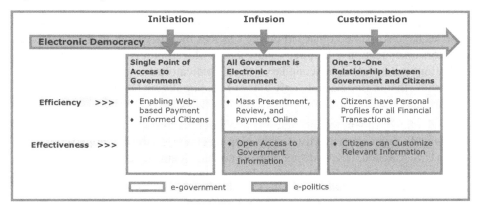

When the e-democracy proceeds to the *infusion phase*, nearly all governments adopt the principles of e-government. Online review and payment applications are widely installed. Citizens can make most government payments via the Web and electronic bill presentment is the standard. Government becomes more efficient via two major approaches. Small governments opt for an application service provider (ASP) solution, while large governments implement in-house systems. An initiation stage is necessary because governments need to create the infrastructure (e.g., software firms, methodologies, consulting skills), acquaint governments and citizens with the concept of e-government, and learn how to scale from a handful to tens of thousands of online government services. Once the foundation of skills and knowledge has been built and the idea has gained currency, large-scale adoption is feasible.

With the further development of e-government, citizens will not be satisfied with a one-size-fits-all solution, and customization will be demanded. During the *customization phase*, electronic democracy implements a one-to-one relationship between citizen and government. To further improve their personal efficiency, all citizens have an electronically maintained, personal profile of their financial interactions with government. An address change, for example, is a single transaction that automatically notifies all government systems. In addition, citizens can get a detailed breakdown of their particular government payments so that they are more directly connected with how their taxes and fees are spent (e.g., amount contributed to education).

Developed vs. Developing Countries

Every year the United Nations releases a report on the least developed countries (LDC) and compares their economic conditions in several different categories. For 2002, 49 countries were designated as the least developed. These countries were decided based on their low GDP per capita, their weak human assets, and their high degree of economic vulnerability (UNCTAD, 2002). E-government implementation and development is a high-priority issue on various countries' agenda. Some countries have surpassed others in online services that they offer to their citizens. Indicators on education and literacy show that in Mozambique, only 7% of the total population was enrolled in secondary school. Indicators on communications and media show that in Bangladesh, only 3.4% of the population has a telephone, while 9.3% are in the circulation of daily newspapers (UNCTAD, 2002).

Although e-government technologies have a potential to improve the lives of 80% of the world's population that lives in developing countries, the developed countries such as U.S., Canada, UK, and Australia are so far leaders in e-government (Annual Global Accenture Study, 2002), reaping the vast majority of initial gains of e-government implementation. Actually, the gap between developed and developing countries in Internet technological infrastructures, practices, and usage has been wider rather than narrower over recent years. Besides the lack of sufficient capital to build up expensive national information infrastructure (NII) on which e-government is based, developing countries also lack the sufficient knowledge and skill to develop suitable and effective strategies for establishing and promoting e-government.

An estimated 500 e-government programs were launched in the year 2001 by governments worldwide (Palmer, 2002). E-government strategies have had a tremendous impact on the way governments interact with their citizens. More than 75% of Australians file income taxes online, while the mayor of Minnesota receives about 13,000 emails from the public each week (Palmer, 2002). According to the 2002 Annual Global Accenture (former Anderson Consulting: AC) Study, Canada is the leader in e-government implementation. The remaining top 10 countries are (in order): Singapore, the U.S., Australia, Denmark, the United Kingdom, Finland, Hong Kong, Germany, and Ireland. A survey by the United Nations found that of its 190 member states, only 36 out of the 169 available Web sites had one-stop portals, and less than 20 offered online transactions (Jackson, 2002). This clearly shows a big gap in current e-government implementation status in different countries. A more recent study, using United Nations data, empirically proves that e-government development and implementation differ in three areas: income level, development status, and region (Siau & Long, 2005).

In comparison with other countries, the United States, along with Australia, Singapore, and Canada, are the early leaders in the march toward e-government. Governments in the United Kingdom, France, Germany, Spain, Norway, Hong Kong, and New Zealand have vowed to change their policies towards the implementation of e-government in order to take full advantage of the digital information age. Other cautious implementers include Italy, Japan, Netherlands, and South Africa. Though there has been significant progress made in developed countries in e-government implementation, many developing countries have been left behind with a long way to catch up. Table 1 summarizes differences between developed and developing countries in various aspects of government.

History and Culture

The history and culture between developed and developing countries are different in many aspects. Developed countries are known more for their early economic and governmental growth, with many governments forming in the 1500s. Several of the developing countries have just recently gained their independence, and still do not have a specific government structure. Culture is also a major difference between developed and developing countries. Religious and other backgrounds among citizens of developing countries defer them from doing certain activities that are commonplace among developed countries. War is also notorious among

Table 1. Main differences between developed and developing countries

	Developed Countries	Developing Countries
History and Culture	• Government and economy developed early, immediately after independence • Economy growing at a constant rate, productivity increasing, high standard of living • Relatively long history of democracy and more transparent government policy and rule	• Government usually not specifically defined; economy not increasing in productivity • Economy not growing or increasing productivity; low standard of living • Relatively short history of democracy and less transparent government policy and rule
Technical Staff	• Has a current staff, needs to increase technical abilities and hire younger professionals • Has outsourcing abilities and financial resources to outsource; current staff would be able to define requirements for development	• Does not have a staff, or has very limited in-house staff • Does not have local outsourcing abilities and rarely has the financial ability to outsource; current staff may be unable to define specific requirements
Infrastructure	• Good current infrastructure • High Internet access for employees and citizens	• Bad current infrastructure • Low Internet access for employees and citizens
Citizens	• High Internet access and computer literacy; still has digital divide and privacy issues • Relatively more experienced in democratic system and more actively participate in governmental policy-making process	• Low Internet access and citizens are reluctant to trust online services; few citizens know how to operate computers • Relatively less experienced in democratic system and less actively participate in governmental policy-making process
Government Officers	• Decent computer literacy and dedication of resources; many do not place e-government at a high priority	• Low computer literacy and dedication of resources; many do not place e-government a high priority due to lack of knowledge on the issue

some developing countries in the Middle East and Asia (e.g., Afghanistan), which depletes their economy and their government structure.

Technology Staff

The in-house staff for most developed countries has been in existence and well established. Although many of them are old, with half of the existing United States government information technology (IT) workers eligible to retire within the next 3 years (Ledford, 2002), the existing department is up and working. In contrast, many developing countries do not have an IT department in place, or have an IT department that is low skilled and insufficiently equipped. Education in these countries is a major problem, as well as lack of financial resources to pay skilled workers. This brings up major issues with the development and maintenance of systems.

Governments in many developed countries choose to outsource e-government projects. Developed countries often house companies specialized in e-government development within their border, which makes outsourcing an affordable and convenient alternative. Though companies specialized in e-government development may be available in developing countries, the competitive systems development rates they charge may not be affordable for many developing countries. Even if outsourcing is affordable, without appropriate understanding of IT, many government officials of developing countries will find it difficult to specify requirements and resources to devote for the projects to be outsourced.

Infrastructure

The size and abilities of infrastructures between developed and developing countries differ dramatically. For example, India's capacity for international telecom traffic reached just 780 mbps by the end of 2000, which is a mere 1.4% of the capacity available in the neighboring country, China (Dooley, 2002). Developed countries have the infrastructure size and abilities to make Internet and telephone access available to almost all of their residents, with some populations over 300 million. The insufficient infrastructure of developing countries is due to economic conditions, war, or destruction that may have recently occurred, and governmental regulations of the telecommunications industry. A dilemma of government regulations also exists in India, where the sector has been a monopoly since its independence from Great Britain in 1947 (Dooley, 2002). All of these factors unfortunately hinder the progress of e-government in developing countries.

Citizens

The difference of Internet accessibility between developed and developing countries is a reflection of the country's infrastructure and telecommunication abilities. As mentioned previously, developing countries lack financial resources and government stability and structure to contain a sizable infrastructure. This results in low access to the Internet and telephone. One third of the world's population has never made a phone call, and 63 countries have less than 1% access to the Internet (ICeGD, 2002). In developed countries, almost every citizen has access to the Internet, and the rate of computer literacy surpasses that of developing countries.

Government Officers

It is imperative that government officials understand and value e-government. The level of resources they are willing to allocate is dependent on their understanding of technology and the benefits that will ensue. In developed countries, most government officials use the Internet or computers on a daily basis. Therefore, government officials in developed countries are familiar with technology and realize how efficient it is. This increases their dedication to allocating additional resources for further implementation. In developing countries IT is a vague concept, and government officials are somewhat unwilling to allocate already scarce resources towards something they are not familiar with.

A Conceptual Framework of E-Government Implementation

Most, if not all, e-government strategies and implementation plans in developing countries have been based on theories and experiences of developed countries (Huang et al., 2002). Feeling the pressure and demand from citizens to provide e-government services online, many developing countries have no choice but to hastily jump into the e-government implementation wagon by following e-government development strategies proposed and carried out by developed countries. However, due to substantial differences in many key aspects of e-government-related technological and social conditions between developed and developing countries, e-government development strategies and experiences from developed countries may not be directly applicable to developing countries. Even in developed countries, about 20%-25% of e-government projects are either never implemented or abandoned immediately after implementation, and a further 33% fail partially in terms of falling short of major goals, causing significant undesirable outcomes or both (Heeks, 2000).

The Center for International Development at Harvard University supported by IBM, identified four key factors describing differences between developing and developed countries in terms of implementing e-commerce (Kirkman, Osorio & Sachs, 2002). These four factors, which are termed as National e-Government Infrastructure (NeI) factors, are adapted to study e-government in this research.

NeI Factor 1: Network Access

Network access is measured by the availability, cost, and quality of information and communication technology (ICTs) networks, services, and equipment. More specifically, it includes the key elements presented in Table 2.

NeI Factor 2: Network Learning

Network learning concerns two key issues: (1) does an educational system integrate ICTs into its processes to improve learning, and (2) are there technical

Table 2. Network access key elements

Infrastructure Development
Infrastructure development is a necessity before countries can consider any large projects dedicated to e-government. Citizens must have access to services before any of the cost-saving benefits will apply. Also, with a lack of back-end infrastructure, governments and their employees will be unable to move into transactional process and further stages of e-government implementation.
Resources and IT Support
Outsourcing can be an option for countries to implement e-government. The private sector has an obligation to support governments throughout the world in their dedication to e-government. Developing countries need financial discounts and support from the private sector to successfully develop applications, due to their lack of resources and staff.
Utilization
The citizen utilization of the Internet is based on the access to the Internet and the Web site. Technical support must provide 24/7 access, in addition to providing a better infrastructure so that more citizens can utilize the Internet. Much like in developed countries, citizen utilization is an important part of the cost savings for countries.

training programs in the community that can train and prepare an ICT workforce? Technical staffing and training is a major issue in e-government implementation. In developing countries, the problems lie in the lack of financial resources to hire full-time in-house support, and in the inability to find such support due to the lack of education in these countries. Outsourcing is an alternative, however, affordable and competent companies may not be available. Even if a country can find the finances to support an outsourcing project, stability and maintenance of the application are often difficult.

NeI Factor 3: Network Economy

Network economy concerns how businesses and governments use information and communication technologies to interact with the public and with each other. Key issues involved include collaboration, partnership, public-private sector partnership, e-community creation, and so forth. Boundary removal between different agencies in a government is a major issue in e-government. In many developing countries, government structure is undefined and destabilized by corruption and communism. Consequently, boundary removal and department collaboration is a difficult and slow process. In many countries, war and terrorism is a constant issue that disrupts government operations on a daily basis. Government departments must collaborate with each other, with private sectors, and with related communities in order for e-government to be implemented in an efficient way. Due to the low computer literacy and high cost of online access, long and unnecessary transactions need to be cut down in processes to allow users to quickly access documents and print them or fill them out online.

NeI Factor 4: Network Policy

Network policy concerns the extent that the policy environment promotes or hinders the growth of ICT adoption and use. Some related key issues include legislations, laws, strategies (visions and missions), accountability, and so forth. Government agencies and departments must be accountable for their information and the processes they support. It is essential for processes and duties to be segregated and responsibilities to be assigned to appropriate agencies and departments. These agencies and departments then need to work together to design their Web pages and IT flows. After implementation, they must have the abilities, and be held accountable to support the Web pages and troubleshoot them. Governments must also be accountable for their financial and accounting systems. Many developing countries have issues and economic problems due to their lack of reliable accounting systems.

Culture and Society Factors

E-commerce largely deals with business transactions in the private sector, whereas e-government deals with services in the public sector. Due to key differences between private and public sectors (e.g., Bozeman & Bretschneider, 1986; Caudle, Gorr, & Newcomer, 1991; Rainey, Backoff, & Levine, 1976), factors other than the ones identified by the previously-mentioned Harvard University e-commerce research project may also be important to e-government strategies and implementations. Prior relevant research suggested some key factors for e-government strategies and implementations that can be used to identify differences in e-government between developed and developing countries. Those suggested factors include society factors like *history, citizens* (Huang et al., 2002), *government staff and governance* (Wimmer, Traunmuller, & Lenk, 2001), *organizational structure* (Baligh, 1994); and cultural factors like *national culture* (Hoftstede, 1980; Hofstede, 1991), *organizational culture* (Hoftstede, 1980; Schein, 1993), and *social norms* (Ajzen, 1988). Other than those suggested by literature, society factors like *politics* and *information availability* should also be considered. Developing countries are often less democratized, with underdeveloped press communication resulting in unbalanced and deficient information availability. These politics and information factors have significant impact on the speed of infrastructure establishment in developing countries, and thus should be considered in creating e-government strategies.

Figure 2. A conceptual research framework

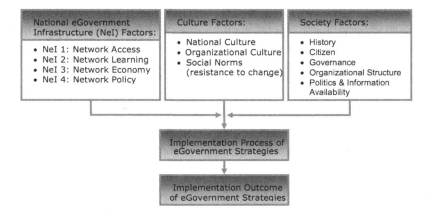

Based upon this literature review and discussion, a research framework incorporating critical success factors (CSFs) that influence e-government strategies and implementations is proposed and shown in Figure 2. Some CSFs identified in proposed framework could be more important to developed countries than to developing countries, or vice versa. The framework can also be used to assess and guide the strategic development of e-government implementation in developed and developing countries.

Case Study

The following case study is used to demonstrate how the proposed e-government implementation framework can be used to analyze different e-government strategies adopted in developed and developing countries. It presents a snapshot of current e-government implementation in the U.S. (the largest developed country) and China (the biggest developing country in the world, with a focus on Shanghai, the biggest city and economic center of China) in comparing their e-government implementation strategy.

E-Government Implementation Strategy in the United States

The U.S., as the largest developed country, has one of the most advanced national e-government infrastructures (NeIs) in the world, and it also has a long history and culture of a democratic government structure and a capitalist economic system. As a result, the U.S. government adopted the following three strategic principles in the implementation of e-government: (1) citizen centered, not bureaucracy centered; (2) results oriented; and (3) market based, actively promoting innovation (source: http://www.firstgov.gov). In short, the e-government implementation strategy of the U.S. is market-based, with the aim of serving and supporting citizens' specific requirements, which is assessed by clear and specific results.

The policy environment in the United States is an important consideration in understanding the strategy for e-government implementation. A complete set of laws relating to the development of e-government had been in place already, including Privacy Act, Computer Matching and Privacy Protection Act, Electronic Freedom of Information Amendments, Computer Security Act, Critical Infrastructure Protection, Government Paperwork Elimination Act, and Electronic Government Act (Relyea, 2002).

According to the white paper of the U.S. federal government's e-government strategy (eGovernment Strategy, 2002, 2003), more than 60% of all Internet users interact with government Web sites. Moreover, by leveraging information technology (IT) spending across federal agencies, the U.S. federal government will make available over $1 billion in savings from aligning redundant investments. Federal IT spending in the United States exceeded $48 billion in 2002 and $52 billion in 2003. That level of IT spending provides enormous opportunities for making the transformation of government into a citizen-centered e-government. Indeed, a good portion of current federal IT spending is devoted to Internet initiatives, yielding over 35 million Web pages online at over 22,000 Web sites. However, past agency-centered IT approaches have limited the government's productivity gains and ability to serve citizens. As a result, the federal government is determined to transform the way it does business with citizens through the use of e-government.

A September 2002 report from the Pew Foundation found that 71 million Americans have used government Web sites—up from 40 million in March 2000. A June 2002 United Nations report, *Benchmarking E-Government: A Global Perspective,* rated the United States as the world leader in e-government on the basis of achievements over the last year. The United States Web portal, FirstGov.gov, which integrates various government services internally and externally for the enhancement of efficiency, usability, and effectiveness, is currently in stage 4 of its implementation (Hiller & Belanger, 2001). FirstGov.gov, which is America's Gateway to more than 180 million Web pages from federal and state governments, the District of Columbia, and U.S. territories, attracts almost 6 million visitors a month. Named one of the "50 Most Incredibly Useful Web Sites" by Yahoo, July 2002, and to *PC Magazine's* "Top 100 Classic Sites," March 2003, FirstGov.gov was most recently awarded the prestigious *Innovations in American Government Award* for transcending traditional government boundaries.

In January 2003, the current e-government project managers met with the members of the 2001 e-government task force. This group of more than 100 government managers shared a number of insights about unresolved e-government challenges that the 2003 strategy should address. None of the identified challenges involved technological barriers (as discussed earlier, the U.S. has one of the best NeIs in the world, so that its main strategic issues for successfully implementing e-government are largely nontechnical issues). The challenges were centered around behavioral or policy changes needed, such as leadership support, parochialism, funding, and communication. Another challenge in 2003 is to physically migrate agency-unique solutions to each cross-agency e-government solution, reducing costs and generating more citizen-centered results. The suggested solutions to these challenges include establishing single sources of information, accessible by citizens in no more than three clicks (one stop portals such as Recreation.gov and Regulations.gov); developing tools that provide a simple one-stop method to access government programs; and establishing common sets of standards for data collection and reporting.

In 2003 and 2004, the overall e-government strategy addressed the following areas:

- **Driving results and productivity growth:** IT and management reform investments that create an order of magnitude improvement in value to the citizen, especially in the areas of homeland security information sharing and knowledge flow;
- **Controlling IT costs:** Consolidating redundant and overlapping investments, enterprise licensing, fixing cost overruns, and competing away excess IT services charges;
- **Implementing the E-government Act of 2002:** Including government-wide architecture governance and Web-based strategies for improving access to high-quality information and services; and
- **Improving cybersecurity:** Desktop, data, applications, networks, threat and vulnerability focused, business continuity, and privacy protection.

In summary, due to the relatively long history of a democratic system, the main goals of the U.S. e-government focus on increasing effectiveness and efficiency of government work and, at the same time, to reduce cost.

Differences Between The U.S. and China

The first e-government implementation project in China began in 1994. According to the 11th Report of the Statistic of China National Network Development (RSCNND) by China National Network Information Centre (CNNIC), up to the end of 2002, the Internet had achieved 59.1 million users. It added up to 9% of the Internet users in the world (655 million). There were 371,600 Web sites, among which 291,323 were in com.cn, 6,148 in gov.cn, 54,156 in net.cn and 1,783 in org.cn. The number of computers linked to the Internet was more than 20.83 million.

Though China has maintained its position as the fastest growing economy in the world in recent years, there still exists a big gap in terms of national e-government infrastructure (NeI) between China and other developed countries like U.S. Even though its economy has developed fast in the last decade, China is still in the process of transitioning from a centrally controlled planned economy to a market-based capitalist economy. Using the proposed framework, we assess the e-government implementation status in China with a focus in Shanghai, the economic centre of China. Shanghai is one of the most developed regions/cities in China. If there exist differences between the U.S. and Shanghai in terms of NeIs and e-government implementation based on the proposed theoretical framework, the differences between the U.S. and China can be even bigger.

1. **Network access:** The information infrastructures in Shanghai have undergone mega changes and made some big progress in recent years: Up to the beginning of year 2002, the bandwidth of Shanghai's Internet connection to the outside world was expended to 2.5G, the network cable lines were stretched out for more than 550 kilometers, which covered more than 99% of the whole city. The number of broadband Internet users in Shanghai reached 125 thousand that year; the number of fixed phone users exceeded 6 million, while mobile phone users exceeded fixed phone users. More than 3.1 million families had access to the Internet, which almost doubled the number of the previous year. However, even in Shanghai, one of the most advanced cities in China, subscribing to Internet service is still more costly in China than in developed countries such as the United States. In China, the charge of ISP (internet service provider) is bidirectional; users pay for not only sending but also receiving information.

2. **Networked learning:** The development of network learning is speeding up in Shanghai. The broadband of the main network of Shanghai Science & Education Network (SSEN) was expanded to 1.25G from the 64k in its budding stage. The fibro-cable connecting the educational institutions in Shanghai was longer than 200 kilometers in year 2001. More than 19 Universities in Shanghai made their effects to launch a common-shared database of the book information in their universities' libraries. In this system, people could also search for the key academic periodicals, and borrow through the Remote Borrowing/Lending Service. Up to year 2001, the SSEN had a sea-sized collection of materials including 12 thousand periodical databases, 200 thousand e-book resources, business subdatabases, science and technology subdatabases, digital periodical system database, and so forth. More than 100 multifunctional databases provided a wide range of selections to the students' content. Furthermore, several universities in Shanghai have gotten permission from the government to develop their "net-school" projects, which made the e-learning in Shanghai more professional and orderly. According to the *Human Development Report in 2001* by the United Nations Development Program (UNDP), which first published the Technical Achievements Index (TAI) in the world, China is listed as 45th among the 72 countries, whereas the U.S. is ranked as number 2 on the list.

3. **Networked economy:** The information industry in Shanghai is keeping a fast-developing momentum in recent years. The turnover of the information industry in Shanghai was 130.225 billion yuan by its growth rate of 24.4%, which maintained its strategic position as Shanghai's first pillar industry. The proportion of the added value in this industry in the GDP amounted to 8.1%,

which was 0.7% more than the previous year. Among the information industry in Shanghai, the turnover of the information product manufactory industry reached 101.3 billion yuan; its growth rate even hit 37.4%. The product sales percentage was also increased by 1.8% and summed up to 97.5%. Meanwhile, the information services and software in Shanghai also achieved an output of 28.8 billion yuan, 52.2% more than the previous year. The information industry in Shanghai has maintained the top three throughout the whole country in terms of its scale, which draws the attention from the worldwide. The network economy is thus greatly enhanced by the strategy Shanghai adopted, "To promote the Industrialization by Informationization." Among the 1,500 industry companies, 80% of them have set up an IT department; 97% of them have popularized the use of computers; 89% of them have gotten familiar with common software; 12% of them have conducted ERP; 8% of them have implanted CRM. More than 500 marketplaces have adopted their MIS; Most Convenient chain stores, supermarkets have launched POS and also have gotten them linked with each other to form a value-added network system. As a whole, China's e-commerce turnover is relatively small in size, accounting for only 0.23% of U.S.' annual e-commerce turnover.

4. **Network policy:** Network policy might be the weakest part of the four NeI factors for China. China has been transforming its economic system from the old Soviet Union's "planned economy" model to the capitalist's "market economy." The transition period, though it seems to be on the right track, is painful and far from completion. The legal systems, laws, and regulations have been gradually established, yet they are far from maturity in managing the big developing economy, not to mention the completeness of its network economy policy and related laws.

Due to its relatively short history of modernized society and long history of feudal governmental system, China's democratic system and policy still has a long way to go, even though it has achieved much more progress in the last decade. For example, up to the year 2002, 12 policies, statutes and regulations were taken into consideration by Shanghai municipal government. The major ones are listed as follows:

•   Regulations on Shanghai's Informationization Projects Management

•   Detailed Rules of the Regulations on the IC Industry and Software Promotions in Shanghai

•   Decision on the Overall Informationization Construction in Shanghai

•   Suggestions on the Information Security in Shanghai

•   Management Measures on the Social Insurance Card System

•   Management Measures on the Public Mobile System

Besides these policies, statutes, and regulations, the implementations are also of the same importance. Shanghai's municipal government is dedicated to the administration, supervision, and mutual discussion of the confusions, in order to achieve a better legal environmental situation.

5. **Culture and society factors:** Developed countries have a long history and culture of democratic governmental structure and capitalist economic system, with many governments forming in the 1500s. Many developing countries have not completed the process of establishing an effective and transparent governmental structure, as well as an efficient capitalist economic system. China only started its "open door" policy in the late 1970s, and its "market-driven economy" in the 1990s. The differences in history and culture, citizens, government officers, and technical staff, between China and other developed countries, like U.S., are also noticeably large.

   For example, China was under the feudal government system for nearly 5,000 years, where the dictator of the country, the emperor, has absolute power and possesses absolute wealth in the country. Only until the early 1910s, such a governmental structure was overturned. However, such a very long history of ruling by an absolute powerful emperor would have an impact on modern governmental structure and system. Even now, national and provincial governments still have certain privileges to access and use valuable resources, such as financial, human, and production resources. Governmental agencies and organizations are generally more effective/powerful than private sectors in carrying out e-government implementations. The level of transparency of governmental management mechanism and the decision-making process is relatively low. Because of those historical reasons and the advantages existing in governments, many university graduates and talents favour to work for governments. As a result, governmental officers and/or technical staff in governments are generally more knowledgeable than those in the private sector in using information technologies and systems in their daily work.

In summary, due to the differences in NeIs and other social issues, it may not be feasible for the private sector to play a leading role in e-government implementation; instead, it may be governments that drive the progress of e-government implementation. Therefore, the e-government implementation strategy between the U.S. and China, which will be discussed, are largely different.

E-Government Implementation Strategy in China

As analyzed, due to the substantial differences in all four key aspects/factors of NeI and other CSFs between China and developed countries like the U.S., instead of adopting the e-government implementation strategies developed in the U.S. directly, China should adopt a strategy that fits well with its current position in terms of the four aspects of NeI and other CSFs, as specified in the proposed assessment framework. For example, as the center of China's economy development, Shanghai's e-government implementation can function as a role model for other cities and provinces in China to follow up. Three specific e-government implementation strategies of Shanghai are specified. They are (1) to increase the transparency of government work, (2) to provide the convenience and better services to citizens and enterprises, and (3) to improve the efficiency of the government administration.

Compared with the U.S.'s e-government strategic principles—"citizen-centered," "results-oriented," and "market based" (eGovernment Strategy, 2003), Shanghai has largely different strategic goals. The ultimate goal of e-government implementation could be quite similar, which is to improve the performance and efficiency of the government work, and lead to better interactions/cooperation between government and the public, and between the government and private enterprises. The unique feature of Shanghai's e-government strategy is to "increase the transparency of the government work." Other than achieving its usual goals, e-government in Shanghai is used as an instrument in expediting government transformation and conformity. Via the implementation of e-government, civil rights are concretized, bribability is minimized, and governance by law and democracy are enhanced.

In general, the e-government implementation in China, as a whole, is aiming to serve its overall economic development goal, which is to completely transform China's former Soviet Union style "planned economy" to "market economy." Such changes in the overall mechanism of the country will definitely have profound effects on e-government implementation strategy and practice. On the other hand, the U.S. has a long history of market economy and democratic system. The government work is relatively much more transparent than that in China. Therefore, "increasing the transparency of government work" may not seem to be as important as it is to China.

In fact, based upon the successful experience of e-government implementation strategies in developed countries, China adopted a different e-government implementation strategy, which could be characterized as "government-driven and partnership with private sector." In this strategy, governmental departments consolidate all forces and resources available in a society (a city or a province) to lead the implementation of e-government while establishing partnership with private sector for the implementation purpose. So far, China's e-government implementation is still at stage 1, with some features in stages 2, 3, and 4 in some economically more-developed cities and provinces, whereas the U.S. may already be at stage 3, according to the 5-stage model (Hiller & Belanger, 2001), and it has achieved some initial results. Chinese government perceived that the rapid development of the Internet in the U.S. resulted from effective and significant direct support and sponsorship from the government through the military, education, and government procurement policies, which has been regarded as a good example and effective means for driving the development of e-government in China by Chinese government.

The dominant role played by Chinese government generally fits well with the historical and cultural characteristics, as well as the NeI of China. In fact, the Chinese government could be the only possible entity in the society that has enough power and capability to coordinate all related government agencies, organizations, and private sectors, as well as consolidate all available resources to effectively implement e-government. The government has also had successful experience in playing the leading role in modernizing its previous out-dated telecommunication industry, which is perhaps the most successful contemporary example of China's interventionist economic strategy. By mid-2001, China's public switching capacity was 300 million circuits, which is the world's largest. This was largely due to the supply-driven program of network rollout by the government, with the growth rate of double digits through the 1990s (Lovelock & Ure, 2001).

The fund for e-government implementation is being mainly covered by governments both at central and provincial levels. For example, the investment by the central national government alone is reportedly standing at over $120 million U.S.D. at the very least (Lovelock & Ure, 2001). By 1998, China has set up 145 gov.cn domain names in China. According to the China Internet Network Center (CNNIC) annual report, the number of current gov.cn domain names is more than 5,864.

The Chinese government is speeding up the construction of network infrastructure in preparing for its completion of e-government implementation in 2005. Since the initiation of first e-government program "Digital Beijing," which Beijing Municipal Government used on computerization of administration procedure and e-education in 1994, Chinese government has made much progress on e-government. The purpose of e-government construction falls into three categories: building the internal network to handle government affairs at all levels and the external Web to handle business in connection with enterprises, public services, and affairs between government; promoting 12 key services involving customs, taxation, finance, public security, social security, and agriculture and water resource; and accelerating establishment of important databanks such as population and agricultural information. Services currently offered by government Web sites mainly include function/vocation introduction, government announcement/laws and regulations, government news, trade/regional information, work guide, and so forth. (Source: Semiannual Survey Report on the Development of China's Internet at January. 2002, China Internet Network Center).

The Government Online Project (GOP) provides good evidence indicating the government's dominant role and support for e-government development in China, and it has three stages. Stage one focuses upon connecting 800-1,000 government offices and agencies to the Internet; stage two focuses on having government offices and agencies move their information systems into compatible electronic form; and stage three will occur sometime late in the decade, when government offices and agencies become paperless.

The purpose of the GOP is to create a centrally accessible administrative system that collects and transports data to and from users, users being the public and the enterprise system, as well as government departments. In other words, the government's strategy for driving the "information economy" is to first launch the GOP by setting up formal government Web sites so that the public can acquire information and procure specific government services via the Internet. The focus then shifts to promoting office automation via government Web sites in order to cut down on excessive bureaucracy, and hence expenses.

By the end of 2000, 80% of all government agencies, both local and national, had established Web sites. Some examples of the implemented e-government Web sites include:

- State Economic and Trade Commission State Administration of Internal Trade
- Central Committee of the League Commission of Science, Tech & Industry for National Defense
- State Administration of Foreign Exchange Control General Office of CP-PCC
- Supreme People's Court Supreme People's Procurator
- Ministry of Agriculture Ministry of Civil Affairs
- Ministry of Foreign Affairs Ministry of Foreign Trade and Economic Cooperation
- Ministry of Information Industry Ministry of Justice
- Ministry of Labor and Social Security Ministry of Land and Natural Resources
- National Bureau of Oceanography National Intellectual Property Right Office
- China Council for Promotion of International Trade China National Space Administration
- CNNIC General Administration of Civil Aviation of China
- General Administration of Customs (Source: Ministry of Information Industry (MII) http://www.mii.gov.cn/mii/index.html)

These are only a few examples of Chinese e-government implementation projects. However, currently most Chinese people cannot pay their taxes, obtain their driver license, ID, residence certificate, and so forth, from the government Web site, and the paperless government still has a long way to go.

The Chinese government, like all governments, is stricken with turf battles between ministries, commissions, and other organs that all view the Internet as touching on their domain of authority or interest. As noted, the Government Online Project was initiated in early 1999. The following two strategic projects were also planned and will be fully implemented in the near future. *Enterprise Online* is to encourage industries to aggressively adopt the full use of available Internet technologies, and to provide a greater degree of transparency. *Family Online* is to encourage increased use of network resources by families across China, including those in rural areas, and to bring the populace at large onto the government's new communications platform.

In summary, while China has achieved its fast economic development in the late decade, it has also started to move to a more democratic and transparent government system and mechanism. E-government has become one key implementation mechanism for the government to achieve its goal of a more transparent government. China, different from the U.S., adopted a different e-government implementation strategy. Based on its own economic, historic and social factors, China's e-government implementation is, so far, largely driven by government, rather than by market forces. In a relatively short time period, it has achieved some noticeable results, although there is still a long way to go.

Discussion and Conclusion

Although there are some prior studies published on e-government strategies and implementation (e.g., Carter & Belanger, 2005; Chircu & Lee, 2003; Glassey, 2001; Greunz, Schopp, & Haes, 2001; Huang et al., 2002; Wimmer et al., 2001), to our knowledge, most, if not all, published e-government strategies are from the perspective of developed countries, not from the perspective of developing countries. Due to the considerable differences between developed and developing countries, the latter cannot directly adopt e-government strategies used in developed countries. For that reason, the current study intends to do some initial work to bridge this gap. It compares strategic issues and implementations of e-government between developed and developing countries. More specifically, the following issues are addressed:

- Proposing a conceptual framework that includes the critical success factors influencing e-government strategies and implementations for developed and developing countries.

- Using a case study to illustrate how the proposed framework can be used to analyze different e-government strategies in a developed country (U.S.) and a developing country (China).

Due to the substantial differences in four aspects of NeI and other CSFs, as specified in the proposed framework, developing countries cannot and should not directly adopt developed countries' successful e-government implementation strategies. The proposed framework provides a clear structure and guideline for developing suitable e-government implementation strategy. Developing countries should consider their own positions in terms of CSFs, as specified in the proposed e-government strategy framework, and learn from other countries' successful e-government implementation strategies, and then work out the e-government implementation strategies that fit with their countries' characteristics and conditions.

Future studies can be conducted to collect national data in both developed and developing countries to empirically and statistically verify the proposed framework and study the relationships among the specified CSFs. More specifically, the importance of those CSFs to e-government strategies and implementation can be ranked through using survey research methodology. More complicated relationships existing between CSFs can be determined using structure equation modeling technique. In this way, CSFs for implementing e-government strategies can be specifically identified and validated. With the guidance of the proposed framework, e-government strategies and implementations in developing countries can be more effective and efficient.

References

Ajzen, I. (1988). *Attitudes, personality and behavior*. Milton Keynes: Open University Press.

Annual Global Accenture, (2002). *Study report*.

Archer, N. P. (2005). An overview of the change management process in *eGovernment. International Journal of Electronic Business, 3*(1), 1-1.

Baligh, H. H. (1994). Components of culture: Nature, interconnections, and relevance to the decisions on the organization structure. *Management Science, 40*(1), 14-28.

Bozeman, B., & Bretschneider S. (1986). Public management information systems: Theory and prescription. *Public Administration Review*, Special Issue, 47-487.

Carter, L., & Belanger, F. (2005). The utilization of e-government services: Citizen trust, innovation and acceptance factors. *Information Systems Journal, 15*(1), 5-25.

Caudle, S. L., Gorr, W. L., & Newcomer, K. E. (1991). Key information systems management issues for the public sector. *MIS Quarterly, 15*(2), 171-188.

Chen, Y. N., Huang, W., Chen, H. M., & Ching, R. K. H. (2006). eGovernment strategies in developed and developing countries—An implementation framework and a case study. *Journal of Global Information Management, 14*(1), 25-48.

Chircu, A. M., & Lee, H.D. (2003). Understanding IT investments in the public sector: The case of e-government. In *Proceedings of American Conference on Information Systems (AMCIS)*, FL.

Dooley, B. L. (2002, February). Telecommunications in India: State of the marketplace, *Faulkner Information Services*, (Docid 00016872).

eGovernment Strategy. (2002, 2003). US Federal Government. Retrieved from http://www.firstgov.gov

Glassey, O. (2001, June 27-29). Model and architecture for a virtual one-stop public administration. In *The 9ᵗʰ European Conferences on Information Systems* (pp. 969-976).

Greunz, M., Schopp, B., & Haes, J. (2001). Integrating e-government infrastructures through secure XML document containers. In *Proceedings of the 34ᵗʰ Hawaii International Conference on System Sciences*.

Grönlund, A., & Horan, T. A. (2004). Introducing e-gov: History, definitions, and issues. *Communications of the Association for Information Systems, 15*, 713-729.

Heeks, R. (2000). *Reinventing government in the Information Age*. London: Roultedge Press.

Hiller, J., & Belanger, F. (2001). Privacy strategies for electronic government. *E-Government Series*. Arlington, VA: PricewaterhouseCoopers Endowment for the Business of Government.

Hofstede, G. (1980). *Culture's consequences: International differences in work-related values*. Newbury Park, CA: Sage Press.

Hofstede, G. (1991). *Cultures and organizations: Software of the mind*. London: McGraw Hill.

Huang, W., D'Ambra, J., & Bhalla, V. (2002). An empirical investigation of the adoption of eGovernment in Australian citizens: Some unexpected research findings. *Journal of Computer Information Systems, 43*(1), 15-22.

Huang, W., Siau, K., & Wei, K. K. (2004). *Electronic government: Strategic and implementations*. Hershey, PA: Idea Group Publishing.

International Conference on e-Government for Development (IceGD). Accessed September 25, 2002, from http://www.palermoconference2002.org/en/home_a.htm

I-Ways (2005). eGovernment in the European Union: Online availability of public services. *I-WAYS, Digest of Electronic Commerce Policy and Regulation, 28*, 92-95.

Jackson, N. (2002, February). State of the marketplace: E-government gateways. *Faulkner Information Services*, (Docid 00018296).

Jain, A., & Patnayakuni, R. (2003, August). Public expectations and public scrutiny: An agenda for research in the context of e-government. *Proceedings of American Conference on Information Systems (AMCIS)*, Florida.

Janssen, D., Rotthier. S., & Snijkers K. (2004). If you measure it they will score: An assessment of international eGovernment benchmarking. *Information Polity, 9*, 121-130.

Kirkman, G. S., Osorio, C. A., & Sachs, J. D. (2002). The networked readiness index: Measuring the preparedness of nations for the networked world. In *The global information technology report: Readiness for the networked world* (pp. 10-30). Oxford University Press.

Ledford, J. L. (2002). Establishing best practices for e-government within the U.S. *Faulkner Information Services* (February) (DocId: 00018275).

Lovelock, & Ure. (2001). *E-government in China*. Retrieved from http://www.trp. hku.hk/publications/e_gov_china.pdf

Moon, J. M. (2002). The evolution of e-government among municipalities: Rhetoric or reality? *Public Administration Review, 62*(4), 424-433.

Moon, M. J., & Norris, D. F. (2005). Does managerial orientation matter? The adoption of reinventing government and e-government at the municipal level. *Information Systems Journal, 15*(1), 43-60.

Navarra, D. D., & Cornford, R. (2003). A policy making view of e-government innovations in public governance. In *Proceedings of American Conference on Information Systems (AMCIS)*, FL.

Palmer, I. (2002). State of the world: E-government implementation. *Faulkner Information Services* (January) (Docid 00018297).

Quinn, J.B., Anderson, P., & Finkelstein, S. (1996). Leveraging intellect. *Academy of Management Executive, 10*(3), 7-27.

Rainey, H. G., Backoff, R. W., & Levine, C. H., (1976). Comparing public and private organizations. *Public Administration Review*, 233- 243.

Relyea, H. C. (2002). E-gov: Introduction and overview. *Government Information Quarterly, 19*, 9-35.

Schein, E. H. (1993). On dialogue, culture, and organizational learning. *Organizational Dynamics*, 40-51.

Siau, K., & Long, Y. (2005). Using social development lenses to understand e-government development. *Journal of Global Information Management*.

Symonds, M. (2000). The next revolution: After eCommerce, get ready for eGovernment.

The Economist. (2000, June 24). Retrieved from http://www.economist.com/l.cgi?f=20000624/index_survey

Snellen, I. (2000). Electronic commerce and bureaucracies. In *Proceedings of the 11ᵗʰ International Workshops on Database and Expert System Application* (pp. 285-288).

Sprecher, M. (2000). Racing to e-Government: Using the Internet for citizen service delivery. *Government Finance Review, 16,* 21-22.

Tapscott, D. (1995). *Digital economy: Promise and peril in the age of networked intelligence.* New York: McGraw-Hill.

UN (United Nations) and ASPA (American Society for Public Administration). (2001). *Global Survey of e-Government.*

UNCTAD (2002). *Least Developed Countries at a Glance.* United Nation Information Communication Technology Task Force.

U.S. Census Bureau. (1999). *Government Organization: 1997 Census of Governments.* Washington, DC. Retrieved from http://www.census.gov/prod/www/abs/gc97org.html

Watson & Mundy. (2000). Electronic democracy: A strategic perspective. *Communications of ACM.*

Wimmer, M., Traunmuller, R., & Lenk, K. (2001). Electronic business invading the public sector: Considerations on change and design. In *Proceedings of the 34ᵗʰ Hawaii International Conference on System Sciences.*

Chapter XII

Organizational Learning Process:
Its Antecedents and Consequences in Enterprise System Implementation

Weiling Ke, Clarkson University, USA

Kwok Kee Wei, City University of Hong Kong, Hong Kong

Abstract

This chapter uses organizational learning as a lens to study how firms implement the enterprise system. The core research questions are: What are the critical organizational factors affecting organizational learning in ES implementation? How do these elements shape the learning process and thereby influence ES implementation outcomes? To address these questions, we conducted comparative case study with two organizations that have recently adopted ES and achieved significantly different results. Based on the empirical findings, we propose a framework that describes how organizational factors affect the four constructs of organizational learning in ES implementation context—knowledge acquisition, information distribution, information interpretation and organizational memory.

Introduction

Over the past few years, enterprise systems (ES) have generated much interest among researchers and practitioners as a potential means to enhance organizational agility (Davenport, 1998; Sambamurthy, Bharadwah, & Grover, 2003). While interest and investment in ES have been rising steadily, actual experiences with ES have exhibited more ambiguity. Some studies report improvements in efficiency and effectiveness from ES adoption, yet others find that the expected gains are far beyond reach (Al-Mashari & Zairi, 2000). It is imperative to conduct research that can make sense of the apparently-inconsistent ES adoption results.

Most of extant research on ES focuses on discrete critical success factors leading to on-time and within budget implementation (e.g., Bingi, Sharma, & Godla, 1999; Holland & Light, 1999; Parr & Shanks, 2000; Sumner, 2000). Yet, to leverage the business value of ES, it is not sufficient to simply adopt and install the system. Rather, employees and the organization as a whole must learn how to apply the technology effectively while they are implementing the system (Argyris & Schon, 1978; Attewell, 1992; Cooper & Zmud, 1990; Fichman & Kemerer, 1997; Purvis, Sambamurthy, & Zmud, 2001). The learning process plays a critical role in shaping IT adoption results (Tippins & Sohi, 2003). Hence studying how different forces affect the organizational learning process allows us to understand what leads to different ES implementation outcomes.

In this chapter, we use organizational learning as a lens to study how firms implement ES. Extant ES literature alludes to organizational learning sporadically and most of them do so in a cursory fashion, except the work of Robey, Ross, and Boudreau (2002) and Scott and Vessey (2000). Different from these studies, this paper studies all four constructs of the underlying learning process involved in ES implementation—knowledge acquisition, information distribution, information interpretation and organizational memory (Huber, 1991). The core research questions are: What are the critical organizational factors affecting organizational learning in ES implementation? How do these elements shape the learning process and thereby influence ES implementation outcomes? To address these questions, we collect data by conducting case studies with two firms that have implemented ES within budget and on-time, but with significant different outcomes.

This chapter makes three principal contributions. First, drawing on the rich data of two organizations' experiences, the chapter generates an understanding of the organizational learning associated with ES implementation. Second, dealing with the complex links traced in context, this chapter adds substantive content to our understanding of the central role played by organizational factors in the organizational learning enacted in ES implementation. Such an understanding has been absent from the research and practice discourses on ES. Third, the chapter integrates our research findings with the more formal insights available from the IS implementation and organizational learning literature. It facilitates researchers and practitioners to explain, anticipate, and evaluate the organizational learning process associated with the ES adoption. This chapter is organized as follow: First, we briefly describe theoretical background of this study. Second, we discuss our research methodology. Third, we present the empirical findings that emerged from our case study. Last is our discussion and conclusion.

Theoretical Background

Firms' ability to apply IT effectively in their business activity explains the different outcomes of their IT adoption (Armstrong & Sambamurthy, 1999; Boynton, Zmud, & Jacobs, 1994; Cooper & Zmud, 1990; Feeny & Willcocks, 1998; Sethi & King, 1994). When technologies are first introduced, they impose a substantial burden on the adopter in terms of the knowledge needed to understand and use them effectively (Argyris & Schon, 1978; Attewell, 1992; Fichman & Kemerer, 1997; Purvis, Sambamurthy, & Zmud, 2001). Organizations must undergo an intensive learning process to bridge the gap between what they have known and what the new technology requires them to know. Thus, the effectiveness of the organizational learning process plays a critical role in shaping IT adoption results. Indeed, this argument has been widely tested to be valid by the IS implementation literature (e.g., Boynton et al., 1994; Ciborra & Lanzara, 1994; Fichman & Kemerer, 1997; Lyytinen & Robey, 1999; Pentland, 1995; Purvis et al., 2001; Wastell, 1999).

Organizational learning is defined as a process enabling the acquisition of, access to and revision of organizational memory, thereby providing direction to organizational action (Robey et al., 2002). As cognitive entities, organizations are capable of observing their own actions, experimenting to discover the effects of alternative actions, and modifying their actions to improve performance (Fiol & Lyles, 1985). The breadth and depth of organizational learning are positively related to its four constructs—knowledge acquisition, information distribution, information interpretation and organizational memory (Huber, 1991). Knowledge acquisition is the process by which knowledge is obtained (Huber, 1991; Robey et al., 2002; Tippins & Sohi, 2003). Information distribution is the process by which knowledge obtained is shared through formal and informal channels (Maltz & Kohli, 1996; Slater & Narver, 1995). Information interpretation is the process by which functional units reach a consensus with regard to the meaning of information (Daft & Weick, 1984; Slater & Narver, 1995; Tippins & Sohi, 2003) and organizational memory refers to organizations' storing knowledge for future use (Huber, 1991; Walsh & Ungson, 1991).

Extant ES literature alludes to organizational learning sporadically, and most of them do so in a cursory fashion, except the work of Robey et al. (2002) and Scott and Vessey (2000). In addition, the literature suggests a list of critical success factors for ES implementation, such as leadership (Lee & Sarkar, 1999), top management support and change management (Al-Mashari & Zairi, 2000). But there is no study explicitly linking these factors with organizational learning enacted in ES implementation. Different from the extant studies, our research studies how organizational factors affect the learning process, which determines ES implementation outcomes.

Research Methodology

To address our research questions, we employ a case study methodology. As an empirical inquiry investigating a contemporary phenomenon within its real-life context, a case study is particularly appropriate when examining "how" and "why" research questions (Yin, 1994). Given the nature of our research question and desire to obtain rich explanations of organizational learning process in ES implementation, a case study methodology is the most appropriate.

We selected two organizations for their similarities as well as their differences (Glaser & Strauss, 1967), paying attention to theoretical relevance and purpose. With respect to relevance, our selection process ensured that the substantive area addressed—the on-time and within budget implementation of ES—was kept similarly. As the purpose of the research is to generate insight into how organizational factors affect organizational learning enacted and thereby ES implementation outcomes, differences were sought in organizational conditions, such as the motivation of adopting ES, user training methods, and adoption outcomes. We first conducted a study with CPM—a PC and computer peripheral manufacturing company with 800 employees located in South China. The second company we studied was MEM which was a division of a publicly listed multi-national electronic manufacturing company. This division had 750 employees and was located in North China.

In both research sites, we collected data by using multiple methods: unstructured and semi-structured interviews, archival sources, and observation. This triangulation across various techniques of data collection provides multiple perspectives on an issue, supplies more information on emerging concepts, and yields stronger substantiation of constructs and allows for cross-checking (Eisenhardt, 1989; Pettigrew, 1990; Yin, 1994).

In this study, we had both investigators make visits to the case study sites together so that we could avoid biases due to one single researcher's perception. In particular, we followed Eisenhardt and Bourgeois' (1988) strategy and had one researcher handling the interview questions, while the other recording notes and observations.

Table 1. Amount of interviewees

CPM		MEM	
Interviewee's Title	**Count**	**Interviewee's Title**	**Count**
Senior VP in Marketing 1	S	enior VP 1	
Senior VP in Manufacturing 1	G	eneral Manager 1	
CIO 1	V	ice General Manager	1
Departmental Manager 4	D	epartmental Manager	5
Line Worker	5	Line Worker	4

This tactic allows the interviewer to have the perspective of personal interaction with the informant, while the other investigator retains a different and more distant view. The interviews we conducted are shown in Table 1. Each interview lasts between one and one-and-a-half hours. They were all tape-recorded and transcribed within 24 hours after the interview.

Data Analysis

We analyzed data within each site as well as across the two sites. Given the qualitative nature of the data collected, we avoided biases by using the iterative approach of data collection, coding, and analysis. Within CPM, the first site, we relied more on open-ended and generative interview questions. After these interviews, both authors independently read the transcripts of interviews and categorized data into concepts of salient organizational factors, major organizational learning activities, and implementation outcomes. The lists of concepts were compared and contrasted. Any difference was further examined and verified with the informants. This process yielded a broad set of concepts, which guided our second field study conducted in MEM.

Following the constant comparative analysis method suggested by Glaser and Strauss (1967), we systematically compared MEM's experiences with those of CPM. Data collected from MEM were first sorted into concepts generated by CPM's data. However, the list of concepts did not accommodate some findings emerging from MEM. For example, the mistrust among mid-level managers led us to study the organizational culture's effect, which did not seem to be salient to us in CPM's case. In this kind of situation, we went back to CPM to collect data related with these new concepts. The iteration between data and concepts ended when we had enough concepts to explain experiences of both sites.

Research Findings

Organizational Factors and Organizational Learning in CPM

ES Vision. The vision of adopting ES was formulated when CPM was in a crisis. Its management decision-making and inter-departmental coordination became ineffective due to its fast business expansion—more than 25% annual growth rate for four years in a row. As described by the CIO:

Our management encountered severe difficulties due to the lack of information support. The business data located in fragmented systems were inconsistent and difficult to reconcile ... The coordination between departments was chaotic. For example, our accounting system didn't record the sales long after the goods were delivered and we didn't detect these mistakes until we did [a] physical count.

In addition to the internal difficulties, CPM faced a more and more competitive market, and profit margins of its major products were diminishing. To cope with these problems, the top management decided to expand its business scope and adopt the advanced packaged software—enterprise system. As explained by the CIO:

The packaged software in the market was a solution to integrate our system and streamline our business processes ... It (ES adoption) is part of our business strategic plan ... In addition [to] adopting an integrated system, we expected to change our practices and organizational structure in the light of ES functionalities.

With a "transform" vision of ES adoption, CPM treated it as an investment and was committed to it with slack resources. These resources allowed CPM to acquire ES knowledge by hiring consultants (the Consulting Group in our later description), whose service cost USD$400,000. The consultant group transferred its system knowledge to CPM by helping the firm choose the right software/hardware, configure the system, and train end users. In addition, the consultants transferred the knowledge of process-oriented methodology to CPM and taught CPM managers how to use tools to draw business process diagrams. The external knowledge provided by the Consulting Group was critical to jump start CPM's ES project, as commented by the IT manager:

ES is much more complicated than our old systems. Without the external knowledge from the consultants, I don't think we would be able to get it implemented success-fully.

Also, as described by the senior VP of manufacturing:

Though I had heard of the concept of process-oriented thinking, but I didn't know how to describe our business practices by using the tools until I attended the classes ... These business process diagrams were really helpful and greatly facilitated our sharing of business process ideas.

Equipped with process-oriented knowledge and graphically describing business process techniques, CPM managers were able to discuss business practices by representing business processes with a uniform set of notations. It enhanced the effectiveness of communications and facilitated information interpretation—another construct of organizational learning (this sub-process is described in later sections).

Advocacy of ES Vision

The necessity of adopting ES was first perceived by the CEO who had led the firm since it was first set up in 1988. In a top management meeting, CEO presented his idea about ES adoption and asked for attendants' comments. After studying the feasibility of adopting ES for two weeks, the top management formulated its ES vision and started to communicate the vision with mid-level managers. The managers were called upon to embrace this vision and influence their subordinates by articulating the vision as much as possible. In addition, flyers, posters, and brochures about ES were widely distributed. Within two weeks, the message of adopting ES was disseminated across the organization. As described by a line worker about employees' reaction to ES adoption decision:

Some people thought it would be a good opportunity for the firm and individuals to learn, while others were worried about losing their jobs after ES adoption. It took a while for us to be convinced that we would benefit from ES adoption.

Employees' concerns were addressed by the CEO in an assembly meeting, in addition to the departmental meetings. By clearly explaining the rationale for ES adoption, the CEO assured employees that their jobs would be secure as long as the firm grew healthily, which required employees to endeavor as a unit toward a common goal—enhancing the firm's competitiveness and make ES adoption a success. As explained by a line worker:

Since implementing ES was a must-do project for our company's survival, it didn't make sense for us to resist it ... If we accepted the project positively and tried to gain some ES knowledge, mostly likely we would keep our jobs and upgrade ourselves. Especially, a lot of firms were adopting ES. With the ES knowledge gained from the project, we would be more competitive in the job market.

His comments were conferred by another line-worker:

It was a good opportunity for us to learn this advanced technology ... Being positive and supportive was a smarter choice than being worried and resistant.

The advocacy of ES vision allowed CPM to win the majority's support. It also motivated the employee to contribute, receive, and capture ES knowledge. This was revealed by the employees' passion and persistence in learning ES after work twice a week for nearly two months. In recalling the learning experience, one line worker described to us that:

Though we had to perform our job duty as before, staying overtime to learn ES was not unbearable. Since we were excited about this learning opportunity and looking forward to seeing the system implemented successfully. [Those] kind of feelings made us ... take a positive approach and [be] better able to put up with the fatigue.

The employees' endeavor in learning ES allowed CPM to distribute knowledge to the right people. The system knowledge was first transferred to the IT group, which would be responsible for the maintenance and support of the system. Also, knowledge on each module adopted was transferred to all relevant employees by formal training courses. Though the users were mainly trained to master the knowledge on the modules related to their work, a lot of employees proactively studied other modules and how different modules were inter-related. In addition, power users were formally assigned in each business unit. These power users learned about "why" and "how," in addition to "what." Such knowledge empowered them to be able to re-configure the system and make necessary adjustments of parameters to meet the requirements of special events.

Administrative Structure Support

CPM set an administrative structure for the project, which included a steering committee, working committee, project function groups, IT group, and consulting group. The steering committee was consisted of the members of the top management team, while the working committee consisted of senior managers who were respected and trusted in the organization. The project function groups were made up by the managers and key employees of every department. The six members of the consulting group were from a highly-reputable consulting firm specializing in ES adoption. These committees/groups were delegated with appropriate responsibility and authority to make decisions related to ES implementation. For example, the responsibilities of the working committee included formulating project plans and ensuring the progress of the project, guiding, organizing, and promoting the interaction among function groups, analyzing and proposing solutions to problems of business process optimization, organizing managerial and technical training courses, and being in charge of job specifications and standardizing work procedures.

The administrative structure served as a formal communication channel in CPM's learning ES, which was especially important for the acquisition of business knowledge and information interpretation. It called for regular/irregular meetings that allowed people to have formal and informal information exchange. For example, the function groups met four times a week to generate the diagrams of the business process status quo and redesigning the firm's business processes. According to the inventory manager:

Being a member of the function group made me better understand what role I should play in this project ... The meetings and social gatherings provided us chances to communicate with each other. In addition to getting jobs done, they also enhanced cohesion and trust among us, which made coordination and cooperation issues much easier ... It helped a lot with our reaching consensus on the business processes spanning departmental boundaries.

Control Scheme

To ensure that employees would learn and master knowledge required to apply ES effectively, the firm made employees' performance in the ES implementation an important part of individuals' and business units' annual evaluation. For example, it accounted for 60% of the CIO's annual evaluation. As commented by the manufacturing manager:

This evaluation scheme made it clear to everyone that he must be responsible for what he did and how he performed throughout the ES implementation process ... I think this evaluation scheme was really helpful in encouraging people to put in their effort ... As we would also be evaluated as a business unit, we were encouraged to help each other in learning how to use the system.

In addition, CPM formulated strict controlling rules, that is, only when the employees passed skill tests on ES, would they be allowed to take up jobs using the system. Employees who failed these tests would have to undergo the training again or be assigned to do some other jobs. In addition to providing incentives to learning ES, these control schemes ensured minimum operation and manufacturing disruptions after the system went live.

Top Management Involvement

The committee members attended all business process-redesign meetings and training workshops on process-oriented methodology. Also, the steering committee evaluated and approved the refined business process and ES implementation plan. As commented by a mid-level manager:

They worked together with us, even though we had to work overtime continuously for months. Their personal involvement in the project made us well aware of the importance of the project and inspired us to work hard on it ... Also, with their presence in the meetings, we could make decisions on business process changes on the spot, which facilitated the project's progress.

In addition to enhancing employees' morale and facilitating the project progress, top management brought constructive ideas and sound judgments on the refined business processes. Due to their possession of knowledge that was not available to mid-level managers, top management was able to challenge the business model proposed by the groups and evaluate different proposals, which ensured that the most suitable model was adopted.

Organizational Structure and Culture

CPM was organized divisionally with business units representing its major business areas. It had a culture that emphasized cooperation among employees and across functional units. Especially, the management emphasized employees' job satisfaction and career development. The firm organized many formal and informal social gatherings every year, in addition to providing free lunches for employees in its canteen. As commented by the senior VP of marketing:

These social gatherings allowed employees from different, maybe not directly-related, departments to know each other ... It helped us build cohesive and trusting culture.

The firm's culture enabled people to share different opinions openly, which was critical for the organizational learning in ES implementation. In the sub-process of information interpretation, all groups and committees came together to discuss about the possibilities of redesigning the organization's business processes. The discussions mainly focused on further improvement of business processes within the department and the management of activities spanning departmental boundaries and ad hoc business events. Trusting and cohesive culture facilitated the reaching of the consensus on how to get jobs done, as described by the marketing manager:

We benefited a lot from the innovative ideas provided by people from other departments ... We freely expressed our opinion and discussed in greater details when there was any disagreement. While trying to fight for our department, we also tried to put ourselves in others' shoes. There was nothing that couldn't be worked out. Especially, we could always pass controversial issues to the Boss. He had the last say.

With the shared understanding about what the best business practices were after ES implementation, CPM was able to update its organizational memory according to changes in its organizational structure, business processes, and management white paper. The information distribution and interpretation sub-processes decided the types of organization memory for this project. First, all the activities happened during the ES implementation were recorded in the computer system as part of the project. These documents facilitated the review, coordination and communication during and after the ES implementation. Second, the organization memory had humans as carriers. All end users and power users passed ES tests and became carriers of knowledge on how to interact with the system. They served as instructors to new comers of their departments, using the operation documentation of each module compiled by IT group. In addition, function group and committee members are the carriers of knowledge on business processes.

Organizational Factors and Organizational Learning in MEM

ES Vision. Aiming to cut purchasing cost and reduce lead time, the headquarters of MEM decided to integrate the databases in different sites located in different countries. Following this strategy, MEM was required to adopt ES which had been implemented in the headquarters and some other sites. ES implemented in MEM had its configuration and business processes exactly the same as those in other sites.

With the aim to cut costs by ES adoption, MEM was tight with resources contributed to ES project. The knowledge about the new business processes and system was acquired by learning from the expert team sent by headquarters. The experts spoke different languages from MEM employees. Due to the language barrier, it was difficult for MEM employees to capture the knowledge transferred by the experts, just as described by the personnel manager:

Language barrier was a big problem. I couldn't understand them clearly. Even worse, it was hard for them to understand my questions. Sometimes it became so frustrating that I just kept silent. And that might have passed a wrong message, and made them [think] that I didn't have any problems in understanding what they said.

Though the employees complained about the difficulties in learning and suggested hiring native speaking consultants, the top management decided not to do so due for two main reasons: (1) the high consulting fee; and (2) the consultants' lack of knowledge about business processes to be adopted. The senior VP believed that as long as employees in MEM put in enough effort, they could get around the language barrier problem. Hiring consultants was regarded as a waste of money and violated the principle of ES adoption—cost saving.

Advocacy of ES Vision

In one meeting, the general manager informed the top and mid-level managers of the headquarter's decision on implementing ES at MEM and explained the rationale for this adoption. Different from CPM, the vision was not passed to employees at lower levels. Neither did all of the mid-level managers align with this vision. As told by the sales manager:

With all the data shared among different sites, it meant that the discount we offered to our clients would be monitored by other sales people. That would lead us (sales representatives) to compete against each other by offering higher discount rates.

It would harm both the interests of our division and the company as a whole. In my opinion, the adoption of ES was a big strategic mistake.

Some employees were against ES adoption because of their fear of losing jobs after ES adoption. As described by the Purchasing Manager:

The system was bad for each division. With central sourcing, we would lose autonomy in selecting our own supplies ... Since the Boss emphasized cost saving, most likely we would be replaced by the system.

Overall, employees regarded the project owned by headquarters and stayed distant from it. With the lack of support from employees, especially some key mid-level managers, the morale of learning ES was low. MEM employees received knowledge transferred by the expert team passively and did not endeavor to capture the knowledge, which was reflected in their making excuses for skipping or postponing ES lessons.

Administrative Structure Support

MEM did not set up a specific administrative structure to support the ES implementation project, but had the experts from headquarters to lead the project, with assistance of the IS department. The expert team was in charge of the project plan and training organization. Throughout the project, the information flew mainly from the experts to MEM, and there was an insufficiency of communication among MEM employees. This arrangement affected the effectiveness of information distribution and interpretation, due to the lack of inputs from MEM employees.

Treating MEM employees as knowledge receivers, the expert team adopted a hierarchical approach to transfer ES knowledge, that is, the expert team trained the mid-level managers and the managers trained their subordinates. In these trainings, the experts verbally explained the standardized business practices set by headquarters and showed the managers how to enter and retrieve data from the system. Each manager was shown how to use the module related to his/her work only. The managers passed what they had learned to their subordinates in a similar way. Regarding the trainings, a manager made such comments:

The experts just told me what to do, rather than why I should do it that way. So after they left, I was totally lost when I encountered problems. As I was the only one who learned this module with the experts, I couldn't seek help from others within our firm ... I was not confident to give advice to my subordinates when they had problems with the system.

Also, a line worker told us:

The system was too complex to me and learning experiences were really frustrating ... It seemed to me that none of the people in our division really knew the system. Basically we just learned by trial and error ... So our skepticism about the system's capability in supporting our operation turned out to be right.

This training method led to little ES knowledge overlapping within the firm, and the lack of administrative structure deprived the chance for employees to share what they had learned. Thus, the firm did not have managers who knew the new business processes across department boundaries well. The low degree of information distribution made MEM encounter great problems in information interpretation, which was described as, "there was little shared understanding of business processes coming along with the system".

Control Schemes

The top management assumed that all of the employees would put in their best efforts in learning ES and participate in ES project proactively, so the firm did not set up any reward scheme for the employees' performance in the project. Neither did they formulate any control scheme to ensure that employees were able to interact with the system appropriately before the system went live. This lack of control scheme, coupled with the employees' attitude towards the project, did not provide employees enough incentive to seek for and capture ES knowledge.

Top Management Involvement

Trusting the expert team's capability, the top management did not participate in the project as much as in CPM. On the contrary, they almost left the project completely in the hands of the expert team, though they checked whether the project was progressing as expected from time-to-time. The general manager told us:

The Expert Team from headquarter[s] was very experienced in ES implementation after undertaking many projects in other sites. Leaving the project to them was the best choice for us.

Table 2. Differences of organizational factors in CPM and MEM

Organizational Factor	CPM	MEM
ES Adoption Vision	Transform I	nformate up
Advocacy of ES Vision	Strong advocacy across the firm	Limited dissemination
Top Management Involvement	Actively participated in key decision making	Left the decisions to the Expert Team from HQ
Administrative Structure Support	Steering and Working Committees and Functional Groups	No formal structure at MEM side
Control Scheme	Strict rules on the assignment jobs related with ES	No control scheme
Organizational Structure and Culture	Cohesive and trusting	Competitive and mistrusting
Employee's Attitude	Enthusiastic	Resistant and suspicious

With the lack of top management involvement, MEM lost the chance to study the feasibility of copying all business processes from headquarters, as commented by one manager:

Some of the new business processes did not suit our division. I think it would be very helpful if our boss discussed with the Expert Team and got them (business processes) modified ... Well, the processes implemented were so alien to us.

Organizational Structure and Culture

MEM was organized as a matrix with control coming directly from the general manager. It had a particularly competitive culture. The employees' career path was "up or out". The turnover rate was higher than other companies in the same industry. So the employees needed to focus on excelling themselves individually. The working relationship was described as "more competitive than cooperative" by one manager.

This culture made employees concerned about what they talked about and made them unwilling to share their ideas freely. When the general manager called for meetings after realizing the lack of knowledge overlapping and mutual understanding of business practices, the participants chose to be silent most of the time, as described by the general manager:

I really didn't know what went wrong. They simply didn't want to share their ideas openly. If I was in the meeting, I would lead the discussion and they would talk.

But without my presence, the meetings were so silent. But I was too busy to attend all their meetings.

In addition, a manager explained to us:

Some managers didn't get along well and were afraid of being backstabbed. So they wouldn't talk freely. Even with [the] General Manager's presence, they chose to avoid critical problems existing in their departments... Also, some of us just didn't feel like sharing what we had learned with each other, since our exclusive possession of knowledge made us valuable to the firm.

Due to the limited information distribution and little information interpretation, there was insufficient organizational memory to guide ES application. Humans were the main organizational learning carriers in MEM, especially the mid-level managers. In addition, the business process changes were not followed by corresponding organizational structure changes. MEM ended up having a function-oriented, organizational structure and process-oriented, business practices. This situation, coupled with insufficient understanding of business practices across the organization, caused confusion about job specification of posts spanning functional units.

To summarize our research findings described in the previous sections, we present the major differences between organizational factors (Table 2) and the organizational learning processes enacted in CPM and MEM ES implementation (Table 3).

These differences between the organizational learning processes enacted in ES implementation by CPM and MEM caused significant different implementation outcomes, though both firms managed to get the system implemented within budget and on-time. We categorized these outcomes into the following: further business process refinement, users' capability to apply the system effectively and appropriately, more effective and efficient departmental coordination, better decision making, solid organizational memory, and enhanced business performance. To avoid the complexity of presentation, we list our findings one by one, following the order of the earlier-mentioned aspects of implementation outcomes.

ES Implementation Outcomes in CPM

1. By implementing ES, CPM managers learned to evaluate different business practices by analyzing the efficiency and effectiveness of business processes. The group and committee members learned process-oriented methodology, thus they were able to change business processes without the help from the consultant after the system went live. According to the senior VP in marketing,

"we now have a team to keep studying our business processes and continuously refine them. I think this is the most important gain from ES project."

2. The end users and power users mastered system knowledge. End users were effective in interacting with the system. The firm did not run into any chaos due to end users' operation mistakes. In addition, power users were able to reconfigure the system to cater for the requirements of ad hoc events and new business processes.

3. By solving many problems together throughout the ES implementation project, managers knew each other better and established a more trusting relationship. This relationship, coupled with their knowledge about business practices across the whole organization, made inter-departmental coordination more effective and efficient.

4. With real-time operational data stored in the central database, the management was able to make more informed decisions and respond to market changes more swiftly.

5. With many different types of organizational memory carriers and overlapping knowledge among employees, the firm was able to maintain its organizational memory integrity when some key players left for ES consulting jobs.

6. With the support of ES, the amount of bad debts was reduced by four million U.S. dollars in the year 2002. In addition, the firm succeeded in getting around

Table 3. Differences between organizational learning in CPM and MEM ES implementation

Org. Learning Sub-Process	CPM	MEM
Knowledge Acquisition	- System knowledge and process-oriented methodology were acquired from the consultants - Business process status quo was acquired from organizational memory	- System knowledge and new standardized business process information were acquired from experts at headquarters
Information Distribution	- System configuration information was distributed to the IT group and power users in every business unit - System operation knowledge was distributed to all end users - Information about business processes was shared among business units	- System operation knowledge and information about business processes were distributed to the relevant mid-level managers by the experts - Mid-level managers passed what
Information Interpretation	- Function groups and the working committee worked together to streamline the business process, focusing on the activities spanning departmental boundaries and non-routine practices	- Little information interpretation during ES implementation
Organizational Memory	- All information related to the project was documented in computer-based repositories - Standard system operation manuals were compiled - Humans were certified and became organizational memory carriers	- Humans were the main organizational memory carriers -System configuration files were archived

the dealership and set up their own distribution channel across the country. As described by the Senior VP of Marketing:

Without the ES, it wouldn't be possible for us to manage the inventory across the country on our own. By getting rid of the dealership, our profit margin was increased significantly.

ES Implementation Outcomes in MEM

1. There was insufficient understanding of business processes among managers. Since the business processes implemented in the system were straightforward to the Expert Team, they were not aware of the necessity of sharing the rationales for these business practices with MEM managers. This caused managers' incapability in handling ad hoc events and system errors. Thus, MEM had to turn to the expert Team at headquarters whenever problems arose. But being located in different time zones, a difference of 13 hours, MEM couldn't get a response from the experts promptly. The efficiency promised by the ES system was greatly comprised.

2. End users could not interact with the system appropriately. The central database was often corrupted by individuals' mistaken operation. Due to the lack of knowledge about the inter-relationship between different modules, they did not take action to inform related parties of these errors immediately. This allowed the mistakes to cascade across the whole system and caused operation and manufacturing disruptions. Eight months after the within-budget and on-time implementation of the ES, MEM kept experiencing difficulties and encountered problems with this system. MEM had to limit the access privilege of most users or simply switch to manual operation for some processes.

3. With the lack of common understanding of how jobs were done across departmental boundaries, inter-departmental coordination was chaotic and relationships between some managers became distrustful.

4. Since the central database was often corrupted, managers could not make decisions based on these data. Also, since MEM abandoned the old system after ES went live, the managerial decision making could not receive the right data support for months.

5. MEM also suffered a loss of organizational memory due to the leaving of some key end users and managers. Due to the limited information distribution and little information interpretation throughout the ES project, the manager became the single carrier of knowledge transferred by the expert team. This knowledge structure made MEM vulnerable to personnel turnovers.

Table 4. Differences of implementation outcomes in CPM and MEM

Implementation Outcomes	CPM	MEM
Relationship between business units	Trusting and valuing each other	Distrustful and competitive
Inter-department coordination	Became more effective and efficient	Coordination was difficult due to lack of business practice knowledge
Managerial decision making	Got timely and accurate information support	Couldn't use the information due to the inaccuracy of data
Loss due to employee turnover	Did not lose organizational memory	Big loss of organizational memory due to resignation of some key mid-level managers
End user's interaction with the system	Effective and appropriate	Their mistakes caused manufacturing and operation disruption
Capability to deal with ad hoc events	Could handle special events without help from consultant	Must turn to experts at HQ
Significant impact on business performance	Decreased bad debts by about 4 million USD in 2002 and set up distribution channels without new hiring	Inventory cost increased by about 2 million USD in 2003

6.   The operation cost was increased rather than decreased, due to the end users' inappropriate interactions with the system. For example, its inventory cost was increased by two million U.S. dollars in 2003.

The major differences between these two firm's ES implementation outcomes can be summarized by Table 4.

Developed from these two organizations' experiences, the process of organizational learning in ES implementation can be described with a model (Figure 1). This model shows the major organizational factors that emerged as salient from our data analysis. Also, it encompasses how these organizational factors affect the four constructs of organizational learning. This process is proposed as an initial formulation of the key concepts and interactions that portray organizational learning in ES implementation. No claim is made that the concepts and interactions presented here are exhaustive. Further organizational learning studies on ES implementation should modify or extend the ideas presented here.

In this model, the four organizational learning constructs are influenced by organizational factors as follows:

A.   Influenced by environmental and organizational contexts, the top management formulates ES vision. Guided by this vision, the organization decides the amount of resources to be committed to the project, which leads to different ways of knowledge acquisition. The knowledge acquired directly affects the amount of knowledge that is distributed in the organization.

B. The organization takes action to distribute knowledge to its relevant employees. This sub-process is influenced by advocacy of ES vision, top management's involvement, and the control scheme mediated by employees' motivation to receive and capture knowledge. The end users' learning experiences either reinforce or change their perception about ES adoption, which in turn influences their learning motivation. On the other hand, the breadth and depth of information distribution influences information interpretation.

C. Top management's involvement, the administrative structure, and organizational culture, trust in particular, decide the effectiveness and outcomes of information interpretation. The interaction process in information interpretation may affect organizational culture.

D. With top management involvement, the consensus on business practices implemented in ES (the result of information interpretation) was institutionalized and became organizational memory. Employees equipped with ES knowledge (the result of information distribution) are another type of ES knowledge carrier. The knowledge in organizational memory can be brought forth, affecting future learning and affecting the organization.

Figure 1. Organizational factors affecting organizational learning in ES implementation

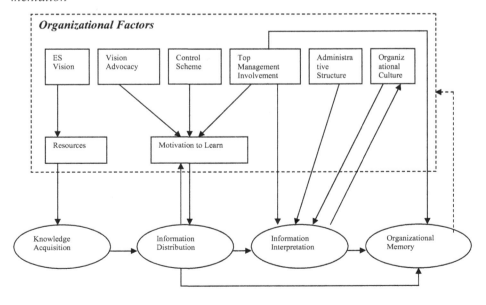

Discussion and Conclusion

While CPM and MEM both implemented ES on-time and within budget, their implementation outcomes differ significantly. The comparative analysis method, which allows contrasting CPM with MEM on a common set of concepts, suggests that these differences can be attributed to variations in the organizational learning process which was affected by organizational factors including the firm's ES vision, organizational culture, the ad hoc administrative structure for ES adoption, employees' motivation to learn ES, leaders' advocacy of ES vision, the top management's involvement, and control scheme. To enhance the internal validity and generality of theory building from this case study, we tie our findings to existing literature (Eisenhardt, 1989).

First, the attitude of the organization's "power elites" is important for ES implementation outcomes. Institutional leadership goes to the essence of the process of institutionalization, concurring with Armstrong and Sambamurthy's (1999) findings. It is particularly needed for ES implementation, which represents a transition to alternative ways of getting jobs done across the whole organization. The central responsibility of the top management is to ensure individuals and the organization as a whole learn how to apply ES effectively. This responsibility can be carried out through four key functions: advocacy of ES vision, personal involvement in the learning, setting up formal communication channels, and ordering internal conflicts.

Second, the firm's IT vision affects the amount of resources dedicated to the organizational learning in ES implementation. Firms with transformative IT vision would treat ES adoption as an investment and devote adequate resources to the project. In contrast, the firm with the vision of "automate" or "informate up" would try to minimize the cost of ES adoption (Scott-Morton, 1991). Thus, the vision about ES adoption affects organizational learning, mediated by the resources dedicated to the project.

Third, effective learning depends on a culture of openness, mutual trust, and a self-critical disposition. Consistent with the literature of organizational learning and learning in information system development, the accessibility to expertise and trusting working environment help the business units and individuals overcome learning anxiety and learn faster (Schein, 1993; Wastell, 1999). Anxiety and uncertainty about sharing "private" knowledge lead to the avoidance of authentic engagement in identifying and solving substantive problems.

Fourth, knowledge structure characterized by extensive knowledge overlaps, and information exchange among managers is important for successful ES implementation outcomes. The information exchange enriches organizational knowledge structure and consequently enhances the firm's absorptive capacity (Boynton et al., 1994; Cohen & Levinthal, 1990; Purvis et al., 2001). In turn, such knowledge and enhanced absorptive capacity enable rich dialogues among managers through which truly innovative ES applications arise (Lind & Zmud, 1991; Watson, 1990). Also, know-how and know-why about the innovation should be distributed to system users. Transferring why and how knowledge to the end users can instill confidence and a sense of control, which helps users to deal with ad hoc events.

In order to ensure that the study's results can be placed in an appropriate context as well as to enable future research, it is important to examine the limitations of this study. First, we neglect the socialization of the learning process from the individual to the organizational level, which might offer insights into how the learning process can be correctly managed. Second, both organizations we conducted the study with are in a culture of high collectivism. Some strategic conducts applicable in this culture might not be appropriate for another culture. Future research on the issues we do not address in this paper can extend our understanding of organizational learning in ES implementation.

References

Al-Mashari, M., & Zairi, M. (2000). The effective application of SAP R/3: A proposed model of best practice. *Logistics Information Management, 13*(3), 156-166.

Argyris, C., & Schon, D. (1978). *Organizational learning: A theory of action research.* Reading, MA: Addison-Wesley.

Armstrong, C. P., & Sambamurthy, V. (1999). Information technology assimilation in firms: The influence of senior leadership and IT infrastructures. *Information Systems Research, 10*(4), 304-327.

Attewell, P. (1992). Technology diffusion and organizational learning: The case of business computing. *Organization Science, 3*(1), 1-19.

Bingi, P., Sharma, M. K., & Godla, J. (1999). Critical issues affecting an ERP implementation. *Information Systems Management, 16*(3), 7-14.

Boynton, A. C., Zmud, R. W., & Jacobs, G. C. (1994, September). The influence of IT management practice on IT use in large organizations. *MIS Quarterly, 18*(3), 299.

Ciborra, C. U., & Lanzara, G. F. (1994). Formative contexts and information technology: Understanding the dynamics of innovation in organizations. *Accounting, Management and Information Technology, 4*(2), 61-86.

Cohen, W. M., & Levinthal, D. A. (1990). Absorptive capacity: A new perspective on learning and innovation. *Administrative Science Quarterly, 35*(1), 128-125.

Cooper, R. B., & Zmud, R. W. (1990, February). Information technology implementation research: A technological diffusion approach. *Management Science, 36*(2), 123.

Daft, R. L., & Weick, K. E. (1984). Toward a model of organizations as interpretation systems. *Academy of Management Review, 9*(2), 284.

Davenport, T. H. (1998). Putting the enterprise into the enterprise system. *Harvard Business Review, 76*(4), 121-131.

Eisenhardt, K. M. (1989, October). Building theories from case study research. *Academy of Management Review, 14*(4), 532-550.

Eisenhardt, K. M., & Bourgeois, L. J. I. (1988, December). Politics of strategic decision making in high-velocity Envi. *Academy of Management Journal, 31*(4), 734-737.

Feeny, D. F., & Willcocks, L. P. (1998). Core IS capabilities for exploiting information technology. *Sloan Management Review, 39*(3), 9-21.

Fichman, R. G., & Kemerer, C. F. (1997, October). The assimilation of software process innovations: An organizational learning perspective. *Management Science, 43*(10), 1345-1363.

Fiol, C. M., & Lyles, M. A. (1985, October). Organizational learning. *Academy of Management Review, 10,* 803.

Glaser, B. G., & Strauss, A. L. (1967). *The discovery of grounded theory: Strategies for qualitative research.* New York: Aldine Publishing.

Holland, C. P., & Light, B. (1999, May/June). A critical success factors model for ERP implementation. *IEEE Software*, 30-36.

Huber, G. P. (1991). Organizational learning: The contributing processes and the literatures. *Organization Science, 2*(1), 88-115.

Lind, M. R., & Zmud, R. W. (1991). The influence of a convergence in understanding between technology providers and users on information technology innovativenss. *Organization Science, 2*(2), 195-217.

Lyytinen, K., & Robey, D. (1999). Learning failure in information systems development. *Information Systems Journal, 9,* 85-101.

Maltz, E., & Kohli, A. K. (1995). Market intelligence dessemination across functional boundaries. *Journal of Marketing Research, 33*(1), 47.

Parr, A., & Shanks, G. (2000, December). A model of ERP project implementation. *Journal of Information Technology, 15*(4), 289-303.

Pentland, B. T. (1995). Information systems and organizational learning: The social epistemology of organizational knowledge systems. *Accounting, Management, and Information Technologies, 5*(1), 1-21.

Pettigrew, A. (1995). Longitudinal field research on change: Theory and practice. In G. P. Huber & A. H. Van de Ven (Eds.), *Longitudinal field research methods: Studying processes of organizational change* (p. 91). Thousand Oaks, CA: Sage.

Purvis, R. L., Sambamurthy, V., & Zmud, R. W. (2001, March/April). The assimilation of knowledge platforms in organizations: An empirical investigation. *Organization Science, 12*(2), 117-135.

Robey, D., Ross, J. W., & Boudreau, M. C. (2002, Summer). Learning to implement enterprise systems: An exploratory study of the dialectics of change. *Journal of Management Information Systems, 19*(1), 17-46.

Sambamurthy, V., Bharadwah, A., & Grover, V. (2003). Shaping agility through digital options: Reconceptualizing the role of information technology in contemporary firms. *MIS Quarterly, 27*(2), 237-263.

Sarker, S., & Lee, A. S. (2003). Using a case study to test the role of three key social enablers in ERP implementation. *Information & Management, 40*(8), 813.

Schein, E. H. (1993). How can organizations learn faster? The challenge of entering the green room. *Sloan Management Review, 34*(2), 85-92.

Scott, J. E., & Vessey, I. (2000). Implementing enterprise resource planning systems: The role of learning from failure. *Information Systems Frontiers, 2*(2), 213-232.

Scott-Morton, M. S. (1991). IT-induced business reconfiguration. In M. S. Scott-Morton (Ed.), *The corporation of the 1990s: Information technology and organizational transformation* (pp. 3-23). Oxford: Oxford University Press.

Sethi, V., & King, W. R. (1994). Development of measures to assess the extent to which an information technology application provides competitive advantage. *Management Science, 14*(2), 1601-1627.

Slater, S. F., & Narver, J. C. (1995). Market orientation and the learning organization. *Journal of Marketing, 59*(3), 63.

Sumner, M. (2000, December). Risk factors in enterprise-wide/ERP projects. *Journal of Information Technology, 15*(4), 317-327.

Tippins, M. J., & Sohi, R. S. (2003). IT competency and firm performance: Is organizational learning a missing link? *Strategic Management Journal, 24*(8), 745.

Walsh, J. P., & Ungson, G. R. (1991). Organizational memory. *Academy of Management Review, 16*(1), 57-91.

Wastell, D. (1999). Learning dysfunction in information systems development: Overcoming the social defenses with transitional objectives. *MIS Quarterly, 23*(4), 581-600.

Watson, R. T. (1990). Influences on the IS manager's perceptions of key issues: Information scanning and the relationship with the CEO. *MIS Quarterly, 14*(2), 217.

Yin, R. K. (1994). *Case study research: Design and methods.* Thousand Oaks, CA: Sage Publications.

This work was previously published in the Journal of Global Information Management, 14(1), 1-22, January-March 2006.

Chapter XIII

Knowledge Management and Electronic Commerce Supporting Strategic Decisions:
The Case of Taiwan

Wen-Jang Kenny Jih, Middle Tennessee State University, USA

Marilyn M. Helms, Dalton State College, USA

Donna T. Mayo, Dalton State College, USA

Abstract

Current literature on e-commerce and knowledge management primarily emphasizes the benefit of knowledge management for innovative e-commerce operations. The Internet-enabled e-commerce field provides capabilities for firms in all sectors to reach global buyers and suppliers. Knowledge management provides frameworks to manage intellectual capital as a valuable organizational and strategic resource. Do knowledge management practices significantly benefit electronic commerce? If so, does the relationship work in the other direction? Does a firm's e-commerce applications significantly benefit knowledge management practices as well? To test these exploratory propositions, empirical data were collected from companies in a variety of industries in Taiwan, a country emphasizing e-commerce initiatives. The results revealed significant relationships between the way businesses implement electronic commerce projects, as well as how they experiment with knowledge management concepts. In addition, the findings reveal interesting benefits and difficulties in implementation. These relationships were found to operate in both directions, offering reinforcing effects as well as connections.

Introduction

Internationally, Internet technology is an integral component of business strategy. Most firms use electronic commerce to reach customers at home and abroad. E-commerce, when properly linked with business processes and aligned with an organization's culture, aids a firm's strategic growth (Ahadi, 2004; Piris, Fitzgerald, & Serrano, 2004). These initiatives can lead to important performance gains (Green & Ryan, 2005). Another global imperative is the widespread recognition of the value of intellectual capital as a major source of sustainable competitive advantage (Marr, Schiuma, & Neely, 2004). To avoid basing competitive strategy on price discounting alone, a company must continuously engage in acquiring and updating the knowledge base. According to Porter (2001), intellectual assets embodied in the total business system are then difficult to duplicate.

Knowledge management provides the mechanism for firms to keep up with innovative activities (Bakhru, 2004; Trethewey & Corman, 2001). As e-commerce information flows freely and sites are easy and inexpensive to duplicate, innovations have an increasingly shorter life span. Thus, these two developments of knowledge management and e-commence would seem to supplement each other (Fahey, Srivastava, Sharon, & Smith, 2001; Bose & Sugumaran, 2003). The integration of major business processes brought about by e-commerce provides a wealth of data and information that can fuel knowledge management (Fang & Wu, 2006; Kocharekar, 2001). Yet most discussions in the literature are largely conceptual in nature (Holsapple & Singh, 2000). Inquiries that examine these global issues, based on actual data, are needed to obtain more insight into the relationship and directionality between the two management themes.

The purpose of this study is to correct this deficiency in the literature by exploring these relationships. Thus, the primary research question is: Do knowledge management practices significantly benefit electronic commerce? If so, does the relationship work in the other direction? Do a firm's e-commerce applications significantly benefit knowledge management practices as well? To test these exploratory propositions, empirical data were collected from companies in a variety of industries in Taiwan. Taiwan was chosen due to its aggressive emphasis on e-commerce initiatives. The paper will first briefly review the existing literature on both knowledge management

(KM) and electronic commerce (EC) individually, and then will present current literature on the linkages or supplementary relationships between the two topic areas. The paper links this literature to the paper's research propositions. Next, the case of Taiwan, a global e-commerce leader, is discussed, along with the questionnaire development and subsequent data collection and analysis. The implications for practice call for future research in other countries to validate these exploratory research findings.

Literature Review

Knowledge Management

In today's volatile business environment, knowledge is an asset and knowledge management must be used to aid in the development of new products as well as in the management of strategic decisions. Su, Chen, and Sha (2006) agree an important task of knowledge management is the conversion of tacit knowledge in to explicit knowledge, allowing information technology to extract customer knowledge from different market segments. KM has captured increased attention in today's global business environment because it views intellectual capital as manageable, and suggests frameworks to help companies utilize this valuable strategic resource (Brand, 1998; Child, 2002; Kim & Mauborgne, 1999).

KM is a set of business processes through which valuable knowledge is identified, collected/created, organized/stored, distributed, managed, and applied to problems or projects (Child, 2002; Davenport & Prusak, 2000; Grover & Davenport, 2001; Kim & Mauborgne, 1999; Leseure & Brookes, 2004; Pan & Scarbrough, 1998; Zack, 1999a).

Early discussions of KM practices range from a human-oriented to a technology-driven point of view. At one extreme of the continuum is the view of knowledge as completely unmanageable and KM as managing knowledge as human networks (Brand, 1998, Porter, 2001, Savary, 1999; Storck & Hill, 2000). Some researchers, however, view KM as an expansion of traditional data and information management. This latter view suggests a holistic approach (joining social and technological factors) to achieve performance expectations (Davenport & Prusak, 2000; Georgopoulos, Koulouriotis & Emiris, 2004; Koch, Chae, & Guo, 2002; Soo, Devinney, Midgley, Diakoulakis, & Deering, 2002).

Researchers argue organizational knowledge can be managed without an explicit definition of the knowledge itself. Rather, the focus should be on measuring its business processes (i.e., problem solving and decision making) and the innovative outcomes (Grover & Davenport, 2001; Soo et al., 2002). Various researchers (see, for example, Ahn & Chang, 2004; Castanho, 2004; Diakoulaki set al., 2004; Holsapple & Joshi, 2004; Wang & Ariguzo, 2004) have studied knowledge management and worked toward a better understanding of the topic as well as moved toward model development.

Data and knowledge is available in various forms and decision makers combine different types of data and knowledge (Mataxiotis, Ergazakis, Samouilidis, & Psarras, 2004; Woods, 2004). KM is emphasized in the computer information systems community and is continuously gaining interest in industries, enterprises, and government (Ahn & Chang, 2004; Davenport & Prusak, 2000). While the research cites IT issues, artificial intelligence, and EC, most experts agree the true goal of KM is to establish a unified, global framework (Stankosky, 2004). Although technology is not a replacement for knowledge, the gap between the two must be bridged (Spiegler, 2003).

There are three major areas of concern characterizing an organization's KM program: (1) the choice of implementation strategy (e.g., system-oriented vs. individual-oriented and top-down vs. bottom-up), (2) the set of objectives expected to be achieved (determined by such factors as top managers' support and involvement, the nature of the industry in which the organization operates, its existing information technology infrastructure, and the organizational culture) (Zack, 1999a, 1999b), and (3) critical successful factors.

Researchers agree much work is required to understand how the conceptualizations that comprise business processes across the extended enterprise can be captured, represented, shared, and processed by intelligent software agents and humans. It is hypothesized these efforts will ultimately lead to transparent and secure information and knowledge flows in services, as well as supply chains to increase the economic efficiency in the digital economy of the future (Singh, Iyer, & Salam, 2005). Mudambi and Navarra (2004) studied multinational subsidiaries' knowledge flows in the United Kingdom and found support for a more creative role for knowledge intensity. Gerstlberger (2004) studied both companies in Upper Austria, Germany, and in the Silicon Valley of the U.S., and found regional innovative systems were important for knowledge sustainability.

Electronic Commerce

E-commerce includes business-to-consumer (B-to-C), business-to-business (B-to-B), and internal business via an Intranet (Kalakota & Whinston, 1996a). The number of organizations offering e-commerce solutions is growing exponentially. E-commerce is no longer a choice for organizations, but rather a necessity if a business is to sustain a competitive advantage, agrees Sharma, Gupta, and Wickramasinghe

(2006). While the expectation for the commercial value of Internet technologies was widely touted during the end of the last century, the sudden collapse of dot-com companies in the spring of 2000 drove many to the other extreme of the expectation continuum.

Recent observations have demonstrated that when used properly, the Internet can become the technological foundation of an innovative international business strategy. It has been generally recognized that *how* the Internet is incorporated in the value-creating business strategy, rather than the Internet itself, enhances a company's competitive advantage (Barua, Konanna, Whinston, & Yin, 2002; Feeny, 2001; Fingar & Aronica, 2001; Garbi, 2002; Jih, 2002; Lee & Whang, 2001; Prusak & Liam, 1998; Wigand, 1997). The Internet provides companies of all sizes and in all industries a convenient, affordable communication infrastructure that is not limited by time and distance. Internet transactions include the purchase of information products (such as software, CDs, and books) to physical products (like automobiles and groceries) (Child, 2002; Feeny, 2001; Turban, Lee, King, & Chung, 2000).

Internet technologies have enabled innovative companies such as Tesco, e-Bay, Rosenbluth International, Dell, and Amazon.com to outperform their competitors. As companies streamline their internal and external business processes, the distinction between the "old economy" and "new economy" continues to fade.

Researchers have analyzed EC business models from many different perspectives and frameworks (Barua et al., 2002; Hogue, 2000; Kalakota & Whinston, 1996b; Mahadevan, 2000; Turban et al., 2000). Electronic commerce has become important to countries across the globe. Salman (2004), for example, studied e-commerce for competitive advantage in developing countries and concentrated on Bangladesh. In their study of e-tourism in Greece, Buhalis and Deimezi (2004) found e-commerce to have a great potential for the country, and confirmed how e-commerce has revolutionized the travel industry, in particular.

Linkages Between EC and KM

EC supports KM. The way companies implement KM concepts often is facilitated by their capabilities in implementing EC applications. The implementation of their EC applications also can benefit from experience acquired from their KM practices. This reinforcing effect results from the following seven characteristics shared by the two management paradigms. Both (1) use the Internet and their related technologies (Grover & Davenport, 2001), (2) emphasize intangible assets, (3) must be tightly integrated with major business processes, (4) are innovation-minded (Srinivasan, Lilien, & Rangaswamy, 2002), (5) lack commonly accepted operational performance indicators and are hard to justify (Soo et al., 2002), (6) have strategic significance (Davenport & Prusak, 2000; Zack, 1999a, 1999b), and (7) both EC applications and

KM implementations are governed, to a certain degree, by the principle of network economies (Brand, 1998; Pan & Scarbrough, 1998; Savary, 1999). Specifically, EC supports KM in both technology and content.

EC applications must be developed with the foundation of information architecture. Hogue (2000) identified nine functional components of one such EC process architecture: profiling, personalization, search management, content management, workflow management, collaboration and trading, event notification, catalog management, and payment. It is evident that the functional components for EC applications also play an important role in KM practices, as evidenced by the first six among the nine EC components in the Hogue model.

In the KM field, Turban, Aronson, and Liang (2005) emphasize the essential role of information technology in KM implementations. In particular, three categories of information technology are instrumental: knowledge discover (e.g., data warehousing and data mining), knowledge distribution (e.g., collaborative software), and knowledge application (e.g., expert systems and intelligent agent). Most of these technologies, such as expert system and intelligent agent, have helped EC companies add a wide variety of customization capabilities to EC applications. The supporting role of EC for KM is evident. EC applications also support KM practices by providing valuable customer knowledge to help better focus the KM program.

Focusing on customer knowledge allows a KM program to be effective in accomplishing its mission and efficient in the use of organizational resources. The importance, as well as the dimensions of customer knowledge, are addressed by Glosch (2000), Bose and Sugumaran (2003), Jarvenpaa and Todd (1997), and Plessis and Boon (2004). EC Web sites constantly collect a massive amount of customer knowledge through daily operations. These knowledge contents represent valuable resource input for KM programs. Alvesson (2004) found key knowledge intensive firms are using e-commerce in their business model and include IT, management consulting, advertising, and life sciences. He further agrees KM is indeed a core competency. The increased sense of urgency for the institutionalization of comprehensive knowledge management programs is driven by e-commerce. A well-designed KM infrastructure facilitates sharing of knowledge and reduces operating cost, improves staff productivity, and increases the knowledge base and expertise sharing (Bose & Sugumaran, 2003).

Spiegler (2003) states the idea of technology is to represent the means and knowledge to the end as well as to support the e-commerce process. He agrees methods for generating knowledge are assisted by using technology or e-commerce.

KM supports EC. Electronic commerce is challenging and is only sustainable for global companies who continue to innovate and strategically use acquired knowledge. Wenger (2004) agrees if knowledge is a strategic asset, it must be managed. For example, the value-added content in Web site design has been recognized as an important factor influencing online shoppers' perception as well as their behavior (Jarvenpaa & Todd, 1997; and Wolfinbarger & Gilly, 2002). True value-added content of an e-commerce Web site can only be produced and sustained through a viable knowledge management program. Huosong, Kuanqu, and Shuqin (2003) agree that while KM has been studied, our understanding of how the design of a KM system affects both its use and definition is still limited. Malhotra (2000) confirms knowledge creation is relevant to both e-business and e-commerce.

KM supports EC in various forms. Singh, Furrer, and Ostinelli (2004) studied Web standardization in Italy, India, the Netherlands, Spain, and Switzerland and found knowledge of local cultural preferences were important for Web customization. In Brazil, Tigre and Dedrick (2004) studied local cultural knowledge for e-commerce adaptation and found local forces were important for driving e-commerce diffusion. Plessis and Boon (2004) studied e-business in South Africa and found knowledge management is a prerequisite for e-business and its increasing customer-centric focus and is an integral part of both customer relationship management and e-business.

Synergy in both directions—KM-to-EC and EC-to-KM. Gathering and using customer knowledge and feedback serves to link KM and EC (Blosch, 2000; Bose & Sugumaran, 2003). The potential synergy between KM and EC has been noted in both the information systems and the marketing literature along three dimensions: process impact, community and content, and system architecture (Holsapple & Singh, 2000; Salazar, Hackney, & Howells, 2003). The "process impact" point of view, in particular, stresses the increasing demand for in-depth knowledge in implementations of e-business processes and views KM as playing a vital role in change management. Fahey et al. (2001) suggest KM is valuable in evaluating the what, how, and why aspects of e-business operations. Through the development of e-business focused knowledge, organizations can evaluate the type of work performed in the global e-business environment, understand how they are doing it, and determine why certain practices in companies are likely to change in the future.

In the implementation of a KM solution in Greek banks, Samiotis, Poulymenakou, and Doukidis (2003) found support for KM in the newly employed and strategically important e-banking role, while Bose and Sugumaran (2003) found a U.S. application of KM technology in customer relationship management, particularly for creating, structuring, disseminating, and applying knowledge.

Rowley (2002) agrees such customer knowledge is an important e-business opportunity since customers in the digital economy depend on knowledge management and the accompanying organization's knowledge management paradigm. Recent developments in information technology, the Internet, enterprise resources planning systems, and KM are all necessary for business survival (Soliman & Youssef, 2001). However, the new business models created by e-business are changing operations.

But most agree it has not been integrated well with internal knowledge management initiatives.

Fahey et al. (2001) stress that with the development of e-business, focused knowledge organizations are needed to enhance customer relationship management, supply chain management and product development. The authors also emphasize the central role of knowledge management in managing e-business changes occurring in organization. Warkentin, Bapna, and Sugumaran (2001) studied e-knowledge networks and found them key in interorganizational collaborative e-business, thus linking KM and EC. KM plays a role in customer retention with value-added service through product-related knowledge and support of the online community. Faced with a great array of vendor choices, customers are often attracted by the Web sites that contain relevant, well-organized information and knowledge relating to product quality and usage.

The rich knowledge information and knowledge content, according to Wolfinbarger and Gilly (2001), represents an important motivating factor by providing online shoppers with freedom, control, and even fun. Williams and Cothrel (2000) argue for the importance of the online community in the Internet-centered business world, and highlight the important role of experience sharing in managing the online community. Lastly, on the system architectural dimension, Kocharekar (2001) contends both KM and EC represent the next movement beyond ERP systems and must converge to a commerce characterized by knowledge intensive activities, which they term knowledge commerce or K-Commerce.

Based on our literature review on KM and EC and their initial linkages, we propose that:

EC facilitates the practices of KM, whereas KM guides and supports EC.

The reasoning behind this proposition is reiterated as follows. Although experience suggests traditional wisdom should not be ignored in running EC businesses, there is also an abundance of evidence indicating innovative thinking is critical to conducting business via the Internet. Facing a massive amount of information, customers' attention will be drawn to the Web sites offering innovative values. KM supports EC by enabling a company to put its entire organizational knowledge base behind such major business processes as new product development, customer service, and supply chain management. The infrastructure constructed for EC applications also provides valuable mechanisms for the implementation of KM programs. The literature also shows successful EC operations must be guided and aligned with business strategy, backed by fully integrated business processes and work flows, and built around a consistent customer-centric system of interactions. This requires a great deal of innovative capability and learning capacity, which can only be achieved with an effective, ongoing knowledge management program. The characteristics shared by EC and KM suggest existence of synergy between the two fields.

To test this linkage, we chose to examine the relationship between the two fields in terms of the basic aspects of each, considering B2B and B2C e-commerce applications as well as strategy, objectives, and critical success factors. Thus, the following research propositions were developed:

P1: *EC applications do not significantly affect KM practices.*

P1.1: *EC applications do not significantly affect the choice of KM implementation strategies.*

P1.2: *EC applications do not significantly affect the objectives of KM initiatives.*

P2: *KM practices do not significantly affect the applications of EC.*

P2.1: *The choice of KM implementation strategy does not significantly affect applications of EC.*

P2.2: *Critical success factors of KM initiatives do not significantly affect applications of EC.*

Research Methodology

The first step to validate our research proposition regarding the mutually reinforcing effect between KM and EC is to test the correlation between the two. For this purpose, a cross-sectional survey was administered to business managers.

Taiwan. Taiwan was selected as the site for this exploratory study for several important reasons. Among other major initiatives, EC has been designated by the government of Taiwan as an important area of investment to stimulate national economic vitality and enhance competitiveness. In the second quarter of 1999, the Ministry of Economic Affairs launched a multiyear project to promote EC applications in 40 industries identified as having the best potential to stimulate long-term national economic development (http://www.ec.org.tw). A primary project objective is to develop Taiwan into an Asia-Pacific regional commercial center. Both business-to-consumer and business-to-business EC applications are included in the promotional campaign. These government-funded promotions include research support, training, systems development, and a national innovative projects contest. In academia, a variety of research projects have been sponsored by the National Science Council, and numerous industrial associations in Taiwan have examined various aspects of EC applications. Based on a field survey, Jih (2002) found that a variety of benefits have been realized by companies in Taiwan who have actively adopted EC.

Taiwan recovered more quickly than other Asian nations from the 1997-1998 financial crises that hit Asian markets, and experienced only a brief period of slow growth. Currently, Taiwan has a solid economic and financial foundation due to their economic transformation from a labor-intensive environment to a capital and technology-intensive environment. This export-oriented economy has grown at a 5% to 6% yearly rate and this growth, in part, is due to the continuous development of a knowledge-based economy (Tang, 2000; Wang, Scherban, & Bonnici, 2005). Taiwan now exports twice as much to China as to the U.S., after decades of relying only on the American market, largely due to their increase in the production of computer chips and laptop computers and notebooks (Bradsher, 2004).

Recognizing the importance of continuous innovation in such major areas as new product development, production process streamlining, and quality assurance, many Taiwanese companies have attempted to implement forms of KM programs in their organizations. Many manufacturing firms in Taiwan play an important upstream role in global supply chains. These companies understand they must continually improve their production cost, quality, delivery, and service. The service industries within the domestic Taiwanese market also face competition from global players with scale advantages (Child, 2002). World Trade Organization membership means almost every company in Taiwan will face unprecedented, larger competitors. Taiwan, a small island nation, is a major exporter with little domestic demand. Thus, e-commerce levels the playing field for the nation. Their commerce must be with international partners, and most of these transactions depend on e-commerce as their means of competition.

Taiwan is growing in their adoption of e-commerce. In 2004, International Data Corporation developed an Information Society Index ranking a nation's capabilities for quickly migrating for an information society. Of 53 ranked nations, Taiwan was number 20 among all nations, and 7th among Asian nations. In addition, *The Economist* and IBM jointly conducted a global e-readiness study. In 2004, Taiwan ranked 22nd among all nations and 5th among Asian nations. The *Global Information Technology Report* (2004-2005), issued by the World Economic Forum, ranked Taiwan 15th among all nations in the area of network readiness. The Network Readiness Index consists of environment, readiness, and usage. Thus, Taiwan is quickly addressing e-commerce capabilities for the future. More recently, a survey sponsored by the Department of Commerce of Taiwan reveals an increasing trend for the retailing segment of electronic commerce. In 2005 alone, the business-to-consumer market size for this important segment was $1.6 billion in Taiwan. The predictions for 2006 are $2.3 billion. Beyond 2006, the estimates increase rapidly to $3.1 billion for 2007;

$4.0 for 2008; $4.8 for 2009. The business-to-business market size for Taiwan has grown at an average annual rate of 85.2%, from $44.1 billion in 2000 to $194.3 billion in 2004. This growth is expected to continue with business-to-business market size predicted to be $399.1 billion in 2009 ("Research Report of the Institute of Information Industry" retrieved July, 2006 from http://www.ec.org.tw).

The successful experiences of the Scientific Industry Park helped develop the various industries of Taiwan, including high-tech industries that were working on behalf of other nation's industries. To increase the competitive capacity of the domestic Taiwanese high-tech industries and to add to the short life spans of high-tech industries themselves, innovation is being emphasized. High-tech industries must give serious consideration to the issues of both internal marketing and knowledge management (Lee & Chen, 2005). Lee and Chang (2006) also studied innovation ability in their study of Taiwanese wire and cable companies, and agreed like leadership, innovation ability is a basic organizational ability.

The emergence of a knowledge-based economy and e-entrepreneurship is important for the entire Asia-Pacific region (Mahood & Yu, 2005). Recent research has investigated the relationship between knowledge management and firm value in Taiwan. Huang, Shih, Huang, and Liu (2006) found that the Taiwan electronic industry's high innovative ability to create new knowledge had a very positive effect on firm value. Similarly, a study of accounting firm branch offices in Taiwan and the United States revealed that knowledge sharing is positively related to organizational marketing effectiveness in setting strategic alliances (Chen, 2006).

In a qualitative study of pharmaceutical manufacturers in Taiwan, results indicated the information cultures of the pharmaceutical manufacturers were negative toward KM, specifically manufacturers are challenged by the financial investment required and the compatibility and interoperability of such computer systems (Wang, 2006).

Survey instrument. The questionnaire was written in Chinese, and contained items designed to address issues related to EC applications, KM practices, the benefits realized, and difficulties experienced in applying the concepts. The questionnaire was pilot tested with a convenience sample of managers to ensure validity and reliability. Some questions were revised for clarity and wording based on the feedback obtained from the pilot test, and the companies involved in the pilot testing were excluded from the final results. The data was collected in 2002 and 2003.

In designing the questionnaire, the EC applications in three categories (business-to-business, business-to-consumer, and intraorganizational EC activities), were considered following the original definition of Kalakota and Whinston (1996b). Three macrolevel aspects of KM practices were also used in the study: KM strategies, KM objectives, and KM critical success factors. Each construct was measured with multiple questions. Except for questions about the respondents' demographic background and company information, all questions used a seven-point Likert-type scale to collect perceptual data, with 7 representing "strongly agree" and 1 representing "strongly disagree." Figure 1 is a graphical depiction of the research proposition and is the study's conceptual framework. The EC and KM components, which serve as the basis for the survey items, are summarized in Table 1. The questionnaire consisted of 4 questions for B-to-B applications, 5 questions for B-to-C applications, and 3 questions for intranet applications. For KM implementation practices, there were 2 questions on KM strategies, 13 questions on KM objectives, and 10 questions on KM critical success factors. In addition, 15 benefits questions and 11 difficulty items were included to advance understanding of KM implementations. For KM strategies, companies were asked to identify the relative emphasis (as a percentage) of system-oriented (technology view) vs. personal-oriented (human resource view) and top-down (revolution approach) vs. bottom-up (evolution approach) KM implementation strategies. Examples of survey questions are included in Table 2.

Data Collection and Analysis

A total of 221 questionnaires were mailed to the chief information officers of a variety of companies in Taiwan. The companies were selected based on their publicly reported EC and KM activities and their positions as recognized leaders in the application of EC and KM concepts within key industries in Taiwan. They were categorized into financial service institutions, information technology, electronics manufacturing, and other industries (representing pharmaceutical, management consulting, and retail chains).

Sixty-three questionnaires were returned, representing an effective response rate of 28.5%. Information technology representatives had the highest response rate (52.6%)—an understandable result given the progressive nature of this industry in Taiwan. A follow-up interview was conducted with a small number of these compa-

Figure 1. Conceptual framework

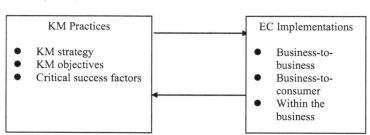

Table 1. Summary of research variables

Research Variables		Definition
EC Activities	Business-to-Business EC Activities	• Electronic financial transaction • Knowledge dissemination and sharing • Workgroup discussion • Workflow integration
	Business-to-Consumer EC Activities	• Organizational information dissemination • Online transaction • Product/service information inquiry • Customer service • Online advertising
	Intraorganizational EC Activities	• Information dissemination and sharing • Workgroup discussion • Workflow integration
KM Activities	KM Strategies	• Systems approach vs. individual approach • Top-down vs. bottom-up approach
	KM Objectives	• Increasing organizational knowledge repository and value • Establishing knowledge network • Improving efficiency of knowledge usage • Facilitating organizational innovation • Promoting organizational learning
	Critical Success Factors for KM	• Linkage with overall organizational performance • Technological and organizational infrastructure • Flexible knowledge organization structure • Organizational culture enables knowledge sharing • Clear and specific objectives • Incentive measures • Multiple knowledge transfer channels • Top management support

Table 2. Sample survey items (All on a 7-point Likert-type scale with 1 as Strongly Disagree to 7 as Strongly Agree)

EC (B2B):

- Our financial transactions with upstream and downstream business partners are all conducted on WWW and/or EDI.

- We exchange information, knowledge, and experience with business partners on WWW and/or EDI.

- We use WWW and/or EDI to communicate and collaborate with our business partners.

- We use computer networks, including the Internet, to integrate with business partners our work flows.

EC (B2C):

- We provide company and products/services information on our Web site.

- We conduct product and service transactions online.

- We provide online search capability for customers' information inquiry.

- We offer online customer service and inquiry capabilities.

- We advertise and promote our products and service online.

EC (Intranet):

- We encourage knowledge and experience sharing among employees using computer networks.

- We provide networking capabilities for employees to communicate with one another and to engage in group discussions.

- We attempt to integrate our workflows using Internet technologies.

KM Strategy:

- Please indicate the relative emphasis on the two knowledge management strategies of your company:

  System-driven: _____ %

  Personally oriented: _____%

  (Please note the two numbers should total 100 %.)

- Please indicate the relative emphasis on the following two knowledge management strategies of your company:

  Top-down strategy: _____ %

  Bottom-up strategy: _____%

  (Please note the two numbers should total 100 %.)

---

continued on following page

Table 2. continued

KM Objectives:

- Our objective for knowledge management implementation is to create electronic databases, digital knowledge bases, document bases, and other digital media, so they can be conveniently accessed by our employees.
- Our objective for knowledge management implementation is creating valuable knowledge repositories in electronic forms.
- Our objective for knowledge management implementation is to strengthen our innovation
- Our objective for knowledge management implementation is to uncover knowledge owned by our employee so it can be utilized more.

KM critical success factors:

- Our knowledge management initiatives are aligned with our overall business strategy.
- Knowledge management is viewed as a long-term organizational effort rather than just a short-term and one-time endeavor.
- A flexible organization structure is employed to promote knowledge management efforts, such as an interdepartmental KM team.
- We have a clear definition for knowledge to distinguish it from data and information.

Table 3. Sample distribution

	Financial Service Institutions	Information Technology Industry	Electronics Manufacturing Industry	Other Industries	Total
Questionnaires Mailed	102	19	50	50	221
Questionnaires Received	37	13	17	11	78
Effective Questionnaires	31	10	14	8	63
Effective Questionnaire Return Rate	30.4%	52.6%	28%	16%	28.5%

Table 4. Reliability measures of the research constructs and the questionnaire

	Cronbach's α	Question Category	Number of Questions	Cronbach's α
E-Commerce	0.94	B-B EC	4	0.8682
		B-C EC	5	0.9775
		Intranet	3	0.9380
Knowledge Management	0.9792	KM Objectives	13	0.9832
		KM CSF	10	0.9762
		Current Implementations	26	0.9592
Entire Questionnaire			0.9795	

nies to obtain anecdotal and supplementary information to augment the quantitative data. The distribution of the respondents is summarized in Table 3.

Statistical analysis was used to analyze the collected data. First, descriptive statistics were obtained for each variable. The correlation between EC applications and KM objectives and between EC applications and KM critical success factors were then analyzed using Pearson Product-Moment Correlations. A one-way analysis of variance was conducted to examine the impact of KM implementation strategy on EC applications and the difference of KM implementation strategies among different industries. In addition, the internal consistency of the questionnaire (measured by the Cronbach's alpha coefficient) was examined to ensure survey reliability. Table 4 shows each individual construct has a Cronbach's α coefficient of at least 0.8682 and Cronbach's alpha for the entire questionnaire is 0.9795. The questions for perceived benefits from KM implementations and for the difficulties encountered were also analyzed. Cronbach's alpha for the former is 0.9827 and the latter is 0.9204, both indicating high degrees of reliability.

Survey Results

Since the effective respondents all had EC and KM programs, the distribution of their sizes (as measured by the number of employees and annual sales) was examined to determine if size had a significant influence. Although there were 23 companies

(36.5%) with 1,000 or more employees, there were also 28 companies (44.4%) with 300 or fewer employees. The largest revenue category was represented by 19 responding companies with annual sales of $800 million USD or above.

The second category was represented by the companies with annual sales between 40 million and $134 million USD. Although larger companies had more resource support for applications of EC and KM, smaller companies were also actively engaged in these activities. In fact, follow-up interviews revealed smaller companies hoped EC and KM applications would help them compete more effectively within their respective industries.

Effects of EC applications on KM Practices

The possible effects of EC applications on KM strategies were examined by obtaining the Pearson product-moment correlation coefficient between EC applications and KM practices. Each EC application type was used as an independent variable, and each knowledge strategy type as a dependent variable.

As summarized in Table 5, the system's approach is positively correlated and the individual approach is negatively correlated with business-to-business EC applications. The fact these are the only significant correlation coefficients (at the 1% level) may be explained by the experimental nature of EC (especially business-to-consumer EC) and KM activities. The system's approach places more emphasis on the use of information technology in implementing KM projects, whereas the individual approach views human interaction as the more important information technology. Both the degree and the direction of the correlation coefficients indicate key aspects of EC applications and KM implementation strategies (system vs. individual) are significantly correlated.

Table 5. Correlations between EC implementations and KM strategies

	B-to-B EC	B-to-C EC	Intranets
Systems Approach	0.461*	0.121	0.178
Individual Approach	-0.461*	-0.121	-0.178
Top-down Approach	-0.101	-0.126	-0.018
Bottom-up Approach	0.101	0.126	0.018

Note: Level of significance less than 0.01

Table 6. Correlations between EC implementations and KM objectives

	B-to-B EC	B-to-C EC	Intranets
Increasing organizational knowledge and value	0.448*	0.669*	0.668*
Establishing knowledge network	0.427*	0.607*	0.578*
Improving efficiency of knowledge usage	0.428*	0.697*	0.617*
Facilitating organizational innovation	0.458*	0.710*	0.676*
Promoting organizational learning	0.383*	0.690*	0.675*

*Note: * Level of significance less than 0.01*

When EC activities are correlated with KM implementation objectives, the correlation coefficients are significant at the 1% level (See Table 6). The degrees of EC implementations are positively correlated with the importance placed on each KM objective. It appears these companies have an understanding of the strategic value of KM to their organizations, and an expectation that EC applications will facilitate successful implementations of KM. In summary, some EC applications do facilitate KM practices. Therefore, Proposition 1 is rejected.

The data from Taiwan about the effects of EC applications on KM practices indicate that KM practices benefit from EC application. This facilitating effect is especially obvious in fulfilling KM objectives: all EC application types have significantly positive impact on both efficiency and effectiveness of KM programs. The technological infrastructure and business processes designed for EC operations, such as the Web-based user interface, product/service customization, and online community, also facilitate important aspects of knowledge management, e.g., knowledge acquisition, knowledge flow, and knowledge application.

The facilitation effect is discussed by Alvesson (2004) and Rowley (2002). Buhalis and Deimezi (2004) also reported similar findings in their study about the travel industry in Greece. Kankanhalli, Tanudidjaja, Sutanto, and Tan (2003) shared this observation by attributing a part of the KM programs implementation success at British petroleum, Buckman Laboratories, and Shell to the capabilities of their EC-enabled information technologies. As a matter of fact, the majority of technological tools discussed in the KM literature are associated with some types of EC applications (Holsapple, 2004). Although successful KM implementation does not solely depend on EC technology, the technological tool is essential to smoothly implement the KM program.

Table 7. Correlation between CSFs for KM and EC applications

	B-to-B EC	B-to-C EC	Intranets
Linkage with overall organizational performance	0.364**	0.563**	0.579**
Technological and organizational infrastructure	0.275*	0.420**	0.503**
Flexible KM organization structure	0.377**	0.494**	0.622**
Organizational culture enables knowledge sharing	0.283*	0.465**	0.525**
Clear and specific objectives	0.318*	0.559**	0.584**
Incentive measures	0.237	0.446**	0.460**
Multiple knowledge transfer channels	0.326**	0.536**	0.551**
Top management support	0.347**	0.685**	0.598**

*Note: • Level of significance < 0.05; ** Level of significance < 0.01*

Effects of KM Practices on EC Applications

A one-way analysis of variance (ANOVA analysis) was used to determine the effects of KM practices on EC applications using each EC application as the dependent variable and KM strategies as the independent variables. The business-to-business EC is the only variable significantly affected by the choice of system's approach vs. an individual approach to KM implementation (F-value: 9.257, Level of significance < 1%). Thus, the choice of KM implementation strategy does significantly affect some aspect of EC application, namely B-to-B EC. When each type of EC application was used as the dependent variable with critical success factors for KM implementation as the independent variables, the result of Pearson Product-Moment Correlation analysis shows all correlation coefficients pass the test at either the 1% or the 5% level of significance. The highest correlation relationship is found between intranets and flexible KM organization structures. Thus the more flexible the organization structure for KM, the more likely company-owned Intranets would be utilized.

It is also worth noting the degree of intranet usage has higher correlations (with all but one KM variable) than the other two types of EC applications (B-to-B and B-to-C). This is an understandable phenomenon given the current similar internal orientation of both intranet and KM applications. The second component of Proposition 2 (P2.2: Critical successful factors of KM initiatives do not significantly affect applications of EC) is rejected.

The companies in Taiwan understand this trend and actively engage in integrating EC in their business models. EC is rapidly emerging as a competitive paradigm in today's global business environment. The key to succeeding in EC applications is to provide attractive customer value (effectiveness) at affordable cost (efficiency). Both effectiveness and efficiency of EC applications can be enhanced by KM. This finding is shared by Singh et al. (2004) in their report on Web standardization in several European nations, by Tigre and Dedrick (2004) in their study regarding using local cultural knowledge for EC adaptation in Brazil, and by Plessis and Boon (2004) in their study in South Africa. In addition, stories abound in Fortune 500 companies about how innovative EC applications derive enormous business value from aggressive KM implementation (Holsapple, 2004).

Perceived Benefits from KM Implementations

Qualitative understanding of the future of KM in Taiwan was addressed by 15 items in the questionnaire. The means and the standard deviations, as well as the rankings, are summarized in Table 8. The top 5 benefit items are: (1) improvement of organizational capability in responding to environmental change, (2) improvement of overall productivity, (3) improvement of overall performance, (4) timely monitoring of competition, and (5) enhancement of organizational innovative capability.

It is interesting to note the breadth of the top 10 benefit items: capability to respond to change, productivity and performance improvement, relationship improvement (customer, supplier, and employee), and product quality improvement. Companies appear to have a good understanding that successful KM requires a broad view of value assessment. This is a sound beginning since it requires an extensive period of time for a company to reap the long-term benefits from a KM investment. These findings are consistent with those reported in the KM literature.

Perceived Difficulties Encountered in KM Implementation

As shown in Table 9, on a 7-point Likert-type scale, the six difficulty items with difficulty averages above 4, as reported by respondents are: (1) difficulty in knowledge flow due to lack of interdepartmental coordination, (2) lack of top management support, (3) weak consensus on the value of knowledge to the organization, (4) lack of innovative capability and motivation to innovate, (5) lack of incentive to encourage knowledge sharing, and (6) lack of clearly defined communication mechanisms across departments

Table 8. Benefits realized from KM initiatives

Rank	Benefit from KM Initiatives	Mean	Standard Deviation
1	Improvement of organizational capability in responding to environmental change	4.92	1.35
2	Improvement of overall productivity	4.90	1.52
3	Improvement of overall performance	4.86	1.62
4	Timely monitoring of competition situations	4.83	1.62
5	Enhancement of organizational innovative capability	4.81	1.48
5	Enhancement of customer satisfaction	4.81	1.62
6	Quicker response to market demand variation through production adjustment or marketing planning change	4.79	1.60
7	Improvement of product quality	4.78	1.53
8	Improvement of relationship with suppliers and customers	4.75	1.44
9	Improvement of employee satisfaction	4.73	1.61
10	Increase of sales volumes	4.63	1.37
11	Reduction of operational costs	4.51	1.53
11	Increase of profitability	4.51	1.51
12	Reduction of maintenance costs	4.41	1.42
13	Reduction of product/service development costs	4.38	1.56

Organizational and human factors ranked higher than technological factors, a confirmation of the observation reported in KM literature about the importance of organization culture for KM implementation (Brand, 1998; Davenport & Prusak, 2000; Koch et al., 2002; Pan & Scarbrough, 1998; Storck & Hill, 2000). The finding suggests, while companies have a clear understanding of the strategic value of knowledge, it is difficult for them to develop momentum. Nonetheless, the fact the highest degree of difficulty is only 4.62 indicates companies do not feel hopeless about coping with these challenges.

Summary and Conclusion

EC represents a promising avenue by enabling companies to interact directly with customers and integrate efforts of supply chain members (Keeny, 1999). The improved innovative capacity resulting from a thorough execution of KM strategies

Table 9. Difficulties experienced in KM implementations

Rank	Difficulties Encountered	Mean	Standard Deviation
1	Difficulty in knowledge flow due to lack of interdepartmental coordination	4.62	1.47
2	Lack of top management support	4.44	1.64
3	Weak consensus on the value of knowledge to the organization	4.33	1.51
4	Lack of innovative capability and motivation to innovate	4.30	1.53
5	Lack of incentive to encourage knowledge sharing	4.16	1.45
6	Lack of clearly defined communication mechanisms across departments	4.11	1.48
7	Employee resistance to sharing knowledge	3.94	1.60
8	Lack of clearly defined objectives for KM	3.92	1.51
9	Lack of trust between employee and management	3.76	1.51
10	Lack of hardware equipment to implement KM projects	3.49	1.74
11	Lack of proper software to implement KM projects	3.46	1.68

helps companies establish and sustain competitive advantage by providing unique, attractive customer values (Zack, 1999a, 1999b). The business environment today requires companies to continually offer new and improved products or services, trim operational costs, shorten delivery time, increase quality, provide value-added customer services, and quickly adapt to unexpected changes. To cope with these multifaceted challenges effectively, companies must diligently engage in activities capable of transforming their businesses into "intelligent-acting" organizations (Wiig, 1994, 1995). The literature reviewed suggests that there is a significant relationship between how companies apply EC and how they practice KM in their operations.

Our empirical study confirms this proposition. More specifically, the choice between systems-oriented and individual-oriented KM implementation strategies is affected by the business-to-business EC, and vice versa. Each of the KM implementation objectives is significantly affected by each of the three types of EC applications, and each of the three types of EC applications is significantly affected by all but one KM critical success factors. Two important implications for information system professionals and e-commerce managers can be drawn from the findings of this study.

First, although information technology itself does not guarantee success of either EC applications or KM implementations, it does represent an essential component as it provides the technological infrastructure. The information technology infrastructure must be properly aligned with business strategy and business processes to create synergies. Only with a high degree of synchronized efforts can a company perform competitively in an open environment. Taiwan is not unique in the pressures for global expansion and increased need for market development. Taiwan's recent success in manufacturing computer-related hardware and software is a natural fit to the need for EC applications and KM implementations.

Second, the investments in EC applications and KM implementations are complementary. As is noted in the Taiwanese example, the hardware and software tools acquired for EC applications can be useful for the promotion of KM activities. EC applications are guided and supported by an active KM program. The companies in Taiwan, as demonstrated in this study, are similar to companies in other parts of the world with regard to the facilitation effect of EC on KM. The enabling and support effect of KM on EC, and the synergistic effect between EC and KM in Taiwan, are also evident in companies throughout the world. These findings add to and extend the EC and KM research by providing empirical evidence obtained in Taiwan. The contributions of this study are largely exploratory.

It is the first study to attempt to empirically test the directional linkage or correlation between KM and EC. Other literature has alluded to the relationship but has not attempted to validate its presence. Since the subjects for this research were Taiwanese businesses, operating in a global business environment, the study has global relevance. It is, however, limited to one country. Other limitations of the research are the questionnaire design limited to subjective judgment, and variable response rates. Future research should work to overcome these limitations.

Three directions for future research are suggested. The first direction extends the scope of coverage by including additional forms of EC application (such as customer-to-business) and other KM practice items (such as knowledge acquisition methods). The second direction should examine in-depth relationships between EC and KM. For example, an interesting research issue might be how communities of practice support EC operations. The third direction involves collecting primary data from companies in the U.S. and internationally to further validate the research propositions, explore additional relationships, make cross-cultural comparisons, and establish further global linkages between these two important management themes.

References

Ahn, J-H, & Chang, S-G. (2004). Assessing the contribution of knowledge to business performance: The KP3 methodology. *Decision Support Systems*, *36*(4), 403-414.

Ahadi, H. R. (2004). An examination of the role of organizational enablers in business process reengineering and the impact of information iechnology. *Information Resources Management Journal, 17*(4), 1-19.

Alvesson, M. (2004). *Knowledge work and knowledge-intensive firms.* Oxford: Oxford University Press.

Bakhru, A. (2004). Managerial knowledge to organizational capability: New e-commerce businesses. *Journal of Intellectual Capital, 5*(2), 326-336.

Barua, A, Konana, P. K., Whinston, A. B., & Yin, F. (2001). Managing e-business transformation: Opportunities and value assessment. *Sloan Management Review, 43*(1), 36-44.

Blosch, M. (2000). Customer knowledge. *Knowledge and Process Management, 7*(4), 265-268.

Bose, R. & Sugumaran, V. (2003). Application of knowledge management technology in customer relationship management. *Knowledge and Process Management, 10*(1), 3-17.

Bradsher, K. (2004, December 13). Taiwan watches its economy slip to China. *New York Times*, C7.

Brand, A. (1998). KM and innovation at 3M. *Journal of KM, 2*(1), 17-22.

Buhalis, D., & Deimezi, O. (2004). E-tourism developments in Greece: Information communication technologies adoption for the strategic management of the Greek tourism industry. *Tourism and Hospitality Research, 5*(2), 103-130.

Castanho, M. A. R. B. (2004). What do college life sciences students need to know about knowledge management. *Journal of Biological Education, 38*(2), 85-9.

Chen, L.-Y. (2006). Effect of knowledge-sharing to organizational marketing effectiveness in large accounting firms that are strategically aligned. *Journal of the American Academy of Business, 9*(1), 176-182.

Child, P. N. (2002). Taking Tesco global. *The Mckinsey Quarterly, 3.* Retrieved from http://www.mckinseyquarterly.com

Davenport, T. H., & Prusak, L. (2000). *Working knowledge: How organizations know what they know.* Boston: Harvard Business School Press.

Diakoulakis, I. E., Georgopoulos, N. B., Koulouriotis, D. E., & Emiris, D. M. (2004). Towards a holistic knowledge management model. *Journal of Knowledge Management, 8*(1), 32-46.

Fang, L.-Y., & Wu, S.-H. (2006). Accelerating innovation through knowledge co-evolution: A case study of Taiwan semiconductor industry. *International Journal of Technology Management, 23*(2/3), 183-195.

Fahey, L, Srivastava, R., Sharon, J. S., & Smith, D. E. (2001). Linking e-business and operating processes: The role of knowledge management. *IBM Systems Journal, 40*(4), 889-907.

Feeny, A. (2001). Making business sense of the e-opportunity. *Sloan Management Review, 42*(2), 41-51.

Fingar, P., & Aronica, R. (2001). *The death of E and the birth of the real new economy.* Tampa, FL: Meghan-Kiffer Press.

Garbi, E. (2002). Alternative measures of performance for e-companies: A comparison of approaches. *Journal of Business Strategies, 19*(1), 1-17.

Gerstlberger, W. (2004). Regional innovation systems and sustainability—Selected examples of international discussion. *Technovation, 24*(9), 749-758.

Green, A., & Ryan, J. J. C. H. (2005). A framework of intangible valuation areas (FIVA): Aligning business strategy and intangible assets. *Journal of Intellectual Capital, 6*(1), 43-53.

Grover,V., & Davenport, T. H. (2001). General perspectives on KM: Fostering a research agenda. *Journal of Management Information Systems, 18*(1), 5-21.

Hoffman, D. L., & Novak, T. P. (1997). A new marketing paradigm for EC. *The Information Society, 13*, 43-54.

Hogue, F. (2000). *E-enterprise: Business models, architecture, and components.* Cambridge University Press.

Holsapple, C. W. (Ed.). (2004). *Handbook of knowledge management* (Vols. 1 and 2). Berlin: Heiderberg-Springer.

Holsapple, C. W., & Joshi, K. W. (2004). A formal knowledge management ontology: Conduct, activities, resources and influences. *Journal of the American Society for Information Science and Technology, 55*(7), 593-605.

Holsapple, C. W., & Singh, M. (2000). Toward a unified view of electronic commerce, electronic business, and collaborative commerce: A knowledge management approach. *Knowledge and Process Management, 7*(3), 151-164.

Huang, H.-W., Shih, H.-Y., Huang, H.-W., & Liu, C.-H. (2006). Can knowledge management create firm value? Empirical evidence from the United States and Taiwan. *The Business Review, 5*(1), 178-183.

Huosong, X., Kuanqi, D., & Shuqin, C. (2003). Enterprise knowledge tree model and factors of KMS based on E-C. *Journal of Knowledge Management, 7*(1), 96-106.

Jarvenpaa, S. L., & Todd, P. A. (1997). Consumer reactions to electronic shopping on the World Wide Web. *International Journal of Electronic Commerce, 1*(2), 59-88.

Jih, W. J. K. (2002). Effects of EC implementations in Taiwan. *Journal of Computer Information Systems*, 56-62.

Kankanhalli, A., Tanudidjaja, F., Sutanto, J., & Tan, B. C. Y. (2003). The role of IT in a successful knowledge management initiatives. *Communication of the ACM, 46*(9), 69-73.

Kalakota, R., & Whinston, A. B. (1996a). *Electronic commerce: A manager's guide.* New York: Addison-Wesley.

Kalakota, R., & Whinston, A. B. (1996b). *Frontiers of EC.* New York: Addison-Wesley.

Keeny, R. L. (1999). The value of Internet commerce to the customer. *Management Science, 45*(4), 533-542.

Kim, W. C., & Mauborgne, R. (1999). Strategy, value innovation, and the knowledge economy. *Sloan Management Review, 40*(3), 41-54.

Koch, H., Paradice, D., Chae, B., & Guo, Y. (2002). An investigation if KM within a University IT Group. *Information Resources Management Journal, 15*(1), 13-21.

Kocharekar, R. (2001). K-commerce: Knowledge-based commerce architecture with convergence of e-commerce and knowledge management. *Information Systems Management*, Spring, 30-35.

Lee, C., & Chen, W.-J. (2005). The effects of internal marketing and organizational culture on knowledge management in the information technology industry. *International Journal of Management, 22*(4), 661-673.

Lee, H. L., & Whang, S. (2001). Winning the last mile of e-commerce. *Sloan Management Review, 42*(4), 54-62.

Lee, Y.-D., & Chang, H.-M. (2006). Leadership style and innovation ability: An empirical study of Taiwanese wire and cable companies. *Journal of the American Academy of Business, 9*(2), 218-222.

Leseure, M. J., & Brookes, N. J. (2004). Knowledge management benchmarks for project management. *Journal of Knowledge Management, 8*(1), 103-116.

Mahadevan, B. (2000). Business models for Internet-based e-commerce: An anatomy. *California Management Review, 42*(4), 55-69.

Mahmood, A., & Yu, C. M. (2005). E-entrepreneurship in knowledge economy: Implications for the Asia-Pacific economies. *The Business Review, 4*(1), 153-160.

Malhotra, Y. (2000) Knowledge management for e-business performance: Advancing information strategy to "internet time" information strategy. *The Executive's Journal, 16*(4), 5-16.

Marr, B., Schiuma, G., & Nelly, A. (2004). Intelectual capital—Defining key performance indicators for organizational knowledge assets. *Business Process Management Journal, 10*(5), 551-569.

Mataxiotis, K., Ergazakis, K., Samouilidis, E., & Pgarras, J. (2004). Decision support through knowledge management: The role of the artificial intelligence. *International Journal of Computer Applications in Technology, 19*(2), 101-119.

Mudambi, R., & Navarra, P. (2004). Is knowledge power? Knowledge flows, subsidiary power and rent-seeking within MNCs. *Journal of International Business Studies, 35*(5), 385-406.

Pan, S. L., & Scarbrough, H. (1998). A socio-technical view of knowledge-sharing at Buckman Laboratories. *Journal of KM, 2*(1), 55-66.

Plessis, M., & Boon, J. A. (2004). Knowledge management in e-business and customer relationship management: South Africa case study findings. *International Journal of Information Management, 24*(10, 73-85.

Piris, L., &Fitzgerald, A. S. (2004). Strategic motivators and expected benefits from e-commerce in traditional organizations. *International Journal of Information Management, 24*(6), 489-499.

Porter, M. (2001, March). Strategy and the Internet. *Harvard Business Review*, 63-78.

Prusak, L., & Liam, F. (1998, spring). The eleven deadliest sins of KM. *California Management Review, 40*, 265-276.

Rahman, B. (2004). Knowledge management initiatives: Exploratory study in Malaysia. *Journal of the American Academy of Business, 4*(1/2), March, 300-335.

Rowley, J. E. (2002). Reflections on customer knowledge management in e-business. *Qualitative Market Research, 5*(4), 268-280.

Salazar, A., Hackney, R., & Howells, J. (2003). The strategic impact of Internet technology in biotechnology and pharmaceutical firms: Insights from a knowledge management perspective. *Information and Technology Management, 2*(2-3), 289-301.

Samiotis, K., Poulymenakou, A., & Doukidis, G. (2003). Understanding knowledge management interventions: Evidence from supporting (e-) banking activities. *Knowledge and Process Management, 10*(3), 175-191.

Savary, M. (1999). KM and competition in the consulting industry. *California Management Review, 41*(2), 41-52.

Sharma, S. K., Gupta, J. N. D., & Wickramasinghe, N. (2006). A framework for designing the enterprise-wide e-commerce portal for evolving organizations. *Electronic Commerce Research, 6*(2), 141-154.

Singh, N., Furrer, O., &Ostinelli, M. (2004). To localize or to standardize on the Web: Empirical evidence from Italy, India, Netherlands, Spain, and Switzerland. *Multinational Business Review, 12*(1), 69-87.

Singh, R., Iyer, L. S., & Salam, A. F. (2005). Introduction. *Association for Computing Machinery—Communications of the ACM, 48*(12), 38.

Soliman, F., & Youssef, M. (2001). The impact of some recent developments in e-business on the management of next generation manufacturing. *International Journal of Operations & Production Management, 21*(5/6), 538-549.

Soo, C., Devinney, T., Midgley, D., & Deering, A. (2002). KM: Philosophy, processes, and pitfalls. *California Management Review, 44*(4), 129-150.

Spiegler, I. (2003). Technology and knowledge: Bridging a "generation" gap. *Information & Management, 40*(6), 533-539.

Srinivasan, R., Lilien, G. L., & Rangaswamy, A.(2002). Technological opportunism and radical technology adoption: An application to e-business. *Journal of Marketing, 66*(3), 47-60.

Stankosky, M. (2004). Tackling a unified KM framework. *KM World, 13*(1), 1-19.

Storck, J., & Hill, P. A. (2000). Knowledge diffusion through 'strategic community.' *Sloan Management Review, 41*(2), 63-74.

Su, C.-T., Chen, Y.-H., & Sha, D. Y. (2006). Linking innovative product development with customer knowledge: A data mining approach. *Technovation, 26*(7), 784-795.

Tang, F. (2000). *Taiwan to become a knowledge-based economy within 10 years.* Retrieved August 17, from http://www.thenews.com

Tigre, P. B., & Dedrick, J. (2004). E-commerce in Brazil: Local adaptation of a global technology. *Electronic Markets, 14*(1), 36-47.

Trethewey, A., & Corman, S. (2001). Anticipating k-commerce. *Management Communication Quarterly, 14*(4), 619-628.

Turban, E., Aronson, J. E., & Liang, T. P. (2005). *Decision support systems and intelligent systems* (7th ed.). NJ: Prentice-Hall.

Turban, E., Lee, J., King, D., & Chung, H. M. (2000). *EC: A managerial perspective.* NJ: Prentice-Hall.

Wang, L. K., Scherban, D. M., & Bonnici, J. (2005). International business: Taiwan's edge in the Asian financial crisis. *Journal of American Academy of Business, 6*(1), 143-150.

Wang, M. (2006). The impact of information culture on managing knowledge: A double case study of pharmaceutical manufacturers in Taiwan. *Library Review, 55*(3/4), 209-221.

Wang, S., & Ariguzo, G. (2004). Knowledge management through the development of information schema. *Information & Management, 41*(4), 445-456.

Warkentin, M., Bapna, R., & Sugumaran, V. (2001). E-knowledge networks for inter-organizational collaborative e-business. *Logistics Information Management, 14*(1/2), 149-162.

Wenger, E. (2004, January/February). Knowledge management as a doughnut: Shaping your knowledge strategy through communities of practice. *Ivey Business Journal Online,* 1-5.

Wigand, R. T. (1997). EC: Definition, theory, and context. *The Information Society, 13*(1)-16.

Wiig, K. M. (1994). *KM: The central management focus for intelligent-acting organizations.* Arlington, TX: Schema Press.

Wiig, K. M. (1995). *KM methods: Practical approaches to managing knowledge.* Arlington, TX: Schema Press.

Williams, R., & Cothrel, J. (2000). Four smart ways to run online communities. *Sloan Management Review, 41,* 4, 81-91.

Wolfinbarger, M., & Gilly, M. C. (2002). *.comQ: Dimensionalizing, measuring and predicting quality of the e-retail experience.* CRITO, University of California. Retrieved from http://www.crito.uci.edu

Wolfinbarger, M., & Gilly, M. C. (2001). Shopping Online for Freedom, Control, and Fun. *California Management Review, 43*(2), 34-55.

Woods, E. (2004). KM past and future: Changing the rules of the game. *KM World, 13*(1), 12-14.

Zack, M. H. (1999a). Developing a knowledge strategy. *California Management Review, 41,* 25-145.

Zack, M. H. (1999b). Managing codified knowledge. *Sloan Management Review, 40*(4), 45-58.

Chapter XIV

An Evaluation System for IT Outsourcing Customer Satisfaction Using the Analytic Hierarchy Process:
The Case Study in Korea

YongKi Yoon, Yonsei University, Korea

Kun Shin Im, Yonsei University, Korea

Abstract

Many companies have recently been choosing information technology (IT) outsourcing in response to complicated information systems and various internal requirements. In order to monitor and maintain a high quality of IT outsourcing vendors' services, it is necessary to develop a system to evaluate IT outsourcing customer satisfaction. The system can be used as a tool for choosing IT outsourcing providers. Through the literature reviews and experts' interviews, we propose the evaluation system of IT outsourcing customer satisfaction. Using AHP (analytic hierarchy process) technique, attributes associated with customer satisfaction in IT outsourcing environments are then rated in terms of their importance. The customer satisfaction evaluation system is applied to IT outsourcing service receivers in Korea to demonstrate its practical implications.

Introduction

Recently, IT outsourcing has been recognized as a strategy for increasing efficiency and cutting costs of the information systems implementations. A properly implemented outsourcing strategy brings together industry knowledge and IT to create systems that help organizations acquire and maintain a competitive advantage and provide better service at a lower cost (Sengupta & Zviran, 1997). In IT outsourcing environments, customers' requirements and feedback are essential to the development of information systems applications and the improvement of the service quality of IT service vendors or companies. From the vendor's perspective, it is important to minimize the reasons for complaints and dissatisfaction, as well as the cost of a service recovery plan (McCollough, Berry, & Yadav, 2000). It is also important for vendors to establish a track of direct feedback from customers on their reactions to the complaints and dissatisfaction (Abubakar, Mavondo, & Clulow, 2001). Therefore, it is particularly useful to develop a customer satisfaction evaluation system for IT outsourcing providers and their customers.

This chapter aims to introduce a systematic evaluation system for the evaluation of IT outsourcing customer satisfaction that reflects outsourcing environments as well as customer feedback. In this chapter, we present an evaluation framework for IT outsourcing customer satisfaction through the literature reviews and experts interviews, and develop the IT outsourcing customer satisfaction evaluation system using AHP analysis. AHP is used for weighting and ranking key customer satisfaction factors. The system is applied to IT outsourcing customer companies in Korea to demonstrate the practical value and effectiveness of the proposed system. This study may be useful and helpful to practitioners, IT managers, and customers who are faced with outsourcing services. Using the evaluation system as a tool for measuring IT outsourcing customer satisfaction, IT outsourcing providers can monitor their service level and understand customers' requirements precisely. The observed values of customer satisfaction can provide important guidelines in the improvement of IT outsourcing services and improve their competitive position in the market. For customers, they can utilize the results of customer satisfaction in choosing IT outsourcing vendors.

First, we review information technology outsourcing, customer satisfaction, and related information system evaluation models in section 2. In section 3, our research method, including AHP, is explained. In section 4, the evaluation system for IT outsourcing customer satisfaction is described, and the weights and priority in the evaluation system are explained in section 5. In section 6, a case study is summarized to prove its practical value.

Literature Review

Information Technology Outsourcing

IT outsourcing is defined as the act of subcontracting part or all of a company's IT function to one or more external vendors (Cheon, 1995; Gelbstein, 2002; Grover, Cheon, & Teng, 1996; Lacity & Willcocks, 1995; Loh & Venkatraman, 1992; Sengupta & Zviran, 1997). Corporations introduced IT outsourcing until the mid-1990s chiefly to achieve cost-effectiveness and thus, mostly pushed ahead with computing-related services or system integration in the form of strategic alliances (Grover et al., 1996; McFarlan & Nolan, 1995). However, recently, with new forms of IT outsourcing models such as ASP having been developed, and existing computing services or system integration or system management outsourcing having been segmented and specialized, new characteristics are appearing that are totally different from those of traditional IT outsourcing (Young & Berg, 2001).

Various approaches to IT outsourcing have been studied. The transaction cost theory offers a method of evaluating the relative advantages of different internal and external organizations for handling transactions (Cheon, 1995). It also provides an excellent framework for analyzing the outsourcing options (Lacity & Hirschheim, 1993). Vining and Globerman (1999) studied IT outsourcing decision factors by using production cost, bargaining cost, and opportunism cost in various outsourcings. They stated that the outsourcing cost rose and the preference of IT outsourcing fell off when asset specificity was high. Kern (Kern & Kreijger, 2001; Kern, Kreijger, & Willcocks, 2002) applied a transaction cost approach to ASP and noted that transaction cost decreased because ASP lowered asset specificity and uncertainty. Nam et al. (Nam, Rajagopalan, & Chaudhury, 1996) analyzed two-phase IT outsourcing decision-making process by taking transaction costs into account.

The resource-based approach views a firm as a collection of productive resources (Cheon, 1995). Roy and Aubert (2000) chose the IS sourcing mode from the viewpoint of resources base. Khalfan and Gough (2002) stated that IS outsourcing was performed because of the shortage of available resources and a poor core resource in the internal situation of a company. As Yang and Huang (2000) performed an IT outsourcing decision-making process through AHP, they classified the corresponding criteria into these five categories: management, strategy, technology, economics, and quality. While a resource-based approach to strategic management focuses on an internal analysis of a firm in terms of resources and capabilities, a resource dependence theory focuses on elements in the external environments (Cheon, 1995). The agency cost theory provides an excellent framework for evaluating the relative advantages of the different internal and external organization forms for handling contracts between an outsourcing service receiver and a provider (Cheon, 1995).

In addition to these traditional types of research, various new approaches to IT outsourcing are being actively studied. For example, strategic alliances and partnerships are new trends, and ideas like these are generating IT outsourcing success (Sun, Lin, & Sun, 2002). Willcocks and Choi (1995) studied the importance of strategic alliance in IT outsourcing based in total IT outsourcing case and asserted their usefulness. Ireland et al. (Ireland, Hitt, & Vaidyanath, 2002) stated that social capital, complementary resources, new capabilities, and knowledge transfer factors make IT outsourcing successful from the strategic alliance point of view. In addition, McFarlan and Nolan (1995) and Quinn (1999) emphasized the importance of relationship management in outsourcing. Some researchers have presented embodied framework related to strategic alliance and applied them to real companies or businesses (Means & Schneider, 2000; Parker, Condon, & Ackers, 2002). Gartner defined strategic sourcing as the dynamic delivery of internal and external business resources and services that ensure that business objectives are met (Rold, 2000). King and Malhotra (2000) presented an IS sourcing analysis framework based on short-term operation impacts, midterm tactical impacts, and long-term strategic impacts. In addition, Lee and Kim (1997) presented the advantages and disadvantages of the process of concluding IT outsourcing agreements among affiliate companies in Korea as well as decision-making models for choosing IT outsourcing providers.

Rushton and Gardiner (1997) presented a decision-making process related to the designing and buying process in software sourcing. Palvia (1995) induced nine decision-making factors, such as cost control in selecting IT outsourcing. Gallivan and Oh (1999) dealt with preference factors related to multivendors and co-sourcing through partnership in a one-to-one relationship in outsourcing. Khalfan and Gough (2002) presented a difference in decision-making factors between the private and public sectors.

Although most of the research related to IT outsourcing has been studied by various scholars and practitioners, the study on customer satisfaction in IT outsourcing environments has been insufficiently conducted. Previous research on customer or user satisfaction had a focus on internal organization or information systems instead of outsourcing vendors and their customers. The customer satisfaction on IT outsourcing service would be one of the most important strategies for IT outsourcing providers and receivers. Customer satisfaction represents a central strategic focus for customer-oriented firms across diverse industries (Szymanski & Henard, 2001). In order to ensure customers enjoy a high degree of satisfaction and a high quality of services, IT outsourcing service providers are needed to track their levels of customer satisfaction. Thus, developing a comprehensive set of measurement tools is an essential step in monitoring the service quality provided by the external vendors (Loh & Venkataraman, 1992; Sengupta & Zviran, 1997. Accordingly, it is necessary to review the general customer satisfaction and information system evaluation models related to user information satisfaction in order to develop an evaluation system for measuring IT outsourcing customer satisfaction and tracing any changes in customer satisfaction.

Customer Satisfaction

Scholars of different academic backgrounds have different analyses of customer satisfaction by looking at it both theoretically and practically (Chien, Su, & Su, 2002). Wong (2000) believes that a customer's total satisfaction is an emotional perception. Leem and Yoon (2004) viewed customer satisfaction as a broad concept that included a perceived evaluation of products and services. Parasuraman, Zeithaml, and Berry (1988) defined customer satisfaction as the difference between perceived quality and expected quality in their SERVQUAL model. They divided service attributes into five categories: tangibles, reliability, responsiveness, assurance, and empathy. They constructed a generic survey that could be used for the measurement of customer satisfaction for all service sectors. SERVQUAL was also suggested as a means to measure the service quality of a given information system (Kettinger & Lee, 1997; Pitt, Waton, & Kavan, 1995, 1997). Even though the SERVQUAL model is accepted in one part of academia, debates on its validity have continued. Moreover, this model is not widely used in commercial settings. Cronin and Taylor, the developers of the SERVPERF model, explained that customer satisfaction could be measured only in terms of perceived quality. Also, this model could reduce survey questions and improve the predictability of customer purchase intentions (Cronin & Taylor, 1992). To utilize the practical values of previous models, the ACSI (America Customer Satisfaction Indices) model in the U.S. (National Quality Research Center, 1995) and the NCSI (National Customer Satisfaction Indices) model in Korea (Korea Productivity Center, 1997) have been developed and are currently being applied in various areas. Chien et al. (Chien, Chang, & Su, 2003) showed the 33 latent variables in the NCSI models of different countries, and compared the relationship between the NCSI model and the various concrete issues within customer satisfaction programs.

Typical customer satisfaction evaluation models are difficult to apply directly to customers or users of IT outsourcing service vendors. They do not assume that customers possess a certain level of professional knowledge about the products or services that are often required to use information systems or services provided by IT outsourcing vendors.

Information System Evaluation Models

The assessment of IS effectiveness is an important issue for both IS practitioners and general management (Sengupta & Zviran, 1997). Many pieces of research on user satisfaction, information system usage, and information value have been done to evaluate IS effectiveness (Cho, 2000). Several studies have employed user information satisfaction (UIS) as a dependent variable to demonstrate IS effectiveness and acceptance (Igbaria & Machman, 1990; Ives & Olson, 1984). Although there is no standard measure of satisfaction in these studies, it is argued that user satisfaction is an indicator of system usage and effectiveness (Sengupta & Zviran, 1997). Bailey and Pearson (1983) measured user satisfaction as the weighted sum of the user's positive and negative reactions to a set of factors regarding an information system and identified 39 factors that can represent the user satisfaction domain. Ives et al. (Ives, Olson, & Baroudi, 1983) suggested some modified factors that are based on the study of Bailey and Pearson (1983). Baroudi and Orlikowski (1989) developed simple and short form measures that include 13 questions with two response scales per question. Cho (2000) mentioned that the measurement tool of Ives et al. (1983) were not suitable to measure end-user computing satisfaction. However, Doll and Torkadeh (1988) verified that five factors, such as content, accuracy, format, ease-of-use, and timeliness, are suitable to measure end-user computing satisfaction.

Typical user information satisfaction models are not suitable for evaluating overall customer-oriented service quality and satisfaction regarding IT outsourcing vendors or companies. This is because those kinds of methods are not directly related to the service and product quality of vendors and their end users; rather, they focus on the information system itself and an internal information department. Finally, Sengupta and Zviran (1997) stated that the development of a comprehensive measure of user satisfaction in outsourcing environments and the construction of new instruments for serving IT outsourcing environments were needed in academia and industry.

Research Method

We developed an evaluation framework for IT outsourcing customer satisfaction using the AHP applications. First of all, we reviewed the related literature and extracted key elements or factors that have an effect upon customer satisfaction in IT outsourcing environments. Second, we conducted interviews with nine IT outsourcing experts, who are related to the IT outsourcing service industry, academia, and government, to generate customer satisfaction-affecting factors and verify extracted key factors from the literature reviews, and then we defined all customer satisfaction-affecting factors. Subsequently, we constructed an evaluation framework for IT outsourcing customer satisfaction that was classified into consulting service satisfaction, customer supporting service satisfaction, and performance satisfaction. In order to determine the weights and rank the importance of the elements in the evaluation system for IT outsourcing customer satisfaction, the AHP method was used. Finally, we conducted a series of personal interviews with three IT professionals, composed of one CIO and two professors, to confirm the validity of our evaluation system. They have work experiences for IT outsourcing companies for over 6 years or have studied various projects related to IT outsourcing. They are also well-known professionals of IT outsourcing in Korea. The interviews confirmed that our proposed system was suitable for studying IT outsourcing customer satisfaction. We then developed a five-point Likert-style questionnaire based on the evaluation system. We think that a professional group is suitable for evaluating the validity of the evaluation system because our study has exploratory characteristics and the studies on customer satisfaction of IT outsourcing are insufficient. The following section deals with why and how AHP can be used in weighting and ranking elements of IT outsourcing customer satisfaction. And then, a cast study was conducted to apply our evaluation system for evaluating customer satisfaction of IT outsourcing in Korea.

Analytic Hierarchy Process (AHP)

The AHP, introduced by Saaty (1990), is a mathematically based, multiobjective decision-making tool (Udo, 2000). AHP mainly addresses how to solve decision-making problems having uncertainty and multiple criteria characteristics (Yang & Huang, 2000). It is an extensively used multicriteria decision-making method, and has been applied to a wide variety of decisions and applications (Chan, Kwok, & Duffy, 2004; Hafeez, Zhang, & Malak, 2002; Ngai, 2003; Yang & Huang, 2000). Moreover, the AHP is a suitable approach for undertaking quantitative as well as qualitative analysis (Hafeez et al., 2002). Ngai (2003) stated that the AHP was aimed at integrating different measures into a single overall score for ranking decision alternatives, and its main characteristic was that it is based on pair-wise comparison judgments. IT outsourcing customer satisfaction evaluation has multicriteria and weights for each factor of the customer satisfaction. The development of weights and priority for the customer satisfaction factors would be an important step in implementing an evaluation system for IT outsourcing customer satisfaction in a practical manner. For those reasons, the AHP was selected in this study. The AHP is used to find key customer satisfaction factors and determine weights of the factors in the evaluation system.

Evaluation System for
IT Outsourcing Customer Satisfaction

The evaluation system for IT outsourcing customer satisfaction comprises an evaluation framework, evaluation areas, evaluation factors, evaluation attributes,

Figure 1. Evaluation framework for IT outsourcing customer satisfaction

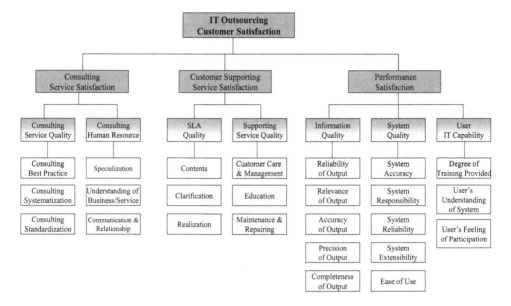

and evaluation measurements. First, the evaluation framework for IT outsourcing customer satisfaction is presented in Figure 1 to outline the whole structure of the system.

The evaluation framework for IT outsourcing customer satisfaction is divided into three areas: consulting service satisfaction, customer supporting service satisfaction, and performance satisfaction. Consulting service satisfaction is related to consulting service quality in such areas as the business capability and human resources of IT outsourcing vendors. Customer supporting service satisfaction refers to various supporting service issues such as SLA (service level agreement), education, and maintenance and repairing coming from the IT outsourcing vendors. Performance satisfaction concerns performance issues from the services and products of IT outsourcing vendors.

In this framework, evaluation factors and attributes are developed for consulting service satisfaction, customer supporting service satisfaction, and performance satisfaction. Evaluation measurements are generated from the evaluation attributes. These factors, attributes, and measurements are presented in Tables 1, 2, and 3.

Consulting service satisfaction has two evaluation factors: first, consulting service quality related to consulting best-practice, systematization, and standardization, and second, consulting human resource corresponding to specialization, understanding of business and service, and communication or relationship. The evaluation factors for

Table 1. Evaluation factors, evaluation attributes, and measurements of consulting service satisfaction

Evaluation Area	Evaluation Factors	Evaluation Attributes	Evaluation Measurements	Related References
Consulting service satisfaction	Consulting service quality	Consulting best-practice	• Advanced methodology • Advanced business adaptation	Paulk, Curtis, & Chrissis (1991, 1992, 1993), ISO/ IEC TR 15504 (1998), Frank & Hans (1999), Yeo & Nam (2003), Leem & Yoon (2004), Sengupta & Zviran (1997),
		Consulting systematization	• Consistency of consulting goal • Systematical consulting • Risk management	
		Consulting standardization	• Documentization • Standard management system • SLA management regulations	
	Consulting human resource	Specialization	• Consulting knowledge • Consulting experience	Sengupta & Zviran (1997), Baroudi & Orlikowski (1988), Byrd & Turner (2000), Leem & Yoon (2004)
		Understanding of business/ service	• Understanding of business structure • Understanding of business environments • Understanding of business characteristics • Understanding of business process • Understanding of IT infrastructure • Project comprehension	
		Communication & relationship	• Participant intention • Communication ability • Presentation skill	

customer supporting service satisfaction are divided into supporting service quality and SLA (service level agreements) quality. The supporting service quality attributes are categorized according to service types that are offered by IT outsourcing vendors. These attributes are customer care and management, education, and maintenance and repairing. SLA forms an essential part of the IT outsourcing service (Gartner, 2000), for it sets up expectations between the consumer and provider. It helps define the relationship between the two parties. Yoon et al. (2004) suggested the development and management of SLA's measurement are needed to obtain a success in IT outsourcing. SLA quality includes SLA contents, reliability, and clarification, while

Table 2. Evaluation factors, evaluation attributes, and measurements of customer supporting service satisfaction

Evaluation Area	Evaluation Factors	Evaluation Attributes	Evaluation Measurements	Related References
Customer supporting service satisfaction	Supporting service quality	Customer care and management	• Quick response • Customer care regulation	Paulk et al. (1991, 1992, 1993), ISO/IEC TR 15504 (1998), Frank & Hans (1999), Yeo & Nam (2004), Leem & Yoon (2004)
		Education	• Instructor's specialty • Kindness and response • Continuity of education service • Continuous contents development • Education effectives	Paulk et al. (1991, 1992, 1993), ISO/IEC TR 15504 (1998), Frank & Hans (1999), Yeo & Nam (2004), Leem & Yoon (2004)
		Maintenance and repairing	• Quickness in emergency • Continuous and periodical service • Reflection of updated requirements and changes • Service's attitude • Specialty	Paulk et al. (1991, 1992, 1993), ISO/IEC TR 15504 (1998), Frank & Hans (1999), Cho (2000), Yeo & Nam (2004), Leem & Yoon(2004)
	SLA quality	Contents	• Contents specification and requirement • Accuracy	Doll & Torkzadeh (1988), Gartner (2000), Lee (2002), Yoon, Seo, & Kim (2004)
		Reliability	• Realization • Reality of SLA	
		Clarification	• Clarification and clearness	

performance satisfaction has three evaluation factors: information quality, system quality, and user IT capability.

In order to measure all of the 52 evaluation measurements of IT outsourcing customer satisfaction, we developed a five-point Likert-style questionnaire that is based on 52 measurements that are 19 consulting service satisfaction measurements, 17 customer supporting service satisfaction measurements, and 16 performance satisfaction measurements. The questionnaire is used in a case study.

Table 3. Evaluation factors, evaluation attributes, and measurements of performance satisfaction

Evaluation Area	Evaluation Factors	Evaluation Attributes	Evaluation Measurements	Related References
Performance satisfaction	Information Quality	Reliability of output	• Information reliability	Baroudi & Orlikowski (1988), Sengupta & Zviran (1997)
		Relevance of output	• Information relevance	
		Accuracy of output	• Information accuracy	
		Precision of output	• Information precision	
		Completeness of output	• Information completeness	
	System Quality	System accuracy	• Accuracy	Baily & Pearson (1983), Ives & Olson (1984), Doll & Torkzadeh (1988), Kettinger & Lee (1994), Pitt et al. (1995, 1997), Leem & Yoon (2004)
		System responsibility	• Responsibility	
		System reliability	• Reliability	
		System extensibility	• Extensibility	
		Ease of use	• Compatibility • User friendly	
	User IT Capability	Degree of training provided	• Professional knowledge • Education level	Baroudi & Orlikowski (1988), Broadbent et al. (1996), Sengupta & Zviran (1997), Stratman & Roth (2002)
		User's understanding of system	• General understating of IT or system • Business application	
		User's feeling of participation	• Feeling of participation	

Weights and Priority in the Evaluation System

In order to assign weights to evaluations areas, factors, and attributes, we used the AHP analysis that is based on the evaluation framework. We conducted questionnaires for 30 IT experts who are consultants and managers related to IT outsourc-

Table 4. The weights and priority of the evaluation areas, factors, and attributes for IT outsourcing customer satisfaction

Evaluation areas	Weights of areas Local	Evaluation factors	Weights of evaluation factors Local	Weights of evaluation factors Global	Priority of factors	Evaluation attributes	Weights of evaluation attributes Local	Weights of evaluation attributes Global	Priority of attributes
Consulting service satisfaction	0.105	Consulting service quality	0.500	0.0525	4	Consulting best-practice	0.105	0.0055	20
						Consulting systematization	0.637	0.0334	7
						Consulting standardization	0.258	0.0135	14
		Consulting human resource	0.500	0.0525	4	Specialization	0.637	0.0334	7
						Understanding of business and service	0.258	0.0135	14
						Communication and relationship	0.105	0.0055	20
Customer supporting service satisfaction	0.637	Supporting service quality	0.250	0.1593	3	Customer care and management	0.088	0.0140	13
						Education	0.243	0.0387	6
						Maintenance and repairing	0.669	0.1065	4
		SLA quality	0.750	0.4778	1	Contents	0.405	0.1935	2
						Reliability	0.114	0.0545	5
						Clarification	0.481	0.2298	1

continued on following page

Table 4. continued

Perfor-mance satisfaction							
0.258	Information quality	0.258	0.0666	6	Reliability of output	0.326	0.0217	10
					Relevance of output	0.137	0.0091	17
					Accuracy of output	0.326	0.0217	10
					Precision of output	0.137	0.0091	17
					Completeness of output	0.074	0.0049	22
	System quality	0.105	0.0270	7	System accuracy	0.460	0.0125	16
					System responsibility	0.108	0.0029	24
					System reliability	0.260	0.0070	19
					System extensibility	0.120	0.0033	23
					Ease of use	0.052	0.0014	25
	User IT capability	0.637	0.1643	2	Degree of training provided(Specialty)	0.747	0.1228	3
					User's understanding of system	0.119	0.0196	12
					User's feeling of participation	0.134	0.0220	9

ing service. The weights are evaluated by Expert Choice, which is a multiattribute decision support software tool based on the AHP methodology and a tool that can help the decision makers to examine and resolve problems involving multiple evaluation criteria (Udo, 2000). Questionnaires or data that has the inconsistency ratio of more than 0.1 were ruled out. The priority and weights of the evaluation areas, factors, and attributes of the evaluation system for IT outsourcing customer satisfaction are shown in Table 4.

In Table 4, "Local" means the weights in the criteria that are calculated by Expert Choice software directly. "Global" means the weights calculated by multiplying "Local" values. "Global" values are used in ranking the evaluation area, factor, and attributes. For example, the "Global" weight of consulting service quality (0.0525) is calculated by multiplying the "Local" weights of consulting service satisfaction (0.105) by "Local" weights of consulting service quality (0.500). The "Global" weight of consulting best practices (0.0055) = 0.105×0.500×0.105.

Customer supporting service satisfaction has the highest weight among the three evaluation areas. The evaluation factors and attributes that have the most effect upon IT outsourcing customer satisfaction are SLA quality and SLA clarification. SLA contents and reliability have the second and the fifth rank in the priority of evaluation attributes. Maintenance and repairing has the fourth priority, and education the sixth in evaluation attributes. Thus, one may say that IT outsourcing users have higher expectations of satisfaction in SLA and supporting service quality. In the survey, most of the interviewees also stated that service issues such as SLA and maintenance and repairing are important in IT outsourcing services as factors for attaining IT outsourcing customer satisfaction. User IT capability is also an important consideration factor that has the second priority in evaluation. It is a potent influence on IT outsourcing customer satisfaction. Especially, the degree of training provided or the specialty existing is a dominant influence in user IT capability and performance satisfaction.

A Case Study

To show the practical implications of the IT outsourcing customer satisfaction evaluation system, we applied it to IT outsourcing customer companies in Korea. In Korea, the IT outsourcing market is rapidly increasing, and many corporations introduce IT outsourcing in many fields. Outsourcing has become a very important issue to outsourcing service receivers and providers. IT outsourcing providers focus on customer satisfaction to retain existing customers as well as attract new customers, and service receivers want to select a good vendor among various service providers in Korea. In the survey, IT outsourcing services are classified into five areas: application

Table 5. The IT outsourcing service classification and participants

Outsourcing areas	Detailed classes	Participants
Project process	Application Service Provider (ASP)	4 companies
	Hosting and Data Center Operations	6 companies
	System Operations and Support	4 companies
Project work	Application Development and Maintenance	8 companies
	An Outsourcing Hybrid	3 companies

Table 6. The overall evaluation results of IT outsourcing customer satisfaction

Outsourcing Areas	IT Outsourcing Customer Satisfaction	Consulting Service Satisfaction	Customer Supporting Service Satisfaction	Performance Satisfaction
		Mean	Mean	Mean
Application Service Provider (ASP)	2.582	2.919	2.402	2.888
Hosting and Data Center Operations	2.960	2.721	3.030	2.883
System Operations and Support	2.595	3.120	2.499	2.617
Application Development and Maintenance	3.067	3.155	3.035	3.110
An Outsourcing Hybrid	2.668	3.141	2.511	2.865
Total average	**2.774**	**3.011**	**2.695**	**2.873**

service provider, hosting and data center operations, application development and maintenance, system operations and support, and an outsourcing hybrid based on the classifications of IT outsourcing service (Bennett & Timbrell, 1999; Gelbstein, 2002; Young & Berg, 2001). We sent 120 questionnaires to 40 customer companies that outsource IT functions. A total of 25 companies from the five outsourcing areas participated in the survey. We received 32 usable and meaningful data, a response rate of 27%, through the questionnaires. IT outsourcing service classification and the participants are presented in Table 5.

Table 7. The evaluation results of IT outsourcing customer satisfaction by the size of outsourcing vendors

Size of Outsourcing Vendors	IT Outsourcing Customer Satisfaction	Consulting Service Satisfaction	Customer Supporting Service Satisfaction	Performance Satisfaction
		Mean	Mean	Mean
Large enterprises	3.105	3.309	3.066	3.119
SMEs	2.832	3.033	2.776	2.889

Table 6 shows the overall evaluation results of IT outsourcing customer satisfaction. Table 7 represents the service level by the size of IT outsourcing vendors—large enterprise and SMEs.

IT outsourcing customer satisfaction, calculated by using the weights of evaluation areas in Table 4, is the weighted sum of consulting service satisfaction, customer supporting service satisfaction, and performance satisfaction. IT outsourcing customer satisfaction regarding the application development and maintenance area is higher than that of any other outsourcing areas. One can deduce that application development and maintenance is relatively stable regarding market and IT trends. Thus, its results in customer satisfaction seem to be superior to other outsourcing areas.

The total average of customer supporting service satisfaction is lower than consulting service satisfaction by 0.316, and is lower than performance satisfaction by 0.178, due to the weakness in SLA quality and education in customer supporting service. The resulting customer satisfaction tends to decrease easily, as customer expected values increase. Thus, this data may be interpreted to mean that customers have higher expectations of satisfaction in SLA quality and supporting service than they do in the consulting services.

The average customer satisfaction of a large enterprise is higher by 0.273 than SMEs is. This may mean that large enterprises provide more stable information systems and continuity of service to customers than SMEs because large vendors have more systematic IT outsourcing departments and experienced service knowledge. Based on these results, SMEs appear still to be weak in terms of their enterprise resource and service levels.

Conclusion

We proposed an evaluation framework for IT outsourcing customer satisfaction through the literature reviews and experts' interviews, and developed the IT outsourcing customer satisfaction evaluation system using AHP analysis. AHP is used for weighting evaluation factors and ranking customer satisfaction areas and factors. The areas include consulting service satisfaction, customer supporting service satisfaction, and performance satisfaction. The developed evaluation system is applied to companies that introduced IT outsourcing in Korea, and we evaluated their customer satisfaction using the system directly. Consulting service satisfaction is the highest and customer supporting service satisfaction is lowest among the three areas in Korea. The Korean customers satisfied the consulting service quality and consulting human resource, but dissatisfied SLA quality and education service from IT outsourcing vendors. IT outsourcing vendors in Korea have to focus their services on improving SLA quality and education service to increase customer satisfaction.

To our knowledge, our study is a first study that introduces the AHP application in developing an evaluation system of IT outsourcing. Our system has strengths in handling complex, multicriteria, qualitative variables, and in improving the system easily by adding or deleting evaluation factors by the purpose of each company. And our evaluation system can be used to evaluate IT outsourcing customer satisfaction by outsourcing areas such as application service provider, hosting and data center operations, system operations and support, and application development and maintenance.

We view the evaluation system as a useful tool to monitor or manage IT outsourcing companies' service level and understand customers' requirements precisely. By using it, IT outsourcing providers can evaluate their customer satisfaction levels by themselves, and give customers a high degree of satisfaction. They can also utilize the weights of the customer satisfaction factors to improve the outsourcing services quality. From the viewpoint of customers, enterprises can utilize our evaluation system in choosing IT outsourcing vendors or deciding the level of IT outsourcing.

On the basis of this research and current issues, we consider our findings in the light of several limitations of the evaluation system and directions for future research. First, the proposed system did not consider the characteristics of each outsourcing service type and the new IT outsourcing services, such as BPO (business process outsourcing) and strategic alliance. The continuous improvement of the proposed customer satisfaction evaluation system is needed to maintain the reliability and applicability of the system by including more relevant factors of the IT outsourcing customer satisfaction. Such efforts could facilitate the development of a theory for the IT outsourcing customer satisfaction. Second, the results of our study may have to be carefully interpreted since the sample was restricted to Korea. Our evaluation system has limitations in comparing the level of IT outsourcing customer satisfaction among the nations. In further studies, it can be tried to develop the maturity model of IT outsourcing customer satisfaction for systematical comparison of the customer satisfaction levels among IT outsourcing vendors and nations. As a result, our framework could be corrected to make it better.

References

Abubakar, B., Mavondo, F., & Clulow, V. (2001). *Customer satisfaction with supermarket retail shopping.* Retrieved from http://130.195.95.71:8081/WWW/ANZMAC2001/ anzmac/AUTHORS/pdfs/Abubakar1.pdf

Bailey, J., & Pearson, S. (1983). Development of a tool for measuring and analyzing computer user satisfaction. *Management Science, 25*(5), 530-45.

Baroudi, J. J., & Orlikowski, W. J. (1988). A short-form measure of user information satisfaction: A psychometric evaluation and notes on use. *Journal of Management Information System, 4*(4), 513-24.

Bennett, C., & Timbrell, G. T. (1999). Application service providers: Will they succeed? *Information Systems Frontiers, 2*(2), 195-211.

Broadbent, M., Weill, P., O'Brien, T., & Neo, B. S. (1996). Firm context and patterns of IT infrastructure capability. In *Proceedings of the Seventeenth International Conference on Information System* (pp. 176-94).

Byrd, T. A., & Turner, D. E. (2000). Measuring the flexibility of information technology infrastructure: Exploratory analysis of a construct. *Journal of Management Information Systems, 17*(1), 167-208.

Chan, A. H. S., Kwok, W. Y., & Duffy, V. G. (2004). Using AHP for determining priority in a safety management system. *Industrial Management & Data Systems, 104*(5), 430-45.

Cheon, M. J., Grover, V., & Teng, J. T. C. (1995). Theoretical perspective on the outsourcing of information systems. *Journal of Technology Information, 10*, 209-19.

Chien, T. K, Su, C. H., & Su, C. T. (2002). Implementation of a customer satisfaction program: A case study. *Industrial Management & Data Systems, 102*(5), 252-59.

Chien, T. K., Chang, T. H., & Su, C. T. (2003). Did your efforts really win customers' satisfaction. *Industrial Management & Data Systems, 103*(4), 253-62.

Cho, H. M. (2000). *An empirical study on IT outsourcing service satisfaction assessment: Focused on ERP project.* Kyunghee University, Korea.

Cronin, J. J., & Taylor, S. A. (1992). Measuring service quality: A reexamination and extension. *Journal of Marketing, 56*, 55-68.

Doll, W. J., & Torkzadeh, G. (1988). The measurement of end-user computing satisfaction. *MIS Quarterly, 12*(2), 259-74.

Frank, N., & Hans, V. V. (1999). *IT service capability maturity model* (Tech. Rep. No. IR-463, release L2-1.0).

Gallivan, M. J., & Oh, W. (1999). Analyzing IT outsourcing relationships as alliances among multiple clients and vendors. In *Proceedings of the 32ⁿᵈ Hawaii International Conference on Systems Sciences-1999.*

Gartner, (2000). *Strategic analysis report: A guide to successful SLA development and management.*

Gelbstein, E. (2002). Outsourcing. In H. Bidgoli et al. (Eds.), *Encyclopedia of information systems 3* (pp. 428-430). Academic Press.

Grover, V., Cheon, M. J., & Teng, J. T. C (1996). The effect of service quality and partnership on the outsourcing of information systems functions. *Journal of Management Information System, 12*(4), 89-116.

Hafeez, K., Zhang, Y. B., & Malak, N. (2002). Determining key capabilities of a firm using analytic hierarchy process. *International Journal of Production Economics, 76*, 39-51.

Igbaria, M., & Nachman, S. A. (1990). Correlates of user satisfaction with end user computing. *Information & management, 19*(2), 73-82.

Ireland, R. D., Hitt, M. A., & Vaidyanath, D. (2002). Alliance management as a source of competitive advantage. *Journal of Management, 28*(3), 413-46.

ISO/IEC TR 15504 (1998a). *Software process assessment—Part 1: Concepts and introductory guide.* Retrieved from http://www.qasoft.demon.co.uk/page4.html

ISO/IEC TR 15504 (1998b). *Software process assessment—Part 2: A reference model for processes and process capability.* Retrieved from http://www.qua. soft.demon.co.uk/page4.html

Ives, B., & Olson, M. H. (1984). User involvement and MIS success: A review of research. *Management Science, 30*(5), 586-603.

Ives, B., Olson, M. H., & Baroudi, J. J. (1983). Measurement of user information satisfaction. *Communication of ACM, 26*(10), 785-93.

Kern, T., & Kreijger, J. (2001). An exploration of application service provision outsourcing option. In *Proceeding of the 34ᵗʰ Hawaii International Conference on System Sciences-2001.*

Kern, T., Kreijger, J., & Willcocks, L. (2002). Exploring ASP as sourcing strategy: Theoretical perspectives, propositions for practice. *Journal of Strategic Information Systems, 11*(2), 153-77.

Ketler, K., & Walstrom, J. (1993). The outsourcing decision. *International Journal of Information Management, 13*, 449-59.

Kettinger, W. J., & Lee, C. C. (1997). Pragmatic perspectives on the measurement of information systems service quality. *MIS Quarterly.*

Khalfan, A., & Gough, T. G. (2002). Comparative analysis between the public and private sectors on the IS-IT outsourcing practices in a developing country: A field study. *Logistics Information Management, 15*(3), 212-22.

King, W. R., & Malhotra, Y. (2000). Developing a framework for analyzing IS sourcing. *Information & Management, 37*, 323-34.

Korea Productivity Center. (1997). NCSI.Retrieved from http://www.ncsi.or.kr

Lacity, M. C., & Hirschheim, R. (1993). *Information systems outsourcing.* London: Wiley.

Lacity, M. C., & Willcocks, L. P. (2001). *Global information technology outsourcing* (1st ed.). John Wiley & Sons.

Lee, G. H. (2003). ITIL service desk: Service support set. *Epitomie.* Retrieved from http://www.eptitomie.com

Lee, J. N., & Kim, Y. G. (1997). Information systems outsourcing strategies for affiliated firms of the Korean conglomerate groups. *Journal of Strategic Information Systems, 6*(3), 203-29.

Leem, C. S., & Yoon, Y. K. (2004). A maturity model and an evaluation system of software customers satisfaction: The case of software companies in Korea. *Industrial Management & Data Systems, 104*(4), 347-54.

Loh, L., & Venkataraman, N. (1992). Diffusion of information technology outsourcing: Influence sources and the Kodak effect. *Inform. Syst. Res., 3*(4), 334-58.

McFarlan, F. W., & Nolan, R. L. (1995). How to manage an IT outsourcing alliance. *Sloan Management Review, 36*(2), 9-23.

Means, G., & D. Schneider, D. (2000). *META-CAPITALISM; The e-business revolution and the design of 21st-century companies and markets.* Pricewaterhousecoopers.

Nam, K., Rajagopalan, S., & Chaudhury, A. (1996). A two-level investigation of information systems outsourcing. *Communications of the ACM, 39*(7), 36-44.

National Quality Research Center. (1995). *ACSI.* University of Michigan Business School. Retrieved from http://www.acsi.org

Ngai, E. W. T. (2003). Selection of web sites for online advertising using the AHP. *Information & Management, 40*, 233-42.

Palvia, P. C. (1995). A dialectic view of information systems outsourcing: Pros and cons. *Information & Management, 29*, 265-75.

Parasuraman, A, Zeithaml, V. A., & Berry, L. L. (1988). SERVQUAL: A multi-item scale for measuring consumer perceptions of service quality. *Journal of Retailing, 64*, 12-40.

Parker, A., Condon, C., & Ackers, G. (2001). *Justifying exSourced processes*. The Forrester Report.

Paulk, M. C., Curtis, B., & Chrissis, M. B. (1991). *Capability maturity model for software*, (CMU/SEI-91-TR-24), Software Engineering Institute.

Paulk, M. C., Curtis, B., & Chrissis, M. B. (1992). *Key practices of the capability maturity model* (CMU/SEI-92-TR-25).

Paulk, M. C., Curtis, B., & Chrissis, M.B. (1993). *Capability maturity model for software*, version 1.1, (CMU/SEI-93-TR-24).

Pitt, L. F., Waton, R. T., & Kavan, C. B. (1995). Service quality: A measure of information systems effectiveness. *MIS Quarterly.*

Pitt, L. F., Waton, R. T., & Kavan, C. B. (1997). Measuring information systems service quality: Concerns for complete canvas. *MIS Quarterly.*

Quinn, J. B. (1999). Strategic outsourcing; Leveraging knowledge capabilities. *MIT Sloan Management Review, 40*(4), 9-21.

Rold, C. D. (2001). *The five dimensions of strategic sourcing*, Gartner.

Ross, S. (1973). Economic theory of agency: The principal problem. *American Economic Review, 63*, 134-39.

Roy, V., & Aubert, B. (2000). A resource-based view of the information systems sourcing mode. In *Proceedings of the 33rd Hawaii International Conference on System Sciences-2000.*

Rushton, P. J., & Gardiner, G. S. (2000). A design or buy process for determining software sourcing strategy. *5th International Conference on FACTORY 2000* (pp. 251-256).

Saaty, T. L. (1990). How to make a decision: The analytic hierarchy process. *European Journal Operation Research, 48*, 9-26.

Satty, T. L. (1994). How to make a decision: The analytic hierarchy process. *Interfaces, 24*(6), 19-43.

Sengupta, K., & Zviran, M. (1997). Measuring user satisfaction an outsourcing environment. *IEEE transactions on Engineering Management, 44*(4), 414-421.

Stratman, J. K., & Roth, A. V. (2002). Enterprise resource planning (ERP), competence constructs: Two-stage multi-item scale development and validation. *Decision Sciences, 33*(4), 601-28.

Sun, S. Y., Lin, T. C., & Sun, P. C. (2002). The factors influencing information systems outsourcing partnership. In *Proceedings of the 35th Hawaii International Conference on System Sciences-2002.*

Szymanski, D., & Henard, D. (2001). Customer satisfaction: A meta-analysis of the empirical evidence. *Journal of the Academy of Marketing Science, 29*(1), 16-35.

Terdiman, R., & Berg, T. (2000). Application sourcing: Application service providers, legacy systems and more. Retrieved from http://www.gartner.com

Udo, G. G. (2000). Using analytic hierarchy process to analyze the information technology outsourcing decision. *Industrial Management & Data Systems, 100*(9), 421-29.

Vining, A., & Globerman, S. (1999). A conceptual framework for understanding the outsourcing decision. *European Management Journal, 17*(6), 645-54.

Willcocks, L., & Choi, C. J. (1995). Co-operative partnership and "total" IT outsourcing; from contractual obligation to strategic alliance. *European Management Journal, 13*(1), 67-78.

Wong, A. (2000). Integrating supplier satisfaction with customer satisfaction. *Total Quality Management, 11*(4-6), S826-9.

Yang, C., & Huang, J. B. (2000). A decision model for IS outsourcing. *International Journal of Information Management, 20*, 225-39.

Yeo, M. K., & Nam, Y. M. (2004). Strengthening IT outsourcing service considering customer's expectation. *Entrue Journal, 3*(1), 1-10.

Yoon, S. C., Seo, H. J., & Kim, M. S. (2004). The validity investigation of IT outsourcing costing/pricing model based on SLA. *Entrue Journal, 3*(1), 75-87

Young, A., & Berg, T. (2001). *The future of outsourcing.* Gartner.

Appendix A

Analytic Hierarchy Process

The application of the AHP is based on the following four principles (Satty, 1994):

1. **Decomposition:** A complex decision problem is segmented into a hierarchy, with each level consisting of a few manageable elements; each element is then further divided, and so on.

2. **Prioritization:** Involves pair-wise comparisons of various elements residing at the same level with respect to an element in the upper level of the hierarchy.

3. **Synthesis:** The priorities are pulled together through the principle of hierarchic composition to provide an overall assessment of the available alternatives.

4. **Sensitivity analysis:** The stability of the outcome is determined by testing the best choice against a "what-if"-type of change in the priorities of the criteria.

The following steps for computing the weight of the elements in each level in the analytic hierarchy are stated by Yang and Huang (2000).

1. **Paired comparisons:** The elements in a level of the hierarchy are compared in terms of their importance or contribution to a given criterion that occupies the level immediately above the elements being compared. It requires the comparison of $n(n-1)/2$ times if the number of elements are n. The numbers used for comparisons will be 1/9, 1/8, ..., 1/2, 1, 2, ..., 8, 9. The meaning of the numbers is explained in Table A-1. The magnitudes we obtain from paired comparisons would be set into the upper triangle of the square matrix, the main diagonal of the matrix must consist of 1's, and the magnitudes of the down triangle would be the reciprocals of the reverse position in the matrix. Based on mathematic symbols, it can be expressed as follows:

    Let C_1, C_2, ..., and C_w be the set of criteria or attributes. The quantified comparisons on pairs C_i, C_j can be represented by an $n \cdot n$ matrix:

$$A = a_{ij}, (i, j = 1, ..., n) = \begin{array}{c|ccccc} & a_1 & a_2 & \cdots\cdots & & a_n \\ \hline a_1 & & a_{12} & \cdots\cdots & & a_{1n} \\ a_2 & a_{21} & & \cdots\cdots & & a_{2n} \\ \vdots & \vdots & \vdots & \vdots & \vdots & \vdots \\ a_n & a_{n1} & a_{n2} & \cdots\cdots & & \end{array}$$

where a = integer and $0 < a < 10$; and if $a_{ij} = a$, then $a_{ij} = 1/a$, and then $a_{ij} = 1$ if $i = j$.

2. **Computing a vector of priorities:** We can compute the principal eigenvector, which becomes the vector of priorities wA, and then is normalized. The formula to arrive at the principal eigenvector is: $wA = \lambda_{max} w$, in which λ_{max} is the largest eigenvalue of A, w is the eigenvector.

3. **Measuring consistency:** It may be difficult for decision makers to reach consistency in the process of deriving the positive reciprocal matrix. A measure of consistency for the given pair-wise comparison is needed. Consistency means $a_{ij} \cdot a_{jk} = a_{ik}$. A consistency ratio (CR) provides a measure of the probability that the matrix was filled in purely at random. The number, a consistency ratio of 0.1, is considered the acceptable upper limit (Hafeez et al., 2002). This measurement of consistency can be used to evaluate the consistency of decision makers as well as the consistency of the entire hierarchy.

Table A-1. AHP scale and meaning

Intensity of Importance	Definition
1	Equal importance of C_1 and C_2
3	Weak importance of C_1, over C_2
5	Essential or strong importance of C_1, over C_2
7	Very strong demonstrated importance of C_1, over C_2
9	Absolute importance of C_1, over C_2
2, 4, 6, 8	Intermediate values between adjacent scale values

Appendix B

Simplified AHP Questionnaire for Evaluating Weights of IT Outsourcing Customer Satisfaction

The following is the overall framework of the evaluation system for IT outsourcing customer satisfaction:

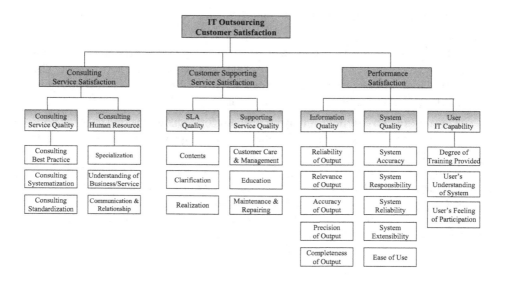

Please, check (✓) for the following questions:

1.   For IT outsourcing customer satisfaction:

Items			← A is more important than B					B is more important than A→			
A		B	9	7	5	3	1	3	5	7	9
Consulting service satisfaction	vs.	Supporting service satisfaction									
Consulting service satisfaction	vs.	Performance satisfaction									
Supporting service satisfaction	vs.	Performance satisfaction									

1.1. For consulting service satisfaction:

Items			← A is more important than B					B is more important than A→			
A		B	9	7	5	3	1	3	5	7	9
Consulting service quality	vs.	Consulting human resource									

1.2. For supporting service satisfaction:

Items			← A is more important than B					B is more important than A→			
A		B	9	7	5	3	1	3	5	7	9
SLA quality	vs.	Supporting service quality									

1.3. For performance satisfaction:

Items			← A is more important than B					B is more important than A→			
A		B	9	7	5	3	1	3	5	7	9
Information quality	vs.	System quality									
Information quality	vs.	User IT capability									
System quality	vs.	User IT capability									

1.1.1. For consulting service quality:

Items			← A is more important than B					B is more important than A→			
A		B	9	7	5	3	1	3	5	7	9
Consulting best-practice	vs.	Consulting systematization									
Consulting best-practice	vs.	Consulting standardization									
Consulting systematization	vs.	Consulting standardization									

1.1.2. For consulting human resource:

Items			← A is more important than B					B is more important than A→			
A		B	9	7	5	3	1	3	5	7	9
Specialization	vs.	Understanding of business/service									
Specialization	vs.	Communication and & relationship									
Understanding of business/service	vs.	Communication and & relationship									

1.2.1. For SLA quality:

Items			← A is more important than B					B is more important than A→			
A		B	9	7	5	3	1	3	5	7	9
Contents	vs.	Reliability									
Contents	vs.	Clarification									
Reliability	vs.	Clarification									

1.2.2. For supporting service quality:

Items			← A is more important than B					B is more important than A→			
A		B	9	7	5	3	1	3	5	7	9
Customer care and management	vs.	Education									
Customer care and management	vs.	Maintenance and repairing									
Education	vs.	Maintenance and repairing									

1.3.1. For information quality:

Items			← A is more important than B					B is more important than A→			
A		B	9	7	5	3	1	3	5	7	9
Reliability	vs.	Relevance									
Reliability	vs.	Accuracy									
Reliability	vs.	Precision									
Reliability	vs.	Completeness									
Relevance	vs.	Accuracy									
Relevance	vs.	Precision									
Relevance	vs.	Completeness									
Accuracy	vs.	Precision									
Accuracy	vs.	Completeness									
Precision	vs.	Completeness									

1.3.2. For system quality:

Items			← A is more important than B					B is more important than A→			
A		B	9	7	5	3	1	3	5	7	9
Accuracy	vs.	Responsibility									
Accuracy	vs.	Reliability									
Accuracy	vs.	Extensibility									
Accuracy	vs.	Ease of use									
Responsibility	vs.	Reliability									
Responsibility	vs.	Extensibility									
Responsibility	vs.	Ease of use									
Reliability	vs.	Extensibility									
Reliability	vs.	Ease of use									
Extensibility	vs.	Ease of use									

1.3.3. For user IT capability:

Items			← A is more important than B					B is more important than A→			
A		B	9	7	5	3	1	3	5	7	9
Degree of training provided	vs.	User's understanding of system									
Degree of training provided	vs.	User's feeling of participation									
User's understanding of system	vs.	User's feeling of participation									

About the Authors

M. Gordon Hunter is a professor of information systems in the Faculty of Management at The University of Lethbridge, Alberta, Canada. Hunter has previously held academic positions at universities in Canada, Singapore, and Hong Kong. He has held visiting positions at universities in Australia, Monaco, Germany, New Zealand, and the U.S. In July and August of 2005, Hunter was a visiting Erskine fellow at the University of Canterbury, Christchurch, New Zealand. He has a Bachelor of Commerce from the University of Saskatchewan in Saskatoon, Saskatchewan, Canada and a doctorate from Strathclyde Business School, University of Strathclyde in Glasgow, Scotland. He has also earned a Certified Management Accountant (CMA) designation from the Society of Management Accountants of Canada. He is a member of the British Computer Society and the Canadian Information Processing Society (CIPS), where he has obtained an Information Systems Professional (ISP) designation. Hunter chairs the executive board of The Information Institute, an information policy research organization. He has extensive experience as a systems analyst and manager in industry and government organizations in Canada. Hunter is an associate editor of the *Journal of Global Information Management*. He is the Canadian World Representative for the Information Resource Management Association. He serves on the editorial board of *Information and Management*, *International Journal of e-Collaboration*, *Journal of Global Information Technology Management*, and *Journal of Information Technology Cases and Applications*. Hunter is also a member of the advisory board for *The Journal of Information, Information Technology, and*

Organizations. He has published articles in *MIS Quarterly, Information Systems Research, The Journal of Strategic Information Systems, The Journal of Global Information Management, Information Systems Journal,* and *Information, Technology and People.* He has conducted seminar presentations in Canada, the U.S., Europe, Hong Kong, Singapore, Taiwan, New Zealand, and Australia. Hunter's current research interests relate to the productivity of systems analysts with emphasis upon the personnel component including cross-cultural aspects, the use of information systems by small business, the role of chief information officers, and the effective development and implementation of cross functional information systems.

Felix B. Tan is a professor of information systems and associate dean of research for the Faculty of Design and Creative Technologies at AUT University, New Zealand. He serves as editor-in-chief of the *Journal of Global Information Management.* He is on the executive council and is a fellow of the Information Resources Management Association. He also served on the Council of the Association for Information Systems as the Asia-Pacific Representative. He has held visiting positions with the National University of Singapore, The University of Western Ontario, Canada and was a visiting professor at Georgia State University (USA) in May/June 2005 and the University of Hawaii at Manoa in January 2006. Dr. Tan is internationally known for his work in the global IT field. Dr. Tan's current research interests are in electronic commerce, global information management, business-IT alignment, and the management of IT. He is actively using cognitive mapping and narrative inquiry methods in his research. Dr. Tan has published in *MIS Quarterly, Information & Management, Journal of Information Technology, IEEE Transactions on Engineering Management,* as well as other journals, and refereed conference proceedings. Dr. Tan has over 20 years experience in information systems management and consulting with large multinationals, as well as university teaching and research in Singapore, Canada and New Zealand.

* * *

Roman Beck is an assistant professor at the Institute of Information Systems at the Johann Wolfgang Goethe University, Frankfurt, Germany. His research focuses on the role of IT in creating new business models, the diffusion of IT innovations, IT project management, and the role of network externalities on the adoption of new standards. He publishes on a wide array of topics in the field of IT standards, globalization, and networked economies. His academic research has been presented at ICIS and other international IS conferences, and has been published in academic journals such as *EM-Electronic Markets, Wirtschaftsinformatik, JGIM, Information Polity*, or *CAIS*.

Carole Bonanni is an instructor at the University College of the Fraser Valley. Her current research interests are in the areas of m-banking, industrial organization, and competitive strategy.

John Bowes specializes in the transition of media industries from print and broadcast in the early 20th century to computer-mediated technologies of the present. Related interests are in health communication, electronic commerce, and trust in online communities. Dr. Bowes is coordinator of Simon Fraser University's EC3 Lab, a research facility devoted to electronic commerce, usability, computer-mediated education, and social research analysis. He has taught at the University of North Dakota, Dublin City University (Ireland) and Charles Stuart University (Australia), where he was a Fulbright visiting scholar. For 28 years prior to coming to Simon Fraser University, Canada, he was on the faculty of the University of Washington's School of Communication. He presently is a professor and director of the School of Interactive Arts and Technology at SFU.

Erran Carmel's area of expertise is global software development. His co-authored book *Offshoring Information Technology* was released in 2005 (Cambridge University Press). His 1999 book *Global Software Teams* was the first on that topic. He has written over 50 articles, reports and manuscripts. His academic articles have appeared in *MISQ Executive*, *IEEE Software*, *Communications of the ACM*, and many other journals. He is an associate professor at the Kogod School of Business at American University in Washington, DC, USA, where he co-founded and led the program in management of global information technology (MoGIT).

H. M. Chen is a professor and associate dean of the Management School, Shanghai Jiaotong University (SJTU), China. He earned his PhD from Shanghai Jiaotong University (1991). He was a visiting scholar at Sloan School, MIT (1999-2000). His main research interests are in industrial organization (mergers and acquisition), negotiation and bargaining theory, transportation management (air transportation), and technology innovation. Professor Chen published dozens of papers in academic journals and conference proceedings.

Y. N. Chen, Marry R. Nixon professor of accounting at Western Kentucky University, USA, specializes in accounting information systems and auditing. Her current research focuses on the effectiveness of analytical review procedures and implementation of information systems. Dr. Chen earned her PhD from the University of South Carolina. Before joining Western Kentucky University, she was an associate professor of accountancy at Ohio University and assistant professor of accounting at Concordia University, Canada. Professor Chen has authored articles in many leading academic and professional journals, including *Auditing: A Journal of Practice & Theory, Issues in Accounting Education, Journal of Management Information Systems, Information & Management, Review of Quantitative Finance & Accounting, Internal Auditing, Journal of End User Computing, Journal of Computer Information Systems, Journal of Global Information Management, Journal of Education for Business, Assessment & Evaluation in Higher Education*, and *Journal of Applied Business Research.*

R. K. H. Ching is a professor of information technology and information systems in the College of Business Administration, California State University, Sacramento, USA. Dr. Ching received his PhD from the University of Arkansas, Fayetteville. His publications have appeared in various journals, including the *Journal of the Operational Research Society, Information Systems Management* and the *Journal of Global Information Management*, and numerous conference proceedings.

Dianne Cyr is an associate professor in the Faculty of Business at Simon Fraser University, Vancouver, Canada. She leads a government-funded research project titled "Managing E-loyalty through Design." This investigation is focused on how trust, satisfaction, and loyalty are built in online business environments through Web site design. Unique features of this work are comparisons across cultures, genders, and concerning applications to mobile devices. Further details of these research projects may be accessed at http://www.eloyalty.ca. Cyr is the author of five books and over 40 research articles. Career details may be found at http://diannecyr.com.

Marilyn M. Helms is the sesquicentennial endowed chair and professor of management at Dalton State College, USA. She earned her BBA, MBA, and DBA from the University of Memphis. She works closely with the area community on research projects and training programs. She teaches production management, quality, and entrepreneurship. She is the author of numerous journal articles and writes a column for the *Dalton (GA) Daily Citizen* newspaper. She earned her doctorate from the University of Memphis. Prior to joining DSC, she was the George Lester Nation Professor of Management at UT-Chattanooga. She was awarded a Fulbright teaching award to Coimbra, Portugal. Her research interests include manufacturing strategy, quality, and international management.

Wayne W. Huang is a professor with the MIS Department, College of Business, Ohio University, USA. He has worked as a faculty in universities in Australia, Singapore, and Hong Kong, and has received research awards in universities of Australia and U.S. His main research interests include group support systems (GSS), electronic commerce, e-learning, knowledge management systems, and software engineering.

He has published more than 80 academic research papers (peer-reviewed), including papers being published in leading IS journals such as the *Journal of Management Information Systems (JMIS); IEEE Transactions on Systems, Man, and Cybernetics; Information & Management (I&M); IEEE Transactions on Professional Communication; Decision Support Systems (DSS); Communications of AIS*; and *European Journal of Information Systems*. He is senior editor of the *Journal of Data Base for Advances in Information Systems* (an ACM SIGMIS Publication), and on the editorial board of *I&M, Journal of Global Information Management (JGIM)*, and *Journal of Data Management (JDM)*.

Joe Ilsever is a full-time business faculty member at Douglas College in Vancouver. He has a PhD from Simon Fraser University. His areas of research include "flow," customer online engagement, and modeling of online behaviour with structured equation models (SEM, AMOS). His particular research interests include application of advanced statistical models to e-commerce. Dr. Ilsever currently teaches corporate finance, statistical methodologies, and management simulation studies.

Kun Shin Im is an assistant professor of information systems at Yonsei University, Korea. He holds PhD in MIS from University of South Carolina and a PhD in accounting from Yonsei University. His research interests include IT impacts on organizational structure, IT investments evaluation, IT adoption, and IT training effectiveness. He has published several studies in these areas in *Information Systems Research, Journal of Information Technology Management*, and *Journal of Organizational & End User Computing*.

Wen-Jang Kenny Jih is currently a professor of computer information systems at the Jennings A. Jones College of Business in Middle Tennessee State University, USA. He obtained his doctorate degree in business computer information systems from University of North Texas in 1985. He previously taught at Longwood University in Virginia, University of Tennessee at Chattanooga, Auburn University in Alabama, and Southern Methodist University in Dallas. From 1997 to 2001, Dr. Jih served as the Dean of School of Management of Da-Yeh University, a comprehensive private institution in Taiwan. His recent research interests include knowledge management, e-commerce, m-commerce, and innovative approaches to information systems education.

Weiling Ke is an assistant professor in information systems at the School of Business, Clarkson University, USA. She received her PhD from the National University of Singapore. Ke has been doing research on inter-organizational knowledge sharing, e-government development, and enterprise system implementation. She publishes with the *Communications of ACM, Journal of Global Information Management*, and proceedings of major IS conferences.

Helen Kelley is an associate professor of information systems in the Faculty of Management, University of Lethbridge, Canada. Her research focuses on the individual user of information and enterprise resource planning technologies, viewed from social cognitive and attributional perspectives. Her current interests investigate understanding what management of organizations can do to enhance individual adoption of and learning about information systems technologies plus information systems security effectiveness. Her research has been published in *Information Systems Research* and *Business Quarterly*.

Wolfgang Koenig is a professor of information systems at the Institute of Information Systems, Johann Wolfgang Goethe University, Frankfurt, Germany. Koenig chairs the "E-Finance Lab Frankfurt am Main," a joint research program with Accenture, Bearing Point, Deutsche Bank, Deutsche Postbank, Finanz IT, IBM, Microsoft, Siemens, and T-Systems. Moreover, he serves as editor-in-chief of the leading mid-European IS journal *Wirtschaftsinformatik*. His research interest is in e-finance, standardization, and information management. His research has been published in academic journals such as *MIS Quarterly, International Journal of Electronic Markets, Wirtschaftsinformatik, JGIM, JISeB, JITSR, CAIS*, and elsewhere.

Sumit Kundu serves as the Ingerson-Rand professor in international business at Florida International University, USA. His doctoral degree is from Rutgers University. His primary research areas a internationalization of service industries, theories of multinational enterprise, global strategic alliances, international entrepreneurship, and emerging multinationals. He has published in the *Journal of International Business Studies, Journal of Business Research, Journal of International Management, Journal of International Marketing*, and *Journal of Small Business Economics*, among many others. He is on the editorial board of the *Management International Review*.

Karen D. Loch is the director of the Institute of International Business and associate professor at Georgia State University, USA. She holds a PhD in MIS from the University of Nebraska – Lincoln and an MA in French language and literature. She has published in leading scholarly journals such as *MISQ, CACM, JAIS, CAIS, JGIM, IEEETrans, ISJ, Journal of Business Ethics, IRMJ, DATA BASE*, and *AME*, as well as popular trade journals.

Yuan Long is an assistant professor of computer information systems (CIS) at Colorado State University – Pueblo, USA. Her research interests include open source software development, e-government, and social network. She has publications in journals such as the *Journal of Global Information Management, Industry Management & Data Systems*, and *Journal of Information Technology Cases and Applications*. She has also published in conferences such as International Conference on Information Systems (ICIS'2004), and Americas Conference on Information Systems (AMCIS'2005 & AMCIS'2006). In addition, she served as a committee member of IRMA 2005 International and as a reviewer for several journals such as *Journal of Information Technology Cases and Applications, Electronic Government, Information Resources Management Journal, Journal of Computer Information System*, and *International Journal of Innovation and Learning*.

R. C. MacGregor is an Associate Professor in the School of Information Technology and Computer Science at the University of Wollongong in Australia. He is also the former Head of Discipline in Information Systems. His research expertise lies in the areas of information technology (IT) and electronic commerce (e-commerce) in small to medium enterprises (SMEs). He has authored a number of journal and conference publications examining the use and adoption of IT in SMEs. Along with Lejla, Rob was the recipient of the Australian Prime Minister's Award for Excellence in Business Community Partnerships (NSW)(2004). Rob is also the founding Editor of the Australasian Journal of Information Systems and was Conference Chair of the Australian Conference of Information Systems (1992). In his spare time, Rob writes music. His most recent work is the symphony 'Alba'.

Donna T. Mayo is chair of the Division of Business Administration and associate professor of Marketing at Dalton State College, USA. She holds a PhD in Marketing from the University of Alabama. Donna has published numerous scholarly and applied works in a variety of journals, including *Journal of Marketing Theory Practice, Journal of Business Research*, and *Journal of Internet Commerce*. Her research interests include entrepreneurship, marketing communication, e-commerce, and customer service. She has consulted with more than 30 private and public organizations in the areas of marketing research and customer service.

Brian Nicholson is a senior lecturer in information systems at Manchester Business School, UK. His interests lie in global software development, business process outsourcing and developing countries. He is co-author of *Global IT Outsourcing* (Cambridge University Press, with S. Sahay and S. Krishna) and has published journal articles in *IEEE Software, Information and Organisation* and others. He has recently undertaken research and consultancy projects in Costa Rica, Iran, and India.

Fred Niederman serves as the Shaughnessy endowed professor of MIS at Saint Louis University, USA. His doctoral degree is from the University of Minnesota (1990). His primary research areas pertain to global information management, information technology personnel, and using information technology to support groups and meetings. He has published more than 30 refereed journal articles including several in top MIS journals such as *MIS Quarterly, Communications of the ACM,* and *Decision Sciences.* He has presented papers at several major conferences and serves as associate editor of the *Journal of Global Information Systems.*

Ana Ortiz de Guinea received her Master of Science in MIS from the University of Lethbridge (Canada). Her master's studies were sponsored by the International Council of Canadian Studies and the Fundación de Estudios La Caixa (Spain). She has a five-year undergraduate degree in computer engineering from the Universidad de Deusto (Spain). During her undergraduate program, she studied for one year at the University of Bath (UK) with a scholarship from the European Union. She has teaching experience and has worked for PriceWaterhouseCoopers and the Altran Foundation Group as a consultant in management information systems.

Silvia Salas studied with the Department of Decision Sciences Information Systems at Florida International University, USA. Her research interests are in the areas of global information management, intersections between organizational behavior and technology, and ethics in information management.

Keng Siau is a professor of MIS at the University of Nebraska-Lincoln (UNL). He is the editor-in-chief of the *Journal of Database Management* and the Book Series Editor for *Advanced Topics in Database Research.* Dr. Siau has over 200 academic publications. Dr. Siau is the author of over 85 refereed journal articles that appear in journals such as *MISQ, CACM, IEEE Computer, Information Systems, IEEE Transactions on Systems, Man, and Cybernetics, IEEE Transactions on Professional Communication, IEEE Transactions on Information Technology in Biomedicine,* and *IEEE Transactions on Education.* In addition, he has published over 95 refereed conference papers, edited/co-edited over 10 scholarly and research-oriented books, and written more than 15 scholarly book chapters. He served as the Organizing and Program Co-chairs of the International Workshop on Evaluation of Modeling Methods in Systems Analysis and Design (EMMSAD) (1996–2005).

Detmar W. Straub, J. Mack Robinson distinguished professor of information systems at Georgia State University, has conducted research in the areas of Net-enhanced organizations (e-commerce), computer security, technological innovation, and international IT studies. He holds a DBA (Doctor of Business Administration) in MIS from Indiana and a PhD in English from Penn State. He has published 130 papers in journals such as *Management Science, Information Systems Research, MIS Quarterly, Organization Science, Communications of the ACM, Journal of MIS, Journal of AIS, Information & Management, Communications of the AIS, IEEE Transactions on Engineering Management, OMEGA, Academy of Management Executive*, and *Sloan Management Review*. Former senior editor for *Information Systems Research* and *Journal of the AIS (JAIS)* and co-editor of *DATA BASE for Advances in Information Systems*, he is currently senior editor for *DATA BASE*. He has previously served as associate editor for *Management Science and Information Systems Research*, and associate publisher/associate editor for *MIS Quarterly* (as well as editorial board member on a host of other journals). Former VP of publications for *AIS*, he has served as co-program chair for AMCIS and ICIS. He was elected an AIS fellow in 2005.

L. Vrazalic is an Associate Professor in Information Systems at the University of Wollongong in Dubai (UOWD). She is also the Chair of the UOWD Research Committee and co-ordinator of the Program for the Enhancement of Learning and Teaching (PELT). Her interests are in human computer interaction and e-commerce, and she was awarded the University Medal for her research (1999). Lejla received the Vice Chancellors Award for Outstanding Contribution to Teaching and Learning (OCTAL) and a Carrick Citation for Outstanding Contributions to Student Learning (2004 and 2006 respectively). She is also the recipient of the Australian Prime Minister's Award for Excellence in Business Community Partnerships (NSW) for her work on community portals in Australia (2004).

Kwok Kee Wei is the head and chair professor in the Department of Information Systems, City University of Hong Kong. He was elected president of the Association of Information Systems in 2003. He has published widely in the information systems field with more than 100 publications including articles in *MIS Quarterly, Management Science, Journal of Management Information Systems, Information Systems Research, European Journal of Information Systems*, and *ACM Transactions on Information Systems*. He is serving on the editorial boards of several international journals including the *IEEE Transactions on Engineering Management*. He was the senior editor of *MIS Quarterly* (2000-2003). His research focuses on human-computer interaction, innovation adoption and management, and knowledge management systems.

Rolf T. Wigand is Maulden-Entergy Chair and Distinguished Professor of Information Science and Management in the Departments of Information Science and Management at the University of Arkansas at Little Rock, USA. He received his PhD in Organizational Communication from Michigan State University. Wigand researches electronic markets, e-business, standards development, disintermediation, and the impact of electronic commerce technologies on firms, markets, and professions. His research has been published in the *Sloan Management Review, MIS Quarterly, Information Management, Information Management Review, Computers in Human Behavior, Human Organization, International Journal of Technology Management, International Journal of Electronic Markets, Journal of Information Technology, Journal of Management Information Systems, The Information Society*, and elsewhere.

YongKi Yoon is a senior manager at LG Electronics. He received his PhD degree in Technology Management from Yonsei University, Korea. His research interest includes information technology valuation, information strategy planning and IT outsourcing in e-business environments.

Index

A

acculturation 13–15
American University in Cairo 41, 51
analytic hierarchy process (AHP)
    354, 360
application service provider (ASP)
    278, 367
Australia 156–200
Australian Bureau of Statistics 161
average variance extracted (AVE) 258

B

brand 227
business-
    to-business (B-to-B) 328
    to-consumer (B-to-C) 328

C

Cairo 23
Canada 89, 245–274
chief
    executive officer (CEO) 238
    information officer (CIO)
        85, 91, 94, 305
    technology officer (CTO) 230
China 281, 303
Chinese 104
client firm 230
collectivism 88, 106
communication 220
competitive advantage 326, 329
confidence interval chart 148
consultant 311
consulting group 308
consumer 109, 112
contact
    cost 235
    stage 223
continuity 5
contract stage 224
control
    environment 236
    stage 225
cost 276
    of living 65
    saving 222

critical success factor (CSF) 286, 328
cross-cultural
  investigation 85
  research 85–102
cross-loading 258
culture 6–8, 18, 34, 47–
    48, 78, 88, 103–
    106, 111, 141, 279–
    280, 285, 310
customer
  intimacy 163
  relationship management 331
  satisfaction 354–382
    evaluation system 355
  service 332
customerisation 164
customization 164
  phase 278

D

data
  envelopment analysis (DEA) 201–217
data gathering 21, 24
decision-making unit (DMU) 212
design element 121
developing country 147, 275–299
digital literacy 33, 59, 218
disintermediation 168
downsizing 76

E

e-business
  integration 201–217
  readiness 208
  satisfaction index 206
  solution 202
e-government 276
  development 137–155
  implementation 275–299
e-loyalty 103, 105, 107, 111
efficiency 207
Egypt 39
electronic
  commerce 157, 283, 325–353
    adoption 156–200
    adoption barrier 169

  benefits 167
  democracy 278
  emic 96
  English 104
  enterprise system (ES) 301
    implementation 300–324
  ethnicity 106
  etic 96
  export 73

F

federal government 277
femininity 88, 106
foreign
  direct investment (FDI) 71
  language training 71
functionality 225
funding 5, 46

G

Gates, Bill 276
Georgia State University 2, 11–13
German 104
global organization 103–136
Globtel 227
government 49, 277
  information 277
  official 282
  Web site 287
government-to-business (G2B) 138
government-to-customer (G2C) 138
government-to-employee (G2E) 138
government-to-government (G2G) 138
grants 36, 42
grounded theory 88
growth theory 140

H

Harvard University 283
high income country 138
Hill, Dr. Carole 37
human
  capital 72
    theory 65
  development index (HDI) 142

I

immigration 77
income level 140
India 69
individualism 88, 106
information
  and communication technology (ICT)
        137, 283
  availability 285
  distribution 300–302
  exchange 162
  interpretation 300–302
  system 245–274
  technology (IT) 60
information and communication technol-
        ogy (ICT) 2
infusion phase 278
initiation phase 277
intellectual
  capital 326
  property 67, 69
internal cost 68
International Data Corporation (IDC) 203
Internet 204, 277, 326
  access 86
  accessibility 282
  environment 108
  shopping 103
  store 109
  vendor 108
interview 114, 254, 303

J

Japanese 104
Jordan 16

K

Kamel, Dr. Sherif 34, 37
Kamel, Sherif Dr. 8–10
Karlstad 156–200
knowledge 4, 44
  acquisition 300–302, 319, 342
  distribution 330
  flow 218, 342

management 325–353
transfer 5, 357
worker 90
Korea 354–382

L

language 104
least developed countries (LDC) 278
local
  government 277
  loyalty 115
  satisfaction 115
  trust 115
localization 110
longevity 4
low income country 138

M

management support 248–249
masculinity 88, 106
mass customisation 164
measurement model 257
memory 310
Meso, Dr. Peter 37
Microsoft 225
mixed influence model 204
Motorola 227
multi-culture 96
multinational corporation (MNC) 23

N

narrative inquiry 85, 94
National
  Customer Satisfaction Indices 358
  Science Foundation (NSF) 34
national
  culture 285
  e-government infrastructures (NeIs)
        283, 286
  information infrastructure (NII) 279
National Science Foundation (NSF) 2
native speaker 52
network
  access 283
  economy 284

learning 283–284
    policy 284
non-governmental organization (NGO) 23

O

offshore
    contract 235
    outsourcing 225
    software 219
        outsourcing 218–244
    vendor 230, 234
offshoring 59–84
one-to-one relationship 357
online shopper 104
onshore
    personnel 229
    presence 234
    software 219
opportunism 226, 232–233
organizational
    agility 301
    culture 285
    learning 300–324
    memory 300–302
outsourcing 60, 354–382

P

parsimonious
    model 14
    testing 14–16
partial
    e-commerce 162
    least square 257
personal
    construct theory 85
    interview 359
poverty 92
power distance 88, 106
principal investigator (PI) 36
privacy policy 104
production flow 44
program of research (PR) 3–6, 33–58
public administration 276
pure e-commerce 162

Q

qualitative research 87
quality 233

R

regional development theory 141
reliability 228, 340
religion 279
Repertory Grid 85
reputation 104
research questions 3
resource poverty 161, 246
revenue 62
risk 161

S

satisfaction 201
scanners 201
security 116, 168, 171
September 11 61
service level agreement 361–362
SERVQUAL 358
Sierra 221
Singapore 89, 247
single-culture 96
small
    business 245–274
    firm 220, 224, 226
    large business 157
    to medium enterprise (SME) 156–
        200, 201–217
socialization 108
social norm (SN) 24, 285
software development 219
Spanish 104
stakeholder 36, 231
state government 277
steering committee 308
strategic
    alliance 156–200, 171
    management 221
structural model 258
subcontracting 356

supply chain 164, 208, 328
survey 43, 114
Sweden 156–200

T

Taiwan 325, 333
technological culturation (acculturation)
     13–15
Texas Instruments 227
theory of reasoned action (TRA) 250
think-aloud interview 254
transaction cost 70, 221
   theory 218
trust 103–104, 107
turnover 314

U

uncertainty 161
   avoidance 106
unemployment 162
United Nations 137
user
   information satisfaction (UIS) 359
   satisfaction 250

V

vendor 104, 108, 224, 230, 236, 252, 2
     55, 332, 354, 369
   familiarity 116
   support 264

W

Wahba, Dr. Khaled 37
Wahba, Khaled Dr. 8–10
war 279
Web
   -based survey 43
   measure index (WMI) 142–145
   site
      culture 107
      design 103–136, 330
      satisfaction 107
      trust 107, 116
   standardization 331
Wollongong 156–200
working committee 308

Y

Y2K 61, 219